CRIME AND ELDER ABUSE

ABOUT THE AUTHOR

Brian K. Payne received his Ph.D. in Criminology from Indiana University of Pennsylvania in 1993. He is professor and chair of the Department of Sociology and Criminal Justice at Old Dominion University. He has published over fifty articles in scholarly journals on topics such as elder abuse, white-collar crime, and methods of social control. He is the author of four previous books including *Drugs and Policing: A Scientific Perspective, Incarcerating White-Collar Offenders, Crime in the Home Health Care Field,* and *Family Violence and Criminal Justice: A Life Course Approach* (co-authored with Randy R. Gainey).

Second Edition

CRIME AND ELDER ABUSE

An Integrated Perspective

By

BRIAN K. PAYNE, PH.D.

Department of Sociology and Criminal Justice
Old Dominion University
Norfolk, Virginia

CHARLES C THOMAS • PUBLISHER, LTD.
Springfield • Illinois • U.S.A.

Published and Distributed Throughout the World by

CHARLES C THOMAS • PUBLISHER, LTD.
2600 South First Street
Springfield, Illinois 62704

©2005 by CHARLES C THOMAS • PUBLISHER, LTD.

ISBN 0-398-07566-2 (hard)
ISBN 0-398-07567-0 (paper)

Library of Congress Catalog Card Number: 2004062028

Printed in the United States of America
GS-R-3

Library of Congress Cataloging-in-Publication Data

Payne, Brian K.
   Crime and elder abuse : an integrated perspective / by Brian K. Payne--2nd ed.
     p. cm.
   Includes bibliographical references and index.
   ISBN 0-398-07566-2 -- ISBN 0-398-07567-0 (pbk.)
   1. Older people--Abuse of. 2. Older people--Abuse of--Investigation. 3. Older people--Crimes against. I. Title.

HV6626.3.P39 2005
364.15'55--dc22

                                             2004062028

To Kathleen, Chloe, and Charles

PREFACE

About twenty-five years ago, the concept of granny battering appeared in British medical journals and was used to describe a host of abusive acts committed against elderly persons. Since then, a number of other concepts have been used to replace this politically incorrect concept. Perhaps the most popular concepts are elder abuse and elder mistreatment. Attention from social scientists from various disciplines has increased in the eighties and nineties. Noticeably rare, however, is criminological input into the study of elder abuse. This book offers a criminological foundation from which increased understanding about elder abuse will evolve.

It is my belief that the interdisciplinary nature of the elder abuse problem requires a cooperative effort among scholars researching the topic. Indeed, elder abuse is an issue that relates to several different disciplines including criminology, gerontology, social work, social welfare, sociology, psychology, victimology, medicine, and a host of other social sciences. Further, an integrated effort among practitioners responding to abuse is needed to effectively handle cases of elder abuse. Given the steady increase in the proportion of older persons in our society, it is expected that there will be more elderly victims in the future. Therefore, it is imperative that attention be given to the victimization experiences of elderly persons.

The reader will note that I refrain from using a specific age to describe when abusive actions become elder abuse as opposed to some other type of crime. I avoid setting an age restriction, such as sixty-five which is the age that the Social Security Administration uses to describe what is meant be "elderly," because I am more interested in the general ways in which older victims (as opposed to younger victims) are perceived, handled, studied, and treated. Also of interest is the way that consequences of victimization are experienced differently by elderly persons. It is my belief, however, that "classifying the elderly into a single group can do more disservice than good" (Doerner & Lab, 1998, p. 204).

The basis of Doerner and Lab's quote is that there is tremendous variation in the characteristics of persons over a certain age, such as sixty-five. Age is certainly a relative concept. As an example, one day I was talking to my neighbor, Alice, who is in her late seventies, when another neighbor who is in his nineties drove by in his automobile. The neighbor I was talking to quickly said, "I hope I'm like him when I get old. I want to be able to get around the way he does." Neither of my neighbors define themselves by their age; rather, they seem to define themselves by what they are able to do.

So, when I refer to the phrases "crimes against elderly persons" and "elder abuse," I am talking about general trends and am not suggesting that all persons who are older are going to experience victimization in the same way. In general, though, older victims experience abuse in different ways than younger victims do.

This second edition of *Crime and Elder Abuse: An Integrated Perspective* builds on the earlier edition in five ways. First, new research has been added into each chapter. Second, the tables and figures have been updated, with applied critical thinking questions now included in order to make the tables and figures more interactive with readers. Third, various sections have been added in different chapters—in Chapter 3, discussion about homicides and home health care fraud has been added; in Chapter 5, different law enforcement strategies have been described, and so on. Fourth, Chapters 2 through 7 now include box inserts titled "Voices from the Field," which include brief over-views written by professionals who are discussing some aspect of elder abuse. Finally, Chapter 7, Preventing Elder Abuse: An Integrated Approach, has been added. It is my hope that this new edition will shed some light on what can be done to prevent elderly persons from being victimized or at least min-imize the consequences of victimization when abuse does occur.

B.K.P.

ACKNOWLEDGMENTS

I am indebted to many persons whose input, insight, and assistance made this book possible. Randy Gainey (Old Dominion University), Garland White (Old Dominion University), Ed Stevens (Troy State University), and countless undergraduate and graduate students at Old Dominion University read various parts of this book and challenged me to see and explain ideas from an integrated perspective. I am also indebted to Crystal Carey for her help in her capacity as the graduate intern for the Center for Family Violence Education and Research. She performed numerous tasks that were invaluable.

I express my gratitude to Old Dominion University and the College of Arts and Letters for the research leave granted to work on this second edition. Chandra DeSilva, Dean of the College of Arts and Letters at Old Dominion University, offered much support that helped me complete this project. Thanks also to my friends in the Sociology and Criminal Justice Department at Old Dominion for their encouragement and support.

Also, let me thank the many fine scholars whose works are cited throughout this book. May their efforts continue to expand our understanding of this devastating problem. Thanks also to the professionals who supplied their words of advice in the box inserts in Chapters 2 through 7 in this edition. Their insight will prove to be extremely valuable.

Finally, and most importantly, I would like to thank my family–Kathleen, Chloe, and Charles–for their patience and support.

CONTENTS

CRIME AND ELDER ABUSE

Chapter 1

THE YOUNG GET OLDER
AND THE OLDER GET VICTIMIZED

1. Why is it important to study crime against older adults?
2. How does the demographic makeup of society influence crime?
3. What does the author mean by gero-criminology?
4. What are mandatory reporting laws? How effective do you think they are?
5. How does victimization among older adults compare to the victimization of other groups?
6. Is it ageist to separate out crimes against older adults? Why or why not?
7. Why would people who work in criminal justice be concerned about older victims of crime?

INTRODUCTION

At seventy-seven years old, Mary Ann was a retired real estate professional, the widow of a judge, and the parent of a prosecutor. She and her husband had built up a respectable amount of savings that should have ensured that Mary Ann would live comfortably for the rest of her life. Con artists who swindled Mary Ann out of $74,000 with bogus investments and promises of phony prizes nearly shattered that comfort. Not long thereafter, she moved to North Carolina and got an unlisted phone number. One day a man identifying himself as Virgil Hastings called Mary Ann to say that he was a lawyer who was in charge of her case and that he had recovered her lost money, and that he would be able to send her the money if she sent Hastings $1,950 to cover legal fees. She sent the money and, as you may have guessed, never heard back from Hastings. This scam is referred to as a "recovery room scam" in that persons who are known to have already been scammed are targeted, contacted, and promised reimbursement in exchange for legal fees (Church, 1997).

Mary Ann is not alone. In fact, elderly persons make up only 12 percent of the population but 30 percent of fraud victims (Wangrin, 1994). Fraud, however, is not the only type of crime committed against older adults. Indeed, there is great variation in the kinds of offenses that threaten the financial, physical, and emotional lives of older adults. Consider the following examples:

1. A woman paid roofers $4,000 for getting a layer of tar in one spot on her roof. The tar left the roof in worse condition than before (Calvan, 1998).
2. An elderly nursing home patient was blinded because he was punched by his nurse's aide (Payne & Cikovic, 1995).
3. A fraudulent investor convinced a woman in her sixties to pay $4,000 for a fraudulent living trust (Tighe, 1994).
4. In Buffalo, an elderly woman was charged $100,000 to have a water line installed. Authorities learned of the scam only after the woman told a neighbor she didn't have the money for the final payment (Kalter, 1995).
5. A home care provider pled guilty to stealing a woman's credit card and running up a $1,500 bill. The same caregiver had previously been charged with stealing rings from nursing home patients (*St. Petersburg Times,* 2003: 3).
6. An elderly man was pulled from his bed by his nipples because a nurse's aide thought he wasn't being cooperative (Payne, 1998a).
7. A sixty-five-year-old man died "after his wife held him down and hit him repeatedly" (Nelesen, 2003, p. E5).
8. A seventy-five-year-old woman was murdered by her nephew. The murderer placed peeled onions around the room to cover up the smell of the deceased body. Ironically, it was the smell that led concerned neighbors to call the police.
9. A paid caregiver stole $30,000 from a ninety-year-old woman who was in her care (Mitchell, 2003).
10. A certified nursing assistant was arrested and subsequently admitted to sexually abusing two elderly women (*St. Petersburg Times,* 2003).
11. A fifty-seven-year-old male forcefully entered his eighty-two-year-old father's mobile home and tied him up with nylon rope. Then, he gagged his father with a pillow case and assaulted him (Tisch, 2003).

The list could go on and on; the point is that older adults are victimized in a variety of ways. While official statistics show older adults are less likely to be victimized than younger individuals, the very nature of aging in the United States creates certain situations where older adults are more likely to be targeted for certain crimes than younger people. For example, children and younger adults would rarely, if ever, be victims of patient abuse in nursing homes. Likewise, younger adults are less likely to need health care; therefore, they are less likely to be victims of medical crimes (see Jesilow, Pontell, & Geis, 1985; Geis, Jesilow, Pontell, & O'Brien, 1985; Rosoff, Pontell, & Tillman, 2003). Further, fraudulent telemarketers, repair technicians, and investors are more likely to target older adults who have more money saved for their future (Church, 1997). These offenses (telemarketing fraud, occupational fraud, patient abuse, and medical crimes) are typically not included in official crime statistics. Conversely, older adults are not as apt to join gangs, do drugs, and engage in other risk-taking activities that ultimately lead to much of the crime and the subsequent victimization that official statistics measure. Thus, assumptions about the victimization of older adults should not be made from official statistics.

Rather, what is needed are focused examinations that isolate and specifically consider the social and political ramifications of crimes against older adults. This book represents one of the first discourses that integrates elder abuse issues within the framework of a criminological paradigm. To adequately integrate these issues, the way that the victimization experiences of elderly persons can be conceptualized as involving various types of abuse warrants consideration. This will be followed by a discussion of various myths about elderly victimization that continue to limit our understanding about this important issue.

INTEGRATING CRIME AND ABUSE

A *social harm* approach is useful in integrating the notions of crime and abuse. A social harm definition of crime argues that criminal acts are best defined as "activities that involve demonstrable harm to human beings" (Friedrichs, 2003, p. 6). Because many abuses against older adults are not universally defined as illegal, a social harm conceptualization of crime offers a broader base from which we can begin to understand abuses against older adults. This is important because states vary in their definitions of abuse, and it would be virtually impossible to get all to agree on a consistent legal definition of what many refer to as elder abuse (Macolini, 1995; Wolf, 1996a). Indeed, every state in the U.S. has adopted legislation addressing abuse of elderly persons. The complexity and breadth of the statutes are evidenced by the fact that the state laws vary in at least six important ways: (1) their definitions of elderly; (2) their definitions of abuse; (3) whether the abuse is classified

diff. def. of what is elderly state to state. Med. (65+) CJ (50+)

TABLE 1. LEVELS OF ELDER ABUSE

I. Collective Abuse
   A. Ageism—systemic unfair treatment of elderly persons because of their age.
   B. Discrimination in hiring practices—practice of hiring younger as opposed to older employees.
   C. Discrimination in maintaining employment—practice of firing older employees or downsizing organizations giving older employees less pay forcing early retirement.

II. Institutional Abuse
   A. Health care crimes—instances where health care organizations charge for services that were not needed or provided services that were unnecessary.
   B. Patient dumping—refusing care to older adults because coverage has lapsed.
   C. Institutional financial fraud—instances where organizations defraud elderly persons.
   D. Regulatory violations by nursing homes.

III. Individual Abuse
   A. Physical abuse—using physical force or committing violent acts, includes forced drug use.
   B. Psychological/Emotional abuse—causing pain through verbal threats or non-verbal actions.
   C. Financial abuse—wrongful use of elder's money, assets, or property.
   D. Sexual abuse—illegal non-consensual sexual activity with older adult.
   E. Neglect—failing to fulfill obligations that would assist person's daily needs.
   F. Self-neglect—instances where elderly person refuses care.
   G. Duty-related abuse—instances where employees violate organizations' rules describing how elderly persons are to be treated.
   H. Abandonment—instances where an elderly person is deserted by legal caregiver.

Sources: Littwin, 1995; National Center on Elder Abuse, 1996; Payne and Cikovic, 1995; Payne, 1998a; Virginia Coalition for the Prevention of Elder Abuse, 1998; Rosoff et al., 2003.

Critical Thinking Questions:

1. Which type of abuse do you think is the most common? Why?
2. Why is it important to categorize abuse types?

as criminal or civil; (4) their standards for reporting the abuse; (5) how the abuse should be investigated; and, (6) their recommended sanctions for the abuse (Stiegel, 1995). Because of the variation in the legal statutes, a broad social harm definition of crime allows the integration of diverse criminological concepts and abuse themes. A model proposed by Drowns and Hess (1990) that addresses child abuse can be used to better understand elder abuse. Specifically, they (1990) argue that three types of child abuse exist: *collective abuse, institutional abuse,* and *individual abuse.* This typology is useful in showing how elder abuse themes fit within this broader conceptualization of crime.

Table 1 outlines the way that these three types of abuse can be used to address crimes against elderly persons. Each type of abuse will be discussed in detail in later chapters but warrants a brief introduction at this point. At the broadest level, *collective abuse* (a.k.a. societal abuse) refers to instances where society as a whole undertakes activities that result in harm (or victimization) against elderly persons. For instance, many argue that policies and legislation are often systematically biased against older adults (Butler, 1987). The following comments from a nursing home director reflect the view that society's treatment of institutionalized elderly is ageist:

> The biggest problem is our society does not value our elderly. Most of us working in nursing homes love our elderly residents and do our best to care for them with very little money and lots of negative treatment from state agencies and the public. We have a new prison here with cable TV in every room and free dental services, but I have to struggle to find a dentist to provide dentures for our residents. The government needs to adjust its priorities. (Payne, Berg, & Byars, 1999, p. 75)

Those who point to discrimination in societal policies and legislation argue that the end result of the ageism is harm to the elderly person (Butler, 1969).

Some cite the development of laws which are intended to protect older adults as an example of ageism. Kalish (1979) uses the concept of "new ageism" to describe instances where programs, actions, and policies, though designed to help elderly persons, are based on the assumption that older adults are in need of special care because old age is treated as an illness. It can also be argued that employment policies preventing older adults from entering the workforce, or forcing them to leave the workplace earlier than they desire, are examples of discrimination against older adults. When such societal policies increase the existence of age discrimination in the employment arena, the result is collective abuse.

Institutional abuse involves instances where the actions of various organizations and institutions, or the actions of the employees of those organizations, result in either direct or indirect harm to the consumer (Drowns & Hess, 1990). It is analogous to what criminologists refer to as corporate crime, organizational occupational crime, or corporate deviance (Clinard & Yeager, 1990; Ermann & Lundman, 1982; Green, 1990). Clearly, older adults are potential victims of various forms of institutional abuse. There are at least four different types of offenses involving elderly victims that can be characterized as institutional abuse. First, health care crimes include instances of Medicare fraud where health care organizations (and doctors) either perform unnecessary services or bill for services that were never even performed. Estimates suggest that the state of Florida alone loses 1.6 billion dollars annually due to Medicare fraud, with the United States losing up to $40 billion each year due to health care crimes (de Pommereau, 1998; Rosoff et al., 2003). The fact that the majority of elderly persons have at least one chronic health problem (Treas, 1995) increases older adults' vulnerability when health care crimes are considered.

A second type of institutional abuse is called "patient dumping." This involves instances where hospitals or nursing homes either discontinue or refuse to provide care to those in need of care because their insurance will not cover the costs. In one case, for example, an assistant director of nursing was convicted for "refusing emergency room treatment to an eighty-one-year-old woman in severe respiratory distress and then [directing] an ambulance crew to take her to another hospital three miles away" (Medicaid Fraud Report, 1990, January, p. 30). Estimates from the mid-eighties suggested that hospitals "dumped" 250,000 poor, uninsured patients each year (Taira & Taira, 1991). This alarming figure led Congress to pass the Emergency Medical Treatment and Active Labor Act (EMTALA) in 1986. The EMTALA stipulated that emergency rooms must provide screening and stabilization to all patients who request it, regardless of their ability to pay (Fiesta, 1999). Penalties for violations include $50,000 fine per incident. From 1997 to 1998, the federal government was instrumental in obtaining settlements in sixty-seven dumping cases and recovering 2.3 million in penalties (Gemignani, 1999). Problems that have surfaced include determining workable definitions of "stabilizing care" and "appropriate medical screening" (Ellis, 1998).

Third, and on a related level, instances of financial fraud by nursing homes are also types of institutional abuse. In fact, a study by Braithwaite (1993) reveals that some nursing homes file false claims with insurance providers. These false claims include billing for care that was never provided, filing claims for services by staff members who are not actually staff members, and simply providing a poor quality care but billing as if the best care possible was provided. In fact, some argue that not providing adequate care is in the economic interests of some nursing homes. Specifically, Townsend (1971) writes, "The more bed ridden patients there are in a home, the better for the institution [because it means] less work, more money" (p. xv). Braithwaite (1993) also notes that some nursing homes "conspire with residents to conceal assets so that they satisfy the eligibility threshold for Medicaid benefits" (p. 14).

Fourth, nursing homes must abide by a host of complex regulatory standards the violation of which could result in criminal and/or civil penalties. Bua (1997) annually rates nursing homes on their ability to abide by the rules and keeps track of 188 different standards broadly categorized as residents' rights violations, quality of care standards, resident assessments, dietary services, physical environment standards, infection control standards, and so on. When nursing homes violate these standards, the end result is harm to the resident.

Individual abuse involves instances where a specific individual (in this case an elderly person) is directly harmed as the result of an offender's misdeeds. With individual abuse, the offender is generally an individual rather than an organization. Commentators vary on their definitions of and distinctions between types of abuse. An exhaustive list of the specific types of individual abuse researchers have considered yields at least nine different types of individual abuse.

Physical abuse is a common form of individual abuse that likely comes to mind. The National Center on Elder Abuse (1996) defines physical abuse as the "use of physical force that may result in bodily injury, physical pain, or impairment" (p. 1). Definitions of physical abuse vary, but the common ingredient among the definitions is that the victim experiences some form of harm physically. Instances where older adults are punched, kicked, hit, slapped, or assaulted in other ways are obvious examples of physical abuse. In one case, for instance, an eighty-one-year-old woman was repeatedly beaten by her sisters with canes because the sisters "wanted to make her behave" (Campbell, 1988, p. 18). After several visits to the emergency room to get treatment for the beatings, the woman was eventually killed by her sisters. Clearly, this is an example of physical abuse. It is worth noting, however, that cases are not always this obvious. In fact, some suggest that physical abuse "includes the use of physical restraints or the use of drugs to keep a person immobile" (Virginia Coalition for the Prevention of Elder Abuse, 1998, p. 2). However, restraining elderly persons, whether with drugs or physical restraints, is not defined as abuse by all social service agents.

A similar case arises when *psychological* or *emotional abuse* is considered. Basically, law enforcement officers are less likely than nursing home employees to define psychological or emotional mistreatment as types of elder abuse (Payne et al., 1999). For those who consider such mistreatment to be abuse, a typical definition is the "infliction of anguish, pain, or distress through verbal or nonverbal acts" (National Center on Elder Abuse, 1996, p. 1). Consider a case prosecuted by authorities where a caregiver told a patient, "I'll be glad when you die" (*Medicaid Fraud Report,* 1991, September, p. 11). In another case described in the same report, a nurse's aide taunted a resident as she "danced in front of the victim and stuck her tongue out at him" (May, 1991, p. 9). One author argues that psychological abuse "can be as crippling as broken bones" (Littwin, 1995, p. 38). Although these cases involve caregivers, children and relatives of the victim are those most likely to commit psychological abuse against the victim (Lachs & Pillemer, 1995).

A third type of individual abuse, *financial/material exploitation,* "means the adult's money or other property is being taken without his or her consent and used for someone else's benefit" (Virginia Coalition for the Prevention of Elder Abuse, 1998, p. 2). Cases of financial exploitation cost elderly persons up to 40 billion dollars each year and include a host of scams such as home repair frauds, phony prize winning contests, money offers for stuffing envelopes, pigeon drops, and fraudulent charities (Barker, 1993; Tighe, 1994). Offenders often search for potential victims by "trolling for prospects by visiting churches, country clubs, or senior citizen centers" (Church, 1997, p. 57).

Scam artists are not the only ones involved in the financial exploitation of elderly persons. Indeed, older adults with large amounts of cash or property "can be targets for adult children" (Hoberok, 1997, p. A1). In cases such as these, exploitation occurs when elderly persons yield legal guardianship or power of attorney to a relative they trust (Mathis, 1994). When cases of neglect are excluded, financial abuse becomes the most prevalent form of elder abuse in some states (Coker & Little, 1997).

Sexual abuse is a fourth type of individual abuse that involves instances where offenders commit "non-consensual sexual contact of any kind with an elderly person" (National Center on Elder Abuse, 1996, p. 1). Although official statistics suggest that older adults are rarely sexually abused (as compared to younger victims), interviews with adult protective services employees show that most, if not all, individuals working in adult protective services have encountered instances of elder sexual abuse (Ramsey-Klawsnik, 1991). Ramsey-Klawsnik (1991) argues that elderly persons are prime targets of sexual abuse because many are vulnerable and either unwilling or unable to report the abuse. The central premise of her approach to understanding elder sexual abuse is that sexual offenses are more often about power and control, and abusive caregivers find themselves in a position of power through which they use sex to maintain the power and subsequently exert even more control over the victim. She further suggests that official statistics underestimate the extent of elder sexual abuse.

The fifth type of individual abuse is *neglect*, which the National Center on Elder Abuse (1996) defines as "the refusal or failure to fulfill any or part of a person's obligations or duties to an elderly person" (p. 1). This is the most common form of abuse and is particularly devastating because it can lead to a host of illnesses and premature death (Lachs et al., 1998; Minaker & Frishman, 1995; Zuzga, 1996). Potential offenders include paid caregivers as well as relatives. In one case involving a paid caregiver, a patient died from an acute case of bedsores. The *Medicaid Fraud Report* (1990), a publication of the National Association of Attorneys General, describes the case in the following way:

> It is alleged that she neither provided [the victim] with a nutritional diet to prevent infection nor, after the decubiti (bedsores) began to appear, did she properly medicate the sores or regularly turn him over to prevent their growing worse. In addition, she allegedly neglected to properly clean the patient or change his bedding at regular intervals, allowed unlicensed, untrained, and unsupervised staff to treat him, and continuously ignored staff requests that he receive medical attention and hospitalization or that she attend to him in her professional capacity as a registered nurse. (October/November, p. 20)

Expressing his horror over this incident, then Deputy Attorney General Edward J. Kuriansky said, "Not even in the darkest days of New York's nursing home scandal in the mid-seventies was a patient made to endure more deplorable and inhumane treatment at the hands of a supposed caregiver" (*Medicaid Fraud Report,* October/November, 1990, p. 20). These forms of inhumane treatment continue as we enter the next century with relatives and adult children also involved in neglect cases. For instance, once they have guardianship or power of attorney, some family members refuse to spend money on needed supplies that would mitigate elderly persons' health problems. Littwin (1995) calls this "protecting the will" because the relative does not want to see the money he or she would receive when the elderly person dies "wasted" on the elderly person's health care needs.

Self-neglect is another type of individual abuse and is defined as "behaviors of an elderly person that threaten the elder's health or safety" (National Center on Elder Abuse, 1996, p. 2). As a type of elder abuse, self-neglect is described as "a controversial category" (Littwin, 1995, p. 37). The controversy centers on whether actions that adults do to themselves, or fail to do, can be considered abuse. On the one hand, it can be argued that viewing self-neglect as a type of abuse is in the best interest of those who neglect themselves. On the other hand, there are those who would argue that the inclusion of self-neglect as a type of elder abuse is a type of "new ageism" as described by Kalish (1979). The fact is that many non-elderly adults engage in activities (i.e., excessive alcohol use, poor diet, poor exercise routines, etc.) that are detrimental to their physical and mental health. Those opposed to including self-neglect as a type of elder abuse might ask why these sorts of acts are referred to as abuse for older persons but not for younger persons. Moreover, many cases of self-neglect are the result of medical conditions (dementia, Alzheimer's, etc.). To critics, categorizing those who have these illnesses as victims, self-neglect borders on the criminalization of illnesses.

Another type of individual abuse, *duty-related abuse,* is not specifically defined by the National Center on Elder Abuse but has received some attention in the academic literature (Payne & Cikovic, 1995). Duty-related abuse refers to instances where caregivers or other professionals "misperform specific occupational routines" (Payne & Cikovic, 1995, p. 64). Examples of this kind of abuse include not dispensing the patient's medication, tampering with the client's records, changing bandages improperly, not reporting suspected abuse, and so on. Payne and Cikovic (1995) describe a case where one caregiver saw another caregiver abuse an eighty-seven-year-old Alzheimer's patient and chose not to report the incident to authorities. The prosecutor offered the abuser a plea bargain if the abuser would testify that the witness did not report the abuser. This case demonstrates that some authorities, including justice professionals and nursing home administrators, are prepared to do what it takes to make sure that caregivers abide by both institutional rules and the law of the land. Note also that duty-related abuse is closely related to neglect and some would likely argue that duty-related abuse is a type of neglect.

The distinction between the two is that duty-related abuse involves instances where caregivers violate either occupational standards or the law, but their actions do not constitute neglect.

Abandonment, as the last type of individual abuse, entails "the desertion of an elderly person by an individual who has physical custody of the elder or by a person who has assumed responsibility for providing care to the elder" (National Center on Elder Abuse, 1996, p. 2). Disparagingly referred to as "granny dumping," Tanne (1992) describes a case where a family "'parked' their elderly relative in the emergency room while they went to work" (p. 332). Very little has been written about abandonment except for claims in the media which suggest that abandonment is becoming an increasing problem for hospitals in that families and nursing home staffers have been known to leave elderly persons at hospitals without providing valid addresses (Beck & Gordon, 1991). As with duty-related abuse, some may see abandonment as a type of neglect. However, laws of many states and policies of many adult protective services agencies treat abandonment and neglect as separate categories with different penalties and different recommendations for intervention.

In concluding this discussion on the types of elder abuse, three points warrant attention. First, professionals do not agree on the definitions of abuse or the types of acts that should be considered abuse (Hall, 1989; Ogg & Munn-Giddings, 1993; Payne et al., 1999; Wolf, 1996a). Second, in most cases of abuse, the acts are not isolated incidents but occur in conjunction with one another. That is, acts of emotional abuse "might include repeated threats of abandonment or of physical harm" (Morris, 1998). Third, the way that society defines elder abuse will affect how society and social service professionals (social workers, health care providers, law enforcement officials, and others) respond to allegations of abuse. The problem is that a limited understanding among policy makers and members of the public has restricted social service agents' abilities to intervene in cases of elder abuse. The limited understanding of the way that crime affects elderly persons stems from certain myths about elderly crime victims that permeate various individuals' beliefs about crime.

MYTHS ABOUT CRIMES AGAINST OLDER VICTIMS

Myth 1–Most crimes committed against older adults are violent street crimes.

When the idea of elder abuse is considered, some automatically think that violent acts are at the center of the concept. This is likely due to a belief that crime in general is more likely to be of a violent nature and occur on the streets as opposed to in the victim's home. Crime statistics will be considered in more detail later; for now, estimates suggest that property crimes occur five times more often against older adults than violent crimes (Kalter, 1995). Even so, when individuals talk about the crime problem, they tend to speak about violent crime.

It is also important to question our conceptualization of violence (Friedrichs, 2003). Most often when crimes of violence are considered, murder, robbery, rape, and assault are the examples provided. Excluded from this conceptualization are white-collar crimes, environmental crimes, and various instances of corporate deviance that clearly result in physical harm (Friedrichs, 2003; Payne, 1998a). These offenses are not violent street crimes but are violent crimes that occur either in the victim's residence or a location where he or she supposedly feels safe (such as a hospital or a business establishment). As will be shown, elderly persons are more vulnerable to victimization in these areas than are younger persons (Nieves, 1995). Yet, when the crime problem is discussed, there is a tendency to consider the violent street crimes as opposed to these other types of crimes. As an example, the Bureau of Justice Statistics (1999) points out that one in eleven persons between the ages of twelve and fifteen were victims of violent crime in 1997, compared to one in 227 who are sixty-five or older. These statistics show that older adults are not as likely to be victims of street crime. But, if these statistics are used to portray the total crime problem as it affects older adults, then a very distorted picture of crime will evolve.

Myth 2–The consequences of victimization are the same for elderly persons as they are for young people.

Though not tested empirically, comments I have heard in the media and from students who research elder abuse seem to suggest that elderly persons would experience the same form of harm from victimization as younger persons do. Part of this belief likely stems from the fact that very little research has focused solely on what the consequences of elder abuse are (Payne & Cikovic, 1995). What happens, then, is that people assume that the results of traditional victimology research, which has for the most part examined younger victims, can be used to understand the consequences of elderly victimization.

Recent comments show that some have begun to recognize the consequences of elderly victimization, and these comments show that the consequences are indeed different for elderly victims. For example, Jackson-Lee (1996) points out that older crime victims are more likely to be injured than younger crime victims. Consequently, some suggest that increased risk is tied to a higher fear of crime which is consistently found among elderly persons (Pain, 1995). In a similar vein, Bachman, Dillaway, and Lachs (1998) analyzed data from the National Crime Victimization Survey (NCVS) and found that older victims were more likely to be injured by violent attacks and were more likely to need medical assistance due to the injuries.

The loss of trust is another consequence that older adults may experience differently than younger victims (Kalter, 1995). One author writes that some older victims "have plunged into such despair that they have lost their will to live" (Church, 1997, p. 55). This suggestion was recently supported by a study of over 2,800 older adults that found that older victims of abuse and neglect were three times more likely to die earlier than non-abused older adults (Lachs et al., 1998).

Myth 3–The best way to deal with elder abuse is to pass laws that will protect the elderly.

When elder abuse first surfaced as a social problem in the late seventies and the early eighties, a surge of legislation that was designed to protect older persons was passed in the United States. To some, it appeared that "the laws were hastily written substituting the word elder in child protection statutes" (Littwin, 1995, p. 37). According to the American Bar Association, the fact that many of the laws were developed over two years ago, using child abuse statutes as models, has limited the ability of the statutes to respond to many offenses involving financial exploitation. Or, since the laws were based on child abuse statutes and children were not likely to be financially exploited, legislation was aimed at curbing physical abuse as opposed to economic abuse (Steigel, 1995).

Another problem with relying on a child abuse model is that individuals look for signs of child abuse in attempting to identify elder abuse. As will be seen later, the warning signs for the two types of abuse are different (Young, 2000). Macolini (1995) is even more critical of elder abuse legislation stating, "Elder abuse laws have arisen without a cogent rationale for their existence" (p. 354).

Mandatory reporting laws are an example of a highly debated, yet successfully passed, type of elder abuse legislation. Mandatory reporting laws state that certain professionals must report suspected cases of elder abuse. Table 2 outlines the way that states across the United States have developed their reporting laws. Basically, those professionals who, in theory, must report suspected elder abuse cases vary by state and include health care professionals, human service professionals, clergy, law enforcement professionals, financial professionals, and long-term care professionals. Sixteen states mandate that any person who suspects abuse must report it, while Colorado, Illinois, Iowa, Kentucky, New York, North Dakota, South Dakota, and Wisconsin have no forms of mandatory reporting (Stiegel, 1995). According to Zborowsky, (1985) the aim of the mandatory reporting laws was "to assure the well-being of older people and at the same time protect their civil rights" (p. 80). At the same time,

TABLE 2. STATES' REPORTING REQUIREMENTS

	Health Care Empl.	Human Service Empl.	Clergy	Police	L-T-C Empl.	Financial Prof.	Other	Any Person
Alabama	*							
Alaska	*	*	*	*	*			
Arizona	*	*		*	*	*	*	
Arkansas	*	*		*	*			
California	*		*	*		*		
Colorado								
Connecticut	*	*	*	*	*			
Delaware					*		*	*
D.C.	*	*		*	*			
Florida	*			*	*	*	*	
Georgia	*	*	*	*	*		*	
Hawaii	*	*		*	*		*	
Idaho	*	*		*	*		*	
Illinois								
Indiana	*	*		*	*			*
Iowa								
Kansas	*			*			*	
Kentucky								
Louisiana								*
Maine	*			*				*
Maryland	*	*		*				*
Massachusetts	*	*		*			*	
Michigan	*	*		*			*	
Minnesota	*	*		*	*		*	
Mississippi	*	*			*			*
Missouri	*	*	*	*	*		*	*
Montana	*	*		*	*		*	
Nebraska	*	*		*	*		*	
Nevada	*	*	*	*	*		*	
New Hampshire								*
New Jersey	*	*					*	
New Mexico								*
New York								
North Carolina								*
North Dakota								
Ohio	*	*	*	*	*		*	
Oklahoma					*			*
Oregon	*	*	*	*			*	
Pennsylvania								
Rhode Island	*	*		*	*		*	*
South Carolina	*	*		*	*		*	
South Dakota								
Tennessee								*

(*continued*)

TABLE 2. (CONTINUED)

	Health Care Empl.	Human Service Empl.	Clergy	Police	L-T-C Empl.	Financial Prof.	Other	Any Person
Texas								*
Utah								*
Vermont	*	*		*	*		*	
Virginia	*	*		*			*	
Washington	*	*		*	*			
West Virginia	*	*		*				
Wisconsin								
Wyoming								*

Critical Thinking Questions:

1. What are the advantages of mandatory reporting laws?
2. Why is there so much variation in who is required to report abuse across states?

the laws were designed to protect employees from liability as long as they report the suspected abuse in good faith.

Though the intent of these statutes may have been to protect older citizens, some have argued that they have done more harm than good. Those who question the usefulness of the mandatory reporting laws point to the following criticisms: (1) the laws were not based on research; (2) they have been expensive to enforce; (3) they can be used in vindictive ways; (4) there are problems defining what should be reported as abuse; (5) they are ageist; (6) they violate patient-client confidentiality; (7) the subsequent investigations do more harm than good; (8) victims are revictimized by the justice process; (9) they threaten the autonomy of the older adult; (10) they are an invasion of privacy; and (11) they show disregard for the older adult's autonomy (Crystal, 1986; Daniels, Baumhouver, & Clarke-Daniels, 1989; Faulkner, 1982; Macolini, 1995; Utech & Garrett, 1992). Central to each of these criticisms is the result of some of the reported cases–the older family abuse victim ends up being sent to a nursing home (Breckman & Adelman, 1988).

These comments are not to say that passing laws to protect against abuse is wrong; rather, unless those who are involved in responding to and dealing with crimes against elderly persons agree with the law, it really does not matter what the law says. A decade ago, only one in three physicians who suspected abuse reported it (Campbell, 1988). By the mid-nineties, many physicians still failed "to address the problem of elder abuse at the clinical, research, and policy making levels" (Lachs, 1995, p. 11). The best way to get doctors, and other social service professionals, to engage in activities to protect victims of elder abuse is not to pass laws, but to get all groups involved in detecting and responding to elder abuse to work together to protect the victim (Payne et al., 1999).

Myth 4–Elder abuse is quite similar to child abuse.

When laws, policies, research, and theories were initially developed, they relied on child abuse models to respond to questions arising out of elder abuse scenarios (Stiegel, 1995). The problem is that although children and some older adults are similar in their dependency status, older adults "are not simply old children" (Anetzberger, 1987). Indeed, to some comparing elder abuse as it compares to child abuse is ageist and assumes that older adults need protection just like children do (Breckman & Adelman, 1988). As Macolini (1995) sees it, "statutes appear to presume reduced competency in elders, more similar to the level of competency ascribed to children than to younger adults" (p. 354).

Myth 5–Children who abuse their parents do so because they were beaten as children.

On the surface, this myth makes some sense logistically. After all, research shows that children who are beaten are more likely to be violent when they get older (Browne & Hamilton, 1998; Drowns & Hess, 1990; Maxfield & Widom, 1996). Various phrases such as "violence begets violence" and the "cycle of violence" try to describe this process by which abused kids become abusers later in life. It would follow then that if violence in one's childhood causes one to become violent as an adult, then perhaps the child victim would be prone to "pay back" his or her parents with abuse once the child becomes an adult. Korbin, Anetzberger, and Austin (1995) interviewed elder abuse offenders and child abuse offenders, focusing specifically on violent episodes the offenders experienced during their childhoods. Testing the "violence begets violence" hypothesis, they found that the "intergenerational transmission of family violence" applies to child abuse but not elder abuse. Or, kids who are beaten are likely to become adults who beat their kids but do not tend to become adults who beat their parents. Pillemer (1986) found similar results.

Myth 6–Adult family members who abuse their parent do it because their parent is dependent on them.

This is another myth that some may have difficulties with initially. A widespread belief has been that older adults are dependent on their caregivers and that this dependency overwhelms the caregiver who experiences daily stresses trying to deal with the dependent adult. The notion that once again surfaces is that the older adult has become the child and subsequently a burden on the caregiver. Research by Pillemer (1986) found the exact opposite. Specifically, he found that offenders are more likely to be dependent on the victim, and they commit abuse to gain some sort of control over the offender. The dependence, Pillemer noted, involved both mental and financial dependence. He also found that the abusers had emotional problems, problems with alcohol dependence, and long-term dependency relations with the elderly victim. The underlying reason authors suggest that the dependency leads to abuse is that the perpetrator is acting out against the dependency (Pillemer, 1986; Wolf & Pillemer, 1989; Breckman & Adelman, 1988). So, it is often the offender who is likely to be dependent on the victim, rather than the other way around.

Myth 7–Many older people are victims because they are in the wrong place at the wrong time.

Some believe that older adults are victimized because they are in the wrong place at the wrong time. Indeed, because so many older adults themselves seem to accept this premise, they utilize a host of protective measures to reduce their risk of victimization (Pain, 1995). But, elderly persons are more likely to be victimized by someone they know as opposed to a stranger. In fact, seventy percent of all elder abuse cases involve offenders who are relatives of the victim with half of the relatives being adult children (Littwin, 1995). In physical abuse cases, spouses and adult children are the most common abusers (Lachs & Pillemer, 1995). Even more disturbing is the suggestion that elder persons are nearly "twice as likely as younger victims to be raped, robbed, or assaulted at or near their home" (Jackson-Lee, 1996, p. H4491). Building on this idea, Bachman, Dillaway, and Lachs (1998) note that elderly persons are just as likely to be murdered in their home by strangers as they are by known offenders. They write, "while most think of the home as a refuge from the evils of the outside world, it does not seem to serve that purpose for the elderly" (p. 197). Also recall the fact that elderly persons are more likely to be targets of telemarketing fraud, fraudulent charities, and other scams. By the very nature of these scams, the offenses would have to occur in the home rather than somewhere "where the older person was at the wrong time."

Another point that would help debunk myths 6, 7, and 8 (each dealing with why the offenses occur) is that there is no one reason that suitably explains why all of the abusive acts occur. Causes cited in the literature include abuse socialization, social isolation, retaliation, lack of money, vulnerability, intimacy problems, impairment, external stresses, ageism, acute stresses, and external stresses (Anetzberger, 1987; Paveza et al., 1992; Pillemer & Finkelhor, 1989; Wolf, 1988). The point is that it would be foolhardy to suggest that these acts are caused by one single factor.

Myth 8—Crimes against older persons are not really a serious problem in our society.

This is likely the most important myth because believing it limits our ability to deal with the problem that does exist. Official statistics seem to support this myth. Table 3 shows the percentage of violent crime victims by age. As shown in the table, elderly persons are significantly less likely than adolescents and younger adults to be victims of violent crime.

Table 4 shows how many individuals there are in each age group per victim. Again, the numbers strikingly suggest that elderly persons are very rarely victims of violent crime. In fact, the Bureau of Justice Statistics suggests that the serious violent crime rate is seventeen times higher for individuals eighteen to twenty-one years old than it is for those sixty-five or older. Because of these "unequivocal findings," elderly victims of violence are paid very little attention in the literature (Bachman et al., 1998, p. 1).

The attention that has been given questions the wisdom of assuming that these findings give an accurate picture of the crime problem as it impacts elderly persons' lives. For instance, the Bureau of Justice Statistics says that one

TABLE 3. AGES OF VIOLENT CRIME VICTIMS

| | | Percent of Victims | | |
Age of Victim	Percent of Population	All Violent Crime	Rape/Sexual Assault	Robbery
12 to 14	5	10	8	11
15 to 17	5	12	12	10
18 to 21	7	17	21	14
22 to 24	5	11	14	9
25 to 29	9	13	9	12
30 to 34	11	11	13	12
35 to 39	10	8	9	8
40 to 49	17	12	10	12
50 to 64	16	5	2	6
65 or older	15	2	1	4

Source: Perkins, C. (1997). *Age Patterns of Victims of Serious Violent Crime.* Washington, D.C.: U.S. Department of Justice.

Critical Thinking Questions:

1. Why do you think these patterns exist?
2. How would these patterns influence criminal justice policies?

TABLE 4. PROBABILITY OF VICTIMIZATION BY EACH AGE GROUP

| Age of Victim | *Number of Persons in the Population for Each Victim* | | | | |
	All Serious Violent Crime	Murder	Rape/Sexual Assault	Robbery	Aggravated Assault
12 to 24	23	5945	168	83	39
25 to 34	42	6170	378	132	73
35 to 49	67	10891	591	219	116
50 or older	424	23376	4272	494	424
Total	50	9241	416	164	86

Source: Perkins, C. (1997). *Age Patterns of Victims of Serious Violent Crime.* Washington, D.C: U.S. Department of Justice.

Critical Thinking Questions:

1. Why do you think these patterns exist?
2. How would these patterns influence criminal justice policies?

in 265 older adults are victims of violence each year. Littwin (1995) cites a separate official report that suggests that one in twenty elderly persons, or 1.5 million, may be victims of elder abuse each year. A prevalence study by Pillemer and Finkelhor (1988) found that thirty-two out of 1,000 older adults reported mistreatment, with twenty out of 1,000 reporting physical abuse. So, why is there disparity between these figures? Part of the answer lies in the decision to view "violent crime" as the type of crime which is a problem in our society. According to the Federal Bureau of Investigation's *Uniform Crime Reports,* these violent crimes are murder, robbery, rape, and assault. The FBI's definitions are based entirely on activities that are more central to younger members of society. Of course, we would find that younger persons would more often be the victims of these offenses. Gauging the seriousness of crime according to the FBI's measure of violent crimes ignores many of the offenses of which elderly persons are primary targets (Church, 1997; McCabe & Gregory, 1998; Payne, 1998b).

To examine whether the FBI's statistics adequately reflect crime in the lives of older adults, McCabe and Gregory (1998) analyzed data from the FBI's National Incident Based Reporting System (NIBRS) in South Carolina. Using this comprehensive data base, results of their study reveal that older adults (sixty-five and older) are "more at risk than are younger segments of the population for crimes of robbery, intimidation, vandalism, and forgery/fraud" (p. 363). But intimidation, vandalism, and fraud are not seen as "violent offenses." One could argue, however, that the effects experienced by the victims are more important than whether the FBI and the BJS decide to label certain acts as violent. The problem is that the labels are misleading and they tend to mask the real crime problem as it affects older adults.

It would be unfair to say that the labels are misleading without providing further support for why the crime problem as it affects elderly persons is an important area of study. Notwithstanding the facts that older adults experience the effects of victimization differently and that up to one million elderly persons are abused each year, when dollar figures are considered, estimates suggest that consumer frauds targeting the elderly cost nearly $40 billion each year (Barker, 1993). Even more important is the future of the crime problem as it affects older adults. Surely we have witnessed steady growth in the number of elderly persons living in the United States. In fact, at the turn of the twentieth century, only four percent of the population were "elderly." Today, roughly thirteen percent of the population fits under that label. Demographers estimate that elderly persons will make up one fourth of the U.S. population by 2025 (Treas, 1995). Many believe that more elderly residents means more crime victims in the next few decades (Lachs et al., 1996; Minaker & Frishman, 1995). Interestingly, the trend may have already started. Recent crime statistics from the Bureau of Justice Statistics show that between 1993 and 1997, crime went down for all age groups except for older adults (Rand, 1998). Yet, there is still a misconception that crimes against elderly persons are not that problematic. As will be discussed in the next chapter, the crime figures alone are not the only reason for this misguided perception about the victimization of older adults, but the official statistics have certainly restricted the way social scientists have examined crimes against elderly persons.

Myth 9–In order to best prevent elder abuse, criminal justice agencies must proactively search out offenders and punish them as severely as possible.

Now that a crime problem has been declared, some might argue that the best way to solve the problem is to treat it like many other crime problems–declare a war and attack it forcefully with law enforcement and strict sanctions. This would result in a dismal failure. Instead, what needs to occur is an integrated effort among criminal justice agents and social service professionals. This integrated effort requires cooperation among the actors involved in detecting and responding to elder abuse. To encourage this cooperation, researchers and scholars must approach elder abuse from a broad perspective, linking ideas from various disciplines together so that those learning about the phenomenon see it as the pervasive type of social problem which it really is. The tying together of these ideas could be referred to as *gero-criminology*, which links assumptions of various disciplines and approaches crimes against the elderly from a holistic perspective.

The fields that have examined either crime or the lives of elderly persons include, but certainly are not limited to, criminal justice, criminology, gerontology, psychology, social work, sociology, and victimology. As social sciences, these disciplines focus on various dynamics associated with human behavior. It is important to note that when crimes against elderly persons are considered, ideas from each of these fields potentially contribute to an increased understanding of the way that crime affects elderly persons. Using the strengths of each of these disciplines, and the strengths of the various human service employees who emerge from these disciplines, will increase society's understanding of, and response to, crimes against elderly persons. What follows is a brief introduction to each discipline with particular attention given to the way that each discipline offers insight into offenses against elderly persons. Note that the overview of the disciplines is purposefully succinct. Within each discipline, there are numerous subareas and subfields that help define each discipline. Also, there is no single definition of any of the disciplines that would be agreed on by all members of one particular discipline. However, by keeping the descriptions of the disciplines broad and discussing only how the disciplines either have, or could, address crimes against elderly persons, a base from which this integrated effort can evolve will be created.

For example, sociology is a social science concerned with the role that social forces have in shaping behavior. The strength of sociology has been its ability to illuminate the interplay between various segments of the contemporary society and offer insight into ways that programs and policies can be used to improve society. The weakness, in the area of crimes against elderly persons, is that sociologists who study crime typically focus on the more youthful offenders and victims.

Criminology and criminal justice, two closely related fields, are concerned with the patterns of crime and the formal and informal responses to crime. Though some would argue that the two fields have more differences than similarities, when I refer to criminologists or criminology in this text, I am including ideas from both fields. The strength of criminology concerns its ability to understand causes of crime and assess the approaches used to respond to various crime problems. The weakness of criminology, as far as elder abuse is concerned, is that historically its focus has been oriented more toward street crime and younger offenders than toward the victimization experiences of elderly persons.

The discipline of psychology examines human behavior from the inside out. Or, psychologists focus more on an individual's internal psyche in understanding behavior. The strength of psychology is its ability to understand individual behavior and subsequently offer and evaluate various treatment methods that can be used to help victims, or to rehabilitate offenders. The weakness is that psychologists, like other social scientists, have given relatively little attention to older victims of crime.

Victimology focuses primarily on the victim and the victim-offender relationship. Its strength is obvious in that increased understanding about victimization has been forthcoming since the field evolved in the fifties and sixties. The weakness, as with the other approaches, is that primary attention has been directed more toward younger victims and street crimes, which by their very nature exclude many elderly crime victims.

Social work can be described as a discipline and a practice. As a discipline, social work is concerned with how to best utilize casework methods to assist those who are in need of care. As a practice, social workers regularly use those methods to help individuals in need of certain services. The strength of the social work approach is that it has a long history of studying elder abuse. The weakness is that relying solely on the social work approach, without including criminological themes, tends to decriminalize elder abuse.

Finally, gerontology is the study of aging, focusing primarily on dispelling myths that have contributed to ageism against older persons. It has both biological and sociological orientations. Several gerontologists have examined how older adults are victimized. However, few have integrated criminological or criminal justice themes that would help us understand the role of both formal and informal responses to crimes against older adults.

By integrating and examining the way each of these disciplines has considered crimes against elderly persons, a better understanding of the issue will surely follow. This increased understanding will provide the information needed to better educate various professionals on how to deal with crimes against older adults. Also, by offering an integrated approach to understanding crimes against elderly persons, the reader will see that an integrated approach would also be useful in responding to these offenses. In other words, all actors involved in the detection, intervention, prosecution, and treatment of elder abuse offenders and their victims need to work together to best respond to crimes against elderly persons. These actors include social workers, applied gerontologists, case workers, law enforcement officers, prosecutors, psychologists, probation officers, nursing home employees, and numerous other human service employees who come into contact with elder abuse victims and/or elder abuse perpetrators.

SUMMARY AND PLAN OF PRESENTATION

We have a crime problem in our society. Like other social problems, the crime problem seems to be influenced by broader structural factors. For example, the economy changes with various shifts in the political, educational, and technological systems (Van Gigch, 1978). Crime and consequences of crime also change along with the overall structural changes. The demographic makeup of society, for instance, has been correlated with crime and other social problems. Specifically, the more younger people there are (between fourteen and twenty-four), the higher the crime rate. Also, study after study shows that age is related to victimization in that younger people are more likely to be victimized than older people (Rand, 1998). All too often it seems that we interpret these findings as if they indicate that crime among older adults is not as important of an issue as crime among the younger population. As shown earlier, this is misleading and underestimates the victimization costs experienced by elderly crime victims. In my opinion, since crimes against elderly persons have been overlooked so much by criminologists, they may be even more important to study than the traditional types of crime. Five caveats support my belief.

First, Steffensmeier and Harer (1991) predicted the crime rate would go down in the nineties due to the decreased number of younger people in the United States. Official statistics suggest that their prediction was entirely accurate. In general, the crime rate has gone down since the early nineties and politicians are finding this the perfect opportunity to attribute the decreases in crime to their implementation of truth in sentencing laws, increased law enforcement efforts, and a tougher justice system in general. Not found in these comments, however, is any discussion about the fact that crime among older adults has not decreased. The supposed "get tough on crime" approach has done little or nothing for older adults whose crime rate remained stable while it decreased among the other age groups.

Second, given the demographic and technological changes occurring in our society, it is expected that crimes against older adults will increase. Most, if not all, demographers agree that in the future there will be more older persons than ever before (Treas, 1995). Based on this, all other factors held constant, there will be more older victims than ever before (Lachs & Pillemer, 1996). At the same time, with all of the technological changes occurring in our society, an increase in different types of white-collar crimes, which target elderly persons, is virtually inevitable (Friedrichs, 2003). It is imperative that those dealing with crimes against elderly persons become aware of the issues and concerns that face elderly persons so they are not revictimized by the justice process.

Third, and on a related level, when issues surface due to political, social, and technological changes, educators are often reluctant to confront the issues due to the fear that spending too much time on the issues will be unproductive in the classroom and in the research arena. My colleagues who study gender issues, for instance, tell me that they faced numerous obstacles from curriculum committees, journal editors, and publishers in convincing the respective parties that gender issues were relevant and noteworthy. I have other colleagues who teach courses dealing with race issues who had to justify the importance of integrating racial issues into their criminological and sociological endeavors. Likewise, I have friends who study environmental crime who indicate that they were forced to confront similar obstacles in their attempt to develop environmental crime courses, publish environmental crime works, and produce textbooks dealing with environmental crime.

Today, courses on gender studies, race and crime, and environmental crime are common in most criminology and criminal justice programs. At the very least, these issues are accepted as important issues that need to be discussed at some point within various programs designed to educate future social service professionals. Introducing discourse on older victims of crime has faced similar obstacles. However, because the issue is not clearly defined is not a reason to ignore the issue; rather it is a reason to confront the issue head on and use existing sociological, criminological, psychological, and gerontological principles to make sense of the issue.

Fourth, although I have argued vehemently that official statistics severely underestimate the extent of crime against elderly persons, even if older adults are victimized less often than younger adults, that does not mean we should not be concerned with the issue. Research consistently shows that crime occurs far more often in urban areas than rural areas (Bachman, 1992; Weisheit, Wells, & Falcone, 1995). Likewise, research shows that men commit far more crime than women (Broidy & Agnew, 1997; Steffensmeier & Allan, 1996).

Should we ignore these issues (rural crime and criminal women) because they do not represent the vast majority of the so-called crime problem? Of course not. By paying attention to these issues, insight into similarities and differences between the majority (urban crime and male offenders) and the minority (rural crime and female offenders) has been forthcoming. This sort of understanding has yielded important implications for policy, research, and theory. The fact that there are age differences in how groups experience crime is reason enough to examine crimes against elderly persons. For example, a great deal of research suggests that older adults are more afraid of victimization than younger adults. Measures that would reduce both fear of crime and victimization risks need to be taken.

One of the first articles I ever wrote was a piece that examined the characteristics of elder abuse cases reported in nursing homes (Payne & Cikovic, 1995). It was based on reports to Medicaid Fraud Control Units. Two years after this article was in print, I received a letter from a woman who had read the article. With the letter were two pictures of an elderly woman's bruised face. Both eyes of the woman in the picture were blackened, and bruises stretched from across her forehead to the entire width of her neck. The pictures were, to say the least, horrific. The following letter was included with the pictures:

> I read your article on elder abuse and was very interested in it. Something happened to my aunt in a nursing home. She was 102 years old and had been in a fetal position only moving her arms for over two years. They are trying to tell me she did this to herself on the bed railing, which would have been impossible. Every one in the nursing home covered this incident up, and because of the fact that the administrator worked for the state for 12 years, I am getting no help from state officials. I would like your idea about what you think might have happened to her and where I can go next for help to get to the bottom of this.

I sent the niece a note describing the agencies I was aware of that might assist her in her efforts to investigate the abuse of her aunt. I am not sure how the case was resolved, but I am certain that it was not an easy process for the niece. Unfortunately, this woman had no one to turn to and no where to go. It is my hope that this text will be a resource for all individuals who are concerned or confronted with crimes against elderly persons, and that it will stimulate new research into this crucial subject.

As you read this text, I want you to think about something I saw several years ago that reminded me of the overall theme of this text. In particular, I noticed two older women who appeared to be in their late seventies leaving a gathering together. I had noticed these women at this regular gathering several times before. One of them was severely visually impaired, and the other was confined to a wheelchair but was unable to maneuver the chair on her own; they typically sat next to one another at this particular gathering. What I had overlooked in the past was the way that the women used their combined strengths to offset the other's weakness. On this particular day, I noticed the blind woman holding the handles of the wheelchair and pushing it in the direction indicated by the woman sitting in the wheelchair. So, using the other woman's vision, the blind woman was able to "see" and the woman confined in the wheelchair was able to move. Once I noticed this process, without fail each week the two women followed the same ritual when leaving the gathering. I am sure they had used this practice for a long time prior to my noticing it. Upon seeing it, it made absolute sense to me. In a similar vein, if only the agents involved in detecting and responding to crimes against seniors worked together as smoothly as these two women. If only the agencies would recognize and utilize each other's strengths and weaknesses the way these two women did! Along a similar line, imagine what would happen if the diverse academic disciplines which study fragmented elements of the problem could integrate and blend their efforts in a cohesive paradigm! It is my hope that the reader will see the strengths and weaknesses of each approach and that understanding will promote vision, movement, and cooperation on the part of various actors in the agencies involved in detecting and responding to crimes against older adults. Only through increased understanding will policy makers, practitioners, and educators be prepared to limit the negative consequences associated with the victimization of older adults.

To move toward this increased understanding, each chapter in this text starts with a case scenario describing an elderly person's victimization experience and concludes with the consequences of that experience. Chapter 2 discusses the way that social scientists have gauged the victimization experiences of older adults and the way that certain disciplines have ignored these incidents. Chapter 3 considers in full detail the specific types of offenses of which elderly persons are targets. Chapter 4 considers the specific consequences of offenses against elderly persons and compares those consequences to those experienced by younger victims. Chapter 5 offers some insight into the way that the criminal justice system and other decision makers detect and respond to crimes against elderly persons. Chapter 6 considers various explanations of crimes against elderly persons and contrasts those explanations with theories aimed at describing youthful offenses. Chapter 7 addressed strategies for preventing elder abuse and suggestions for individuals, caregivers, health care providers, and criminal justice and social services professionals provided. Finally, Chapter 8 offers recommendations for future research, policy, and programs dealing with offenses against elderly persons.

Chapters 2 through 7 include a box inset titled "Voices from the Field." These insets were written by professionals with expertise in the study of elder abuse. Their "voices" are provided to bring to light the various issues considered throughout the chapters. Interestingly, these individuals represent the vastly different occupations (e.g., academics, advocates/writers, ombudsmen, police officers, and social services) that need to work together to respond to elder abuse cases. Through it all, it is hoped that the reader will see the usefulness of promoting cooperation among the various social service agencies in preventing and responding to these offenses and come to appreciate the consequences of these offenses.

Recall Mary Ann's case. She lost a large portion of her retirement income. Unlike many others, she was able to recover and now gives crime prevention speeches for the American Association of Retired People. But imagine for a moment the horror she felt when she realized she had lost $74,000. More than that, however, think about the broader but immeasureable impact that this one event had on others. There are secondary victims including relatives, friends, and associates who experience losses and mental anguish as a result of Mary Ann's exploitation (Breckman & Adelman, 1988). Individuals who were not directly victimized hear of events such as this one and experience a loss of trust which yields consequences for those who heard about the event as well as other legitimate businesses who use telephones to solicit customers (Friedrichs, 2003; Payne, 1998a). Citizens read about it and many likely come to believe that other businesses are like this fraudulent business. These beliefs result in a loss of investor confidence which subsequently leads to higher costs for the consumer (Friedrichs, 2003; Rosoff et al., 2003). Can these losses be easily measured? Of course not. But, destroying trust and increasing fear are nonetheless two of the most important consequences of crimes against older adults. The loss of trust and the spread of fear can be countered with research and policies that will provide a better understanding of the crime problem as it influences older adults.

Chapter 2

CRIMES COMMITTED AGAINST THE ELDERLY: WHY HAVE THEY BEEN IGNORED FOR SO LONG?

1. What is white-collar crime? How does it relate to crimes against elderly persons?
2. Compare and contrast elder abuse and family violence.
3. How has politics influenced the way social scientists study crimes against seniors?
4. What does the author mean by magnitude issues?
5. What methods do social scientists use to study crimes against elderly persons?
6. What are the strengths and limitations of each research method?
7. What is meant by a multi-method approach?

INTRODUCTION

A seventy-eight-year-old woman died weighing only seventy-five pounds at her death. She had not been fed in over a month. It was not because her family did not have the resources; rather, more than $300,000 was in a trust fund that the family members were supposed to use for the woman's care. Her caregivers, who were relatives, allegedly denied her food and medical care so they would inherit the trust fund (Rozek, 2003).

A number of issues arise in considering this case. Did elder abuse occur? If so, what type of abuse was it? How should it be counted—as abuse or neglect? Is it murder? From a social harm orientation, one might call acts such as these which lead to death murders; however, official statistics would not capture these acts as murders or any other common criminal offense for that matter.

In the mid-1970s, the concept of "granny bashing" began to appear in British medical journals and described instances where children, grandchildren, and even health care personnel committed a host of violent, abusive, and/or inappropriate acts against older citizens (Baker, 1975). Practitioners and social scientists quickly recognized the "ageist assumptions that lay behind its labeling" and turned to the more accepted notion of elder abuse to describe these acts (Ogg & Munn-Giddings, 1993). After the inception of these concepts, attention to the problem soared in the early eighties throughout the world. In fact, concern was noted among various groups including law makers, practitioners, and scholars. Though the attention did not increase in the nineties, it did not decrease either. It is safe to suggest that elder abuse has received an abundance of scholarly attention resulting in an interdisciplinary focus. Indeed, social workers, gerontologists, psychologists, legal scholars, and a host of other social scientists have spent a great deal of time examining elder abuse. One of the issues that crosses these disciplines involves the inability to agree on an acceptable definition of elder abuse. However, an examination of many of the definitions offered by experts from outside the field of criminology imply that what they are calling elder abuse are typically examples of two distinct types of offenses considered by criminologists—white-collar crime and domestic violence.

However, empirical examinations by criminologists are rare in this area, and questions about white-collar crimes against the elderly, and domestic violence against elderly victims, have been relatively ignored by criminologists. This lack of attention is likely caused by the following: *conceptual ambiguity, political issues, magnitude issues,* and *methodological problems.* By addressing the reasons for the lack of attention given to the crimes against the elderly, it is expected that ways to increase attention in this area will evolve.

CONCEPTUAL AMBIGUITY

Four points regarding the *conceptual ambiguity* of crimes against the elderly are virtually inarguable. First, there is considerable disagreement about the definition of white-collar crime (Friedrichs, 2003). Second, there is very little agreement about the definition of elder abuse (Childs et al., 2000; Eleazer, 1995; Ogg & Munn-Giddings, 1993; Pritchard, 1996a). Third, there has been little agreement about what constitutes domestic violence (aka family abuse, family violence, and domestic abuse), which many cases of elder abuse are (Arbetter, 1995; Littwin, 1995). The lack of agreement about definitions of crime and abuse led to inconsistent and questionable responses to potentially criminal and harmful behavior (Faulkner, 1982; Wolf, 1992). Fourth, variations in state laws, with twenty-eight different terms for elder abuse and neglect, have made it difficult to compare empirical data from different states and implement programs across state lines (Roby & Sullivan, 2000). A review of the definitions of white-collar crime, elder abuse, and family abuse should shed some light on ways to better understand and define these crimes.

White-Collar Crime Definitions

To say that definitions of white-collar crime are varied is an understatement. Edwin Sutherland introduced the concept in 1939 at the annual meeting of the American Sociological Society and later defined white-collar crime as "crimes committed by a person of respectability and high social status in the course of his occupation" (Sutherland, 1949, p. 112). Since then, debates have centered on exactly what sorts of acts, occupations, and victims are captured under this concept (Friedrichs, 2003; Rosoff, Pontell, & Tillman, 1998). Rosoff et al. (2003) note that, "Sutherland's work was ground breaking, forging a new theoretical path and setting a research agenda for many future scholars" (p. 3). Sutherland's concept has broadened considerably to the point that the specific types of white-collar crime are now accepted, albeit debated, by researchers and practitioners. For example, in a recent addition to the white-collar crime literature, Rosoff et al. (2003) describe the following types of white-collar crime: crimes against consumers, environmental crime, fiduciary fraud, crime by the government, corruption of public officials, computer crime, and medical crime. In a similar way, Friedrichs (2003) describes the following categories of white-collar crime: corporate crime, occupational crime, political white-collar crime, technocrime, finance crime, enterprise crime, contrepreneurial crime, and avocational crime. Clearly, a host of different types of white-collar crime exist.

In addition to an increased focus on the specific types of white-collar crime included in its definition, the concept itself has broadened and led to the introduction of a host of related issues that relate to, yet are functionally distinct from, Sutherland's definition. Among these new labels are corporate misconduct (Vaughn, 1983), corporate crime (Clinard & Yeager, 1980), corporate deviance (Ermann & Lundmann, 1982), and organizational crime (Braithwaite, 1989). The problem that arises with regard to white-collar crimes against the elderly concerns attempts to decide what type of crimes they are. For example, are they occupational crimes, white-collar crimes, or corporate crimes? Even more problematic is the answer: crimes against the elderly, whether they are referred to as elder abuse or some other concept, can be examples of each of the aforementioned types of crime.

First, regarding occupational crimes, seniors can be victims of either physical or property offenses. Cases of nursing home abuse committed by nurses' aides or other nursing home employees are known to occur (Braithwaite, 1993; Payne & Cikovic, 1995). It is also known that various employees defraud senior citizens of their limited funds. How these acts are defined by practitioners, scholars, and citizens is of critical import.

Second, seniors can also experience all forms of white-collar crime victimization. Rosoff et al. (2003) describe a host of examples of patient abuse in nursing homes that are clearly examples of white-collar crimes. The growing body of medical crime research (Geis, Jesilow, Pontell, & O'Brien, 1985; Jesilow, Pontell, & Geis, 1993; Pontell, Jesilow, & Geis, 1982; Tillman & Pontell, 1992) demonstrates that crimes in the health care field are potentially crimes against seniors. For example, cases of Medicare fraud ultimately lead to losses in Medicare funding which results in less quality care for seniors (Pontell et al., 1982). In fact, Medicaid and Medicare fraud research has represented the bulk of research on white-collar crimes against seniors. Only a limited amount of research has examined corporate crimes against seniors.

It is this third area, the area of corporate crime, that is the most ambiguous when crimes against seniors are considered. This ambiguity is due to at least two factors: (1) variations in definitions of corporate crime; and (2) difficulties determining whether these acts even occurred (Friedrichs, 2003). For example, proving that a nursing home abides by the regulations set forth by the Occupational Safety and Health Administration (OSHA) is virtually impossible. In one of the first criminological endeavors examining corporate crimes against seniors, Braithwaite et al. (1990) note that nursing homes are actually more successful at monitoring their own behavior than many believe. Elsewhere, Braithwaite (1993) notes that "[N]ursing home enforcement . . . is tougher than at any other point in American history, tougher than nursing home regulation in the rest of the world, and much tougher than most other domains of business regulation in America" (p. 25). However, he also states that interviews with abuse inspectors show that abuse in nursing homes in the U.S. is far worse than abuse in other countries (p. 15). Cases of murder, rape, and assault against seniors are regularly noted in the U.S., while rarely found other places. More importantly, he suggests that cases of neglect are the most serious problems surfacing in all nursing homes, regardless of culture, environment, or geography.

A related problem is that the problems remain hidden. Indeed, it is possible that many of the white-collar crimes committed against seniors are not recorded in official records due to one of four reasons: (1) the individual does not know s/he was a victim; (2) the elderly person is unable to report the victimization due to failing health; (3) the victim feels more harm might occur from reporting; or (4) the elderly person does not define the actions as criminal (Friedrichs, 2003; Payne & Cikovic, 1995; Sundram, 1986).

In sum, depending on the situation, crimes against the elderly can be described as occupational crimes, white-collar crimes, or corporate crimes. Complicating the problem even more is the addition of other concepts to describe these acts. In particular, are these offenses one of the aforementioned types of crime or are they better understood as *elder abuse*?

Elder Abuse Definitions

As mentioned earlier, the concept of elder abuse can be traced to the concept of "granny bashing." While the history of the concept is agreed on by most, the actual definition is, like the definition of white-collar crime, somewhat disputed. Eleazer (1995) begins an article on elder abuse with a quote by J. Callahan: "Abuse, like beauty, is in the eye of the beholder." This statement seems to be particularly accurate when one considers the differences in definitions offered by elder abuse scholars. This is not simply an academic argument. In fact, there is tremendous variation in elder abuse laws across the states, potentially resulting in inconsistent responses to offenses against elderly citizens (Winter, 1986). This ambiguity has prompted some to suggest that a consistent definition among legislatures, academicians, practitioners, criminal justice officials, and the elderly is needed in order to effectively detect, intervene, and prevent elder abuse. To affect change, these groups must come to terms with what the concept "elder abuse" actually means (Ogg & Munn-Giddings, 1993; Pritchard, 1996a).

Part of the problem is that variations in definitions will undoubtedly affect estimates about the extent of abuse, how laws should deal with abuse, and whether family members or caregivers are guilty of abuse. Therefore, conceptual ambiguity is of paramount concern to elder abuse researchers (Wolf, 1988). This ambiguity is not a nineties phenomenon (Wolf, 1988; Hudson, 1991; Hudson, 1994). Ever since the concept of elder abuse became a national concern in the late seventies (Katz, 1979), debate has focused on the kinds of acts captured under this broad heading. In 1982, one elder abuse expert wrote that a "concrete and hopefully narrow definition of the problem should be agreed upon by academic, professional, and legislative persons" (Faulkner, 1982, p. 71). The lack of agreement continued throughout the eighties, leading Wolf (1988) to write: "This lack of uniformity has hindered efforts to determine the scope of the problem and to build the knowledge base necessary for the development of intervention and preventive programs"

(p. 759). As Griffin (1994) notes, although a lot of research has examined issues related to elder abuse, "a clear understanding of the phenomenon has not been forthcoming" (p. 1).

As we enter the next century, a consistent definition of elder abuse is still missing (Wolf, 1996a). As with the white-collar crime definitions, concepts used to describe elder abuse also changed. However, some concepts have become even more ambiguous with some now choosing to use the concept of mistreatment to refer to acts that used to be called elder abuse (Bruce, 1994). This ambiguity makes it more difficult to study, respond to, and prevent elder abuse (Harshbarger, 1993). Stein (1991) describes a gathering of ten experts whose aim was to "identify, organize, and prioritize the most important research questions in the field of elder abuse and neglect" (p. 91). Stein notes that the collection of experts had problems coming to terms with elementary issues such as the definition of abuse and the types of acts that should be considered abuse. Clearly research needs to determine the similarities and differences in various definitions of abuse in order to learn how to get the groups to work together in detecting, intervening, and preventing elder abuse (Munro, 1977). Just as important is the fact that variations in definitions of elder abuse likely underestimate the extent of abuse in the other settings. Conceptual ambiguity also surfaces in an examination of concepts related to family abuse and domestic violence.

Family Abuse Definitions

It is important to note that acts of elder abuse need not be cases of white-collar crime. Indeed, many cases of elder abuse fall far out of the realm of white-collar crime. Rather, abuse can occur just about anywhere (Meddaugh, 1993; Payne & Cikovic, 1995; Ramsey-Klawsnik, 1991) and be committed by a host of different types of offenders (Menio, 1996). It may occur in the home of the victim (Pillemer & Wolf, 1986; Sayles-Cross, 1988), in nursing homes (La Rocco, 1985; Stannard, 1973; Pillemer & Moore, 1990), or other places that are not as familiar to the victim (Lee, 1982). Abusers could be relatives (Jones, 1987; Mitchell & Smith, 1994; Paveza et al., 1992), caregivers (Pillemer & Finkelhor, 1989; Pillemer & Bachman-Prehn, 1991; Sundram, 1986), or complete strangers (Fashimpar & Phemister, 1984; Ferraro, 1995). Most substantiated cases of elder abuse are committed by relatives, with adult children being the group implicated most often (Littwin, 1995). Of course, the fact that they are implicated more often does not mean that most offenses against elderly persons are necessarily committed by relatives. Indeed, cases of white-collar crime noted earlier are particularly difficult to substantiate and have a rather high "dark figure" of crime.

Even so, the fact that many of the cases of abuse are committed by relatives makes the whole field of domestic violence (aka family violence, family abuse, and domestic abuse) relevant. Indeed, as with definitions of white-collar crime and elder abuse, definitions of domestic violence have been rather ambiguous. Domestic violence is "complex in its nature" (Chalk & King, 1998, p. 39). Generally, when individuals consider domestic violence, they are inclined to discuss spouse abuse or partner abuse. In fact, some have defined domestic abuse as being something committed by a man against a woman. For instance, Consalvo (1998) defines domestic violence as "an instance of physical, emotional, or sexual violence against women by their husbands, ex-husbands, boyfriends, or ex-boyfriends" (p. 62). Mills (1998) recognizes that domestic violence may include male victims as she defines the concepts as "violence between adult partners" (p. 306). After her definition, however, she quickly notes that domestic violence "kills an average of four women every day," thus suggesting that domestic violence essentially includes instances where men attack women.

The ambiguity that arises is that domestic violence, because of its complex nature, involves acts other than those where a man physically harms a woman. To deal with this ambiguity, some have selected the broader concept of family violence to describe instances where family members harm one another (Chalk & King, 1998; Ohlin & Tonry, 1989; Wiehe, 1998). The forms of family violence include child abuse, spouse abuse, sibling abuse, and elder abuse (Chalk and King, 1998; Wiehe, 1998).

Spouse abuse and child abuse receive the bulk of attention where family violence research is concerned, with other types such as elder abuse and sibling abuse receiving minimal attention (Chalk & King, 1998; Ohlin & Tonry, 1989). Ohlin and Tonry (1989) write,

> lacking the visceral and emotional appeal of child victims and the political organization and ideological commitments of the women's movement, much less attention has focused on [elder abuse and sibling abuse], many fewer services and resources have been created, and there have been fewer associated statutory and case law developments. (p. 2)

What it comes back to is that the way the concepts are defined by society, and the academic community, will influence the way the abusive actions are examined by researchers.

Ohlin and Tonry (1989) note that one of the problems with family violence research has been disjointed efforts by scholars from vastly different disciplines, with scholars researching different types of family violence. They argue the following:

> Different scholarly and research communities studied different forms of family violence, published in and read different journals, belonged to different

professional and scholarly organizations, and attended different conferences and meetings. Child sexual abuse . . . was for long primarily within the province of medical researchers and social workers. Child physical abuse and neglect was studied preponderantly by medical, social work, and psychology-based researchers. Spouse assault was investigated by feminist activists and clinicians and by sociologists. Abuse of the elderly and of adolescents and violence between siblings were investigated by virtually no one until the last few years. (p. 3)

A related problem has to do with the use of the concept "violence" to describe acts of elder abuse. As Consalvo (1998) notes, the name *domestic violence* "hides the true nature of the crime" (p. 62). When individuals think of domestic violence, they tend to think of the picture painted by the media. In essence, cases of domestic violence portrayed in the media involve horrific cases where the criminal justice system repeatedly arrests certain offenders who are placed in a treatment program, only to commit more violent offenses in the future (Hanna, 1998). Certainly cases such as these are serious; however, there are other types of family violence.

What happens is that some of the crimes committed against elderly persons by family members cannot be described with the word violence (e.g., domestic violence and family violence). For example, cases of financial exploitation or verbal abuse, though they may have very severe consequences for the victim, are generally not seen as violent offenses. So, when the concept of elder abuse is used as a subcategory of family violence, many crimes that truly hurt older citizens are potentially excluded from the conceptualization. Likewise, using the concept of abuse potentially limits the kinds of acts elder abuse scholars examine to the purely physical acts. Due to the vastly different approaches of the various disciplines, and the lack of clear definitions labeling instances of elder abuse as criminal, criminologists, then, were isolated from all types of family violence research (Ohlin & Tonry, 1989). As a result, criminologists' involvement in elder abuse investigations has been limited.

What needs to occur is an integration of the following concepts: elder abuse, family abuse, domestic violence, white-collar crime, occupational crime, and corporate crime. The combination of these concepts fits well within the ideals of gero-criminology, which links assumptions of various disciplines and approaches crimes against the elderly from a more holistic perspective, resulting in an approach integrating the various human service fields and disciplines. By integrating and examining the relationships between these concepts, a setting in which criminologists can better study crimes against the elderly will form. To better study these offenses, however, attention must be given to the political issues arising when examining crimes against seniors.

POLITICAL ISSUES

A second reason crimes against elderly persons have received only nomi-
nal attention from behavioral scientists involves the political issues surrounding the crimes and the subsequent empirical examinations of the crimes. As a
political issue, it can be argued that research on crimes against elderly persons
has confronted, and continues to confront, various obstacles stemming from
the political reaction to these crimes. The political reaction is evident in three
areas: the history of elder abuse, the responses to domestic violence, and the
funding for white-collar crime research.

History of Elder Abuse

Describing the way that political issues actually become issues is not an exact science. Rather, a certain amount of speculation is needed. Nonetheless,
Cobb and Elder (1983) developed an agenda building framework that outlines
the way that issues change, broaden, and become significant to the general
public. According to Cobb and Elder, this model includes four levels: issue
creation, issue awareness, agenda entrance, and issue resolution (see Figure 1).
Applying this model to elder abuse helps demonstrate the way that history has
affected the way that behavioral scientists have examined this area.

The first stage, issue creation, involves the development of an issue. In the
case of elder abuse, Pillemer and Moore (1990) cite a study by Stannard (1973)
as being one of the first examinations of crimes against nursing home residents. It is important to note that the actions did not begin at that point.
Rather, the offenses against senior citizens, which Stannard referred to as
patient abuse, simply did not receive a great deal of attention prior to the
seventies. Even so, the issue of crimes against the elderly did not capture the
attention of the public until long after Stannard's ground-breaking report. Indeed, Cobb and Elder (1983) suggest that an issue must be broadened so that
it appeals to as many members of the public as possible in order to garner
widespread support for change.

Increased support, then, led to the second part of Cobb and Elder's model:
public awareness. In the case of crimes against seniors, the concept was broadened after the concept of granny battering first appeared in British medical
journals (Ogg & Munn-Giddings, 1993). The notion of granny battering (aka
granny-bashing) was a concept that caught on and seemed to offend the
majority of the public (Hugman, 1995). In a way similar to changes in domestic violence-related concepts (e.g., wife assault, spousal assault, domestic abuse
and so on), the notion of granny-battering eventually evolved into the more
politically correct concepts such as the "battered parent" and elder abuse. The

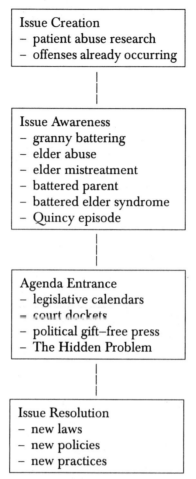

Figure 1. Cobb and Elder's agenda building framework and elder abuse.

Critical Thinking Questions:

1. How does politics influence the development of social issues?
2. How can this model be used to explain other social problems?

concept of "battered parent," however, was seen as "catchy but inaccurate" (Katz, 1979, p. 695). At the same time, an episode of Quincy, a famous late seventy's drama, depicted a case of elder abuse. Katz (1979) argues that the Quincy episode built support for the elder abuse agenda and contributed to public demands for changes in state and federal statutes. Also, *The Battered Elder Syndrome* was published by Block and Sinnott (1979) around the same time, giving increased attention to problems of abuse encountered by older adults. Indeed, the broadening of the elder abuse concept in the scholarly arena and the media increased public support for the need to address the issue. This increase in support leads to the third stage of Cobb and Elder's model—agenda entrance,

Agenda entrance involves instances where an issue is placed on a legislative calendar or court docket for debate and subsequent resolution. With regard to crimes against the elderly, politicians were essentially given a political gift. Specifically, crimes against the elderly, regardless of the label, was an issue that politicians were able to use to get free press without offending constituents. Who would be for elder abuse? This "free press" led to an escalation in elder abuse laws and statutes passed in the early eighties in a way similar to increases in legislation governing other white-collar crimes (Michalowski & Pfuhl, 1991). Regarding specific elder abuse laws, the surge of mandatory reporting laws requiring professionals to report suspected elder abuse cases that occurred in the workplace or the home "offer[ed] politicians an opportunity to go on the record in opposition to beating elderly grandmothers, while spending relatively token sums" (Crystal, 1987, p. 65).

The passing of these laws and statutes is related to Cobb and Elder's fourth stage—issue resolution. In this stage, policy makers decide how the issue should be resolved. In 1979, the House Select Committee on Aging held a hearing called "The Hidden Problem" and addressed the problem of elder abuse (Crystal, 1987). The resolutions since then have been extremely varied. States, for example, have passed laws governing the commission of abuse (Crystal, 1986), the reporting of abuse (Crystal, 1986), and the way the system should respond to abuse (Macolini, 1995).

The problem that once again surfaces is that the issue that developed and was resolved was one focusing primarily on the violent abusive acts society generally fears. Because the law and the political arena implicitly delineated a distinction between these crimes, subsequent research efforts by criminologists were likely affected. As well, the non-violent property offenses, which are often white-collar crimes, were ignored by policy makers throughout the eighties. According to Friedrichs (2003), "politicians have generally found it more attractive to attack street crime and call for 'law and order' than to attack the crimes of powerful corporations" (p. 32). The lack of attention given to many of these offenses in the political and legal arena undoubtedly contributed to the lack of attention criminologists have given to these offenses. A similar pattern arises when the political system's response to domestic violence is considered.

Responses to Domestic Violence

Traditionally, the political arena has approached family violence as a social problem rather than a criminal problem (Chalk & King, 1998). The result has been an unwillingness on the part of the political and justice systems to get involved in these acts, which were seen as family matters (Chalk & King, 1998; Mills, 1998; Schulhofer, 1995). Feder (1998) cites an 1873 court decision (from State v. Oliver) as saying, "If no permanent injury has been inflicted, nor malice, cruelty or dangerous violence shown by the husband, it is better to draw the curtain, shut out the public gaze, and leave the parties to forgive and forget" (336). Jolin and Morse (1997) argue that society has been reluctant to see domestic violence as a crime because of cultural norms allowing violent acts to be committed against females.

It was not until the mid-eighties that the criminal justice system began to treat domestic violence as a crime (Jolin & Morse, 1997). Politicians followed the same "get tough on crime" orientation, discussed by Friedrichs (2003), in passing laws about domestic violence. In particular, mandatory arrest laws and "no-drop prosecution" laws "have been implemented despite empirical evidence that arrest and prosecution may not in fact deter future violence" (Mills, 1998, p. 306). Even if the laws were questionable in utility, attention was still more focused towards spousal and partner abuse than it was towards elder abuse. Only after the criminalization of domestic violence did we see the criminalization of elder abuse (Jolin & Morse, 1998; Wolf, 1992).

So, the way politicians have approached white-collar crime and domestic violence has had repercussions for the way elder abuse was developed as a political problem. These repercussions will carry over into the way behavioral scientists explore issues about elder abuse. A related political issue concerns the degree to which certain behavioral scientists receive funding for research examining crimes against seniors.

Funding of Crimes Against Elderly Persons Research

Funding is an aim of many behavioral scientists. Regardless of discipline, there is widespread belief, perhaps rightfully so, that the research that is most likely to be funded is that which meets the stated and unstated aims of the various funding sources. Some point out that resources are limited for family violence research (Chalk & King, 1998), while others note that an inherent bias limiting funding for white-collar crime research exists (Friedrichs, 2003; Longmire, 1982). Friedrichs (2003) suggests that "[O]n a practical level it has traditionally been easier to obtain research support for projects that explore conventional forms of juvenile delinquency and crime than for research on white-collar crime" (p. 39). Research on white-collar crimes against the elderly is less likely to be funded because it excludes street crimes, it focuses on older rather than younger subjects, and it is victim-oriented rather than offender-oriented. Moreover, elder abuse, as a type of family violence, receives much less attention from politicians and the media than the other types of family violence (Chalk & King, 1998; Ohlin & Tonry, 1989). This lack of attention likely decreases the likelihood of funding for family violence research focusing specifically on elder abuse.

Some also suggest that research examining victims is less likely to be funded than other research. The fact that funding is restricted for white-collar crime research, victimology research, and family violence research stacks the cards against research examining elder abuse crime victims. The lack of funding initiatives for research examining senior citizens issues in criminal justice granting agencies compounds the problem even more. Several granting agencies exist for the sole purpose of funding aging research. However, those agencies rarely seek out criminological endeavors, as their focus is more often given to the biological, medical, and psychological issues confronting older Americans. This roadblock has made it difficult for criminologists to apply their principles to issues (patient abuse, elder abuse, Medicare abuse) often treated as social service issues, or social problems, rather than as the crimes which they actually are.

Suggesting that criminologists are not researching crimes against the elderly because of a lack of funding does not mean that criminologists are selfish researchers who will examine only those issues that are fundable. Rather, to fully address the questions and issues surrounding crimes against seniors, some sort of funding is necessary. Otherwise, practical and economic constraints make it nearly impossible to answer the questions and address the issues empirically. Also, the lack of funding makes it difficult to address elementary issues such as the extent of these sort of offenses, which in fact relates to a third reason crimes against the elderly have been neglected by behavioral scientists.

MAGNITUDE ISSUES

A third reason crimes against the elderly have received little attention has to do with magnitude issues. It is important to note that research consistently shows that older citizens are less likely to be victims of crime than younger victims (Covey & Menard, 1988; Fox & Levin, 1991). This is particularly interesting since older citizens have a higher fear of crime than younger citizens. The implicit suggestion is that because crime is so rare among seniors, our attention should be given to the areas where crime occurs the most.

Table 5 presents the number of murder and non-negligent manslaughter victims by age, and Table 6 presents the number of victims of other crimes broken down by age category. The statistics in these tables come from the Federal Bureau of Investigation and the Bureau of Justice Statistics. The figures clearly suggest that older adults are victimized at much lower rates than all other age groups. It is important to stress a point established in the first

TABLE 5. MURDER AND MANSLAUGHTER RATES
(PER 100,000 IN EACH AGE GROUP)

Year Older	Total	Age			
		14 to 17 Years	18 to 24 Years	25 to 34 Years	50 &
1976	8.7	4.6	14.0	15.6	6.9
1977	8.8	4.9	14.5	15.7	6.7
1978	9.0	5.2	14.8	16.3	6.4
1979	9.8	5.3	16.9	17.8	6.8
1980	10.2	6.0	17.8	18.8	6.9
1981	9.8	5.1	16.3	17.8	6.9
1982	9.1	4.8	15.2	16.0	6.3
1983	8.3	4.5	14.0	14.8	5.5
1984	7.9	4.3	13.5	14.1	5.2
1985	8.0	5.0	13.5	14.2	5.1
1986	8.5	5.3	15.6	15.5	5.1
1987	8.3	5.8	15.7	14.9	5.0
1988	8.4	6.6	16.6	15.5	4.7
1989	8.7	8.0	18.4	15.7	4.6
1990	9.4	9.9	21.5	17.0	4.5
1991	9.8	11.3	24.4	17.0	4.0
1992	9.3	11.4	23.7	16.4	4.3
1993	9.5	12.3	24.7	16.3	4.3
1994	9.0	11.4	24.0	15.7	3.9
1995	8.2	11.2	21.8	14.1	3.9
1996	7.4	9.2	19.8	12.5	3.5
1997	6.8	7.5	19.7	11.6	3.2
1998	6.3	6.2	17.5	10.7	2.8
1999	5.7	5.9	15.4	9.9	2.6
2000	5.5	4.7	14.9	10.2	2.5

Source: U.S. Department of Justice: Bureau of Justice Statistics. (2003). "Homicide Trends in the United States" [Online].

Critical Thinking Questions:

1. What patterns do you think are most telling from these figures?

chapter: official statistics are not reliable indicators of the extent of crimes committed against elderly persons.

The Federal Bureau of Investigation administers the Uniform Crime Reporting Program, which was initially developed in 1929 by the International Association of Chiefs of Police (IACP). Each year, over 16,000 police departments across the United States report the crimes they know about to the UCR program (FBI, 1999). There are questions about whether the police report all of the crimes they know about, with some suggesting that probably 75 percent of the crimes reported to the police are reported to the UCR program (Inci-

TABLE 6. AGE OF VICTIM BY CRIMES, 2001 (PER 1,000 PERSONS)

Crime Type	12 to 15	16 to 19	20 to 24	25 to 34	65+
			Age		
All personal crimes	55.6	58.8	46.5	30.3	3.8
Violent Crimes	55.1	55.8	44.7	29.3	3.2
Completed Vio.	17.4	18.9	17.8	10.0	1.2
Attempted Vio.	37.7	36.9	26.9	19.3	2.0
Rape/Sexual Assault	1.7	3.4	2.4	1.1	.1
Robbery	5.2	6.4	4.2	3.6	1.3
Assault	48.3	46.1	38.1	24.6	1.8
Purse Snatching & Pocket Picking	.5	3.0	1.8	1.0	.7

Source: U.S. Department of Justice, Bureau of Justice Statistics, *Criminal Victimization in the United States, 2001 Statistical Tables,* NCJ 197064, Table 3 [Online].

Critical Thinking Questions:

1. How accurate do you think these statistics are?
2. Why are there such large differences between the victimization rates of younger and older individuals?

ardi, 1999). The offenses are divided into Part I offenses, which are theoretically more severe offenses, and Part II offenses, which are seen as less severe.

Part I offenses include murder, robbery, rape, assault, burglary, motor vehicle theft, larceny, and arson. These offenses are also referred to as index offenses. Thus, the term "crime index" refers to the total number of these offenses (excluding arson) in a community. The "modified crime index" includes arson figures (FBI, 1996). Traditionally, very little information about the criminal incident has been provided in the UCR. Part of the UCR program includes the Supplemental Homicide Reports, which provides quite detailed information about the circumstances surrounding homicides (Fox & Levin, 1991). Recently, the FBI began to develop the National Incident Based Reporting System, which includes more detailed information about the crime, including information about the relationship between the offender and the victim, the type of injuries suffered by the victim, whether drugs were involved, and a host of other factors. As will be seen, one picture of crime arises out of the use of UCR data to understand crimes against seniors, and a quite different picture arises when a more complete data set is used.

In conducting the National Crime Victimization Survey, the Bureau of Justice Statistics uses a longitudinal research design to survey 101,000 people from 50,000 households every six months over a period of three and a half years (Bachman, 1998; Lynch, 1996). Respondents over the age of twelve are asked whether they were victimized, and whether they reported the victimization to the police. Each year the BJS publishes their findings in various reports, the most comprehensive one being *Criminal Victimization in the United States.* Information about crime patterns and the extent of crime is included in this report and is also available on the internet.

The National Archive of Criminal Justice Data (at the University of Michigan) archives the NCVS and UCR data files, which are available to researchers who want to use data bases to address certain research questions. The data sources have certain limitations that are particularly relevant concerning crimes against elderly persons. For example, unreported crimes are not included in these statistics gathered by the FBI and BJS. On the one hand, citizens will not report offenses to the police, thus distorting the UCR's figures. On the other hand, those in the BJS sample may not share complete information with the interviewers, again distorting the figures. For elderly persons in particular, there is a tendency to not report family abuse because they are ashamed and embarrassed that their spouse or child violated their trust (Breckman & Adelman, 1988). Also, fears about the consequences of reporting, including retaliation, abandonment, and institutionalization, also keep many elder abuse victims from reporting their victimization to authorities (Swagerty et al., 1999).

When unreported crimes are included in these figures, estimates indicate that anywhere from one to two million people over the age of sixty-five are abused each year by family members, caregivers, and various significant others (Baron & Welty, 1996, p. 33; Simon, 1992, p. 4). Wolf (1996a) estimates that reported cases of elder abuse and neglect increased 206 percent between 1987 and 1994. These estimates mean that anywhere from 4 to 10 percent of elderly individuals are victims of elder abuse annually (Heisler, 1991; Wolf, 1996a). Some researchers suggest that elder abuse is almost as prevalent as child abuse (All, 1994; Arbetter, 1995). Others seem to agree, suggesting that even these estimates potentially underestimate the actual extent of the problem (Baron & Welty, 1996; Bruce, 1994; Goldstein, 1995). In fact, Voelker (2002) argues that just one in five elder abuse cases is reported, while others suggest that only about one in fourteen cases of abuse is reported (Bruce, 1994).

Not only are unreported crimes not included in these figures, white-collar crimes in which the victims do not know they are victims are excluded. Recall that many elderly victims are actually victims of white-collar crimes. Cases of theft, neglect, or unnecessary surgery occur regularly against elderly victims. The NCVS samples households, thus potentially excluding violations occurring in nursing homes. Also excluded are households without telephones, many of whom would be elderly, have less money, and be vulnerable to victimization (Lynch, 1996). This also distorts the figures arising out of the victimization survey.

As well, reports of scams against the elderly have become increasingly common in the media. These scams are not, however, included in official crime statistics as Part I offenses. As noted earlier, by calling the crimes against the elderly "elder abuse," many other crimes against seniors are potentially ignored. In fact, some suggest that seniors are targets of specific crimes, such as fraud and other white-collar crimes (Friedman, 1998; Rosoff et al., 2003).

The problem that surfaces is that summary statistics are used to determine whether crime is a problem for older adults. Since older adults are, according to official statistics, less likely to be victimized than younger persons, the automatic assumption is that crime is not a big problem in their lives. When more complete data sets are used to examine crime in older adults' lives, a different picture appears.

For instance, Fox and Levin (1991) examined the Supplemental Homicide Reports (a more detailed report collected as part of the UCR) and found that older persons were more likely to be murdered during the commission of a robbery than younger persons were. Likewise, using data from the NCVS, Bachman et al. (1998) found that older victims were more likely to be injured during an attack, and require medical care, than younger victims. Bachman et al. (1998) also found that older men and women are equally likely to be victims of robbery. This may not seem striking except for the fact that this pattern is not found in younger populations. Instead, men under the age of 65 were "twice as likely to experience a robbery victimization as women younger than 65" (p. 204). They go on, stating, "At no other time in the life course are men and women equally vulnerable to becoming the victims of robbery" (p. 204). Also, recall from Chapter 1 that research using the NIBRS, a more complete data set than the standard UCR data found that elderly persons "are more at risk than are younger segments of the population for crimes of robbery, intimidation, vandalism, and forgery/fraud" (McCabe & Gregory, 1998, p. 363).

Based on the results of these studies, which examined characteristics and consequences of elderly victimization, it is clear that the victimization experience is different for older adults than it is for younger persons. These differences are not always evident in summary data that is typically reported by the UCR or NCVS. When more complete data is added, a different picture of the way crime affects older adults appears. Thus, the NCVS and UCR should not be used to determine the actual extent of crime against elderly persons, but they can be used to garner understanding about the way crime affects older persons, at least those whose crimes are reported to the police or the BJS interviewers.

So to rely on official statistics as an indicator of what the important problems are in our society is inaccurate. It is not only inaccurate; it is immoral. To say that it should not be researched because it does not happen that often takes away from the very dignity that should be given to every person re-gardless of race, age, gender, and so on. Even if crimes against the elderly are rare, they are still problematic. A lot of rare diseases receive a great deal of attention from medical scientists because a cure of these endemic illnesses will prevent the diseases from escalating and will potentially contribute to cures of other diseases. Likewise, increased research on crimes against seniors will prevent these crimes from escalating and will contribute to the growing body of criminological research in this area.

METHODOLOGICAL ISSUES

In examining the way that methodological issues inhibit research on crimes against the elderly, it is important to note that these issues are not inherently "topic specific." That is, the issues to be addressed below arise in all types of studies. However, the ways the issues manifest themselves in research concerning elderly crime victims are slightly different. It is also important to stress that research has very real applications and relates to the other concerns addressed in this chapter (e.g., determining the extent of elder abuse, defining elder abuse, and developing appropriate policies). See Box 2.1 for more detail about the importance of applied elder abuse research.

Methods most often used by social scientists to examine criminal behavior include surveys, field studies, archival research, and experiments. Experiments are rare in elder abuse research, with the exception of "quasi-experiments" that attempt to evaluate particular services offered to abusers or victims (see Braun et al., 1997). Generally, research on victim-related aging issues have primarily involved the first three methods.

Survey Research and Crimes Against Elderly Persons

Some might argue that survey research is the cornerstone of social science research. This research involves questions asked of the respondent by the researcher. Forms of survey administration include the following: on-site self-administration, mail-return survey, face-to-face interviews, and telephone interviews. The nature of these forms also varies in that the questions may be open-ended or close-ended with responses provided by the researcher. Each of these methods has been used by social scientists from various disciplines to address crime-related issues among the elderly.

Three significant problems with asking seniors whether they have been a victim of a crime arise in each method. First, many victims of crime, in

BOX 2.1. RESEARCHING ELDER ABUSE

By Loree Cook-Daniels

In 2003, the National Research Council (NRC) of the National Academies published an authoritative tome: *Elder Mistreatment: Abuse, Neglect, and Exploitation in an Aging America*. Despite its size (more than 522 pages) and density (much of it is written in Academic/Government Speak), its analysis of the state of research on elder abuse was neatly summed up in two paragraphs on page two:

When the body of published and unpublished research reports on elder mistreatment is examined as a whole, a number of weaknesses emerge:

- *Unclear and inconsistent definitions*
- *Unclear and inadequate measures*
- *Incomplete professional accounts*
- *Lack of population-based data*
- *Lack of prospective data*
- *Lack of control groups*
- *Lack of systematic evaluation studies*

Among the factors accounting for these deficiencies are:

- *Little funding and few investigators*
- *Methodological uncertainties, especially about surveys*
- *Ethical uncertainties regarding research practices*
- *Inadequate links between researchers and service agencies*
- *Impoverished theory*
- *Intertwined and varying research definitions and statutory definitions*
- *Divergent research traditions in gerontology and family violence*

As a writer and publisher specializing in elder and vulnerable adult abuse, I need not only the findings of carefully-designed and -conducted studies that meet the standards of peer-reviewed academic journals and the NRC, but also answers to far more mundane questions: "How many cases of elder abuse were referred to Adult Protective Services nationwide last year?" "To whom should I report a case of suspected abuse of a resident of an assisted living facility in Elkhart, Illinois?" "Where are people finding emergency housing for abused male elders with significant health problems?" Unfortunately, even straightforward, basic elder abuse facts such as these are hard to come by.

Some of the problem, of course, is endemic to the United States' justice and service systems. As is true of many crimes, in this country there are more than fifty different legal definitions of "elder abuse." As with domestic violence, the various states' elder abuse service "systems" include unique mixes of disparate players such as state and local law enforcement officials, health care providers, privately-sponsored social services, publicly-funded agencies of various sorts, and many others.

Yet the nature of elder abuse and the level of attention (or inattention) it has received has created additional complexities. Because abuse and neglect of elders commonly occurs in residential facilities as well as in private homes, an additional layer of players and complexity is introduced: licensing and certification departments, Medicaid Fraud Control Units, long-term care ombudsmen, and many others may hold pieces of the complete picture. Even computer systems are often more limited when it comes to elder abuse; some states still have not computerized their case records and so have no better way to generate data than hand-counting file folders.

Typically such complexities are dealt with in other criminal justice specialties by federal agencies that help track and reconcile state definitions, reporting systems, and data. This is *not* true in elder abuse. There is neither specific funding nor an agency dedicated to elder abuse on the federal level. There is no nationally-funded clearinghouse of information, no federally-mandated collection of statistics. The Administration on Aging has funded a National Center on Elder Abuse (NCEA) for over a decade, but this small consortium of national volunteer and professional organizations (the largest of which has fewer than 300 members) sets its own, unpublished goals, timeline, and work plan without the assistance of an advisory board or other input and accountability structures. Neither NCEA nor any other national group has produced a model state law or model investigation or service provision policies that could guide programmatic maturing of the field, and authoritative analyses of how to improve the state of research in the field, such as the new NRC book, are just beginning to emerge. There is not even a national, annual elder abuse prevention and treatment conference people can point to as the place to go to learn what innovations are being piloted.

The pending federal Elder Justice Act would address many of the field's information gaps, but its passage is far from certain. Without federal interest in and support of the field, and until an organized, visionary, and national multidisciplinary organization committed to filling those gaps emerges, those of us with questions to answer–be they basic referral information or complicated theoretical constructs–will have to largely rely on our own investigative skills and personal networks. It's not a great way to serve victims of life- and family-destroying crimes, but it's currently all we have.

Reference

National Research Council. (2003). *Elder Mistreatment: Abuse, Neglect, and Exploitation in an Aging America.* Panel to Review Risk and Prevalence of Elder Abuse and Neglect. Richard J. Bonnie and Robert B. Wallace, Editors. Committee on National Statistics and Committee on Law and Justice, Division of Behavioral and Social Sciences and Education. Washington, DC: The National Academies Press.

Loree Cook-Daniels, M.S., is the owner of the consulting firm WordBridges and founder of ASAAPS, the American Society for Adult Abuse Professionals and Survivors. She is also the publisher of Adult Abuse Review and the editor of a daily elder/vulnerable adult newsfeed. She has spent 30 years in the aging field, focusing particularly on public policy issues and elder abuse awareness, prevention, and intervention methods. Prior to designing her own responses to the needs of adult abuse survivors and the people who serve them, she spent more than a decade as a writer and analyst for the National Center on Elder Abuse. She has published hundreds of articles, reports, and news stories onabuse of elders and vulnerable adults and other topics. She lives with her son and partner in Milwaukee, Wisconsin.

particular white-collar crime victims, do not know that they were victimized. Thus, surveys face serious problems of validity (Breckman & Adelman, 1988; Friedrichs, 2003). Second, questions about victimization are sensitive issues (Pillemer, 1985) and may raise fear of crime in some of the subjects (Ferraro, 1995). Ferraro (1995) notes that "[I]t is possible that face-to-face interviews may heighten fear of crime reporting of adults" (p. 71). Based on this admittedly untested assertion, it is likewise plausible that questions about crime make older citizens think about crime when they otherwise would not, thereby increasing their fears. The ethical implications of increased fear place restrictions on the methods of asking older subjects certain questions. Third, elderly victims may choose not to share information about victimization with researchers because of shame, a fear of retaliation from the abuser, or denial that the abuse occurred (Breckman & Adelman, 1988). Other strengths and limitations of each survey type as they relate to seniors and crime are also noteworthy.

First, on-site self-administration of surveys involves the administration of surveys to a group of subjects in one particular setting. In many cases, the subjects are university students who are accessible and familiar with the survey routine. Regarding research on elderly victims of crime, it is difficult to administer surveys on site to both offenders and victims. For example, with offenders, there is no collection of domestic violence, elder abuse, or white-collar offenders that researchers can access readily (Chalk & King, 1998; Friedrichs, 2003). Even if surveys were administered to a group of offenders, there is likely so much variation in the educational level of the offenders that it would be difficult to develop one specific research instrument that could be given to all offenders. Indeed, were one interested in surveying white-collar offenders, developing one survey appropriate for doctors, auto mechanics, telemarketers, retail salespeople, and lawyers would be a formidable task. More realistically, I would expect research examining offenders who commit crimes against the elderly to focus on one specific type of offender. But again, finding a setting where a group of one type of offenders is present is difficult if not impossible.

Problems arise with asking a group of seniors to complete surveys asking whether they have been victimized. Although there are plenty of instances where large groups of elderly congregate (nursing homes, group activities, association meetings, etc.), it is not an easy task to use these large groups as a sample. Gaining entrance and the trust of the group is an initial problem that develops (Berg, 1998; Curry, Johnson, & Sigler, 1994). Also, "older adults may be less likely to recall a particular incident than younger people" (Eve, 1985, p. 400). Further, as with the offenders, there is tremendous variation in the educational level of seniors, so developing a reliable and valid survey instrument may be problematic. In addition, the older adult may experience certain health problems such as impaired vision, hearing problems, or dementia, making it difficult to complete the survey (Pillemer & Moore, 1989). In fact, those with these ailments may be particularly vulnerable to victimization (Rounds, 1996). Unless measures are taken to include these other adults, those who are more likely to have been victimized are potentially excluded from the sample.

There have been instances where groups other than offenders or elderly victims are asked to participate in an on-site administration of a survey. These other groups include students, police officers, and health care workers (Dolon & Hendricks, 1989; Pillemer & Moore, 1989; Payne et al., 1999). Due to the problems associated with surveying older adults, Pillemer and Moore (1989) suggest that staff surveys "are the most feasible way to obtain systematic information on this topic" (p. 316). However, the problem that arises here concerns the significance of the research as it applies to the broader crime problem. In essence, research on the attitudes of students, police, and health care workers is important in that it paints a picture of the way that members of these groups actually define and respond to crimes against seniors. However, this research is limited in that the actual experiences of those directly involved with the offenses are not completely assessed.

Face-to-face interviews are also used to examine various types of crimes committed against older citizens. Face-to-face interviews usually are more time consuming and more expensive for the researcher. In addition to the sampling problems experienced with on-site administration of surveys, other sampling problems develop. Where to find subjects and actually do the interview is of paramount concern. Whereas other subjects may be more mobile, it is often imperative that interviews with elderly persons be done in their residence. The problem that comes up is one of gaining entrance.

Indeed, in studies using a sample from a long-term-care setting, it may be difficult to get past administrators who place obstacles in from of researchers wanting to interview residents. In these situations, researchers are forced to alter research strategies accordingly (Filinson, 2001).

Regardless of whether the respondent lives in his/her own home or an institutional setting such as a nursing home, the interviewer must establish a rapport and increase the level of trust the older person has for the interviewer. In cases where the senior citizen lives in nursing homes (where white-collar offenses occur regularly), the researcher must, in many cases, first gain the permission of the nursing home administrators. Plenty of horror stories about failed master's theses and doctoral dissertations are heard in the hallways of graduate departments where students or advisors were unable to convince administrators of external agencies that their research was significant, but not threatening, to the institution or its residents.

Once access is permitted to older institutionalized adults, a number of other problems arise. First, gaining the trust of the older person who may have been victimized or witnessed such acts is an arduous task (Curry et al., 1994). Also, many of the respondents may have vision or hearing problems that make it difficult to communicate about their experiences with crime. Furthermore, problems with dementia may make it difficult for the older person to recall the events in accurate ways (Coyne, Potenza, & Berbig, 1996; Pillemer & Moore, 1989).

Curry et al. (1994) experienced each of these problems in their attempt to interview fifty residents of nursing homes and fifty non-institutionalized adults. First, two out of six nursing homes were unwilling to allow Curry et al. entrance into the institution. Second, once entrance was permitted, Curry et al. had to gain permission from relatives of the subjects before being permitted to interview the nursing home residents. Many relatives refused, and the nursing home staff had to devote hours of effort trying to arrange these interviews. Third, once the interviews were arranged, some relatives insisted on being present during the interview. Although they were able to analyze data gathered from the interviews of the non-institutionalized adults, due to the problems of selective attrition and the presence of relatives in the nursing home interviews, they had to discard all of the data gathered from the nursing home residents. However, their experiences can be used to inform future research. Although Curry et al. (1994) did not experience as many problems with the non-institutionalized sample, similar problems may occur with these other older adults as well. Gaining trust seems to be the most significant issue with seniors living in non-institutional settings. Research suggests that older people may have the highest fear of crime. Thus, it is likely that this group would also be more concerned about interviews with complete strangers in their own home. Those who have been victimized in the past are less likely to trust strangers and subsequently potentially less likely to allow interviewers into their homes. In short, using face-to-face interviews for criminological research examining victimization experiences of older adults may systematically exclude an important segment of the population.

Berg (1998) shares an example where gaining entrance and trust for face-to-face interviews was problematic because of recent crimes in a particular neighborhood. In the example shared by Berg (1998), the neighborhood watch group showed residents a film showing how criminals will mask their identities to get into the victim's home. One of the impostor identities included in the film was that of an interviewer. The researchers had little success gaining entrance into the respondents' homes. To deal with the dilemma, the researchers attended a neighborhood civic meeting where they introduced themselves and described the nature of the research. This gesture was enough to gain entrance into many of the homes. The point is that researchers may have to take special measures to convince seniors that participating in the study will be a safe and a useful endeavor for the respondent and for society.

Mail-return surveys are a less costly way to survey a large number of subjects, but problems similar to using the other survey methods surface. Some may not be able to physically complete the instrument. Others may not fully understand the questions as the questions are intended to be understood by the researcher. A unique problem with the mail surveys and seniors concerns the development of a sample. Basically, there are very few lists available that would include the names and addresses of all older persons in a particular area. Some states, such as Massachusetts, publish an annual listing of residents' addresses and phone numbers that include age-specific data (Pillemer & Finkelhor, 1989) while other states, such as Alabama (Curry et al., 1994), have no such list available. Developing a comprehensive list of older residents can be done by combining various lists in a community, including driver's license lists, church rolls, pension lists, and membership lists of volunteer organizations (Curry et al., 1994). However, the economic and time costs associated with the task are enormous. Also, excluded from most of these lists are residents of nursing homes, who are prime targets for various crimes. Researchers may choose to mail surveys to all residents of a particular population and focus only on the respondents over a certain age. However, many subjects are systematically excluded from the mailing list. Further, the cost of mailing questionnaires to subjects who may not be included in the final analysis is prohibitive.

Telephone interviews, the fourth survey method, involve instances where researchers telephone citizens and ask them a series of questions. Of the elder abuse research that has been done, two separate telephone interviews by Pillemer and a host of associates (c.f. Pillemer & Finkelhor, 1989; Pillemer & Moore, 1989; Pillemer & Moore, 1990; Pillemer & Bachman-Prehn, 1991) represent perhaps the most comprehensive examinations of crimes against seniors. In one phone interview, nursing home staff were asked about their experiences with and perceptions about abuse, while the other phone interview asked people over the age of sixty-five about their abuse experiences. Results showed that abuse was somewhat common and occurred because of staff burnout and the level of staff-patient conflict (Pillemer & Bachman-Prehn, 1991). Elsewhere, Pillemer and Moore (1989) note that due to the sampling problems with older victims "staff interviews appear to be the most feasible way to obtain systematic information on [elder abuse]" and telephone interviews were potentially more valid than other survey types because respondents seemed to be more open when interviewed by phone (p. 316).

In the phone survey of people over the age of sixty-five, abuse occurring in the victim's home was examined (Pillemer & Finkelhor, 1989). Using a Boston area population that kept a public listing of all residents in a dwelling along with their age and other demographic information to contact a random sample of residents over the age of sixty-five, the researchers interviewed subjects to determine the relationship between the victim and the offender. The researchers found that abusers were spouses in 58 percent of the cases and that contrary to stereotypes about dependency, the abusers tended to be dependent on the elder in some way. This sort of information probably could not have been obtained through any other method.

Of course, a number of problems with phone interviews inevitably surface. Here again, some (e.g., those who are institutionalized) will be omitted from the study because they do not have their own telephones or their phone numbers are unlisted. Also, if researchers want to focus only on the experiences of people over a certain age, they may have to go to extra lengths to develop the sample. For instance, they may have to make phone calls to subjects who will not be included in the final sample or spend a great deal of time going through the lists noted earlier to develop an accurate sampling frame (Curry et al., 1994). Further, with increases in phone calls from telemarketers and the use of call identification packages, some may not answer the phone at all. This potentially eliminates an important segment of the population as well.

Field Studies

Field studies involve various methods where the researcher enters the "field" and uses a variety of techniques to gather information (watching, listening, interviewing, and so on). Four roles are typical in field studies: participant as observer; observer as participant; complete participant; and complete observer. The distinction between each role has to do with the degree of participation the researcher has in the particular setting. The degree of participation, in turn, is determined by a host of practical, empirical, and ethical issues.

Using field studies to examine victimization among the elderly is perhaps the most time consuming method. Nonetheless, a field study by Stannard (1973) was one of the first instances where researchers began to examine patient abuse in nursing homes. Following a method similar to Goffman's (1961) *Asylums,* Stannard (1973) observed activities in one nursing home over a period of about two years. His observations revealed a host of different types of patient abuse occurring throughout the nursing home. In particular, he witnessed or heard about actions including "pulling a patient's hair, slapping, hitting, punching or violently shaking a patent, throwing water or food on a patient, tightening restraining belts so that they cause a patient pain, and terrorizing a patient by gesture or word" (p. 334). Based on his observations, he concluded that the acts occurred because of patient isolation, communication problems between nurses and aides, and the ease by which abusers could offer accounts for their abusive behavior. Again, it would have been impossible for Stannard to make his observations and reach these conclusions through any other method. However, Stannard and other field researchers will face a number of problems in trying to examine offenses against seniors through the use of field studies.

For instance, as with surveys of adults in institutional settings, it may be difficult to gain entrance into the field. In fact, it may be even more difficult to gain access due to the fact that the researcher must be present for a longer period of time in field studies. This extended researcher presence, in turn, increases the likelihood that those being observed might act in certain ways because of the presence of the researcher, subsequently affecting the validity of the researcher's observations. Such a phenomenon, known as the "Hawthorne Effect," was first identified by Roethlisberger and Dickenson (1939) and is now well-accepted in social science research (Berg, 1998). Also accepted, however, is the suggestion that good research practices extended over a long period of time minimizes that impact of the Hawthorne Effect (Berg, 1998; Lofland, 1971).

Recall Stannard's (1973) study. He spent the first year and a half visiting the nursing home, using the identity of a sociologist who was writing a book on nursing homes. Three months after leaving as a sociologist, he returned and spent six weeks working as a janitor in the same home. Even though his identity was clear in the beginning, the actions of those he observed did not seem to change. Indeed, if those he observed were changing their behavior because of the presence of Stannard, one would expect that he would not have seen or heard about abusive acts in the nursing home.

Archival Research

In *The Study of Sociology,* Herbert Spencer (1873) points out that most social phenomena cannot be fully addressed by direct observations. Therefore, social scientists often rely on other methods to examine various social issues. In addition to surveys and field studies, archival research is a common method used to examine crimes against seniors. Briefly, an archive can be viewed as any record, whether it is written, audiotaped, videotaped, or chronicled in some other way (Berg, 1998). Logically then, archival research entails the use of those archives to address research questions. As a form of unobtrusive research (Webb et al., 1966), archives include both official and unofficial (i.e., personal or informal) accounts or descriptions of various patterns of behavior. Adams and Schvaneveldt (1985) argue that archival records are the most readily available, yet among social scientists, perhaps the least used data collection tool. Though relatively rare as a research method in the United States, Berg (1998) points out that archives may actually be a "gold mine" of information.

With regard to crimes against seniors, several different "gold mines" have been used by social scientists to examine the various crimes committed against seniors. As an example of some of these archives, the way that five archives have been used by researchers to address concerns elderly persons face will be addressed. These five archives include the following: (1) the *Medicaid Fraud Report*, published by the National Association of Attorneys General; (2) the *Vital Statistics of the United States*, published by the National Center for Health Care Statistics; (3) various states' records describing the results of mandatory reporting laws; (4) the Health Care Financing Administration's annual reporting of the number of violations of patient's rights; and (5) *The Inside Guide to America's Nursing Homes: Rankings and Ratings for Every Nursing Home in the United States*, published Robert C. Bua. After discussing how these archives have been used, and could be used in the future, the strengths and weaknesses of archival research will be considered.

The *Medicaid Fraud Report* includes specific information about cases of patient abuse occurring across the United States. The report is published ten times a year by the National Association of Attorneys General (NAAG) and includes information about various cases prosecuted by Medicaid Fraud Control Units (see Chapter 5). The cases prosecuted by the units include Medicaid fraud cases committed by health care providers, prescription fraud cases committed by pharmacists billing Medicaid, and patient abuse cases in nursing homes that receive funding from Medicaid. What happens is fraud control units from across the United States send information to the NAAG about arrests, indictments, prosecutions, and convictions of these cases. The Medicaid Fraud Report publishes case descriptions that provide information about the case that, though intended for consumption by those dealing with Medicaid fraud, can be quite useful to researchers. For example, one case in the fraud report describes a case involving an eighty-five-year-old, bed-stricken resident who suffered a broken arm, extensive bruises on her face, and a fractured nose:

> During the course of the investigation, it was determined that two aides had discovered the patient's injuries while making rounds. The aides both suspected a third aide because she had been the one to feed the resident and because she had been drinking prior to coming to work. The resident was questioned and

she stated that an aide had hurt her with her hand. She also stated that she was afraid of retaliation for telling what had happened.

The resident's orthopedic specialist stated that when he examined the resident, her left arm was turned completely backwards. The physician further stated that it takes a lot of force to break the large bone of the upper arm, and that it would be unusual for the arm to have sustained a spiral fracture from an accidental fall. (*Medicaid Fraud Report,* 1990, May/June, p. 22)

The case description goes on noting that after pleading guilty, the defendant was given a fifteen-year sentence in the department of corrections, and was issued a minimal fine. Clearly, a great deal of information is included in this description. Some are not as long, while others are longer. A section in the fraud report, referred to as "case update," describes information about cases that were previously described in the fraud report but were unresolved. For instance, one issue of the fraud report might include a description of a case where an individual pleaded guilty to sexually abusing an elderly person. A few issues later, the sanction given to the offender might be included in the case update section. The way the cases are described makes the descriptions suitable for content analysis. Because the data were not developed for research purposes, there are limitations associated with using the data to address research questions. These limitations will be discussed below. For now, it is important to note that the fraud report can be and has been used to address important research questions about elder abuse, prescription fraud, and Medicaid fraud (Payne & Cikovic, 1995; Payne & Dabney, 1997). Using the fraud report to study elder abuse, Payne and Cikovic (1995) analyzed incidents of patient abuse in nursing homes by examining offenses included in the report and found that violators are actually punished as severely as other offenders in a process similar to the justice process used for street offenders.

The *Vital Statistics of the United States* is another source of information about certain aspects of elderly victimization. In particular, this data source, which is published by the National Center for Health Statistics, provides information about mortality and other social issues (e.g., marriages and divorces) of concern across the United States. Data about deaths are placed on death certificates, which are completed by a legal official in cases of homicides. The funeral director receives the death certificate and then gives it to the local registrar who will review and record the report before sending it to the state registrar. The state registrar will then send information about the death to the National Office of Vital Statistics (Riedel, 1990). Riedel (1990) notes that the next thing that occurs is that "coders prepare the case according to the International Classification of Diseases and enter the case into the national mortality data published as Vital Statistics of the United States" (p. 188). Most public and university libraries are provided the report free of charge. Thus, it is readily available to students and researchers alike.

Researchers have made use of the data, though its use for examinations concerning elderly victims has been somewhat limited. The *Vital Statistics of the United States* has been used to examine infant homicide rates (Straus, 1987), the relationship between gun control and personal violence (Lester & Murrell, 1986; Clarke & Jones, 1989), and suicide (Boyd, 1982; Leenars & Lester, 1990; Males, 1991). When the report is used to examine deaths of elderly persons, it is more often used to examine causes of natural deaths rather than homicides (see Smith, 1998). In one of the few studies using data from *Vital Statistics of the United States* and examining deaths among older persons that were caused by something other than natural causes or diseases, McIntosh (1991) examined suicide rates among various age groups. He found that the suicide rate is highest for males at the age of sixty-five and for females who are between forty-five and fifty-four years old.

There are limitations that probably explain why the database has not been used widely to address the victimization of elderly persons. For example, the *Vital Statistics of the United States* only includes information on the number of homicides each year, and determining which ones were caused by elder abuse, family violence, or white-collar crime is impossible. Causes of homicides are coded into the following categories: firearms and explosives; cutting or piercing instruments; fight, brawl, and rape; other and unspecified; corrosive or caustic substance; poisoning; hanging or strangulation; drowning; child battering or other maltreatment; and, late effects of injury (Riedel, 1990). Also, there is questionable reliability and validity about the initial death certification made at the local level where the whole process of data gathering initiates (Riedel, 1990). If local officials error in their coding, the rest of the process is virtually useless for that particular case. Even so, because the database is so readily available, and rich in historical data (several decades worth), it is a "gold mine" that could be used to address many questions about the deaths, both legal and illegal, of elderly persons.

Official records housed in state and local agencies are also an example of archival records that can be used to address issues confronting elder abuse victims. In fact, most of the archival research that has addressed elder abuse has used state and local records. Hall (1989), for example, examined 288 case records categorized as elder maltreatment by the Texas Department of Human Resources in its attempt to provide adult protective services and found that maltreatment is a diverse phenomenon that cannot be described with traditional maltreatment measures. A study by Choi, Kulik, and Mayer (1999) analyzed county level adult protective services data to see the risk factors associated with financial exploitation. Based on their review of the records, they found that 60 percent of financial abusers were relatives, with most of the relatives being adult children. Their analysis led to important implications concerning case management, prevention, and collaboration among various agencies involved in responding to elder abuse.

A study by Neale et al. (1997) is also illustrative of the way that archives have been used to address concerns facing older victims. In particular, the authors examined the types of services provided by an adult protective services agency and considered the reasons for those services. After reviewing 2,769 case closures over a twenty-six-month period, they found that one-third of the cases were closed because there was no risk for future abuse, one-fifth resulted in placement in a care facility, and a little over ten percent of the victims refused care. The authors would not have been able to gather this information through any other method (e.g., survey, experiment, etc.) than a review of case records.

Countless other studies have also relied on state and local records to gather a better understanding about elder abuse. Sengstock, Hwaleck, and Petrone (1989) reviewed 204 cases of elder abuse in Illinois to shed some light on the service needs of elderly victims and to see whether their needs are actually met. Based on their analysis, they found that self-neglect cases required completely different services than other elder abuse cases, and that case management, homemaking assistance, and legal services were the most common services provided to elder abuse victims. In a similar fashion, Greenberg, McKibben, and Raymond (1990) examined 204 cases of elder abuse committed by adult children in Wisconsin. Their results showed that offenders were generally dependent on the victims, who in turn showed "substantial depression" (p. 73).

The results of all of these studies using archives will be considered in more detail later when issues directly pertinent to the questions addressed in the studies are discussed. For now, the important point to note is that the findings could not have been obtained through any other methods. This is not to say that archival research is the best method, but it is certainly appropriate for certain research questions.

As another example of archival research, some researchers use data from the Centers for Medicare and Medicaid Services (CMS) to address concerns of older adults. The CMS, a part of the U.S. Department of Health and Human Services, administers the Medicare and Medicaid programs. Among other responsibilities, the CMS determines the quality of health care facilities (including nursing homes) and enforces standards as needed. Indeed, one of the goals of CMS is to make sure that nursing homes meet federal health care standards (Dessoff, 1999).

The CMS offers an assortment of information and databases to researchers who are interested in researching various social issues related to the administration of health care. These databases include, but are not limited to, information about health care indicators, health care expenditures, estimates of the extent of fraud, and patient's rights violations in nursing homes (Desoff, 1999; Hyatt, 1999). Because the CMS are responsible for ensuring that nursing homes are meeting appropriate standards, it is in a position to develop a particularly solid database on patient's rights violations. Even so, studies using CMS data more often focus on the financial aspects of health care (see, for example, Baker, 1999; Cromwell et al., 1997; Gardner, 1996; Scalzi et al., 1994). This is particularly surprising because the information about nursing home violations gathered by the CMS is available to the public under the Freedom of Information Act. Robert Bua (1997) is one author who makes great use of CMS data on nursing home violations.

In particular, each year Bua uses information from the CMS to develop *The Inside Guide to America's Nursing Homes.* As such, he used archival data to compile his report, but he also has produced a database that can be used by other archival researchers interested in examining violations by nursing homes. Each year, he ranks over 17,000 certified nursing homes in the United States by using public records made available by the CMS, the United States Postal Service, and the Joint Commission on Accreditation of Health Care Organization (JCAHO). Based on this information, he ranks and rates the nursing homes using a formula that considers the quality of care, number of violations, seriousness of violations, and a host of other factors. Bua (1997) writes that the homes are "evaluated and compared based upon objective, trustworthy, resident-focused inspections that monitor the quality of life and quality of care of nursing home residents" (p. 97).

Each nursing home is compared to other nursing homes in the county, in the state, and in the nation. In particular, the following information is included for each nursing home: total number of beds, number of Alzheimer's beds, percentage of Medicaid supported residents, current county rank, current state rank, historical state rating, national rating, fire safety rating, JCAHO indicator, and a summary of the violations noted in the government inspection report.

JCAHO accreditation simply reflects whether the home successfully completed an accreditation process offered by the Joint Commission on Accreditation of Healthcare organizations, which is a private organization unaffiliated with Medicaid and Medicare that "compiles comprehensive health care standards" (Bua, 1997, p. 98). Because nursing homes are not required to seek JCAHO accreditation, one must not assume that homes that have not been accredited by JCAHO are problematic. At the same time, because all of the nursing homes in his guide are certified, they have met the minimum level of standards needed in order to operate as nursing homes in the U.S.

As far as the summary of inspection violations, the guide includes information on 180 different violations which will be summarized in the next chapter. Some nursing homes had very few, while others had several. Bua's guide can be useful to researchers in two different ways. First, because it includes addresses of nursing homes, researchers can use the guide to develop a sample for a mail survey (Payne et al., 1999). Second, as an archival record, the data in the guide could serve as a data source for various endeavors. For example, one could examine the characteristics of inspection violations, whether the characteristics are regionally determined, or whether the number of beds of percentage of Medicaid residents influences violations. Because editions are published annually, changes over time could be assessed to see if any legislative or policy changes reduced or increased violations. There are clearly dozens of questions that could be addressed using the guide as a data source. As yet, I am not aware of any studies that have utilized this guide to address these areas. This is likely because the guide is marketed as a tool consumers can use to find their loved ones a nursing home. Nonetheless, the guide could be a "gold mine" for graduate students seeking thesis or dissertation data related to nursing home violations.

These are not the only data sources available. With the onset of the computer age, other archival sources become even more accessible than archives were in the past. For example, the "CMS's Nursing Home Search" homepage (www.medicare.gov/nursing/home.asp) has links that will give consumers information that can be used to compare and contrast nursing homes. Also included are the descriptions of license violations of all certified nursing homes throughout the United States. The harm or potential for harm from each violation is included in the information provided on the internet. As with Bua's guide, although the information is not intended specifically for social science consumption, it can be quite useful given the appropriate research questions.

The benefits of unobtrusive research such as archival research are noteworthy. The first benefit is what some refer to as nonreactivity. In particular, when examining crimes against older victims, the subjects, whether they are victims, offenders, or another group, are not aware of the observations and therefore will not react to the observation. Brewer and Hunter (1989) note that archival records give researchers access to data occurring naturally in society.

Historical benefits are a second advantage of archival methods. Basically, archival research gives researchers the ability to analyze patterns, trends, and behavior over time (Fox & Levin, 1991; Covey & Menard, 1988). Historical analyses can also be used for comparative purposes in that cultures, subcultures, and other groups can be compared with one another. An excellent example of this comparative orientation are Max Weber's historical studies (e.g., *The Agrarian Sociology of Ancient Civilization* and *Roscher and Knies: The Logical Problems of Historical Economics*). Changes in orientations, beliefs, customs, norms, and laws can be easily examined. In fact, regarding crimes against seniors, social scientists have used archives to study changes in definitions, variations in elder abuse statutes, and responses to criminal offenses (Crystal, 1987; Payne & Cikovic, 1995).

The third benefit of archival research is that it allows access to subjects who otherwise would be inaccessible. As indicated earlier, gaining entrance into various settings to study crime is often difficult. Using archives, on the other hand, gives the researcher more than access; it provides access to a large number of subjects who otherwise would be unavailable. For example, locating and interviewing 300 victims of elder abuse would be costly, time-consuming, and impossible without some sort of support. However, using the previously mentioned fraud report, Payne and Cikovic (1995) were able to examine the characteristics and structural factors contributing to the abuse. Likewise, Fox and Levin (1991) point out that using official records lets researchers gain information on elderly homicide victims, a group who would be excluded in the other methods.

As with all of the other methods discussed, there are limitations of archival research that potentially limit its use for crimes against seniors. The developer of the data source creates the source for informational rather than research use. For example, the researcher is usually at the mercy of the individual creating the archive when the nature of the variables is considered. The researcher, in essence, engages in a passive role (Brewer & Hunter, 1989) which reduces his or her flexibility with variable construction and analysis (Berg, 1998; Monette, Sullivan, & DeJong, 1990).

A second problem has to do with changes in coding over time which make comparisons problematic. Criminologists, for example, recognize that the style of the *Uniform Crime Reports* has changed as society changed (Hashimoto, 1987). Attempts to examine changes in victimization of various age groups would be useful only if the comparisons were made between years when the data was maintained the same way.

The third problem with using archival records for research on crimes against seniors is missing records. Court records, for example, are usually edited. This is related to what Webb et al. (1966) refer to as selective deposit. Briefly, some records may not contain all of the information needed by researchers. As noted earlier, police departments may not report all of the crimes they know about to the FBI. This certainly affects the validity of official crime records. Hall (1989) used case records to study elder abuse but notes that case records "often represent a service population rather than the general population of interest" (p. 192).

Not getting all of the information needed to paint an accurate picture of crimes against seniors is the result of the missing records. Lack of information then leads to questionable findings. Recall the discussion of the limitations of UCR data. Based on UCR data and fear of crime research, a growing body of research has shown that the elderly have the highest fear of crime but the lowest victimization rate (Clarke et al., 1985). Further analysis with more complete data sets, however, revealed that the elderly actually had a higher probability of homicide from botched robberies (Fox & Levin, 1991). Based on the data available, neither conclusion was incorrect. The point is that the available data influences the research findings, which in turn may influence policy.

A related problem with the use of archival records concerns the use of official statistics. The word official may distort what the data source is actually able to provide. "Official" implies correctness, rightness, and accuracy. As already indicated, the official reports of crime are not a perfect indicator of crime, especially for offenses committed against elderly persons. Rather, they are reports of what victims and law enforcement officials decide to share with various agencies. Even so, the information can be quite helpful when used correctly.

To sum up the methodological issues and why these offenses against seniors are somewhat ignored, it is safe to suggest that a host of problems limits the use of surveys, field studies, and archival research. There are two potential ways to address these issues. The first, and the most scientific way, is replication and/or triangulation. What this actually means is more work for the researchers, which is often unrealistic. The "multi-method" approach (Brewer & Hunter, 1989) entails the use of a combination of research methods to address the same question. A problem as dynamic as elder abuse sometimes requires a multi-method approach. Consider a recent study by Dunlop et al. (2000) in which researchers interviewed professionals encountering elder abuse and content analyzed 319 case report substantiated by protective services in order to assess risk factors and practices.

To be sure, researchers could examine the official records in a particular area, interview subjects, and observe actions occurring in a nursing home to fully gauge the patterns, characteristics, and causes of occupational crime in that setting. Essentially, what one loses in one method is gained by the strengths of other methodologies (Brewer & Hunter, 1989). However, economic and practical factors limit the use of the multi-method approach.

A second way to address these issues is to use performance measurement systems whereby elderly individuals are involved in the development, collection, and analysis phases of the research (Besleme & Mullin, 1997; Gross & Straussman, 1974). The development of the performance measurement systems is important in that "indicators can play an important role in mobilizing citizens to set priorities and goals and participate in community planning and problem-solving efforts" (Besleme & Mullin, 1997, p. 43). Though viewed as less scientific by some, the advantages of subject involvement in the research process offsets the limitations described above. The problem that comes up is convincing and training subjects.

CONCLUDING REMARKS

Some of the cases considered throughout this book were lifted from the *Medicaid Fraud Report,* one of the archives I highlighted earlier in this chapter. It is relevant not just because it provides an interesting data source. Rather, using information gathered by criminal justice practitioners provides researchers with an opportunity to get involved in the collaborative response to elder abuse.

To be sure, these crimes have not been completely ignored by behavioral scientists. However, what so far has amounted to disjointed examinations of the same phenomenon by experts from various disciplines needs to become an integrated approach to examine these misdeeds. Such an approach would increase the ability of social scientists to better deal with crimes committed against elderly citizens. As Pillemer (1986) points out, "any attempt to understand the dynamics of the abuse situation must take into account theory and research related specifically to the aged" (p. 245).

Indeed, an integrated approach involving the following groups is needed in order to better understand crimes against seniors: scholars from various disciplines, practitioners involved in responding to the crimes, practitioners employed in settings where many of these crimes occur, and older citizens who are often preyed on by various offenders. This integrated approach, again, can be referred to as gero-criminology and is not just about establishing collaboration among practitioners involved in responding to elder abuse; rather, it entails the scientific examination of the patterns, trends, and patterns of criminal behavior against seniors and integrates various disciplines' approaches to offenses against seniors. As a consequence, a more holistic approach allowing for broader understanding about these issues is formed. More importantly, applying criminological principles to the issues increases the likelihood of viewing these offenses as criminal acts rather than service problems. The trend of "decriminalizing" these acts in practice and research must change.

Chapter 3

ABUSE IN THE LIVES OF OLDER ADULTS

1. What types of abuse are committed most often against elderly persons?
2. What is the difference between physical abuse and elder abuse?
3. Describe the types of elder sexual abuse.
4. Compare and contrast fraud and collective embezzlement.
5. What types of crimes are committed in nursing homes?
6. What is self-neglect? Should society be concerned with self-neglect? Explain.

INTRODUCTION

The following comments were made by Hubert Humphrey at a hearing entitled "Consumer Fraud and the Elderly: Easy Prey?" held before the U.S. Senate's Special Committee on Aging in September, 1992:

> Contrary to the occasional stereotypes, most older Americans are not frail or befuddled or easily parted from their savings. For the most part, they are self-sufficient, they manage their affairs with sound judgement; and they have the good sense that comes from a lifetime of experience. Their days are full, and their lives are rich.
>
> But the jackals of fraud know there are exceptions to this rule. And like their counterparts in the wild, these predators never attack the strong. Their defining characteristic is their singular ability to find the most vulnerable of victims. To wear them down. To play on their fear. To increase their sense of helplessness. And in the process, to rob them not only of their savings, but of their dignity and self-confidence. (U.S. Senate, 1993, p. 82)

The consumer fraud hearing was important because it demonstrated the willingness of Congress to continue to give attention to crimes against seniors.

Also, congressional hearings in the 1980s tended to focus more on physical abuse rather than financial abuse. Humphrey's comments showed an appreciation for other types of offenses committed against older adults. As will be seen in this chapter, elderly persons can be victims of a host of different types of abuse. Consider the following examples

- One morning, a woman was called on the telephone and told that her eighty-eight-year-old mother had died peacefully in her sleep in the nursing home where she resided. The woman later learned that her mother was "left trapped outdoors in a courtyard on a cold night: when she died (Lash & Rotstein, 2003). According to Lash and Rotstein (2003), "employees carried her cold body back to bed, redressed her and cranked up the heat to make it appear as if she'd died in her sleep."
- A sixty-six-year-old woman moved in with her son and daughter-in-law so she could be closer to them. The son and his wife had other ideas about developing their relationship with the older woman. They "took her life savings, barred her from using the telephone, cut her hair, and drugged her so she would appear to be demented on visits to her doctor" (*Times-Picayune,* 2003: 4).
- An auto repair shop engaged in a bait and switch scheme in which elderly persons were targeted. The employees developed intricate strategies to get older persons into the shop and subsequently charged them ridiculous prices for services. They kept customers' cars until they got their money. Five men were eventually arrested (*Motor Age,* 2003).
- A heroin addict confessed to breaking into an eighty-six-year-old women's apartment to rob her in order to support his habit. In addition to robbing her, he beat, strangled, raped, and murdered the woman (Filosa, 2003).

In Chapter 1, I suggested that there were three broad types of abuse: *collective abuse, institutional abuse,* and *individual abuse.* The distinguishing feature in this typology has to do with the victim-offender relationship. *Collective abuse* cases involve instances where society in general is the transgressor. In *institutional abuse,* institutions, or employees of the institutions, are the offenders. Further, the victims of institutional abuse are often a group of elderly persons rather than one specific elderly victim. *Individual abuse* cases include cases where a specific person[s] commits an abusive act against an elderly victim.

This chapter extends that typology by focusing on the specific types of abuse that are experienced by the victim. The majority of attention will be directed toward an understanding of the types of *institutional* and *individual abuse.* The fact that little direct attention is given to *collective abuse* in this work does not diminish the importance of collective abuse. Indeed, many experts believe that ageist attitudes (which are an example of collective abuse) increase an elderly person's risks of victimization (Hudson, 1991). Thus, *collective abuse,* by its very nature, exists in each of the specific types of abuse to be considered in the following pages. The types of individual abuse committed against elderly persons include: *physical abuse, sexual abuse, financial abuse, neglect, self-neglect, abandonment,* and *psychological abuse.* The types of institutional abuse include: *health care crimes, patient dumping, institutional financial fraud,* and *regulatory violations.*

A consideration of these types of abuse is important because a full understanding of elder abuse will evolve only through a consideration of the specific types of elder abuse (Gilliland & Jimenez, 1996; Wolf, 1992). Gilliland & Jimenez (1996) argue, "to explain elder abuse, research must differentiate types of abuse" (p. 88). Thus, distinguishing between these types of abuse will provide further understanding about the nature of elder abuse.

It is important to stress that depending on who the transgressor is, cases where relatives, professionals, or caregivers abuse older adults could be seen as either institutional or individual abuse. For instance, if a son neglects his mother, this is individual abuse. Alternatively, if a nursing home neglects a patient, this is institutional abuse. To avoid repetition, I will avoid discussing physical abuse, sexual abuse, neglect, and the other overlapping types of abuse under both individual and institutional abuse. Thus, in some instances, individual and institutional abuse examples will be combined to illustrate specific abuse types. In other instances, the broader abuse types will remain separated to maintain a distinction between individual abuse and institutional abuse.

Before proceeding, four other points are noteworthy. First, recall that I am basing my definition of elder abuse on a social harm definition of crime. A social harm definition of crime is concerned with the consequences of the offense, not whether the political or criminal justice system labels actions as illegal or criminal. Defining crime in this manner makes each of the types of abuse considered in this chapter criminal. Second, there is variation in how states, professionals, and researchers define these types of abuse. The definitions offered here are meant as general definitions and are not intended to be the only way to define the various types of abuse. Third, as will be seen, each type of abuse is complex, and there are several sub-types of each type of abuse. That is, there are several types of physical abuse, sexual abuse, financial abuse, and so on. Fourth, those who are victims of one type of abuse are often victims of other types of abuse. It is my hope that the reader will see the true complexities involved in cases of elder abuse.

PHYSICAL ABUSE

When individuals think of elder abuse, they likely think of harmful physical acts that are committed against older persons. Or, they think of physical abuse. Physical abuse involves a host of acts that have been committed against elderly persons that range from pinching, slapping, or hitting an older person to committing murder. In all states, these actions are defined as crime; however, they are not always treated as criminal because the cases often do not come to the attention of the authorities. Five related types of physical abuse have been discussed in the literature: *parent abuse, spouse abuse, patient abuse, other violent crimes,* and *homicides.*

Parent Abuse

Children are believed to be the most common perpetrators in elder abuse cases (Young, 2000). Estimates from the National Center on Elder Abuse (1997) suggest that 1.01 million elderly persons were victims of domestic elder abuse in 1996. The majority of those elder abuse cases were cases where an adult child abuses (physically, financially, psychologically, and so on) his or her parents. It is believed that adult children who abuse their parents are more likely to commit psychological abuse or neglect (Wolf, 1996). Even so, according to estimates provided by the NCEA, the percentage of abuse cases involving adult children has increased in the nineties. In 1990, for instance, 30.1 percent of the abuse cases involved adult children as perpetrators, as compared to 36.7 percent in 1996. Of the 1.01 million elder abuse cases in 1996, 14.6 percent were cases of physical abuse. Figures describing how many children physically abuse their parents, however, are not yet available. Nonetheless, experts realize that physical parent abuse occurs.

As an example, a woman who was abused by her son told a group of U.S. Senators about her abusive experiences:

> In January, my son lost his job, his car blew up, and he turned to alcohol. He came home one afternoon and was out of his mind with whisky. He didn't know who I was and called me by different names. He started smashing everything in the house, and then he turned on me. He punched me out. I was bruised all over my face. . . . I wanted to get out the door, but I couldn't move. I finally had to pretend that I was dead or unconscious. (U.S. Senate, 1991, p. 71)

The woman further stated: "No little lady at 72 should be knocked around by her son" (p. 71). As will be seen in Chapter 4, those who are victimized by their children may experience serious emotional and psychological consequences as a result of the victimization.

Spouse Abuse

Some suggest that spouses are more likely to be the aggressors in cases of physical elder abuse (Folkenberg, 1989). Yet, spouses comprised only 12.6 percent of the elder abuse cases examined by the NCEA (1997). This estimate is likely low for two reasons. First, because the NCEA gathered its information from state adult protective services agencies and state units on aging across the United States, cases where spouses reported the abuse to law enforcement officials may not be included in these estimates, particularly if the law enforcement officers did not report the case to the APS agency. Second, many victims of spouse abuse will not report the abuse to the authorities.

As Baron and Welty (1996) write, "spouses who batter are not likely to stop when they turn sixty" (p. 33). However, older spouse victims are typically not included in the domestic violence literature (Harris, 1996; Vinton, 1991). When elder physical abuse was initially conceived, concern was oriented toward abusive acts against nursing home patients (Seaver, 1996). Today, spouse abuse is a common type of elder abuse, but domestic violence older abuse victims "are more likely to be viewed as abused elderly than victims of domestic violence" (Harris, 1996, p. 3). On a related line, Wolf (1996) notes that "the domestic violence and elder abuse movements have been operating essentially in separate domains" (p. 89).

In one study that tried to merge the fields of elder abuse and domestic violence, Harris (1996) analyzed data from the National Family Violence Survey (by Richard Gelles and Murray A. Straus) and found that even though older adults are victims of domestic violence less often than younger individuals, similar risk factors contribute to abuse in both younger and older populations. In fact, Harris found that over half of the older spouse abuse victims were abused for several years. She refers to this notion as "spouse abuse grown old" (p. 26).

Testimony presented by an older spouse abuse victim at a conference sponsored by the AARP reflects this notion:

> My story and those of other battered women goes on and on. There are many of us older battered women. We experience physical, emotional, spiritual and sexual abuse. The pain is unending. I have almost forty years of such experience. . . . The vows I had taken, "until death do us part," nearly did that on more than one occasion. (*Report to the AARP Forum*, 1992, p. 38)

The effects of abuse on older spouse victims are equal to, if not more severe than, the effects experienced by younger spouse abuse victims (Harris, 1996). Only recently have programs been developed that exist primarily for older spouse abuse victims. In Milwaukee, for instance, an older abused woman's program exists to provide safety, education, and case management. Seaver

(1996) reports that nearly 40 percent of the older women who entered the program in a three-year period "freed themselves from the abuse" (p. 16). She suggests that programs can be useful for older victims if the appropriate support is offered.

All available evidence suggests that it is extremely hard for a spouse abuse victim to leave the abusive relationship. However, it is believed to be more difficult for older women to leave an abusive relationship. Many have never worked and have no financial future. Many are caregivers or care recipients. The shame is also more marked. Feelings of loyalty and desire to adhere to family expectations may also inhibit older victims from leaving abusive partners (Nelesen, 2003).

Patient Abuse

Patient abuse refers to the physical abuse cases that occur in nursing homes, adult care centers, hospitals, or other residential care centers. The figures provided by the NCEA focus on domestic elder abuse cases, and thus exclude abuse that occurs in nursing homes. Indeed, it is difficult to gauge the extent of crimes in nursing homes because patients will not report offenses because they are afraid the offender will hurt them more, and they believe reporting would be futile (Wierucka & Goodridge, 1996).

To try to get an estimate of the extent of patient abuse, Pillemer and Moore (1989) surveyed 577 nurse's aides and nurses and found that 36 percent of the respondents had seen an abusive act in the previous year, and ten percent reported committing one in the same time frame. Crumb and Jennings (1998) cite a study by Gitner (1995) that found that "81 percent of the nurses and aides reported witnessing at least one form of employee abuse toward a patient, including insulting, yelling, threatening to commit physical violence, or isolating a patient beyond what is necessary" (Crumb & Jennings, 1998). Like Pillemer and Moore (1989), Gitner (1995) reports that physical abuse was noted by 36 percent of the employees.

Payne and Cikovic (1995) examined patient abuse in nursing homes by content, analyzing 488 cases of patient abuse reported to Medicaid Fraud Control Units across the United States. Physical abuse, the most common type of abuse reported to the fraud control units, was found in 84 percent of the cases. This does not necessarily mean that physical abuse is the type of elder abuse most likely to occur in nursing homes. Instead, their results may reflect enforcement patterns in that physical abuse cases are easier to detect, substantiate, and prosecute than other types of elder abuse. Also, physical abuse is likely seen as more offensive than other types of elder abuse (Payne et al., 1999). Ways to reduce patient abuse include increasing employees'

(1) education, (2) training, (3) social support, and (4) morale (Wierucka & Goodridge, 1996).

A specific type of physical abuse that occurs in nursing homes involves the use of restraints, both physical and chemical, to control a resident's behavior. Physical restraints entail "tying a patient or a patient's limbs to a bed or chair" (Wiehe, 1998, p. 130). The use of chemical restraints, also known as *pacification* and *overmedication,* involves circumstances where patients are given excess medication in order to make them easier to control (Baker, 1975; Kerr, Dening, & Lawton, 1994; Simmons, 1993). In a case described by Kerr et al. (1994), a care assistant was believed to have overmedicated a seventy-seven-year-old woman known to have a violent temper. The belief was that the assistant gave the excessive medication "to keep her quiet" (p. 731). These acts are nothing new. In fact, Baker (1975), who developed the concept of "granny battering," argued that cases where caregivers increase medication of elderly persons to the point of causing overdose are examples of "granny battering" (p. 22).

At the other extreme from pacification are instances where medical providers fail to provide enough medication to elderly patients. In one case, an eighty-five-year-old man was not given medication to battle the pain he was experiencing as a result of lung cancer. After his death, the daughter sued the doctor and nursing home on elder abuse charges and won a settlement. The jury found that undertreating pain in older adults constituted elder abuse (Demner, 2003; Schiff, 2001). Health care professionals must take caution not to undermedicate or overmedicate, which is an example of chemical restraint.

Chemical and physical restraints in hospitals and nursing homes became more of an issue in the eighties and nineties. Some say that the restraints "are used to 'help' the older patient" (U.S. Senate, 1991, p. 13). In testimony before the Senate's Special Committee on Aging, Geriatrician Arnold Greenhouse points out that the United States is the only country in the world to "restrain, tie down, [or] over medicate the elderly" (U.S. Senate, 1991, p. 13). He argues, as do others, that very little evidence supports the need to restrain older adults.

The use of restraints is not just a problem in nursing homes. Mion et al. (1996) point out that "one in five older adults are restrained at some point during their hospitalization" (p. 412). In fact, they argue that the use of physical restraints has declined greatly in nursing homes but remained at high levels in hospitals. Indeed, between 1987 and 1996, the number of physical restraint violations cited by the HCFA was cut in half (Williamson, 1999). The fact that the use of restraints has declined in nursing homes does not mean that restraints are not problematic in the nursing home industry. In fact, Bua (1997) reports that 16.3 percent of nursing homes in the United States were cited for violating the standard protecting residents from being physically restrained for matters unrelated to their medical needs in the previous round of nursing home inspections.

Other Violent Crimes

Not all cases of elder physical abuse are committed by family members or caregivers. I refer to this other type of physical abuse as *other violent crimes* because a host of offenses defined as illegal in all states are excluded from a conceptualization limited to *parent abuse, spouse abuse,* and *patient abuse.* These other violent crimes are offenses that are officially defined as criminal and include those offenses which are often committed by strangers. Broadly speaking, they include homicide, robbery, assault, and variations on each of these offenses (e.g., aggravated assault and simple assault). As such, these are the offenses represented by official crime statistics reported in the UCR by the Federal Bureau of Investigation and the NCVS by the Bureau of Justice Statistics. The figures cited for elder abuse in the previous pages are provided by the NCEA. As will be seen, there are interesting differences in the patterns evolving from each set of statistics.

Table 7 outlines the victimization rates for violent and property offenses broken down by age, gender, and race categories. The violent offenses measured in Table 7 include rape, robbery, and assault as they are defined by the NCVS. In this context, rape is defined as forced sexual intercourse on the victim. Force can include psychological coercion (Bachman & Taylor, 1994). Robbery is using force or threat of force to steal or attempt to steal another's property. Assault includes attacks with or without weapons that may or may not result in injury (Perkins, 1997, p. 4). It seems important to note that the majority of offenders reported in these cases were strangers to the victims. The Bureau of Justice Statistics (1994) reports that older violent crime victims "are more likely than younger victims to face assailants who are victims" and that older robbery victims "are more likely than younger victims to be particularly vulnerable to offenders whom they do not know" (p. 2).

Table 7 shows that younger persons seem to be victimized by robbery, assault, and rape more often than older adults. It has already been established that official statistics cannot be used to gauge the true extent of crime committed against elderly persons. However, as noted previously, findings from national surveys on the crime problem are useful in demonstrating crime patterns and trends. For example, findings from the National Crime Victimization Survey show that:

1. People aged sixty-five to seventy-four have a higher victimization rate than those seventy-five or older.
2. Older blacks are more likely to be victimized than older whites.
3. Elderly persons with the lowest incomes have higher rates of violence than elderly with high incomes.

TABLE 7. NUMBER OF VIOLENT CRIMES BY GENDER, AGE, AND RACE (PER 1000)

	Number of Violent Crimes per 1000
Teenage black males	113
Teenage black females	94
Teenage white males	90
Young adult black males	80
Young adult black females	57
Teenage white females	55
Young adult white males	52
Young adult white females	38
Adult black males	35
Adult white males	18
Adult white females	15
Adult black females	13
Elderly black males	12
Elderly black females	10
Elderly white males	6
Elderly white females	3

Age Categories:
Teenage   = 12–19 years
Young adult = 20–34 years
Adult   = 35–64 years
Elderly   = 65 and older

Source: Bureau of Justice Statistics. (1994). *Elderly Crime Victims: National Crime Survey.* Washington, D.C.: U.S. Department of Justice.

Critical Thinking Questions:

1. How would you explain interactions between age and race?
2. How would you explain interactions between gender and age?

✦ 4. Separated and divorced elderly persons are more likely to be victims of violent offenses than married elderly persons are.

✦ 5. Elderly victims of violence are almost twice as likely to be victimized at or near their home (U.S. Department of Justice, 1994; see also Bachman et al., 1998).

Interesting differences arise between elder abuse research findings and these NCVS estimates. For example, much of the elder abuse research shows that the typical victim is female (Eisenberg, 1991; National Center on Elder

Abuse, 1997; Perick-Cornell & Gelles, 1982; Tatara, 1993; Whittaker, 1995) over the age of seventy-five (NCEA, 1997; Whittaker, 1995), and related to the offender (NCEA, 1997; Oakars, 1991). Official crime statistics such as those from the NCVS, however, suggest that elderly men have higher victimization rates than elderly women, and that people between sixty-five and seventy-four years old have higher victimization rates than those seventy-four and older (U.S. Department of Justice, 1994). These differences suggest that the elder abuse statistics and crime statistics may be measuring different activities. If this is the case, the need to integrate crime concepts with abuse concepts becomes even more important but at the same time more difficult.

Not all elder abuse research agrees that elderly women are more likely to be victimized. Kosberg (1998) argues that older men are overlooked in elder abuse studies and suggests that figures cited in previous elder abuse research underestimate the actual extent and vulnerability of male elder abuse victims. The safest thing to suggest is that there is no way of knowing how many elderly persons are abused each year, but the number of reported cases of elder abuse has increased since the mid-eighties (Goldstein, 1995; NCEA, 1997).

Homicides

Former homicide detective Joseph Soos (2000) has developed a typology to address homicides against elderly persons. Specifically, Soos argues that the following five types of homicides are committed against elderly persons:

- Murder for profit killings
- Revenge killings
- Eldercide
- Gerontophella
- Relief of burden killings

Murder for profit killings occur when an offender kills an older or vulnerable adult for some form of profit. Profits are generally minimal, but these offenses nonetheless occurred because of the profit sought by the offenders.

Revenge killings occur when offenders kill the older or vulnerable adult in order to get even with the victim or his or her family for some perceived injustice. When it is a family member killing his or her relative, these killings are believed to be a result of abuse the offender experienced at the hands of the victim earlier in life.

Eldercide entails the killing of elderly persons simply out of prejudice against older persons. Consider a home health aid who was accused of trying to kill several of her patients. In one incident, this aide placed a garbage bag over one of her patient's heads for thirty minutes in order to "put her out of her misery" (Price, 1997, np). The patient, an eighty-six-year-old woman with

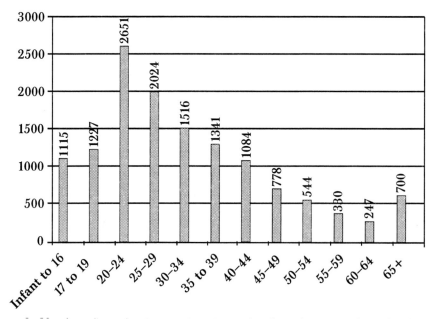

Figure 2. Number of murders/nonnegligent manslaughters known to the police by age, 2001.

Source: *Sourcebook of Criminal Justice Statistics Online* (2003). Table 3.129.

Critical Thinking Questions:

1. Why would it be difficult to detect homicides against older persons?
2. Why are the differences between age groups so large?

Alzheimer's disease, survived this attack because the aide never sealed the bag. When police investigated the incident, they found that the aide had done similar things to other patients in the past.

Gerontophella refers to homicides that are committed in order to cover up an offender's sexual assault against the older victim. Oftentimes, gerontophella cases are never detected. Offenders are, however, sometimes caught. In one recent case, an offender was caught ten years after sexually assaulting an eighty-year-old woman. He was caught when police stumbled on the evidence (Spencer & Anderson, 2003).

Figures 2 through 4 illustrate patterns surrounding the homicides of elderly persons. As shown in these figures, while older persons are less likely than younger persons to be victims of homicide, patterns of homicide vary between age groups. In particular, older persons are far less likely than younger persons to be victimized by firearms. More often, other strategies are used, making it easier for offenders to conceal their offense. Firearms are used in three-fourths of homicides involving victims between the ages of seventeen and thirty-nine.

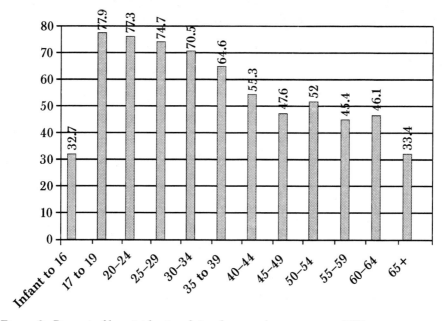

Figure 3. Percent of homicides involving firearms by age group, 2001.
Source: *Sourcebook of Criminal Justice Statistics Online* (2003). Adapted from Table 3.129.

Critical Thinking Questions:

1. Why do you think firearms are rarer in homicides involving elderly victims?
2. What are the implications of these patterns for criminal justice professionals?

Alternatively, just one-third of homicides involving elderly victims entail the use of firearms.

SEXUAL ABUSE

Sexual abuse can be seen as a type of physical abuse (Arbetter, 1995) but is discussed separately because of the different type of harm that victims may experience from sexual assaults. Sexual abuse against older adults occurs when a person has any type of non-consensual sexual relations with an elderly person. Official statistics from the Bureau of Justice Statistics suggest that older adults are victimized far less often than younger people are. In particular, estimates suggest that people under the age of twenty-five make up 56 percent of rape/sexual assault victims. Alternatively, almost a third of the population is over fifty years old, but only 3 percent of the rape/sexual assault victims were over fifty in estimates provided by Perkins (1997). Further, the NCEA

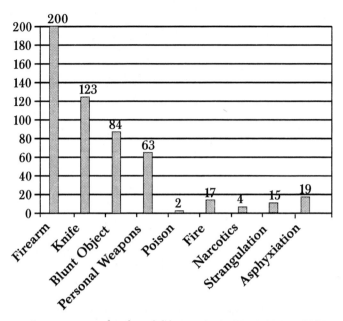

Figure 4. Types of weapons used in homicides against older victims, 2001.
Source: *Sourcebook of Criminal Justice Statistics Online.* (2003). Adapted from Table 3.129.

Critical Thinking Questions:

1. Would certain kinds of weapons be used in different types of homicide?
2. What do these figures mean to you in terms of gun control?

(1997) figures suggest that sexual abuse cases make up about .3 percent of the elder abuse cases. The estimates provided by the NCEA and BJS must be approached with a great deal of caution, however, because elder sexual abuse is believed to be a severely underreported offense (Ramsey-Klawsnik, 1991). As well, one study reveals that older victims are more likely to suffer genital injury than younger victims and that one-third of older sexual abuse victims, as compared to 6 percent of younger victims, needed surgery to repair their injuries (Muram, Miller, & Cutler, 1992). An earlier study, however, finds that genital injuries are not necessarily a consequence of elder sexual abuse (Cartwright & Moore, 1989).

Ramsey-Klawsnik (1999) cites three types of behaviors that are examples of elder sexual abuse. First, *hands-off behaviors* include activities where the offender does not touch the victim but does things that are sexual in nature that potentially harm the victim. Ramsey-Klawsnik cites "exhibitionism, voyeuristic activity, and forcing an individual to watch pornographic materials" as examples of hands-off behaviors (p. 2). Second, *hands-on behaviors* involve behaviors where the offender makes contact with the victim. Third, *harmful genital practices* include "unwarranted, intrusive, and/or painful procedures in caring for the genitals or rectal area" (p. 2).

Based on these behaviors, Ramsey-Klawsnik identifies five different types of elder sexual abuse: (1) stranger or acquaintance sexual assault; (2) caregiver sexual assault; (3) incestuous abuse by a child or relative; (4) partner sexual abuse; and (5) peer sexual assault (see also Ramsey-Klawsnik, 1991; 1993). Along a similar line, Pritchard (1996) identified three types of elder sexual abuse cases that are regularly seen by health care professionals:

1. Those where there is a history of incest (typically between mother and son);
2. Those where a husband sexually abuses his wife; and,
3. Those where older gay men are sexually abused in the community (p. 29).

Victims of elder sexual abuse tend to be female, and the cases are more likely to occur in long-term-care settings than in a community setting. Prosecutions of elder sexual abuse cases are rare, primarily because of a lack of evidence or because victims are unable to participate in the criminal justice prosecution (Teaster et al., 2000). Offenders in these cases are often serial offenders who have histories violence and sexual assault (Mungin, 2002).

Research is mixed concerning the victim-offender relationship in elder sexual abuse cases. Muram et al. (1992) compared the medical records of older sexual assault victims (n = 53) to younger sexual assault victims (n = 55) and found that older adults were more likely to be assaulted by strangers and to have the assault occur in their own home. Johnson (1995) seems to agree, stating, "Most sexual assaults of elderly women occur in the victim's home by an assailant who is unknown to the victims" (p. 221).

Research by Ramsey-Klawsnik (1991) and Holt (1993) suggests slightly different patterns. Ramsey-Klawsnik (1991) asked twenty APS workers to identify and describe cases of elder sexual abuse they had seen in the past. The caseworkers identified twenty-eight cases of sexual abuse, with 81 percent of the cases reportedly committed by caregivers. In fact, 78 percent of the abusers were relatives, with sons representing the majority of offenders. In a similar fashion, Holt, using a methodology similar to Ramsey-Klawsnik's (1993), studied seventy-seven elder sexual abuse cases in Britain and found that 56 percent of the cases were committed by sons of the victims. None of the sexual assaults in Holt's study were committed by strangers.

So, Muram et al. (1992) and Johnson (1995) report that elder sexual abuse offenders are more likely to be strangers, while Ramsey-Klawsnik (1991) and Holt (1993) suggest that offenders are more likely to be sons, who certainly are not strangers to the victim. Two points about these discrepancies are

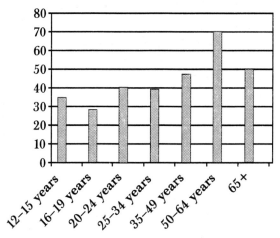

Figure 5. Percent of sexual abuse victimizations involving strangers.
Source: *Sourcebook of Criminal Justice Statistics Online* (2003).

Critical Thinking Questions:

1. What is it about one's age that would influence these patterns?
2. What are the implications of these patterns for professionals?

warranted. First, the disparities are likely due to the differences in the samples. Muram et al.'s (1992) sample included victims who sought out medical services. It seems safe to suggest that victims who seek out medical services are going to be those who truly need help because of their injuries. Official police statistics also suggest that strangers are more commonly the offenders in elder sexual abuse cases (see Figure 5). When a relative is the offender, the victim may be less willing to seek help, due to shame and embarrassment, unless help is absolutely needed (Breckman & Adelman, 1988; Ramsey-Klawsnik, 1991). In the words of one victim, "the reality is that people like me are ashamed to share that the treatment of one of these adult children has been so very hurtful" (Redd, 2003, p. 1). Second, the incongruent findings of these studies suggests that it is very difficult to determine the true extent of elder sexual abuse. Though official statistics suggest it does not occur often, we must not rely on those statistics as indicators of the true extent of the problem.

The one thing these studies agree on is that the abuse is most likely to occur in the victim's home. Cases of sexual abuse in residential care settings also occur in the victim's permanent residence. Many of the instances of sexual abuse in nursing homes involve "unpermitted touching of female victims during bathing, feeding, dressing, and bed time" (Hodge, 1998, p. 27). A problem that comes up in nursing homes has to do with instances of resident-resident sexual abuse. Specifically, there are no clear answers as to what should be done with the perpetrator when the perpetrator is a nursing home resident (Ramsey-Klawsnik, 1999). In many cases, criminal justice officials are unwilling to get involved because of the exorbitant costs in processing elderly offenders through the justice system. In one case, an eighty-seven-year-old man was reportedly raped in a boarding home by a known sex offender who was placed in the home by the Department of Social and Health Services (Welch, 1998). Clearly, greater understanding about elder sexual abuse is needed to ensure that acts are prevented and that the system is prepared to deal with the acts when they do occur.

FINANCIAL ABUSE

According to the National Aging Resource Center, financial abuse is the category of elder abuse that is least likely to be reported (O'Neill & Flanagan, 1998). Roughly 12 percent of the elder abuse cases reported to the NCEA in 1996 were financial abuse cases (NCEA, 1997). There are four types of offenders in elder financial abuse cases: (1) relatives, (2) professional or hired caregivers, (3) friends or others trusted by the victim, and (4) professional groups targeting elder persons (Sklar, 2000).

In many cases, the older victim may not even realize that he or she was financially abused (Wilber & Reynolds, 1996). In part, this stems from the numerous ways that consumers, researchers, and practitioners have defined financial abuse in the past. Different concepts that have been used to refer to financial abuse include material abuse, financial exploitation, fiduciary abuse, exploitation of resources, economic victimization, financial victimization, theft, and fraud (Sanchez, 1996; Wilber, 1990). Some of the specific types of financial abuse include acts such as forgery, misappropriation of money, credit card fraud, and illegal property transfers (Sacks, 1996). The consequences of fraud vary from crime to crime, but they can be quite severe. Some older fraud victims equate the fraud victimization experience with being raped (Deem, 2000).

Part of the complexity of these cases surrounds the range of behaviors that can be seen as financially abusive. Indeed, very different kinds of actions are included under the heading of financial abuse. This range of actions could be viewed as a continuum (Sanchez, 1996). On the one end of the continuum, financial abuse would entail individuals stealing small amounts of money from older adults in subtle ways (Quinn & Tomita, 1997; Sanchez, 1996). Consider for instance a case where "a grandson lives with [his grandmother] the one week at the beginning of each month until her money is gone" (Hall, 1989, p. 198). On the other end of the continuum are cases where offenders steal thousands, or even hundreds of thousands of dollars, from elderly victims.

Unfortunately, when handled criminally, it is difficult for criminal justice officials to prove beyond a reasonable doubt that a crime was committed, that the offender intended to commit the crime, and that the victim did not understand the transaction (Nerenberg, 2000). As a result, these cases are usually treated as civil wrongs, sending a message to victims and the public that these actions are less serious than crimes (Sklar, 2000).

The wide range of fraudulent actions committed against elderly persons was evidenced in testimony presented at a Senate hearing, entitled "Crimes against the Elderly: Let's Fight Back," which was held before the Senate's Special Committee on Aging. In this hearing, an attorney general spoke of a woman who lost her house to fraudulent actions committed by her son:

> Imagine how this woman felt. A lady who had made her home in Sparks for herself and her adult son—imagine how she felt when she fell behind in her mortgage payments. Her son arranged to refinance her house. What he forgot to tell her, though, was that the mortgage company—and the mortgage company also forgot to explain this to her—had the title of her home transferred from her name to his name.
>
> Imagine how she felt when her own son threw her out of her home for which she had literally worked all the years of her life. (U.S. Senate, 1991, p. 2)

In another case, an elderly woman described in more detail the way she was a victim of financial abuse:

> I called the bed company for some information, and they sent me their literature. To my surprise, the bed was over $1,000. You could spend as much as $4,000 on these beds. Shortly after I received my information, the saleswoman from the company paid a visit to me at my home.
>
> . . . She talked me into buying this adjustable bed, gave me a discount, told me I could have the bed for $1,960. It seemed like a lot of money to me at the time, but I was desperately in need of some sleep at night.
>
> The nice saleslady left with my check. She promised that within eight weeks my bed would appear. A couple of months later I got a letter from the bed company saying that the nationwide sales were slow, and that they had filed for bankruptcy.
>
> . . . I never got my money back, nor did I ever get my bed. The loss of this money hurt me badly. It seems like you can't trust anybody anymore. It is mainly senior citizens who buy these beds. I think the people at this company made a fool of me, and probably many other senior citizens, too. (p. 28)

In the "Consumer Fraud and the Elderly" hearing, discussed in the introduction of this chapter, then Illinois Attorney General Roland Burris described the following case:

> One elderly Chicago woman said a man came to her house and told her after an examination that her bungalow had "cancer of the bricks." Unfortunately,

she paid thousands of dollars, hoping for a cure. As might be anticipated, no remedy was offered for the nonexistent disease, and her life savings were depleted. (U.S. Senate, 1993, p. 51)

Clearly, there are different types of financial abuse. The types of financial abuse that elderly persons are victims of that have been considered in the literature are numerous. For purposes of simplicity, I will discuss the following types of financial abuse: *exploitation by primary contacts, nursing home theft by caregivers, fraud by secondary contacts,* and *other property crimes by strangers.* As will be seen, there are variations of each of these types of financial abuse.

Exploitation by Primary Contacts

Primary contacts in this context refers to those individuals who supposedly have a close relationship with the victim (e.g., children, caregivers, relatives, etc.). Exploitation is defined in various ways, depending on one's orientation. As an example of a legal definition, Florida's definition is as follows:

> Exploitation means, but is not limited to, the improper or illegal use or management of an aged person's or disabled adult's funds, assets, or property, or the use of an aged person's or disabled adult's power of attorney or guardianship for another's or one's own profit or advantage. (Mathis, 1994, p. 2)

The exploiter is often a relative of the victim, and is in many cases financially dependent on the victim (Jones, 1996; O'Neill & Flanagan, 1998). These cases can be quite subtle. For instance, Jones (1996) notes that children may force their parents to live on limited incomes, even though they may have hundreds of thousands of dollars. They do this to ensure that they will receive their parents' assets when they die.

Eisenberg (1991) cites four types of financial exploitation. First, direct theft cases involve situations where the offender simply takes items from the victim in various ways. Among other examples, Eisenberg cites cases where caregivers may not return an elderly person's change after a shopping trip. As another example, Jones (1996) quotes one APS worker who said she had "to chase relatives away from the mailbox the day the elderly person's Supplemental Security Income (SSI) check was scheduled to arrive" (p. 20). The second type of exploitation cited by Eisenberg involves coerced property transfers, which entail caregivers "forcing" victims to transfer their property in exchange for better treatment from the caregiver. Third, property conversion involves the "improper use of joint tenancies, powers of attorney, or joint signatures" (p. 68). Fourth, conversion of public benefits or entitlement checks entails situations where children charge their parents, and subsequently the government, for services that are not generally covered by public benefits or entitlement checks.

In some situations, adult offspring may use blackmailing strategies to steal from their elderly parents. Threats of violence or suicide are used to try to make the offender's parents feel guilty. The process generally only ends when the victim passes away or the money dries up (MacDonald, 2003).

Another scenario that arises in financial abuse cases is that a time may come when an elderly person must rely on someone else to help with his or her financial matters (Vezina & Ducharme, 1992). The assistance may be limited to providing help paying bills or shopping, or it may be that the older adult will grant power of attorney to a trusted primary contact, thus giving them the authority to make virtually all financial decisions. As already established, many cases of financial exploitation are cases where the victim places a great deal of trust in a relative, friend, or caregiver (Blunt, 1993).

Blunt (1993) describes three general types of cases that fall into this category. First, the "financial prisoners" include adults who are nearly completely dependent on their caregivers. The caregivers, through isolation and increasing the degree of control they have over the elderly person, eventually gain complete control of the elderly person's finances. Second, "slipping" includes cases where older adults have lost interest in handling their finances, often because of various ailments. The exploiter then steps in and takes control of the finances. Third, the "bereaved widow[er]" involves cases where a widowed spouse who had little experience with handling the finances in the past is approached by the exploiter who "is a welcome relief that reopens the door to the blissful state of allowing someone else to handle the money" (Blunt, 1993, p. 22). (See Box 3.1, Voices from the Field–Shattering the Silence, for an overview of the way that one parent experienced financial abuse.)

In each of these cases, the elderly person may grant power of attorney to the trusted caregiver. Power of attorney is "a written agreement authorizing one or more persons to act for or represent the individual signing the document" (Quinn & Tomita, 1997, p. 263). Reports in the media suggest that power of attorney fraud is a growing problem (Burby, 1994). In fact, one author writes that power of attorney fraud "may be the single most abused legal document in our judicial system" (Mathis, 1994). What happens is that individuals gain complete access to all of the elderly person's assets once they are granted power of attorney. Unfortunately, some misuse this power. One problem that arises is proving that the actions were fraudulent. As Wilber and Reynolds (1996) note, there is a fine line between fraud and simply influencing an older adult. This line is relative and is determined by the dependence and the vulnerability of the adult.

Financial abuse cases are believed to be the most difficult type of elder abuse to identify. With cases of physical abuse, signs surface immediately. With financial abuse cases, warning signs may take months to appear (*Hospital Home Health,* 2002). Bank tellers are believed to be in an especially prime

BOX 3.1. VOICES FROM THE FIELD: SHATTERING THE SILENCE–CONFRONTING THE PERILS OF FAMILY

In October, 2003, the U.S. Senate's Special Committee on Aging held hearings on elder abuse. Below is the testimony provided by an elder abuse victim– Leanna Watts of Grayson, Georgia.

In May of 2002 I relocated from Shreveport, Louisiana to Grayson, Georgia ... to be near family. Upon arrival I learned that my son and his family lived in government subsidized housing, of which there was really no room for me with four children and two adults already living in a 3 bedroom apartment. ... Things began to change after I had settled in and decided to cope with the overcrowded deplorable living conditions that I was subjected to live in. Since I knew that I was relocating to a new area, I withdrew my life's savings of ten thousand in cash to deposit in a bank near my new residence. With that in mind I asked my son to take me to the bank to obtain a safe deposit box to secure my funds until I could decide what next steps to take to protect my savings. After my son found out that I had that sum of money in cash, he and his wife changed dramatically. I was given drugs and forced to sign a "Power of Attorney" form with my son as appointee which gave him control over all of my assets, namely my cash.

Shortly thereafter, one night he and his wife attacked me by standing over my bed yelling and demanding that I give them my safe deposit box keys. After fearing for my life I gave in and surrendered the keys. He and his wife went to the bank, took my $10,000.00 and opened an account in his name at the same bank (Bank One) with my money. ...

I began to feel as though I was in prison. I was not allowed to prepare meals for myself. I was also forbidden to answer the door or go outside. The only times I was allowed outside was on my trips to and from my dialysis clinic to receive my treatment. All of my telephone privileges were suspended and I was even unable to call my own daughter. When she called she was told that I was asleep. In most cases I was asleep because of constantly being given drugs. My son also told me that any conversations that were made on any phones in his house were being monitored and recorded. Subsequently all of the phones were locked in their bedroom while they were away from home. They made all attempts to prevent me from telling anyone about my horrible living conditions.

As my physical condition began to deteriorate they would tell me repeatedly that most dialysis patients die shortly after being on dialysis, and that my death was imminent (at no time did I believe that, since I have been on dialysis for the last 12 years leading a normal life to include traveling on occasions). They then contacted an insurance agent to come to the apartment for them to purchase life insurance on me as they planned my funeral. So they purchased a life insurance policy on me and I was not allowed to speak to the agent or comment on anything regarding my welfare. They sat in the kitchen and made arrangements as I sat on the side of my bed helpless and ignored.

Source: "Shattering the Silence: Confronting the perils of family elder abuse, Testimony by Leanna Watts," Hearing before the Special Committee on Aging, United States Senate, One Hundred Eighth Congress, first session, Washington, DC, October 20, 2003. Publisher: Washington : U.S. G.P.O.

position to identify cases of financial abuse. While most states do not require bank employees to report suspected crimes of abuse, some banks, such as Union Bank in California, train employees how to identify and report such cases (Business Wire, 2003). In some states, bank tellers are required by law to report suspected cases of elder abuse, while most states exempt bank officials from elder abuse mandatory reporting laws.

Nursing Home Theft

Caregivers in nursing homes have also been known to commit financial abuse against nursing home residents. In most cases, the financial abuse cases occurring in nursing homes occur in the form of theft, and the items stolen most often include "money, jewelry, clothing, and food" (Harris & Benson, 1996, p. 176). For whatever reasons, nursing home theft is "one of the most neglected forms of elder abuse in the nursing home literature" (Harris & Benson, 1996, p. 186).

In one of the few studies that has been done, Harris and Benson (1996) surveyed a convenience sample of twenty-three administrators, ninety-six employees, sixty-three relatives, and twenty-two nursing home patients, and focused on the seriousness of theft in nursing homes, the items stolen most often, why they stole, and how the nursing home responded to the thefts. They found that theft was problematic and that various types of items were stolen from residents. They also found that those who stole most often were aides who had been on the job a relatively short time. Interestingly, their findings showed that theft is generally higher around Christmas time. The following quote from one of their respondents is included to shed some light on why the thefts increase at that time: "The employees are underpaid and feel the pressures around Christmas when money is needed more than usual" (p. 177). In addition, they found that thefts may occur around the resident's birthday or any other time gifts were given. Harris and Benson (1996) also report that some administrators advise patients to have fake jewelry made (e.g., wedding bands) and have the real jewelry stored at home by the family. Doing this supposedly protects against theft, whether by employees or other nursing home residents.

A more recent survey of 281 nursing home employees by Harris and Benson (1998) finds that nursing home employees reported seeing patients steal from patients more often than they saw employees stealing from patients. This same survey also reveals that over half of the respondents who reported stealing from patients were in positions other than nurse's aides positions (e.g., food services, maintenance, and housekeeping). Predictors of employee theft included job satisfaction and negative attitudes about patients. That is, employees who did not like their jobs, or who saw residents in an unfavorable light, were more likely to steal than those who liked their jobs and had positive perceptions of the residents.

Harris and Benson (1998) conclude their study suggesting that theft is even less socially acceptable than physical abuse. In no way do they condone physical abuse; rather, they note theft in most cases must be premeditated. That is, the employee likely gave some thought to committing the offense before actually stealing from the patient. On the other hand, many instances of patient abuse are spontaneous reactions to something the patient did. Thus, the offender thinks about theft cases in advance but does not typically plan physical abuse. The implication is that theft is more of a conscious decision, making it less socially acceptable. Just as unacceptable are fraudulent acts by secondary contacts.

Fraud by Secondary Contacts

In this context, the phrase "secondary contacts" refers to individuals with whom the victim has very little interaction. These individuals are not family members, relatives, or trusted caregivers. They are the salespeople, telemarketers, home repair technicians, or others with whom the elderly person has limited contacts. Indeed, the financial abuse committed by secondary contacts is different from the financial abuse committed by primary contacts. When fraud is committed by secondary contacts, the secondary contacts usually form the intent to rip off the elderly victim before they have the elderly person's money. When financial abuse is committed by primary contacts, the intent is generally formed after the offender has already gained access to the older adult's assets. Or, *fraud by secondary contacts* more often involves strangers who do not have access to the victim's money doing things to gain unlawful access to those finances. *Financial exploitation by primary contacts* more often involves trusted caregivers who already have access to the elderly victim's finances, misusing those finances. Fraud by secondary contacts often involve cases of consumer fraud.

There are literally hundreds, if not thousands, of types of fraud that have targeted elderly persons. Estimates from the U.S. Office of Consumer Affairs suggest that one hundred billion dollars a year is lost to fraud, with older adults overrepresented in the losses (Harris, 1995). Offenders will usually

(1) use scare tactics, (2) rush deals, (3) pressure victims for down payments, and (4) make claims of credibility (Special Committee on Aging, 1983). Older adults are often targeted in the following types of fraud: *home repair fraud, insurance fraud, medical fraud, confidence games, telemarketing fraud,* and *phony contests.*

HOME REPAIR FRAUD. Elderly persons are often targets of various home repair or home improvement scams. One estimate suggests that "99 percent of home improvement swindles are committed against older victims, mostly women" (U.S. Senate, 1993, p. 6). One woman asked for a $29.95 air conditioner tune-up but got a tune-up that ended up costing her $3,000. The perpetrators in this scam were eventually indicted for stealing $2.3 million from 400 elderly victims. They preyed on the elderly, confused them, or even broke their appliances so they would have to be replaced (*Contractor,* 1993). Cases where contractors fail to provide services, or provide inadequate services, after being paid are also common examples of home repair fraud. In one case, a contractor defrauded a seventy-four-year-old woman out of $45,000 for home repairs he never finished (National Association of Attorneys General, 1998).

INSURANCE FRAUD. Older adults have also been targets of several different fraudulent insurance schemes committed by fraudulent insurance salespersons (Sullivan, 1997). First, *stacking* is persuading persons to buy more policies than are needed. One older man, for example, was sold seventy-one policies that covered hospitalization, cancer, nursing home costs, and burial expenses. *Rolling over* is persuading the customer to cancel an old policy and replace it with a more expensive "better" policy. *Misrepresentation* occurs when the salesperson deliberately misinforms the customer about the coverage of the insurance policy. *Clean sheeting* is forging the customer's signature. *Switching* occurs when the sales person switches the consumer's policy so that the coverage and the premiums are different than what the victims were told (U.S. Senate, 1983).

Other variations of these schemes have also been known to occur. *Churning* involves agents selling new policies to current customers only to generate commissions (Luchs, 1998; Simon & Hagan, 1999). *Sliding* occurs when agents include insurance coverages that were not requested by customers (Adams, 1998; Pullen, 1998). A recent undercover operation, referred to as "Operation Cheap Tricks," resulted in twenty-nine insurance agents from one insurance company indicted for sliding (Adams, 1998). Also, *vanishing premiums* involves agents misleading customers about future premium payments (Luchs, 1998). Each of these types of fraud are extremely difficult and time consuming to investigate (Bowker, 1999), making it likely they will continue to occur as we enter the next century.

MEDICAL FRAUD. Various medical frauds target older adults with offenders honing in on elderly persons' fears about their current and future health. These medical frauds include quackery, miracle cures, and useless medical aids and cost consumers up to $25 billion a year (Rosoff et al., 2003). Quackery generally refers to useless medical products and services. Consider the following examples:

1. A door-to-door salesperson told an elderly couple that they must purchase the hearing aids he was selling, or they would go deaf or need surgery.
2. A company sold a product at ten dollars a bottle, guaranteed to "revitalize your sex life." The product was just a combination of vitamins consumers could purchase for a dollar. Roughly 36,000 adults were conned.
3. One clinic charged 66,000 individuals $10.95 each for a glaucoma cure, which included exercise directions to be used instead of prescriptions. The exercises could have resulted in blindness (U.S. Senate, 1983, pp. 5–6).

As a testament to the pervasiveness of various medical frauds and useless medical devices, one man formed the "Museum of Questionable Medical Devices" which houses various displays of medical quackery. Located in Minneapolis, the items on display include the electro-matabiograph (e.g., a devise supposedly "capable of diagnosing anything from sleepwalking to sexual obsession," and the Omnipotent Oscilloclast (e.g., a device that assesses "the 'vibration rate' of a blood or saliva sample" (Greene, 1998, p. 68). To guard against increases in medical frauds, Stephen Barrett, author of forty-three books on questionable practices in the medical field, recently developed a homepage (www.quackwatch.com) that is designed to inform consumers about what he sees are current types of quackery (Bowen, 1998).

CONFIDENCE GAMES. Older adults are also the targets of many different confidence games, which are also referred to as "bunco schemes" (Friedman, 1998; U.S. Senate, 1983). A common confidence game that is targeted toward older adults is the pigeon drop. This scheme involves situations where a con artist tells a victim that a large sum of money has been found and the con artist does not want all of the money. Victims are told that they will get half of the money if they give the con artist a small "security deposit" while the con artist puts the money in the bank. Here's an example of what the offender would say to the victim:

I just found $500 over here lying on the corner of the street and I don't want to take all of it myself. I feel very self-conscious about it and I wonder if you could take half of it so I will feel better about it. If you give me 100 dollars to show your good faith, I'll run over and deposit it in the bank and be right back. (U.S. House of Representatives, 1992, p. 296)

A survey of 331 fraud investigators by Friedman (1992) found that pigeon drops are certainly targeted towards elderly persons and that typically the scams originate in stores and shopping malls. In many cases, a team of two offenders will work together in swindling the victim. The team members act as if they do not know each other, making the victims less likely to believe that they are being specifically targeted for a scam. So, one member of the team approaches the elderly person and makes the offer. Then, the second member, appearing to be a stranger, approaches and is offered part of the money that was supposedly found. The victim is sometimes handed a paper bag "with money in it" to hold while the money is deposited in the bank. However, what the victim is actually holding is a bag of cut-up paper (Friedman, 1992).

TELEMARKETING FRAUD. Telemarketing fraud is another type of fraud that is pervasive in the United States, with older adults being overrepresented as telemarketing victims. The AARP (1998) points out that one in six consumers are victims of telemarketing fraud each year, and 80 percent of the fraudulent telemarketers specifically target older adults. The National Consumers League cites FBI statistics (1997) suggesting that there are 14,000 fraudulent telemarketing operations operating in the U.S. on a daily basis. It should not be surprising, then, that the National Association of Attorneys General (1997) indicates that 90 percent of adults have received fraudulent offers from telemarketers. In the mid-eighties, estimates provided by the Federal Trade Commission indicated that consumers lose one billion dollars a year to telemarketing fraud (Rachlin, 1987). More recent estimates from Green and Fogel (1996) suggest that forty billion dollars is lost to telemarketing fraud each year. Even so, Americans still do not see telemarketing fraud as a serious crime.

Pitches such as "You've won a valuable prize," "We'll send you our products at wholesale," "This is the final day of our promotion," and so on are often used to persuade elderly victims to purchase overpriced items (*Consumers Research Magazine,* 1996, p. 27). Rachlin (1987) cites the following three promises as other indicators of fraudulent sales pitches: (1) you will make a lot of money; (2) you will make it quickly; and (3) there's virtually no risk. These pitches are not always used. Clayton (1999) cites a rather brazen telemarketer whose only words to a potential elderly victim were, "Go get your credit card" (p. B3). Fortunately, she did not fall victim to this scam artist's pressure tactics. Others, however, do. Perhaps not surprisingly, whether victims fall prey to telemarketing schemes hinges on whether they believe the telemarketers (Reiboldt & Vogel, 2001).

Telemarketing operations are also known as boiler room operations, in reference to the type of environment where many of them operate. Slotter (1998) cites six stages in these operations. First, *naming* involves deciding who will be solicited, either through using phone lists or bulk mailings that notify individuals they have won a prize (see phony contests schemes below). Second, in the *sales* stage, the scammer uses a written pitch developed by a manager. If the scammer initially fails to persuade the victim to participate in the scam, the scammer will connect the victim to the "no sale room" which includes workers who will not "take no for an answer" (p. 10). Also part of the sales stage is the "reload room," which refers to efforts to convince past victims to participate in the scam. Third, the *verification* stage involves individuals who contact customers after a completed sale and make payment arrangements. The verifiers also "diffuse misrepresentations made by the sales representative" (p. 11). Fourth, *collection* involves collecting the funds as quickly as possible. Fifth, *shipping* is sending the item purchased by the customer. Finally, the *customer service* stage entails handling complaints made by the scammed customers. In this stage, empty promises are made to customers who are belittled to the point of often giving up their attempts to recover their scammed money (Slotter, 1998).

In a brochure titled "They Can't Hang Up," which was designed to protect seniors against fraud, the National Consumer's League (1997) suggests that consumers should ask for a number where they can reach the telemarketer so the consumer can research the purchase. If the telemarketer will not give a number, "it's a red flag of fraud" (p. 2).

Of course, fraudulent telemarketers will victimize all age groups, not just elderly persons. Many, however, will specifically target older adults. One author points out that offenders will listen to the sound of the individual's voice to determine if he or she is older and a possible target of telemarketing fraud (O'Sullivan, 2003). Another author points out that some offenders will "just look through phonebooks for 'elderly-sounding' names like Viola or Henrietta" (Church, 1997, p. 56). Once they are victimized, they become targets for subsequent victimization. When the victim finally decides to put an end to the scams, the fraudulent telemarketers employ what is referred to as the "recovery room scam" on the victim. In this scam, the offender poses as an official whose duty it is to help the victim recover his or her money. The trick is, however, that the victims must pay to get their money back. Recovery room scam artists will tell victims they need the money in order to catch the fraudulent telemarketers and that their money will be returned to them. As an example, Attorney General Janet Reno described the following scam:

> A telemarketer called a previous victim purporting to authorize a tap of the victim's telephone. Next, the crook called back using a different voice and promised to recover the victim's loss for a ten percent fee. In a third call, the crook again posed as an FBI agent and urged the victim to send the money so the telemarketer would be caught red-handed. (*Fund Raising Management,* 1999, p.7)

In some cases, fraudulent telemarketers have placed their fraudulent telephone numbers in phone directories using names that callers would confuse with actual government agencies. For example, one case involved a fraudulent outfit using names and phone numbers similar to the Social Security and Medicare agencies. In 1992, then Iowa Attorney General Bonnie Campbell presented the following testimony in a hearing before the Subcomittee on Social Security concerning this particular case:

> The number looked deceptively like the U.S. Government number, and it referred callers at once to a 900-number call. Both the 800-number and 900-number messages violated Iowa law requiring disclosure of costs, and giving the caller a right to terminate a 900-call without charge. The 800-number recording stated, "we will help you get the benefits you deserve by providing you the information the Social Security information won't."
>
> [An 80-year-old] man looked in his phone book for a number to call with a question about social security benefits. He saw the listings reproduced above. When he dialed the listed 800-number, a recording told him to dial the 900-number. He did so, thinking he was calling the Federal *Government,* thinking he would reach a *real person* who would answer his question, and *not* thinking he would be *charged* for the call. (U.S. House of Representatives, 1992, p. 300–301)

The man hung up after realizing he received another pre-recorded message. He was billed $9.95 for the phone call, which he was eventually reimbursed.

Recent reports in the media suggest that there has been in increase in telemarketing scams that originate in Canada. These scams have become "increasingly elaborate, aggressive, and costly" (Schneider, 1997, p. A21). Schneider (1997) suggests that Canada-based scams "account for about one-third of the telemarketing complaints received by Canadian and U.S. authorities" (p. A21). These cross-border scams are more difficult to investigate because of differences in jurisdictions' approaches to defining and responding to telemarketing fraud (Schupbach, 1998). In one case originating in Canada, a ninety-three-year-old man "paid a $5,000 'processing fee' after being told he'd won a $1 million lottery prize" (The Virginian-Pilot, 1999, p. A7). Associated Press ran the story with an accompanying picture showing the man standing outside of a Tampa International Airport with a sign around his neck that read, "I'm John. Meeting Sgt. Moore from Canada." Of course, Sgt. Moore never appeared. This case is an example of telemarketing fraud but also an example of phony contest fraud.

PHONY CONTESTS FRAUD. Another type of fraud that targets elderly individuals has to do with contests in which consumers are told they are guaranteed to be a winner. Friedman (1998) surveyed 304 seniors who believed they were targets of various schemes but avoided victimization. Not surprisingly, the most common schemes reported by the respondents were sweepstakes swindles. These schemes are well organized. In some cases, those who enter the contest will win a prize, that is for a fee. The prize they get is worth far less than what they invested into the contest. According to Slotter (1998), "most illegal prize rooms operate on a 10 to 1 principle" (p. 11). This means that the prizes received by customers are valued at one-tenth of the price they paid. In one scam, consumers were promised a "car telephone." What they got was a "telephone shaped like a car" (Paulson & Blum, 1989, p. 35).

Of course, there are phony prize contests where victims are told they are guaranteed a prize, and they get nothing. For instance, in one case, six offenders stole millions from elderly citizens in eight different states by making them believe that they had won the Publisher's Clearing House Sweepstakes. Victims were told they would receive their winnings after they sent "prepaid taxes" (ranging from $20,000 to $270,000) to the offenders (*Direct Marketing*, 1997, p. 10). In 1990, then one state attorney general told the Senate's Special Committee on Aging about another scheme where victims receive absolutely nothing:

> A consumer receives a postcard which announces that she is entitled to claim one or more prizes. The "award notice" is professionally designed and appears perfectly legitimate. The post card bears a toll-free telephone number and the consumer is instructed that he or she must simply call to claim the prizes. Once the toll-free number is accessed, a recording instructs the consumer to touch numbers on the telephone which correspond with a "claim number" which appears on the postcard. Ultimately, the consumer receives no prize. What is received is a "telephone bill" which reflects a substantial charge for the call as if a 900 number had been called. The entry of the sequence of numbers that matched the "claim number" engaged an automated information service for which the consumer is charged. (U.S. Senate, 1993, p. 67)

At an earlier hearing, Western Region Chief Post Inspector Jack Swagerty told the same committee about the following phony contest scheme:

> I am sure many of you have seen the contest schemes, where gifts and other prizes are offered to you. All you have to do is fill out a simple contest form. The pitfall is that everyone wins . . . then you must play a second, third, fourth, or fifth, or even more tie breaking rounds in order to be the final winner. Of course, in order to enter these playoff rounds, you have to pay money. (U.S. Senate, 1991, p. 30)

Though the schemes may vary, one similarity is that the fraudulent marketer keeps lists with the names and addresses of previous scam victims. These lists are known as lead sheets (Seeman, 1993). Seeman quotes a law enforcement officer who describes the lists in the following way: "You'll see names with stars, little astericks, red highlights. And right next to it you'll see, handwritten: 'sucker'" (p. 1BR). These lists are referred to as "sucker lists" and are sold to other fraudulent marketers (Harris, 1995).

Other Property Crimes

There are a host of other financial offenses of which older adults are victims. These other property crimes are referred to as personal theft by the NCVS, and include offenses such as larceny, purse snatching, burglary, and motor vehicle theft. The NCVS uses the phrase "household crime" to refer to crimes occurring in the household (e.g., burglary, household larceny, and motor vehicle theft).

Textbook definitions of these offenses are often based on the way the NCVS and UCR define them. For instance, larceny is defined as the taking and carrying away of the personal property of another with the intent to deprive permanently, and burglary is breaking and entering one's home with the intent to commit a crime (Inciardi, 1999). Motor vehicle theft is stealing one's motored vehicle (including cars, trucks, and motor cycles, but excluding tractors and airplanes). Personal larceny with contact includes the crimes of purse snatching and pocket picking (U.S. Department of Justice, 1994).

When elderly victims are considered, as with the "other violent offenses," official crime statistics suggest that, with the exception of purse snatching, older adults are victims of these offenses less often than younger individuals (McCabe & Gregory, 1998). Also like the "other violent offenses," interesting patterns surround these offenses. Of particular interest are the following:

1. In 1992, the personal theft and household crime rates among the elderly were the lowest since the NCVS started collecting data in 1972.
2. Like the rest of the population, older adults are the least susceptible to violent crimes, but most susceptible to household crimes.
3. Those sixty-five and over are about as likely as younger individuals to be victims of purse snatching and pocket picking.
4. Older women are more likely than older men to be victims of personal larceny.
5. Elderly black women are the least likely to be victims of personal theft.
6. Younger victims of personal theft are less likely to tell the police about the act than elderly victims are.
7. Separated and divorced elderly are more likely to be victims of personal theft than married elderly persons are.
8. Elderly renters are less likely than elderly homeowners to be victims of household crimes (U.S. Department of Justice, 1994).

Table 8 outlines some other patterns concerning racial, gender, and age differences in personal thefts reported to the NCVS. In particular, among elderly persons, white females are most likely to be victimized by personal theft, followed by white males, black males, and black females. These figures are particularly interesting when compared to rates of violence reported in the

TABLE 8. NUMBER OF PERSONAL THEFTS BY GENDER, AGE, AND RACE (PER 1000)

	Number of Personal Thefts per 1000
Teenage white males	106
Young adult black males	105
Teenage white females	92
Young adult white males	89
Teenage black males	84
Young adult white females	78
Young adult black females	69
Teenage black females	66
Adult black males	52
Adult white females	48
Adult white males	44
Adult black females	43
Elderly white females	18
Elderly white males	15
Elderly black males	13
Elderly black females	9

Age Categories:
Teenage = 12–19 years
Young adult = 20–34 years
Adult = 35–64 years
Elderly = 65 and older

Source: Bureau of Justice Statistics. (1994). *Elderly Crime Victims: National Crime Survey.* Washington, D.C.: U.S. Department of Justice.

Critical Thinking Questions:

1. How would you explain interactions between age and race?
2. How would you explain interactions between gender and age?

official crime statistics. In contrast, among elderly persons, elderly black males have the highest rate of violence, followed by black females, white males, and white females. So, elderly whites are more likely to be victims of personal theft, and elderly blacks are more likely to be victims of violence.

In an examination of data from the FBI's National Incident Based Reporting System, McCabe and Gregory (1998) also found that older blacks are more vulnerable to violent offenses, and older whites are more vulnerable to personal theft. They contend that, among other things, the differences are related to where the victims live. They write: "one may assert that Blacks, in general, because of the lack of financial resources, are forced to reside in highly violent areas and therefore are more likely to experience violence victimizations" (p. 370). They further argue that "elderly Whites provide would-be offenders with only material possessions to target rather than their physical presence" (p. 370). Others, however, would argue that it is not just location and opportunity that contribute to these differences, but conflict between groups resulting from disparate beliefs and value systems.

NEGLECT

Neglect is a broad concept that refers to a host of different types of abuse that are perpetrated against some elderly victims. Research shows that neglect is more common than any of the other types of elder mistreatment (Pavlik et al., 2001). Over half of the elder abuse cases reported to the NCEA (1997) are allegations of neglect. Severe cases of neglect mimic cases of physical abuse (Poertner, 1986), and can have equally severe consequences. As an example, a seventy-year-old woman who was taken to an emergency room "was covered with bedsores—some as large as a hand—and maggots infested the wounds that cut through to her bone" (Rosado, 1991, p. 47). Some cases of neglect could result in death (Hickey & Douglass, 1981). One of the problems that arises is that neglect is a very complex concept, making it difficult to determine if neglect occurred (Fulmer, 1991). In criminal cases, officials must prove the following:

- That the individual failed to act;
- That the consequences came from neglect rather than aging or disease;
- That the individual was responsible for providing care (King, 2003).

It is just as difficult to distinguish among types of neglect (Hall, 1989). As well, perpetrators could be individuals or institutions. Thus neglect could be seen as individual abuse or institutional abuse, depending on the circumstances surrounding the act. Distinctions to be considered in this book are the distinctions between the following types of neglect: *neglect committed by caregivers, self-neglect,* and *abandonment.*

Neglect Committed by Caregivers

In an article in *Patient Care* (1993), on which six national elder abuse experts served as consultants (see Anetzberger et al., 1993), the following types of neglect are described: *physical neglect, psychological neglect,* and *financial neglect. Physical neglect* is broken down in the article into *active* and *passive neglect.* Others also use the active/passive dichotomy to refer to the types of neglect

(Johnson, 1995; Winter, 1986). *Active neglect* generally refers to actions where intent can be established on the basis that the actions were purposeful and deliberate (Winter, 1986). It involves the "failure to fulfill a caregiving obligation of providing basic life needs—food, water, shelter, clothing, and medical and emotional support" (Johnson, 1995, p. 221). In a survey of nursing home professionals, a nursing home employee described the following actions to Townsend (1971): "It was a prank for revenge for one shift to load the patients with laxatives so the next shift would have to work cleaning up. [One] patient was so weak she was almost dead from laxatives and fleet enemas" (p. 102).

This example clearly involves one where intent to do harm is present in the deliberate actions of the caregivers, who failed to meet the residents' needs. *Passive neglect* is a type of neglect where there is no intent to do harm. Winter (1986) suggests that passive neglect "stems from ignorance" (p. 50). Mitchell and Smyth (1994) seem to agree as they attribute passive neglect to "ignorance, laziness, or lack of skill" (p. 525). Courts generally are reluctant to get involved in passive neglect cases, but APS may certainly need to take actions to ensure that the elderly victim of passive neglect is given the appropriate care (Valentine and Cash, 1986).

Psychological and *financial neglect* can be just as devastating as physical neglect. Among other things, *psychological neglect* involves situations where caregivers cause the older adults to be isolated by restricting their social contacts and their access to the community. *Financial neglect* entails circumstances where caregivers do not use available resources or funds to help older adults (*Patient Care,* 1993). This would include cases where adult children "protect the will" (Littwin, 1995) by not allowing their parents to spend their own money on essential items that would maintain an appropriate level of physical well-being.

Self-Neglect

Self-neglect is a rather controversial type of neglect in that there is disagreement about whether it is a type of elder abuse, and if it is, how it should be defined (Hudson, 1991). Valentine and Cash (1986) note that self-neglect is an important area that various social service professionals will confront on various occasions; but, they note that it does not "clearly fit in the category of elder maltreatment" (p. 23). Part of the problem centers on varied concepts used to refer to cases of self-neglect. Some refer to self-neglect as "Diogenes syndrome" (Clark, Mankikar, & Gray, 1975, as cited in Byers & Lamanna, 1993, p. 70). Hudson (1991) uses the concept of "self-mistreatment" (p. 16) while Kosberg (1998) and Johnson (1995) talk about "self-abuse" as including self-inflicted actions that cause some form of injury to the elderly person (e.g., suicide and substance abuse). Byers and Lamanna (1993) note, "At times, the terms neglect and abuse are used synonymously which may cause additional confusion" (p. 71). The distinction between the concepts seems to be similar to the distinction between active and passive neglect. In self-abuse, as with active neglect, actions are committed that cause harm to the older adult. Self-neglect and self-mistreatment parallel passive neglect in that a lack of action brings about the harm. However, many cases of self-neglect could involve active decisions on the part of the older adult. Byers and Lamanna (1993) cite the example of an older person willfully choosing "to live a life of isolation and squalor shunning dependence" (p. 71).

The NCEA (1997) gathered data about self-neglect and found that self-neglect cases are those that are most often dealt with by protective services employees. Estimates of the extent of self-neglect are likely low because most elderly persons who are neglecting themselves would be unlikely to report their self-neglect to authorities (Hall, 1987). Byers and Lamanna (1993) further note that protective services workers often find these cases the most difficult to handle because efforts to stop the self-neglect are resisted by the victim.

Abandonment

Abandonment can also be seen as a type of neglect. These cases include situations where caregivers leave elderly persons at various locations (usually emergency rooms) because they are unwilling to provide any more care for the older adult. The state of Connecticut defines abandonment as "the desertion or willful forsaking of an elder by a caretaker or foregoing or withdrawal or neglect of duties and obligations owed an elder by a caretaker or other" (Fulmer et al., 1992, p. 506). This definition clearly demonstrates that cases of abandonment are examples of neglect. According to the American College of Emergency Physicians (ACEP) (1999), scenarios of abandonment include family members dropping off elderly persons, boarding homes or nursing homes dropping off elderly persons, and, in some cases, elderly persons seeking out care in emergency rooms on their own because they are unable to care for themselves.

Often family members will take elderly persons to emergency rooms simply because they are exhausted and feel a need to have some time to themselves (Craig, 1991). Doctors refer to abandonment as "red taillight syndrome" because of the way the family members "bolt from the scene," with witnesses seeing only the taillights on the automobile of the person abandoning the older adult (*The Economist,* 1992, p. A29). The abandoned adult does not need emergency room care but cannot be sent home because there is no caregiver available to assist with his or her daily needs. The end result of abandonment is that social services must get involved to develop a plan of action that will provide the abandoned adult the care he or she needs (ACEP, 1998).

PSYCHOLOGICAL ABUSE

Psychological abuse is difficult to define and prove (Gilman, 1993; Quinn & Tomita, 1997). It is hard to assess because many of the behaviors that are examples of psychological abuse "are not concrete" (Johnson, 1995, p. 221). Kurrle, Sadler, and Cameron (1992) define psychological abuse as "the infliction of mental anguish, involving actions that cause fear of violence, isolation, or deprivation, and/or feelings of shame, indignity, and powerlessness" (p. 674). Others argue that the effects of psychological abuse are far reaching, and that most cases of physical abuse will result in psychological abuse (Mickish, 1993).

Of course, psychological abuse can occur without any physical contact whatsoever. Hudson (1991) writes, "If a son throws a punch at his mother but misses, the question is whether this is elder abuse and whether any psychologically harmful effects on the mother can be documented" (p. 16). I would argue that such an act would likely be an example of psychological abuse if the mother experienced any sort of fear in the future as a result of the scenario. So completion of a physically abusive act is not necessary for an act to be psychological abuse. Indeed, the effects of psychological abuse can be devastating.

Some refer to the notion of emotional abuse, which is synonymous with psychological abuse. One woman described her emotional abuse experiences to participants at an AARP (1993) forum. She stated:

> It is emotional abuse when the very soul of the victim is attacked, when her own credibility as a human being is attacked. Physical wounds often heal, leaving no signs of damage, but all victims of emotional abuse that I know have a place in the very depth of their souls that still hurts. (p. 7)

Only 8 percent of the elder abuse cases reported to the NCEA (1997) were cases of psychological abuse. This low figure is likely due to the fact that victims of emotional abuse do not define the actions as inappropriate. Even if they do see them as inappropriate, victims likely see the actions as personal matters rather than concerns they would make public. Pillemer and Moore (1989) found that 40 percent of nursing home employees they surveyed admitted to committing psychological abuse in the previous year. If 40 percent of employees admit they psychologically abused nursing home residents, surely more than 8 percent of all domestic elder abuse cases are psychological abuse cases.

Covert abuse in nursing homes as described by Meddaugh (1993) is an example of psychological abuse. Meddaugh notes that covert abuse is more subtle than overt physical abuse, and it entails actions such as harassment and psychological trauma. An observational study by Meddaugh (1993) found the specific forms of covert abuse to include restrictions of personal choice, increased isolation, labeling, and thoughtless practices.

Restrictions of personal choice entail instances where residents are not given the opportunity to make decisions for themselves. Isolation involves situations where residents are not given opportunities to interact with other residents. Labeling entails referring to residents as "good" or "bad" depending on their aggressiveness. Finally, thoughtless practices include actions such as rushing the residents needs, not providing the care the resident requires, or referring to the resident in derogatory terms (Meddaugh, 1993).

Calling older adults derogatory names and making insulting comments are examples of verbal abuse, which could be seen as a type of psychological abuse (Hickey & Douglass, 1981). Indeed, many cases of elder abuse occur along with instances of verbal abuse. Nandlal and Wood (1997) point out that verbal abuse is defined by the consequences of the abuse as opposed to the literal meaning of the words. They point out that in order for language to be abusive, four criteria must be present: (1) an accountable speaker; (2) an unwarranted assumption about the relationship; (3) unwarranted violation of rights; and (4) a recipient who is harmed (p. 17). An example of verbal abuse would be the use of patronizing speech.

Some cases of verbal abuse are extremely overt. In one case, for instance, workers "threatened, mocked, and insulted" a patient. Evidence in this case was uncovered when suspecting family members of the patient hid a tape recorder in the patient's room. What the tape recorder uncovered was shocking. The workers called the woman a pig and yelled at her. One time, "the patient was told a man was standing outside her window masturbating" (Derfel, 2003: A 6). The consequences from such acts are equivalent to those experienced by victims of physical abuse. Said one victim of elder verbal abuse, "I was actually physically ill for several days, recuperating from that kind of experience" (Redd, 2003).

INSTITUTIONAL ABUSE

The preceding discussion has focused primarily on various types of individual abuse that are committed against elderly persons. In the following section, examples of institutional abuse will be addressed. It is important to recall that institutions can commit a number of the types of abuse addressed in the previous section. For instance, institutions can neglect, physically abuse, or psychologically abuse older adults. Cases of physical abuse in nursing homes could be seen as an example of institutional abuse. To avoid repetition, the dynamics of these overlapping types of abuse as they relate to institutional abuse will not be reiterated. Instead, the following types of institutional abuse will be addressed: *health care crimes, patient dumping, institutional financial fraud,* and *regulatory violations.*

Health Care Crimes

Various health care crimes can be seen as offenses against elderly persons. These health care offenses are outlined in Table 9. Some of the offenses, such as unnecessary surgery, directly involve elderly victims. Many of the other health care crimes may not directly involve elderly persons, but the result is that the elderly population pays the price for the offenses. For instance, fraud in the health care arena costs billions of dollars each year and subsequently results in many older adults not receiving the type of health care they truly need (Pontell et al., 1982). Even though these offenses have drastic effects on society and the elderly population, it is worth noting that most health care professional do not commit these acts (Jesilow et al., 1985). Instead, a very small group of deviant professionals is able to wreak havoc on the entire health care system. A review of the types of crimes committed by professionals in the health care arena will show that these offenses can be seen as crimes against elderly persons.

MEDICARE AND MEDICAID FRAUD. Medicare and Medicaid fraud is a general type of fraud that refers to all of the different types of fraud that health care providers commit against the Medicaid and Medicare systems. Medicaid operates at the state level and provides health care to individuals who are unable to afford it while Medicare operates at the federal level and provides persons over the age of sixty-five access to health care. The providers who

TABLE 9. TYPES OF HEALTH CARE CRIMES

I. Medicare and Medicaid Fraud
  A. Fee-for-Service Reimbursement–Medicaid or Medicare are billed even though no services are provided.
  B. Pingponging–referring patient to other providers even though additional treatment is not required.
  C. Upgrading–provider bills for more expensive service than those provided.
  D. Double-billing–billing more than one agency for the same service.
  E. Drug theft–stealing drug supplies and billing Medicare or Medicaid for the missing drugs.
  F. Unnecessary surgery–performing surgeries that are not needed.

II. Prescription Fraud
  A. Generic drug substitution–provides generic drugs, but bills for more expensive drugs.
  B. Short counting–providing less medicine than prescribed but billing Medicare or Medicaid for the full amount.
  C. Double billing–billing more than one agency for prescription.
  D. Billing for nonexistent prescriptions–billing for prescriptions that were not authorized by doctor.
  E. Forgery–altering writing on prescription.
  F. Overbilling–charging more than regulations permit.

Adapted from Payne, 1998a; Payne and Dabney, 1997; Pontell et al., 1982.

have been implicated in various schemes to defraud these programs include audiologists, physical therapists, physicians, psychologists, podiatrists, psychiatrists, optometrists, chiropractors, and a host of other providers who treat Medicare and Medicaid patients. Agencies such as medical clinics, medical transportation agencies, nursing homes, home health care agencies, health equipment distributors, and shoe companies have also been implicated in these scams (*Medicaid Fraud Report,* 1992).

There are a number of specific types of Medicare and Medicaid fraud that have been discussed in the literature. Pontell et al. (1982) discuss several of them. *Fee-for-service reimbursement* includes situations where providers bill Medicare or Medicaid for services that the client never received (e.g., an elderly person visits a doctor for a physical, but the doctor bills for x-rays that were never provided). *Pingponging* entails instances where providers recommend that patients seek additional services from other providers when those additional services are not needed. *Upgrading* entails situations where providers submit bills to Medicare or Medicaid for services that were more expensive than the services that were actually provided (e.g., a dentist bills for new dentures after simply cleaning old dentures). *Double billing* entails instances where the provider bills more than one insurance company for the same services. Finally, *unnecessary surgery* entails circumstances where unneeded surgery is performed on the victim.

Reiman (1998) cites figures suggesting that 15,000 people die each year as a result of unnecessary surgeries. These unnecessary operations, he suggests, cost up to 4.8 billion each year. In one case, 366 patients sued a hospital after alleging that its doctors had performed unnecessary, or botched, surgeries. Among those who appeared to receive unnecessary surgeries was country music legend Merle Haggard (White, 2003). Given that older adults are more likely to need health care, they are likely overrepresented in cases of unnecessary surgery.

Of course, there is no way of knowing how often any of these acts occur. It is believed that 10 percent of the health care budget is lost to fraud and abuse (Sparrow, 1998; Taylor, 1992). In the Medicare program alone, estimates suggest that 28 billion dollars is lost to fraud and abuse each year (Serafini, 1997). The fraud cases are difficult to substantiate because patients, both young and old, are typically not aware of (1) the services they received from the health care provider or (2) the services billed to the insurance program (Jesilow, Geis, & Harris, 1995). Those detected by authorities do not give an accurate picture of the true problem because the prosecuted cases are usually "the most egregious and stupid cases" (Jesilow et al., 1995, p. 134).

PRESCRIPTION FRAUD. Prescription fraud, as another general health care crime, involves situations where pharmacists commit fraudulent acts against the Medicare and Medicaid agencies. It is a particularly interesting type of fraud because it involves an occupation which has enjoyed a high level of trust from the public for years. In fact, pharmacists "[garner] higher marks for honesty and ethical standards than the clergy" (Wivell & Wilson, 1994, p. 38). Payne and Dabney (1997) and Taylor (1992) describe several of the methods fraudulent pharmacists have used to defraud the health care programs. *Generic drug substitution* involves circumstances where pharmacists provide a generic drug but bill for a more expensive drug. *Short counting* occurs when a pharmacist bills Medicare or Medicaid for the amount prescribed by the doctor but provides less medicine to the patient. *Double-billing* involves situations where pharmacists bill more than one insurance company for the same prescription. *Billing for nonexistent prescriptions* involves billing for prescriptions that were never provided to the patient. Altering the prescription is an example of *forgery*. Finally, *overbilling* occurs when a pharmacist charges Medicare or Medicaid more than regulations permit.

As with Medicaid and Medicare fraud, there is no way of knowing the extent of prescription fraud. It is believed that most pharmacists do not commit these acts. Research on those who do shows that generic drug substitution and billing for nonexistent prescriptions are the actions prosecuted by fraud control units most often (Payne & Dabney, 1997). Of course, this does not necessarily mean that they are the acts committed most often. Rather, they may simply be the acts that are the easiest to detect and prosecute.

Also, keep in mind that there are victims of these offenses. Although these health care crimes (excluding unnecessary surgery) do not involve the typical abusive scenario where an offender directly harms a victim, the fact that rising health care costs result from the fraudulent acts makes society in general a victim of health care crimes. Moreover, the fact that many elderly persons are potentially denied access to health care as a result of the rising health care costs shows that there are indeed victims of health care crimes (Payne, 1998a; Pontell et al., 1982). These costs will be elaborated on in the next chapter. For now, it is safe to conclude that elderly persons are negatively affected by crime in the health care industry.

HOME HEALTH CARE FRAUD. Offending in the home health care industry became a concern in the mid-1990s when a government report suggested that up to 40 percent of home health care bills were submitted in error or fraudulently. The kinds of home health care offenses committed include those described above (e.g., billing for unnecessary services, double billing, fee-for-service reimbursement). Other types of misconduct, however, are specific to the home health field. For example, *negative charting* occurs when home health care providers complete the patient's formal medical record in a way that highlights only the negative aspects of the patient's condition. In these cases, employees are usually directed to include only negative aspects of the patient's well-being in the patient's chart.

When fraud is considered, experts look to agency characteristics to explain patterns surrounding the misconduct. Agencies which are believed to be more likley to engage in fraudulent or abusive activities are those (1) with higher costs, (2) whose owners have questionable backgrounds, (3) that are small family-owned corporations, and (4) whose primary source of income is from Medicare (U.S. Senate, 1997). Four patterns are especially noteworthy in home health care fraud cases:

- Crimes in the home health field are more likely to be committed by providers than recipients.
- Certain types of providers are more prone to crime in the home health care field.
- Offenses generally occur over a period of time.
- Many of the acts are committed in groups.

It is important to note that most home health care professionals do not engage in criminal misconduct on the job; rather, most are called to the profession with a desire to help those who are in need (Payne, 2003; Payne & Gray, 2001).

In one of the few empirical studies on the crime in the home health care field, Matthias and Benjamin (2003) examined whether type of agency (agency based versus consumer directed) influenced the existence of abuse or neglect in the home health care field. They found that type of agency did not influence mistreatment by home health providers. Factors that influenced maltreatment included family ties, social supports, race/ethnicity, and provider turnover (Matthias & Benjamin, 2003).

Patient Dumping

Patient dumping involves situations where hospitals or nursing homes refuse to provide care to a patient because of the patient's lack of health care coverage. To avoid accusations of patient dumping, hospitals should take four steps:

#46

1. Employees must know the law;
2. Doctors must always perform a proper medical screening;
3. The patient must be stabilized; and
4. Employees must ensure that the facility where patient is transferred to is the appropriate facility (Williams, 1998, p. 189).

In addition to hospitals, some nursing homes have dumped patients. Hodge (1998) cites a case where a nursing home administrator evicted an eighty-two-year-old patient whose guardian did not pay the bill by leaving the patient in her wheelchair on the steps of the guardian's home after ringing the doorbell and leaving. This case led the state of Maryland to become the first state to pass a law "making it a crime for nursing home operators or other long-term care providers to illegally evict residents" (p. 32).

Institutional Financial Fraud

Many seniors are targeted for various types of financial fraud, including investment and loan scams. Comments from the media suggest that elderly persons are targeted for these schemes because they have more leisure time, anxiety about future finances, and more money than other age groups (Harris, 1995). On average, older adults have 3,000 dollars more in their checking accounts than other age groups, making them targets for various investment scams (O'Neill & Flanagan, 1998). One type of loan scam involves "tin men" who try to convince elderly persons to take out loans for various home repairs, hospital bills, or other financial needs (Hudson, 1992). Hudson (1992) notes that interest rates sometimes reach 30 percent a year on the loans, which often include ridiculous service fees.

Investment scams have also been oriented toward elderly persons. Some fraudulent investors will tell seniors that the Internal Revenue Service (IRS) has approved an investment in order to convince elderly persons to part with their money. The problem is that the IRS never grants approvals on investments (Clayton, 1999). Many seniors were also targets of investment schemes during the savings and loan crisis (Calavita, Pontell, & Tillman, 1997). What happened is that thrift employees would convince investors to invest money into the thrift industry. Then, the thrift managers would take actions that would make the thrift fail because the managers were assured high reimbursement rates from the insurance companies if their company failed. Calavita et al. (1997) label the thrift manager's actions "collective embezzlement," which is defined as "crime by an organization against an organization" (p. 63). In the end, society lost up to 500 billion dollars as a result of the savings and loan crisis, with elderly persons being overrepresented in losses incurred.

Regulatory Violations

There are literally hundreds of rules that nursing homes, residential care homes, and adult care homes must abide by in order to avoid being cited for violations. These rules exist to ensure that elderly persons are treated with dignity and respect, and protect against financial fraud, quality of care fraud, abuse, illegal restraints, and neglect (Braithewaite, 1993). In some states, laws have been passed to guard against violations of elderly person's Constitutional rights (Utech & Garrett, 1992). Examples of rights violations cited by Berliner (2001) include:

- Not giving the older adult any privacy
- Not allowing the person to vote
- Keeping the individual from worshipping
- Opening or censoring one's mail

The rules guiding the provision of services to elderly persons in nursing homes can be traced to the Nursing Home Reform Law of 1987. Table 10 outlines the rights that nursing residents are afforded as a result of this law.

Evidence about how these rights are violated is provided by the HCFA. The HCFA contracts with state inspectors who will inspect nursing homes at various intervals during the year (Williamson, 1999). The violations of each

TABLE 10. NURSING HOME RESIDENTS' RIGHTS

  I. The Right to be Fully Informed
  - a. The right to be informed of all services available as well as the costs of the services.
  - b. The right to have a copy of the nursing home's rules and regulations.
  - c. The right to assistance with sensory impairments.
  II. The Right to Participate in Their Own Care
  - a. The right to refuse medical treatment.
  - b. The right to refuse chemical and physical constraints.
 III. The Right to Make Independent Choices
  - a. The right to choose their own physician.
  - b. The right to organize and participate in a resident council.
  IV. The Right to Privacy and Confidentiality
  - a. The right to privacy in treatment.
  - b. The right to private and unrestricted conversations.
   V. The Right to Dignity, Respect, and Freedom
  - a. The right to self-determination.
  - b. The right to be treated with dignity.
  VI. The Right to Security of Possessions
  - a. The right to manage their own financial affairs.
  - b. The right to be free from charges for services covered by Medicaid or Medicare.
 VII. The Right to Complain
  - a. The right to present grievances without fear of reprisal.
  - b. The right to prompt efforts by staff to resolve grievances.
VIII. The Right to Visits

Source: Adapted from National Citizen's Coalition for Nursing Home Reform. (1999). *Fact Sheet: Resident's Rights*. www.nccnhr.org/factsheet.htm. A more complete description of the rights is provided by the coalition.

Critical Thinking Questions:

1. Is the violation of any of these rights criminal? Explain.
2. Which rights are the most important?

nursing home are public record and will be made available by state officials upon request. A summary of each home's deficiencies, titled *Nursing Home Compare,* is provided on Medicare's homepage (www.medicare.gov). A review of a few nursing home reports provided on that homepage reveals that inspected nursing homes failed to:

1. Check and update each resident's assessments every three months.
2. Have a program to keep infection from spreading.
3. Give proper treatment to residents with feeding tubes to prevent problems.
4. Make sure that each resident gets a nutritional and well-balanced diet.
5. Try to resolve each resident's complaints quickly.
6. Make sure each resident is being watched, and has assistant devices, when needed, to prevent accidents.
7. Make sure that residents are well nourished.
8. Keep residents free from physical restraints, unless needed for medical treatment.
9. Keep the rate of medication errors (wrong drug, wrong dose, wrong time) to less than 5 percent (Nursing Home Compare, 1999).

Clearly, nursing homes are expected to abide by a host of rules. It is important to note that deficiencies in a few areas do not necessarily mean that the home is problematic. Also, there is tremendous variation in the potential for harm among the types of rule violations. The scope or severity of the deficiencies in each nursing home is provided by the HCFA's summary report on the Internet. The scope ranges from minimal to widespread observations of deficiencies.

Bua (1997) who, as noted in Chapters 1 and 2, uses the information gathered by the HCFA to rank nursing homes in the United States further describes these violations. In all, he summarizes 188 different violations. The top five violations nationwide cited by Bua (1997) from the previous round of inspections were that the nursing home failed to:

1. Make an adequate comprehensive assessment of residents' needs.
2. Store, prepare, distribute, and serve food under sanitary conditions.
3. Develop a comprehensive care plan, with measurable goals and timetables, to meet residents' medical, nursing, and mental and psychosocial needs.
4. Ensure that the resident environment remains as free of accident hazards as possible.
5. Promote care for residents in a manner and in an environment that maintains or enhances each resident's dignity and respect in full recognition of his or her individuality (p. 127).

It is important to stress that the violation of these standards is not criminal per se. In fact, many nursing homes with one or two violations still enjoy high ratings from Bua (1997). A pattern of extensive violations, however, will result in lower ratings from Bua and stiff fines from the government. So, an occasional deficiency is tolerated, while continued deficiencies are not.

Also, it seems safe to suggest that the consequences of violations will play a role in how the violation is conceived by authorities. For example, if a resident dies because he or she received the wrong medication, then the action could be handled criminally. On the other hand, if no harm evolved from such an act, it would be cited as a mere violation. It is akin to exceeding the speed limit. If a driver is caught speeding and no accident occurred, the driver would likely be ticketed simply for speeding. If, however, an accident with injury to others occurred as a result of speeding, then the driver could be held accountable for a host of violations.

Moreover, the fact that some nursing homes are bad does not mean that they are all bad (Garvin & Burger, 1968). However, with growing reliance on nursing homes for various types of care, regulators must remain vigilante in ensuring the safety of nursing homes. Indeed, nursing home populations increased 24 percent between 1980 and 1990 (Brienza, 1995). Although only 5 percent of people over the age of 65 are in a nursing home at any given time, estimates suggest that "43 percent of persons who were age 65 in 1990 will use a nursing home at some point during the remainder of their lives" (Harris & Benson, 1996, p. 173). Certainly more attention needs to be given to offenses occurring in nursing homes.

CONCLUDING REMARKS

At the beginning of this chapter, a quote provided at a Congressional hearing describing instances of financial abuse was included. By now, it should be apparent that elderly persons are victimized by a host of different types of offenses. To be sure, they appear to be less likely than younger persons to be victimized by offenses measured in the official crime statistics (murder, robbery, rape, larceny, assault, etc.). However, older persons are more likely than younger persons to be targeted for financial exploitation, unnecessary surgery, abuse in nursing homes, and many of the other types of elder abuse considered in this chapter.

An interesting irony that arose in this discussion concerns different patterns in elder abuse trends and crime trends. As noted, elder abuse statistics tend to show that older women (over the age of seventy-five) are more likely to be victimized. Alternatively, "official crime statistics" show that men between sixty-five and seventy-four represent the group of elderly persons who are most likely to be victimized. This suggests that elder abuse researchers and criminologists are measuring different types of activities when they research elderly victims. More importantly, it seems that the need for criminologists to get more involved in elder abuse research is manifested in these figures. If crime is defined solely by official reports and official definitions, then criminologists may be ignoring a great number of harmful acts committed against elderly persons.

At the same time, elder abuse research has tended to focus more on instances where acquaintances victimize elderly persons, while criminologists focus more on instances where strangers victimize elderly persons. For example, when elder abuse researchers consider financial exploitation, they tend to focus on cases where a trusted acquaintance (e.g., caregiver or relative) takes advantage of an elderly person's finances. When criminologists look at financial exploitation, they tend to examine acts such as white-collar crimes, telemarketing fraud, and other instances where strangers exploit an elderly victim's assets. An integrated effort among all individuals researching and responding to crimes against elderly persons would help confront these disparities. This integrated effort would have a synergistic effect on the information flowing from such discourse. That is, the sum of the parts would be greater than the whole. A lot more can be learned from elder abuse researchers and criminologists working together in examining elder abuse than would be learned from simply piecing together information after the research has been done separately by the different groups. This integrated effort would fit in within the ideals of gero-criminology.

Chapter 4

VICTIMIZATION EFFECTS, INTERVENTION MEASURES, AND LEGISLATIVE CONSEQUENCES

1. How are elderly persons vulnerable to various consequences of victimization?
2. What does the author mean by deprivational effects?
3. What are experiential effects?
4. How can crimes against elderly persons be perceived as functional?
5. What is the relationship between fear of crime and victimization?
6. What laws have been passed to address crimes against elderly persons?
7. What are the strengths and limitations of mandatory reporting laws?

INTRODUCTION

The last thing 68-year-old Vera Dixon did was lie down in a corner of her son's kitchen, curl up in the fetal position, and die. When the Austin, Texas, police arrived at the scene, they found a vacuum cleaner wrapped around her nearly naked body, diaper-fashion. They also found most of the apartment littered with human excrement. But no sooner had the police arrested Dixon's son, Joe, when they were forced to release him. Though his mother had starved to death, there was no statute under which he could be charged. (Chance, 1987, p. 24)

The preceding case is an example of the way that narrow legislation concerning elder abuse and neglect can make it difficult to help victims of abuse and neglect. A commonly accepted definition of victim is one who is "harmed or damaged by another or by others" (Viano, 1996, p. 182). By this definition, it is clear that Vera Dixon was a victim. Due to the way the law was written, technically she was not a crime victim. Prior to the eighties, crime victims were for the most part ignored by scholars and criminal justice practitioners (Doerner & Lab, 1998; Jerin & Moriarty, 1997). With an increase in victim rights legislation, funding for victimization research, and concern about victims in general, our understanding about the victimization experience has grown tremendously in the eighties and nineties. As will be seen, there are still many areas to be addressed. As a starting point to understanding victimization issues as they relate to older crime victims, this chapter examines elderly persons' vulnerabilities to victimization, the consequences of victimization, fear of crime and victimization, ways agencies have intervened to offset those consequences, positive consequences of victimization, and legislative changes that have reduced the negative effects of victimization.

VICTIMIZATION AND VULNERABILITY

Structural and physical factors influence an elderly person's vulnerability to victimization, as well as the consequences of victimization. The most important, and probably most cited, structural factor increasing vulnerability has to do with the elderly person's isolation (Wilber & Reynolds, 1996). Isolation tends to be a double-edged sword. On the one hand, experts have argued that isolation is a risk factor in elder abuse cases in the community and in the nursing home. This means that isolation can be seen as an element contributing to the existence of crimes against elderly persons. On the other hand, if an elderly person is victimized, and he or she is isolated, then individuals who could help limit the physical and mental effects of the victimization may not become aware of the victimization for some time. The length of time between the offense and the time treatment starts will certainly influence the victimization experience. So, isolation clearly is an important factor that will contribute to whether the victimization occurs and the consequences of victimization (Iutcovich & Cox, 1990; Wilber & Reynolds, 1996).

In considering the consequences of victimization, many argue that older victims experience the criminal event much more severely than younger victims (Eve, 1985; Hirschel & Rubin, 1982; Iutcovich & Cox, 1990). Specifically, Eve (1985) notes that the consequences suffered by older victims "are more serious financially, psychologically, and socially" (p. 399). Eve cites several studies showing that relative losses experienced by elderly victims are far more severe than for younger victims. In burglaries, larcenies, and other household and personal thefts, the amount stolen, as compared to income, is higher for older crime victims. In attacks, they are more likely to suffer injuries. In robberies, older crime victims are more likely to have force used against them. Yin (1985) also argues that the consequences for older crime victims are much more severe than they are for younger crime victims.

It should not be surprising, then, that in addition to the financial, psychological, and social consequences, some would add that the consequences of victimization are more devastating physically to older crime victims (Stiegel, 1995; Yin, 1985). Capturing the physical and financial consequences, Stiegel (1995) writes,

> Elder abuse may have a particularly devastating impact on older persons. They may have fewer options for resolving or avoiding the abusive situation due to their age, health, or limited resources. They may be more vulnerable to and harmed by physical abuse because of their existing physical condition. (p. 1)

Biological factors also put older adults at risk for being vulnerable to victimization and to more severe consequences of victimization. As well, physical and sensory impairments increase older adults' vulnerability to crime (Wilber & Reynolds, 1996). Yin (1985) notes the following:

> Older people are frequently physically weak and fragile. They are often more feeble. They tend to be slow in movement. They do not hear or see as well as younger adults. Their bones are more brittle. In short, elderly people appear to be rather defenseless. (p. 11)

Despite claims that biological and physical changes increase vulnerability, very little research has addressed which biological changes make older adults more vulnerable to the consequences of victimization. Even so, assumptions about the aging process and certain characteristics of illnesses provide the framework from which a better understanding about the vulnerability of older crime victims can evolve. The following discussion considers biological changes in the aging process and ways that the symptoms of some ailments make older adults more vulnerable both to victimization and the consequences of victimization.

There are at least six physical changes occurring in the aging process that potentially increase the elderly victim's vulnerability. These include *bone weakening, changes in sensory abilities, contractures, respiratory ailments,* and *decreases in skin elasticity.* In addition, illnesses and emotional problems such as Alzheimer's, strokes, and bereavement have been suggested to increase older victims' vulnerability to crime.

Many cite *osteoporosis* as an example of bone weakening. Osteoporosis is a "disease that leads to bone weakness" (Anderson, 1997, p. 76). Twenty-eight million people in the United States have osteoporosis, with women being

more susceptible to the disease (Taxel, 1998). In fact, most who have osteoporosis are females who are fifty-five or older (Anderson, 1997). As women get
older, their risk increases. Specifically, 30 percent of women in their sixties, as
compared to 70 percent of women who are eighty or above, have osteoporosis (Taxel, 1998). Osteoporosis is particularly problematic because weak bones
are more likely to result in fractures (Anderson, 1997; Greenspan, 1999). Given
that older crime victims tend to be female more often than they are male, and
that many of the crimes involve the use of force (Eve, 1985), it seems plausible
to argue that the risk of injury increases for those who have osteoporosis.
In many cases, osteoporosis is not identified until a fracture occurs (Taxel,
1998). This means that some potential crime victims may not realize their vulnerability and may try to defend themselves, resulting in fractures or other
problems. Making it even more problematic for older adults is that a broken
bone can lead to a host of other problems. This is not generally the case for
younger individuals who have broken bones, whether they are the result of
crime or an accident. One seventy-three-year-old woman is quoted as saying,
"I have broken a few bones. I broke my elbow, I broke my wrist, and I broke
my hip eight years ago which started all of my other health problems"
(Greenspan, 1999, p. 1531).

Changes in sensory abilities include, but are not limited to, changes in vision
and hearing capacities. Presbycusis is a medical term referring to hearing loss
as a result of aging, and nearly half of the U.S. population suffers from it (Aviv,
1995; Gantz, Schindler, & Snow, 1995). For some, this may involve an inability to discriminate between sounds in that they can hear, but they cannot
make words out of the sounds that are heard. For others, it may simply be that
sounds are not heard unless they are louder and clearer than they were earlier
in the individual's life (Aviv, 1995). Gates and Rees (1997) argue that at some
point hearing loss "affects nearly all people in their senior years" (p. 247).
They suggest that the ability to hear clearly declines as one ages.

Visual impairment is a related sensory problem. Many of those who do have
vision problems either are not aware of them or choose not to seek medical
treatment to fix the problems (Reidy et al., 1998). Cataracts are an example of
visual impairment. Nearly six million individuals in the U.S. have cataracts,
which leads to blindness or double vision. Cataracts are the most common
cause of blindness in the world, with over half of the people between sixty-five
and seventy-four, and 70 percent of those over seventy-five developing
cataracts (Brown, 1999).

One of the problems with regard to victimization that arises is that the consequences of victimization can make the original impairment even worse.
Indeed, there have been instances where an elderly person's partial sensory
impairments were rendered completely impaired as the result of a criminal
act. Payne (1998a), for instance, cites a case where a nurse's aide slapped a par-

tially blind nursing home resident, leaving the resident completely blind. Again, the consequences of the victimization were more severe due to the previous physical condition of the elderly victim.

As well, sensory impairments such as hearing loss and blindness have been regarded as increasing an older adult's vulnerability to crime. Specifically, those with sensory problems might rely more on others for assistance with daily activities (paying bills, shopping, and housekeeping) (Wilber & Reynolds, 1996). This increases their vulnerability to the caregiver (Kosberg, 1998). Further, if they are victimized by a trusted caregiver, the consequences can be far more severe than if they were victimized by a stranger (Fulmer et al., 1984). Also, according to some, "legally blind people may be more vulnerable to certain forms of victimization" (Rounds, 1996, p. 29). In particular, Rounds suggests that blind individuals are susceptible to emotional abuse, verbal abuse, and con games by strangers.

Contractures are another physical condition associated with aging that can increase an older adult's vulnerability to victimization and the consequences of victimization. Contractures entail a stiffening of the joints resulting in shortened muscles and potential paralysis or spasms (Fogel, 1995). They are especially prevalent in nursing homes with increased stays in nursing homes equating to increased likelihood that a patient will "sustain a contracture" (*Brown University Long-Term Care,* 1995, p. 1). Fogel (1995) believes that contractures occur in nursing homes more often because "nursing home patients may be more likely to be immobilized by the use of restraints and/or psychotropic medication" (p. 9). Contractures more commonly occur in hands and knees than other parts of the body with those having them also more likely to have impairments of trunk or limb movement (*Brown University Long-Term Care,* 1995). Regarding victimization and vulnerability, these impairments would make it difficult for individuals to defend themselves (Yin, 1985). For those whose movement is not impaired, contractures are still problematic because they may experience a feeling of pain when they try to grasp objects strongly, again reducing their ability to defend themselves (Schneiderman & Ramakrishnan, 1995). As with sensory impairments, the consequences of criminal victimization can make the impairments associated with contractures, or any other impairment for that matter, even more severe (Tyiska, 1999). Yin (1985) notes, "In the frail condition of the elderly victim, they are more prone to injury if attacked, to require medical attention more often, and to have more expensive medical bills" (p. 67).

Respiratory ailments are common in older adults. Many, in fact, have breathing problems without realizing that certain conditions are present (Connolly, 1996). Estimates suggest that respiratory problems are the "second commonest cause of severe disability among community-dwelling elderly people" (Roomi et al., 1996, p. 12). The problem that resurfaces is that those who have breathing problems might find it more difficult to defend themselves or run from danger, theoretically making them more vulnerable to victimization (Yin, 1985).

Changes in skin elasticity may not increase an elderly person's vulnerability to victimization, but they certainly increase the consequences of victimization. Basically, as people age, their skin becomes drier, less elastic, and more fragile (Gordon & Hecker, 1997). At the same time, their blood vessels flow closer to the skin (Bowers & Thomas, 1995) "as a result of complex biological processes" (Garrett, 1996, p. 10). The result is that older persons are more likely to suffer bruises, which make the skin more susceptible to tears (Bowers & Thomas, 1995). In other words, older adults are more likely to suffer physical harm from a violent act than younger persons are. As Chermak (1993) notes, "even minor injuries can cause serious and permanent damage because of the physical vulnerability of the aged" (p. 111).

So far, the implicit suggestion has been that existing physical conditions may increase an elderly person's vulnerability to victimization and may increase the consequences they experience. However, mental ailments or emotional distress can also increase the victim's vulnerability and make the effects of victimization more severe. For instance, those with Alzheimer's, dementia, or some other disease that reduces that victim's mental capacities are potential victims of con artists or family members who want to defraud the elderly person (Wilber & Reynolds, 1996). Likewise, coping with problems such as a loss of a loved one, a stroke, or loneliness leads to emotional vulnerability with some criminals choosing to target that vulnerability (Wilber & Reynolds, 1996). In *Consumer Rights and the Elderly* (1999), on the state of Maine's worldwide-web homepage, the way that criminals focus on that vulnerability is described in the following way:

> One convicted telemarketer said that he became a telemarketing millionaire before his twenty-eighth birthday because he understood a few things about the psyche of older people: they are lonely, they have financial insecurities dating back to the Depression, and if they get caught in a scam, they are too proud to admit it. "It is incredibly easy to con a person who remembers his or her mother having to pawn their wedding band to put food on this table. . . . Even when an elderly victim didn't want to play anymore, it was easy to keep the game and keep the money going by threatening to expose them to either their spouse, their neighbors, or even to take them to the court" the convicted felon said (p. 9).

What it comes down to is that some elderly persons "suffer mental or physical frailties that leave them helpless against the high-pressure tactics used by telescammers" (Blake, 1996, p. 23). As well, a survey of 331 fraud investigators by Friedman (1992) found that mobility, vision, or hearing problems that could be observed by perpetrators were predictors of home improvement/repair swindles. Those vulnerabilities, or frailties as they are described by Yin

(1985), Blake (1996) and a host of others, are exasperated because the victim has less accessibility to social services, may experience poverty as a result of the victimization (if they aren't already in poverty), or may end up institutionalized as a means to intervene in the criminal event (Tyiska, 1999).

To be sure, not all elderly persons are vulnerable, and aging itself is not a disease or an illness (Wilber & Reynolds, 1996). Even so, some offenders perceive all elderly persons as vulnerable, even if they are not frail, enhancing the likelihood that those offenders will target elderly victims (Hirschel & Rubin, 1982). Tyiska (1999) seems to agree, noting that some "are especially vulnerable to victimization because of their real or perceived inability to fight, to flee, or to notify others and testify about victimization" (p. 4).

So, some may not truly be vulnerable based on their physical condition; however, if criminals perceive elderly persons as vulnerable, then their likelihood for being targeted increases. The result is that the combined changes (biologically, socially, and economically) that come with aging increase the victim's potential for harm. Consider the way a relative of an institutionalized elderly person described the consequences of nursing home neglect:

> The bed sore is the occupational hazard of the nursing home. The old flesh is pinched between the bone and the mattress and hardened by the plastic mattress covers. There is no one to turn the patient over several times a day. There is no evaporation and so the skin is broken and fed bacteria. The ankle bones go first. Then the tail bone. Then the shoulder blades. They are lying in urine; sometimes all night. My God, I have seen sores so big you could put half a grapefruit in them. Filthy with their excrement. Still they are forced to just lay there. (Garvin & Burger, 1968, pp. 22–23)

In this case, the vulnerability of the victim was real, not just perceived.

The vulnerability of elderly crime victims seems to be increased by a lack of understanding about the consequences of elder abuse. Of course, the specific consequences of victimization are difficult to determine. Given that most research has centered on offenders, and the victimization research that has been done tends to consider younger victims, assessing the consequences of elderly victimization requires that we rely on conjecture and comments from the media and other sources to try to understand elderly persons' victimization experiences. To guide this understanding, I will rely on a typology I developed to assess victimization consequences experienced by health care crime victims (Payne, 1998a). This original typology included the consequences of elder abuse in nursing homes, so it is easily applied to all crimes against elderly persons. This will be followed by a discussion of the relationship between fear of crime and victimization, intervention methods, positive consequences from victimization, and legislative and policy changes that have occurred as a result of victimization experiences of elderly persons.

CONSEQUENCES OF VICTIMIZATION

Measuring harm and the consequences of harm is not an easy task. Even so, some suggest that "older victims are less likely to cope successfully with their reactions to crime" (Burke & Hayes, 1986, p. 108). The vulnerability is increased by the fact that these victims have largely been ignored by researchers as well. The victimization typology guiding the presentation of the consequences of victimization for elderly persons is outlined in Table 11. It addresses the "costs of victimization" and is presented as a starting point from which we can begin to understand the experiences of these vulnerable groups.

TABLE 11. A TYPOLOGY DESCRIBING THE CONSEQUENCES OF VICTIMIZATION FOR ELDERLY PERSONS

I. DEPRIVATIONAL EFFECTS
- A. Physical Deprivations
    1. loss of life
    2. loss of physical abilities
    3. loss of peace of mind
    4. deprivation of adequate health care
- B. Time Deprivations
    1. time spent going to doctor, pharmacist, etc.
    2. time spent testifying against abusers
    3. time spent making up for lost productivity
- C. Individual Economic Deprivations
    1. manifest monetary losses–as a direct result of offense
    2. latent monetary losses
    3. health care recovery losses–seeking additional treatment–higher bills (Yin, 1985)

II. EXPERENTIAL EFFECTS
- A. Physical Experential Effects
    1. pain and suffering (physical abuse and sexual abuse)
    2. physical harm from faulty drugs
    3. relatives' pain and suffering
- B. Mental Experential Effects
    1. increased stress due to health problems may lead to more health problems
    2. destroys trust
    3. mental anguish
- C. General Economic Experential Effects
    1. higher costs of prevention needs
    2. family members will experience economic strain

Source: Adpated from Payne, 1999.

Critical Thinking Questions:

1. How does age influence the victimization experience?
2. What are the implications of these experiences for professionals?

In general, victimization effects can be characterized as either deprivations, which are things the victim loses, or experiences, which are things the victim experiences as a result of a crime (Payne, 1998a). As such, my typology includes the following two broad categories: deprivational effects and experiential effects. Three points about the typology need to be stressed. First, the typology focuses primarily on the way the crime impacts the victim with very little attention given to the offender. This is not problematic given the way that victims historically have been ignored by society. Second, the distinction between deprivations and experiences may be somewhat vague in that one could argue that any sort of deprivation is truly an experience. For instance, if one is deprived of money, one has experienced a loss of money. However, I believe it is important to make the distinction because whether a consequence is primarily a deprivation or an experience will play a role in determining the intervention and subsequent treatment provided to the elderly victim. Third, it is important to keep in mind that these consequences are provided as ideal types that would be used to guide our understanding about the consequences of elder abuse. Clearly, those who experience these consequences would not tell their caseworker that they have experienced a mental deprivation or physical experiential effect. Thus, the categories are provided to structure our understanding about the consequences of elder abuse.

Deprivational Effects

The notion of deprivational effects is concerned with the fact that elderly crime victims will be deprived of certain things as a result of victimization. These deprivations can be referred to as *physical deprivations, time deprivations,* and *individual economic deprivations.*

Physical deprivations are concerned with the actual physical losses that are incurred by elderly crime victims. At the most general level, physical deprivations would include death, loss of physical abilities, loss of peace of mind, and deprivations of adequate health care.

Death is inarguably the most serious physical deprivation that elderly crime victims would experience. Other than the FBI data showing that older crime victims are murdered far less often than younger victims, there are no figures available describing how many older crime victims die as the result of criminal behavior. Reiman (1995) estimates that nearly 15,000 individuals die each year as the result of inadequate, inappropriate, or unnecessary medical care (p. 78). Given that the majority of those seeking health care are older, it is safe to argue that older adults are more likely to die from "inadequate, inappropriate, or unnecessary medical care" than younger persons are. Also recall that victims of elder abuse are more likely to die earlier than non-victims (Lachs et al., 1998).

Much of the information about deaths experienced by elderly crime victims is found in anecdotal accounts. In his description of his participant observation study, Stannard (1973) describes a case where a nursing home resident's skin was "coming off in hunks" after the resident was scalded in the bathtub. The resident died shortly thereafter as a result of the scalding. The nursing home administrator described the act as an unfortunate accident caused by a series of events. In particular, the administrator claimed that the laundry person was absent, so no towels were in the usual location when an orderly changed the resident's soiled linens and placed the victim in the bathtub. Supposedly, the orderly had to leave for a few moments to get towels. According to the administrator's version, the victim bumped the hot water handle and was unable to turn it off. Others, however, claimed that the orderly was punishing the resident for cursing at the orderly while the orderly was changing the soiled linens. The case was never prosecuted criminally, though Stannard's presentation makes it seem that the death was not an "unfortunate accident."

These sorts of acts continue to occur in the nineties. One nursing home patient died choking on food, even though the patient was supposed to be fed with tubes (Thompson, 1998). In a similar case, an elderly woman who was only supposed to eat soft foods died after choking on a hot dog (Grier, 1999). Thompson (1998) cites a GAO report that finds that over half of the "suspicious deaths studied in California nursing homes were probably due to neglect, including malnutrition and dehydration" (Thompson, 1998). The GAO report suggests that the problem is not limited to California.

Indeed, neglect can lead to a host of consequences, the most serious of which is death (Zuzga, 1996). Often it is difficult to find out who is responsible for the neglect and whether the consequences are truly a result of neglectful behavior. In a case described by Fiesta (1996), a doctor ordered sun lamp treatment for a ninety-one-year-old woman's decubiti. The licensed practitioner nurse accidentally used a lamp too powerful for the woman, resulting in severe burns. The doctor was notified about the burns, but never examined, or had anyone else examine, the resident. Only after several hours and a follow-up contact by the nursing home supervisor did the doctor refer the resident to an emergency room. As it turned out, the hospital he sent her to did not have a burn unit. The resident died four days later. The doctor was found guilty of neglect and given a civil penalty of $1,000.

For those instances where death does not occur as the result of victimization, the elderly victim may experience the loss of physical abilities. Even minor injuries can interact "with chronic physical conditions interfer[ing] greatly with physical mobility" (Hirschel & Rubin, 1982, p. 365). Some of the injuries are defined as warning signs in the literature. For instance, Anetzberger et al. (1993) describe the warning signs of abuse and neglect as including broken bones, absence of nutrition, absence of dentures, eyeglasses, prostheses, or hearing aids. Clearly, if elderly victims exhibit these warning signs, they will experience physical limitations (e.g., deprivations) as a result of the visible problem. Briefly, broken bones can result in immobility. An absence of dentures will affect a victim's ability to eat or speak. Missing eyeglasses or hearing aids will make it difficult to see or hear. Likewise, missing prostheses will limit the victim's mobility. Further, an absence of nutrition will have an impact on the victim's abilities. In short, each of these losses will lead to a loss of physical abilities.

As expected, very little research has considered the way older victims experience these losses. Nonetheless, they clearly occur. In a neglect case, for example, a nursing home resident "with life threatening bed sores . . . had to have her left leg amputated below the knee due to gangrene" (*Medicaid Fraud Report,* April, 1992, p. 9). Cases of amputation as the result of criminal acts are undoubtedly examples of physical deprivations (Payne, 1998a). Even more troublesome is the fact that the loss of physical abilities can eventually lead to death, which may partially explain why elder abuse victims die earlier than non-victims. For instance, bone fractures are related to high mortality rates (Taxel, 1998). Given that bone fractures are consequences of elder abuse, it appears that some cases of abuse may ultimately lead to an early death for the elderly abuse victim (Zuzga, 1996).

Loss of peace of mind is another physical deprivation that older crime victims may experience. Cohen and Miller (1998) note, "Victims of crime often receive scars that are far deeper than their external wounds" (p. 4). Instances of emotional abuse can have a very drastic effect on the elderly person's peace of mind. One victim said that her abuser "had threatened to poison her food, making her frightened to eat at home" (Breckman & Adelman, 1988, p. 37). This deprivation is related to the other deprivations. For instance, if an elderly victim needs medical attention as the result of a physical deprivation, he or she will experience stress (e.g., will lose peace of mind) as the result of visits to the doctor (Payne, 1998a).

As well, recall from Chapter 3 that sons are believed by some to be the largest category of sex offenders to commit sexual offenses against elderly persons (Ramsey-Klawsnik, 1991). In one case, five nursing home employees reported seeing a man perform assorted deviate sexual acts on his mother (*Medicaid Fraud Report,* 1992, p. 5). Ramsey-Klwasnik (1991) notes that the sons engage in these acts in order to gain control over their elderly mothers. One would expect that the loss of peace of mind for the victim in these cases would be enormous. The fact that some elderly sexual abuse victims engage in self-destructive behavior (Ramsey-Klawsnik, 1991) suggests that they certainly have lost some peace of mind.

Also consider that elderly persons are more likely to be victimized at home than they are in the community. In fact, a survey by Fashimpar and Phemister (1984) revealed that 52 percent of elderly persons in one housing complex were victims of crime, as compared to 19 percent of residents in the entire city. The fact they were victimized at home more often suggests that they will not feel as safe as those who were not victimized. Fashimpar and Phemister (1984) write: "Being elderly, victimized, and threatened with a weapon at home by a known assailant is far more frightening than being middle aged and having one's traveler's checks stolen on vacation by a stranger" (p. 12). Indeed, as will be discussed later, many argue that fear of crime, which can be seen as losing peace of mind in some cases, is a consequence of victimization for older adults (Eve, 1985; Pain, 1995).

Deprivation of health care is the final physical deprivation. Basically, for every elderly crime victim, others who need care are potentially deprived of health care. Beck and Gordon (1991) describe an informal survey from the early nineties that found that some emergency room physicians had at least eight elderly patients abandoned in their emergency room each week. Adding the additional patients into the emergency room will deprive, or at the very least delay, others from receiving health care.

Patient abandonment is not the only example of deprivation of health care. As the result of Medicare fraud, people who need health care do not get it (Longman, 1997; Payne, 1998a; Pontell et al., 1982). Longman (1997) quotes one concerned legislator as saying "every Medicare dollar stolen through fraud and abuse, such as charging the program for Super Bowl tickets, means one less dollar for older Americans' health care" (p. 18). An irony that arises is that crimes such as unnecessary surgery, where a person receives a treatment he or she does not need, results in people who need treatment not receiving it (Payne, 1998a). Crime in the health care system "impacts on programs that must go unfunded due to lack of money, such as eye and dental care for the elderly, or programs that must be limited, such as the monthly prescription limit for Medicaid recipients" (Taylor 1992, p. 20). Undoubtedly, a consequence of some cases of elder abuse is that individuals are deprived of adequate health care.

Time deprivations are not as obvious as physical deprivations, but they nonetheless occur. What they refer to is the possibility that the elderly victim loses time he or she could have spent doing something else because of the victimization. The secondary victims, children, neighbors, and caregivers (see Breckman & Adelman, 1988) will also experience time deprivations in their attempts to help the victim recover from the victimization. In essence, victims, both primary and secondary, will have less productivity at work and at home (Miller, Cohen, & Wiersma, 1996).

The reasons that time is lost have to do with time spent going to the doctor or other treatment programs, time spent worrying about the doctor visit, and time spent engaged in the criminal justice process. With regard to time spent going to the doctor, one survey found that female crime victims make twice as many visits to the doctor as females who were not crime victims did (Koss et al., 1991). Looking at the relationship between medical needs and victimization from a different angle, Tilden et al. (1994) found that one-third of emergency room visits made by women were due to problems resulting from family abuse. Though Koss et al. (1991) and Tilden et al. (1994) did not focus solely on elderly victims, the fact that elderly victims' consequences are potentially more severe than younger victims, and that they are injured more often, suggest that older victims may require even more visits to the doctor than younger victims do.

Beyond the actual physical needs sought from medical treatment, victims lose time visiting doctors. The time deprivation becomes even more complex when the amount of time spent in waiting rooms for medical care is considered. Describing waiting, Schwartz (1974) writes:

> after a certain point, waiting becomes a source of irritation not only because it may in itself be wearisome, boring, and annoying, but also because it increases the investment a person must make in order to obtain a service. . . . This loss to the waiter is related to the fact that time is a finite resource. (p. 844)

In fact, waiting only serves to strengthen the power the provider has over the patient who is already vulnerable (Schwartz, 1974). The fact that crime victims, whether they are elderly or not, are forced to play such a game as a result of the victimization is problematic.

Keep in mind that in many cases secondary victims are going to lose time helping the elderly victim seek medical treatment. This lost time might equate to lost time at work and lost productivity on the job (Miller et al., 1996). This, then, equates to lost wages.

Elderly victims, and their secondary victims, will also lose time if they choose to involve the criminal justice system in responding to the victimization. Even more troublesome is that while they are losing time working with actors in the justice system, elderly victims may in fact experience revictimization at the hands of the justice system. Granted, all victims may experience revictimization, but the elderly victim's revictimization has been described slightly differently in the literature. Hirschel and Rubin (1982) note that some elderly victims will experience disorientation while dealing with criminal justice officials while others are treated as if they are not adequate witnesses. The result is that they experience stress on account of the time and the emotional investment that they place into a process that treats them so poorly.

Further, while they are investing a great deal of time into the process, elderly victims often feel ignored by justice officials. Describing this dilemma in *Defrauding the Elderly,* Geis (1976) writes the following:

> Many victims feel their needs have extremely low priority and that at best, they are tolerated and then often with ill humor. Their role, they say, seems much like that of the expecting father in the hospital at delivery time: necessary for things to have gotten underway in the past but at the moment rather superfluous and mildly bothersome. The offender, at least, is regarded by criminal justice functionaries as a doer, an antagonist, someone to be wary of. . . . The victim, on the other hand, is part of background scenery. (p. 15)

I would argue that the way the criminal justice places low priority on some victims' input increases the impact of time deprivations incurred through involving the justice system in responding to the elder abuse cases. In other words, it's one thing to invest time into a process where one is appreciated; it's quite another when one is devalued and denigrated. As an example, consider the following victim testimony provided by Breckman and Adelman (1988):

> The last time he came to the house, I called the police. They came, and one of the policemen said that they can't keep coming every time I call. He suggested that I get an Order of Protection. They told me that I had to go to court, and I didn't realize what an involved process this was. I thought you go in and say you need it and–bingo–they give you a paper and that's it. But I had to go back twice because at four o'clock they said, "No more today. Come back tomorrow." And, you know, going through that security thing is very degrading. (p. 121)

This example shows that a great deal of time was spent in a process where the victim felt devalued and unguided. The victim experienced "status degradation" during her involvement with the justice system. Many victims of elder abuse choose not to report the case because they believe, justifiably to a degree, that they may experience social devaluation by reporting the crime (Viano, 1996).

Individual economic deprivations are the third and final type of physical deprivations considered in my typology. Essentially, these losses entail the actual economic losses that elderly victims will incur as a result of victimization. Again, all crime victims will experience economic losses. The economic losses experienced by older crime victims are potentially more severe than those experienced by younger victims. For instance, elderly persons, many with less money and fixed incomes, experience more harm from small financial losses than others would (National Center for Victims of Crime, 1995). One reason for this is that they "have fewer resources personally and financially with which to protect themselves from the losses they have incurred" (Iutcovich & Cox, 1990, p. 66).

Also note that the money lost by older victims is generally funds that were reserved for medical care (Scandlen, 2003). As Stiegel (1995) writes, "Older persons may have less ability to recover from financial exploitation if they are already retired or because of their short remaining life span" (p. 1). Younger victims can more easily rebuild their assets over their lifetime through their income received from their jobs. For those elderly persons on fixed incomes, they never regain the money or lost real estate unless they seek legal recourse (Hankin, 1996).

Another problem is that they could experience financial losses as a result of seeking legal recourse. The time the victim, and the secondary victims, would spend meeting with attorneys, filing depositions, and doing other activities necessary in seeking recourse would take away from the time, and subsequent wages, the victims would be getting on their job (Payne, 1998a). Even more troublesome, "Abusers and their lawyers are aware of the financial pressures on the [victim] and may take advantage of that by dragging out litigation and making the victim's lawyers . . . devote more of their costly time to the litigation" (Hankin, 1996, p. 67). Hence, the victim is again "revictimized."

The victim will also incur economic losses as the result of the medical treatment which may be required as a result of the victimization. It has already been established that crime victims need medical services more often than non-crime victims, and elderly crime victims are injured more often than younger crime victims. The fact that the costs of out-patient care for crime victims is 2.5 times greater than it is for non-crime victims is further evidence of economic losses as a result of medical services for crime victims (Koss et al., 1991). One study has even placed dollar figures on losses that take into account pain and suffering, health care needs, lost income, and so on. This research shows that, all things considered, the cost of being a sexual assault victim is estimated at $110,000 for the victim and $87,000 for society (Miller et al., 1996). Keep in mind that relatively speaking these financial costs would hurt elderly victims more because, in general, they have less flexible income (Iutcovich & Cox, 1990; Stiegel, 1995).

Along a related line, a crime victim, elderly or young, may experience increases in their insurance rates if they file claims for the victimization. For some, the insurance coverage may even be canceled (Otis, 1996). Some states have passed laws preventing insurance companies from being able to deny clients insurance on the basis that they were victims of domestic abuse. Otis (1996) notes that the legislation has been opposed by insurance companies who see the restrictions as being a breeding ground for false claims of abuse. Otis (1997) quotes one critic as stating, "I don't contest this is a serious problem. Of course, it is, so is racism in our society, and yet we don't draft racial preference into insurance laws. What we draft is non-discrimination" (p. 4).

Also, in some states, victim compensation will not cover items that are essential to older crime victims (e.g., medical equipment, eyeglasses, hearing aids, and so on) (National Center for Victims of Crime, 1995). The result is that victims may experience economic deprivations because they will need to purchase those essential items in order to get on with their lives. Note that in many cases the secondary victims will also experience economic losses as they try to help the elderly person recover to their previous state. It seems safe to conclude that older crime victims will be subjected to a host of physical, time, and economic deprivations, most of which are felt by all victims, but they seem to effect older crime victims in slightly different ways. A similar case arises in considering what I refer to as *experiential effects*.

Experiential Effects

While deprivational effects are concerned with what the victim loses, experiential effects are concerned with what the victim actually experiences as a result of the victimization. There are three types of experiential effects: *physical experiential effects, mental experiential effects,* and *general economic experiential effects* (Payne, 1998a).

Physical experiential effects are concerned with the actual physical consequences that the victim experiences as a result of the victimization. Many of these experiences are the same as what others refer to as warning signs or indicators of abuse and neglect. Those warning signs that have been suggested in the literature include (1) bruises; (2) welts; (3) burns by cigarettes, ropes, or chains; (4) lacerations; (5) consistent hunger; (6) fatigue; (7) listlessness; (8) hypothermia or hyperthermia; (9) decubitis ulcers; (10) signs of hair being pulled out of the victim's head; (11) injuries to teeth; (12) injuries to the jaw; (13) neck injurines; and (14) injuries to the oral soft tissue (Breckman & Adelman, 1988; Fulmer et al., 1984; Ramsey-Klawsnik, 1991; Rathbone-McCaun & Voyles, 1982; Tilden et al., 1994). Note that if any of these signs appear, and the elderly person was in fact victimized, then it can be assumed that the victim experienced an effect from the victimization. For example, if they are burned, then they have experienced a physical experiential effect. The same could be said for each indicator, so long as the source of the problem was victimization. As another example, one nurse's aide punched a sixty-eight-year-old woman in the face and pushed her to the floor. The fall led to "an open bleeding wound on the resident's head" (*Medicaid Fraud Report,* October, 1990, p. 18). Here, the wound would be an indicator, and a consequence, of the victimization.

As far as the effects of these problems, clearly elderly victims will experience pain and suffering (Miller et al., 1996). However, it is important to note that the physical effects of sexual abuse, though they would include those consequences listed above, potentially include other physical consequences, namely sexually transmitted diseases, genital or urinary infections, problems walking, problems urinating or defecating, and bruises to the pelvic area (Ramsey-Klawsnick, 1991; Teitleman, 1999). For example, in one sexual abuse case, several female residents developed vaginal infections in units where one aide was caught sexually abusing an elderly woman. The elderly woman could not recall the encounter but later said the aide was her husband and that they had sex several times (Fiesta, 1996). Of course, there are emotional consequences experienced by these victims, and they will be discussed a bit later.

Elderly victims of drug theft will also experience physical experiential effects (see Dabney & Berg, 1994). These victims will experience physical harm from receiving improper prescriptions or from not receiving prescriptions at all (Payne & Dabney, 1997). In one case, a licensed practitioner nurse ignored a doctor's orders and "twice neglected to provide the narcotic drug morphine to a patient in her care, and on one occasion, failed to dispense the controlled drug dextropoxphene to another patient" (*Medicaid Fraud Report,* September, 1990, p. 14). She altered records to make it appear that the drugs had been given to the patients, when in fact she kept them for herself. In this case, as in others where caregivers steal drugs from elderly persons, the victim was certainly at a higher risk to experience the pain that the medication was supposed to offset. By depriving the victims of their health care, the caregivers are causing the victims to experience physical experiential effects.

It is also important to note that relatives of victims will experience pain and suffering as a result of crimes against elderly persons. Recall that Breckman and Adelman (1988) describe relatives as secondary victims. As an example, the *Medicaid Fraud Report* describes the effects of one elder abuse case in the following way: "[A]fter this incident, the victim has been extremely withdrawn and [has] not responded in any fashion to family members" (May/June 1987, p. 8). The degree of pain and suffering experienced by family members who could no longer communicate with the patient can only be imagined, but pain certainly would be felt by the family members.

The whole notion of pain brings up a host of related consequences. In essence, physical pain and depression are related, though it is not always clear how the two are related (Parmalee, Katz, & Lawton, 1991). Studying the relationship between pain intensity and depression, Parmalee et al. (1991) conclude that "depression may increase sensitivity to pain caused by an existing physical problem" (p. 15). The relationship between pain and depression ties directly to the notion of mental experiential effects.

Mental experiential effects are concerned with the emotional consequences of victimization for older adults. They are perhaps the most devastating consequences in that the pain is worse than physical pain, and it may take much longer to recover from mental anguish. For instance, a broken bone, though it takes longer to heal in older adults than it would for younger victims, would likely still heal quicker than the loss of trust that may be a consequence of many of the offenses against older victims. In fact, some may never be able to recover from the mental experiential effects.

Depression and stress are common experiences shared by all victims (*Pediatrics,* 1996). Depression and stress can be seen as lowering quality of life, which is regarded as "the largest cost component for crimes of violence" (Miller et al., 1996, p. 23). In fact, long-term medical needs, such as overcoming depression and stress, may be more important than the immediate emergency needs of crime victims (Koss et al., 1991).

As far as how elderly persons handle the mental experiential effects, they seem to show similar, but slightly different experiences as a result of victimization. Similarities arise when the actual emotional consequences are considered. For instance, a residential advisor of a nursing home sexually assaulted a resident by kissing and fondling the resident. The advisor also made sexual advances to a female resident. The *Medicaid Fraud Report* states "both residents were emotionally affected by the advisor's actions" (February, 1992, p. 12). Suffering emotionally as a result of sexual assaults is common in both younger and older victims.

A difference that makes the emotional consequences different for older victims, albeit only slightly different, has to do with the violation of trust that may affect older victims more than younger victims. Recall that many older victims are victims of white-collar crimes. This is important to remember because the consequences of white-collar crime are more widespread than the consequences of street crime (Moore & Mills, 1990). In other cases of elder abuse, the offenses might be committed by trusted relatives or caregivers. In these cases, the victim will distance himself or herself from the caregiver (O'Brien, 1994).

As well, the victim may feel shame that their trust was violated by a trusted caregiver (Brekman & Adelman, 1988). The general point to keep in mind is that victims will experience problems with trust because of the violation of trust committed by the family member, caregiver, or white-collar offender (Pontell et al., 1982; Wilson et al., 1985). Also recall that older victims are more likely than younger to be victimized at or near their homes. Rykert (1994) points out that those who are victimized near their homes "experience a level of fear that continues to affect their quality of life" (p. 10). This is clearly a mental experiential effect, or an emotional consequence.

There are other related emotional consequences that need to be considered. For example, withdrawal is considered to be "the most often reported social response to criminal victimization" (Eve, 1985, p. 399). Payne and Cikovic (1995), for instance, describe a case where a victim completely withdrew from their family as a result of abuse suffered in a nursing home. Other emotional consequences that elderly victims may experience include (1) agitation, (2) confusion, (3) low self-acceptance, (4) loss of appetite, (5) weight loss or weight gain, (6) excessive fears, (7) sleep disorders, (8) speech disorders, (9) compulsion, (10) phobias, (11) conduct disorders, (12) destructiveness, and (13) depression (Breckman & Adelman, 1988; Fulmer et al., 1984; O'Brien, 1994). These consequences could lead to, or in some cases are caused by, stress. Stress could then break down the individual's physical well-being to the point where other health problems result (Tilden et al., 1994).

The mental experiential effects associated with sexual abuse include those listed above but may be even more severe than those consequences. The consequences listed by Ramsey-Klawsnik (1991) and Teitelman (1999) include intense fear, mistrust, sleep disorders, low self-esteem, depression, memory problems, hopelessness, anxiety, confusion, regressive and aggressive behaviors, and self-destructive behavior or suicide. Beebe (1991) notes that sexual assault victims might experience "fear, guilt, shame, anger, and even concern for the offender" (p. 2041). This concern for the offender is likely caused by the fact that many elderly victims tend to be passive, internalize their blame, are loyal, and compliant (Fulmer et al., 1984). Unfortunately, particularly in physical abuse cases, outsiders tend to also be sympathetic with the offender, arguing that caregiver stress caused by the dependent victim causes the offender to lash out. Anetzberger et al. (1993) refer to the caregiver stress hypothesis as the "myth that won't die" (p. 704).

A related consequence is that victims, and those that hear about the victimization of elderly persons, will experience mental anguish just thinking about the actions. This anguish can result in behavioral changes. For instance, because people fear nursing home abuses, they will not report abuse in the community setting because they do not want to end up revictimized in a nursing home (Anetzberger et al., 1993). One relative of a nursing home resident claimed that "the patients were always worrying about nurses or other patients stealing from them" (Garvin & Burger, 1968, p. 22).

To conclude this discussion of mental experiential effects, there are enormous costs associated with the emotional consequences of victimization. Oddly, "mental health care use by crime victims is one of the least known aspects of victimization costs" (Cohen & Miller, 1998, p. 93). Estimates suggest that anywhere from 3.1 to 4.7 million Americans sought mental health treatment as the result of crime victimization in 1991. In fact, one-fourth of all mental health clients are crime victims, leading to expenditures of about billion each year. Granted, there is no reason to believe that elderly crime victims are overrepresented in the need for treatment dealing with the emotional consequences of victimization. Nonetheless, some have argued that elderly persons' higher fear of crime, which is a mental experiential effect, is caused by victimization related experiences (Pain, 1995; Yin, 1982). Thus, in this sense, and in the sense that they are more likely to be victims of offenses where trust is violated, elderly persons' emotional consequences are somewhat different than other victims' consequences.

The last part of the victimization typology is *general economic experiential effects*. In this context, general economic experiential effects refer to the costs of victimization that are incurred by society. For example, forty-five billion dollars is lost to fraud each year, with elderly victims being overrepresented as fraud victims (Miller et al., 1996). Recall from Chapter 1 that elderly persons make up 30 percent of fraud victims but only 12 percent of the population.

Society also experiences general economic experiential effects as the result of Medicare fraud. By some estimates, nearly 40 percent of the Medicare funds for home health care "does not meet the program's reimbursement requirement" (Longman, 1997, p. 18). Estimates such as these mean that the total losses due to fraud and abuse in the health care arena are anywhere from fifty to hundred billion dollars a year–10 percent of the health care budget (Cohen 1996, p. 120; Ford 1992, p. 2; Taylor 1992, p. 17).

The result is twofold. First, members of society end up paying more for health care to offset what is lost to fraud. Second, those who are in dire need of medical services, in many cases elderly persons, are denied access to health care (Longman, 1997). Likewise, instances of patient abandonment end up costing taxpayers due to the increased costs in health care associated with the act of patient abandonment (Hylton, 1992).

It should be noted that family members of elderly victims will sometimes experience further economic strain in an attempt to pay for the services needed for the elderly crime victim. Also, insurance rates of victims, and those in the rest of society, increase as a result of fraud (Miller et al., 1996). These added expenses are also examples of general economic experiential effects.

Certainly, there are drastic consequences suffered by elderly crime victims. Though these consequences are similar in many ways to consequences experienced by other victims, one consequence that is particularly different concerns the fear of crime found among older adults. The following addresses fear of crime and the elderly. Then the way that all of the consequences can be addressed through the different intervention strategies will be considered.

FEAR OF CRIME AND ELDERLY CRIME VICTIMS

The relationship between fear of crime, age, and victimization has received a great deal of attention from criminologists, perhaps more attention than any other issue concerning older crime victims. In fact, fear of crime "has received the bulk of research attention in the U.S." (Eve, 1985, p. 402). To say that the results of this research, ongoing since the mid-seventies, are mixed would be a gross understatement. In general, most of the research indicates that older people are more fearful than younger people, but the extent of the difference in fear between the groups is debatable. Also questioned is whether older individuals' level of fear is justified given their apparent low victimization rate. Again, research is quite mixed in addressing this question. Early studies described fear of crime as "even more of a problem than crime itself" (Clemente & Kleiman, 1976, p. 207). A well cited poll showed that 75 percent of elderly persons rated fear of crime as their most serious problem (Harris, 1975).

Research in the eighties and nineties both confirmed and rejected the suggestion that fear of crime is highest among elderly persons (Iutcovich & Cox, 1990; Skogan & Maxfield, 1981). Today, most studies accept that fear of crime is highest among elderly females, though some argue that the impact of age is significant primarily because of the higher proportion of older females (Pain, 1995). In a similar vein, Ferraro believes that gender is the most important predictor of fear. Others suggest that age interacts with income to produce a high fear of crime (Baldassare, 1986). Others, however, argue that the "unusually high-level of fear" among elderly persons is a result of elder abuse situations (Rathbone-McCaun & Voyles, 1982, p. 191). Lee (1982) also reports that victimization leads to high fear of crime, particularly for elderly females.

Critics of the early fear of crime research point to the way fear of crime was, and still is, measured and argue two points. First, some say that the measures do not actually measure fear of crime but are measuring something else (Eve, 1985; Ferraro, 1995; Lee, 1982; Mawby, 1986). Second, others say that the questions are biased toward certain groups, such as elderly adults, because they ask about behaviors elderly persons would not be engaged in to begin with (Ferraro, 1995; Lee, 1982). In particular, they criticize asking older adults whether they are afraid of walking alone at night because respondents were being asked to indicate perceptions about a behavior that truly would not be a part of their regular activities.

The disparity between older adults' fear of crime and likelihood of victimization became known as the fear of crime and age victimization paradox. This paradox received a great deal of attention from criminologists in the mid-eighties through the mid-nineties. After surveying 1,410 residents in retirement communities in New Jersey and Florida, Akers et al. (1987) conclude that older adults are not as fearful as previously believed and that their personal vulnerability is not related to crime but related to fear. Thus, they were afraid not because of victimization but because of their perceived vulnerability. Others have also found that fear of crime was not as high among older adults as others believed (Iutcovich & Cox, 1990; Ferraro, 1995).

In essence, evidence is mixed regarding the impact that fear of crime has on victimization. Yin (1980) sees victimization as playing an important role in fostering fear but includes what he refers to as "interactions about crime" as a measure of victimization. Interactions about crime are concerned with the extent to which the individual is familiar with individuals who are victims, either personally or through the media. Based on his analysis, Yin (1980) concludes that the "crime-related experience of the elderly's friends is an even stronger predictor of fear than is the respondent's own experience" (p. 498). In a similar vein, a survey of 3,000 North Carolina residents by Belyea and Zingraff (1988) found a relationship, albeit small, between knowledge about victimization and fear of crime.

In interviewing 2,048 elderly persons in Pennsylvania, Iutcovich and Cox (1990) also found that victimization, measured by asking about personal victimization and whether the respondent knew someone who was victimized, was the most significant factor in predicting fear of crime. Similar findings were noted by Kennedy and Silverman (1985) who measured "contact with crime" by asking respondents how often they called the police. They found that those who called the police more often had a higher fear of crime. Alternatively, research by Box, Hale, and Andrews (1988), which shows that age is an important variable in understanding fear of crime, finds that those who were victimized were *less* likely to be fearful, in part because of the self-protective measures they learned to take after victimization.

There are others who argue that the higher fear of crime and low victimization rate among older adults is explained not by vicarious victimization but by the way risk is measured in fear of crime research. Eve (1985), for instance, argues that risk was not controlled for in much of the early research and that this would underestimate the potential for crimes against elderly persons. Briefly, because elderly individuals take greater self-protective measures, they are not at risk for crime; therefore, their victimization rate is reduced. If risk levels were equal across age groups, then the elderly would be more vulnerable to victimization, which would justify their higher fear of crime. Lindquist and Duke (1982) seem to agree, stating the following: "We believe that when the extent to which the elderly are 'at risk' is taken into consideration, the victimization rate for the elderly will equal or exceed the victimization rate for the other age categories" (p. 125). They further argue that the victimization rate is a "function of analytical techniques" (p. 125). On the other hand, research by Clarke et al. (1985) suggests that elderly persons' lower victimization rate cannot be explained by more self-protective risk reducing behavior, thus questioning the role of risk in producing a higher fear of crime.

More recent research by Pain (1995) suggests that elderly persons' level of fear is congruent with their risk. Recall that Pain (1995) saw gender as an important variable explaining why research shows elderly persons are more fearful. Based on her results of surveys of 389 women, she argues that "the na-ture of crime against women ensures that it has a lasting effect on personal fears" (p. 591). She believes that the risks of violence in the home, sexual ha-rassment, and elder abuse explains why elderly individuals, women in partic-ular, have higher levels of fear.

Again, the safest thing to say about fear of crime and the elderly is that fear of crime experts do not agree on the role of victimization in fostering fear or the level of fear among elderly persons. Perhaps a more important issue, how-ever, centers on whether fear, regardless of whether it is higher or lower among elderly persons, impacts the actions of older adults. Indeed, some re-search suggests that there are consequences, both positive and negative, as a result of fear of crime.

Certainly, research suggests that fear of crime will lead to behavioral changes among elderly persons. For example, some have argued that elderly persons are less mobile socially because of their fear (Ginsberg, 1985; Hirschel & Rubin, 1982; Patterson, 1985). Some point out that older adults are more likely to stay at home as a result of their fear (Ginsberg, 1985), while others point out that fear of crime limits elderly citizens' use of public transportation (Patterson, 1985). Gurnack and Zebitz (1993) argue that high levels of fear lead to various lifestyle changes, including withdrawal. In a sim-ilar fashion, Hirschel and Rubin (1982) see fear of crime as producing what they refer to as psychological immobility, defined as "a state of helplessness, powerlessness, and vulnerability" (p. 366).

Yin (1982) sees fear as affecting neighborhood satisfaction and the elderly person's sense of well-being but argues that social isolation is not as problem-atic as others believe. In fact, there are some who see positive consequences associated with fear of crime. For example, Rykert (1994) notes that there are six levels of fear: apathy, concern, apprehension, alarm, tormenting fear, and terroristic fear. He points out that concern is the best level of fear in that it can encourage individuals to take precaution to reduce their risks of victimization. He notes that apprehension can be good, as long as there is not too much ap-prehension. The other levels, he notes, are problematic in producing either social or psychological immobility.

Along a similar line, Norton (1982) surveyed 152 elderly persons who par-ticipated in Seniors Against a Fearful Environment, a crime prevention pro-gram designed to reduce fear and crime and improve seniors' perceptions of the police. Norton found that fear influences protective actions and security conscious behavior. Norton notes, however, as does Rykert (1994), that edu-cation programs may have to raise some individuals' fear of crime in order to achieve the goal of crime prevention. Or, those who would be at Rykert's first level of apathy would likely not engage in security conscious behavior unless they were given a reason to do so. The way to encourage self-protective behavior, according to Rykert and Norton, is to increase fear to the point of concern without raising the level of fear too high.

Though the evidence about fear of crime and elderly crime victims is mixed, anectdotal evidence suggests that fear, whether it is fear of crime or something else, is an important consequence of victimization. For instance, after being assaulted by a therapy aide, one nursing home patient "was frightened by the incident and later in the day became rebellious and wouldn't take his medication. The victim was so intimidated by [the abuser], he was afraid to work in his presence" (*Medicaid Fraud Report,* October, 1992, p. 8). In this case, fear certainly was a consequence of victimization, though this is not what researchers mean by fear of crime.

Tyiska (1999) describes a case where an older woman lived with her family to help with her daily routines because she was unable to walk. Tyiska writes:

> Her grandson, a drug user, frequently stole money from her, especially after the third of each month, when her Social Security Disability Income Check arrived. . . . Once in a state of anger when he could not find her money, he flipped her over and she fell out of bed and onto the floor. She sustained several bruises but was not seen by a doctor. She did not report the abuse or theft to the police out of fear that her family would no longer care for her. (p. 6)

In this case, the consequences of fear were that the victim was unwilling to report the case to anyone.

Perhaps the safest thing to say in summing up the consequences of victimization and the relationship between fear of crime and victimization is that victimization is experienced differently by victims. Understanding these consequences is important, however, because they will dictate the most appropriate intervention strategy. Based on the typology presented previously, and the role of fear, the goals of intervention include the following: restore physical abilities, minimize time losses, recoup monetary losses, deal with physical pain, assist in mental problems, minimize economic losses, and develop the appropriate level of fear within the victim. The following discussion focuses some treatment strategies that have been used to intervene in crimes against elderly persons. This will be followed by a discussion of some of the legislative and policy changes that have been implemented to offset the negative consequences associated with the victimization of elderly persons.

INTERVENTION AND ELDER ABUSE

Intervention strategies have received a great deal of attention from elder abuse scholars. These strategies generally focus on either education or providing social services. One thing that is agreed on is that because experiences are different, treatment must be individualized rather than standardized (Fulmer et al., 1984; Nahmiash & Reis, 2000; Sadler, 1994). Thus, it should not be surprising that authors have considered numerous intervention strategies as being useful in elder abuse cases, depending on the needs of the elderly person. Reflected in each of the models is the fact that treatment requires an interdisciplinary approach (Bradley, 1996).

Biggs et al. (1995) discuss five models that they see as being regularly used in intervening in elder abuse cases. First, the social network model is concerned with enhancing the victims' ties with the community, which interviews with elder abuse victims show is important in assisting in recovery. Second, the advocacy and mediation model involves strategies oriented toward protecting older adults' rights and resolving conflict. Third, the domestic violence model offers immediate protection and uses support services that are similar to those used in serving domestic violence victims (e.g., crisis intervention, support groups, etc.). Fourth, the legal intervention model focuses on using the criminal and civil justice systems to resolve the problem. Fifth, the social work intervention model entails case management with caseworkers coordinating services for the victim.

Like Biggs et al. (1995), Sengstock, Hwaleck, and Petrone (1989) consider the legal intervention model and advocacy model, but they add what they refer to as the mandatory reporting model. This model focuses on the use of mandatory reporting laws to encourage groups to make authorities aware of the problem so that intervention and advocacy can occur.

Harbison (1999), on the other hand, considers completely diffferent models of intervention. First, Harbison (1999) describes the psychopathological model as using strategies that resolve the problesms of the caregiver. Second, the systems model attempts to determine the various causes of the abuse and neglect. Next, the hierarchal model actually ranks the several causes in order of importance. Fourth, the quasi-legal model uses legislative remedies to resolve the problem. Fifth, the child welfare model approaches elder abuse in ways that child abuse would be resolved. Finally, the peer participation model encourages cooperation among elderly persons as a response to elder abuse.

As evidenced by the preceding paragraphs, many models have been proposed as ways to respond to elder abuse. It is important to note that each of these services can be seen as therapeutic and self-protective (Phillips & Rempusheski, 1986). Based on these models, and others presented in the literature, an integrated description of the actual approaches that have been used to deal with elder abuse would give attention to the following services: institutional placement, medical services, social services, therapeutic strategies, educational programs, and legal services.

Before describing how these services are utilized to help elderly victims, a few general points about intervention strategies are warranted. First, the type of service received relates to the type of abuse (Sengstock et al., 1989; Teitelman, 1999). Sexually abused victims would require different services than those who are financially exploited. Next, in many cases, treatment has "to be negotiated with both the caregiver and the victim, neither of whom may desire help" (All, 1994, p. 30). Third, regardless of the type of intervention strategy used, interviews with elder abuse victims show that what helps them overcome their victimization experiences are personal beliefs, external contact, and community services (Sadler, 1994). Finally, one of the problems that arises in these cases is determining when intervention should occur (Myers & Shelton, 1987). Anetzberger et al. (1993) argue that once the abuse occurs, responses should focus on ensuring personal safety, meeting the elderly person's medical needs, utilization of adult protective services (APS), and involvement of multidisciplinary teams to meet the victim's needs. Regarding immediate needs, removal from the threatening environment is sometimes seen as the best alternative for responding to the violent situation (Anetzberger et al., 1993).

Institutional Placement

Unfortunately, ensuring their personal safety may require that the elderly person is removed from the home and placed in an institution (Gurnack & Zevitz, 1993; Sadler, 1994). Salem and Favre (1993) note three types of institutional placement. First, placement in a long-term care unit includes placements in extended care facilities, skilled nursing facilities, and intermediate care facilities. These are generally the places that people refer to as nursing homes. Second, placement in a long-term residential facility entails placing elderly victims in adult foster homes or board and care homes. Third, emergency shelters or safehouses that are available for all domestic violence victims are sometimes used to meet the immediate personal safety needs of victims (Salem & Favre, 1993).

According to Bergeron (2000), a number of problems limit the use of domestic violence shelters for older victims. Many may not have the design required by older persons with disabilities. Also, the noise from younger children may be stressful to older victims. Third, older victims have a tendency to resist using services that are "secret" in nature—as are shelters. Finally, most are not designed to house male victims, meaning that by some estimates, 25 percent of elder abuse victims have nowhere to go.

Note that many victims do not report abuse because they are afraid that they will be removed from their homes. Many recommend that community-based assistance be used instead of institutionalization (Simon, 1992). O'Brien (1994) writes: "When they are reassured that they can remain in their home with the help of various home health services, they are open to appropriate intervention" (p. 411). Though removal from the home does occur, such an alternative is used much less often than the other intervention strategies.

Medical Services

Medical professionals have a rather interesting role in the battle against elder abuse. They are often the first to know about abuse as they are in a position to be the first to recognize cases of abuse (All, 1994; Jorgensen, 1993). As such, they must be prepared to identify abuse and offer appropriate interventions. So, they are "identifiers" and "treaters" in cases of elder abuse.

As far as identifying cases of elder abuse, AMA guidelines suggest that all elderly persons "should be asked about family violence, even in the absence of symptoms potentially attributable to abuse or neglect" (Fiesta, 1996, p. 18). To document abuse, the AMA provides the following guidelines:

1. The chief complaint and description of the incident should be recorded with the patient's own words whenever possible;
2. A complete medical history;
3. A relevant social history;
4. A detailed description of injuries, including type, number, size, location, stages of healing, color, resolution, possible causes, and given explanation;
5. An opinion as to whether the injuries were adequately explained;
6. The results of all pertinent laboratory and other diagnostic procedures;
7. Color photographs and imaging studies, if applicable;
8. Reports of any involvement of law enforcement (Pavlov & Murov, 1994, p. 249).

As far as meeting the victims' medical needs, health care providers will provide typical medical services to make sure that any consequence suffered from the victimization is minimized. Victims' medical needs vary but could possibly entail emergency room treatment, hospitalization, out-patient treatment, or provisions for home health care (Salem & Favre, 1993).

For sexual abuse cases, the role of the physician is particularly important. Beebe (1991) notes that doctors will perform necessary functions in rape cases. First, they will document pertinent history. Second, they will conduct a physical exam. Third, doctors will provide immediate treatment to meet the elderly persons' immediate needs. Fourth, the doctor will provide psychological support and help find follow-up counseling. Fifth, legal evidence will be collected by the doctor. Finally, medical services will be provided to prevent sexually transmitted diseases.

Social Services

Once the abuse is substantiated, the APS caseworker will develop a treatment plan to stop the abuse and to "ameliorate the negative effects of the abuse previously suffered" (Ramsey-Klawsnik, 1995, p. 43). Simon (1992) suggests that the APS worker should involve the victim in developing the treatment plan. As such, many of the social service approaches center on reducing the victim's isolation and using existing social programs to ensure the safety of the victim (Sadler, 1994).

There are numerous social services provided by the caseworker. For instance, caseworkers may be involved in case management, where they organize and structure the services the victim will receive. Case management is, in fact, the most frequent activity performed by the caseworker (Sengstock et al., 1989). These services that are organized, and sometimes provided by the case worker, include the following: home making assistance, meals assistance, counseling services, housing/relocation assistance, transportation assistance, job training, and income assistance (Sengstock et al., 1989).

In providing these services, the least restrictive alternative is sought in an effort to limit intrusion into the older adult's life (Simon, 1992). Of course, there is a delicate balance between protecting older adults from abusers and protecting them from unwanted intrusions from social service workers. There will, in fact, be times where services are provided that are not desired by the victim. To see how often involuntary protective services were provided to the elderly person, Duke (1997) surveyed forty-three (of fifty) state administrators of APS programs. She found that less than 10 percent of elderly APS clients received services after refusing them. In most of these cases, there was a belief that either serious physical harm or death was imminent if the services were not provided. In those cases where involuntary services are provided, the elderly person is appointed an attorney or representative to protect his or her rights.

Therapeutic Services

Next to case management, counseling is the second most common function social service workers will fulfill in responding to cases of elder abuse (Sadler, 1994). In many cases, the victim may refuse treatment. To encourage victims to accept treatment, Breckman and Adelman (1988) describe the "staircase" model. This model is based on the assumption that the victim is independent and the abuser is dependent. There are three stages. First, reluctance entails instances where the victim denies that he or she has been mistreated. Next, recognition entails that time period where the victim realizes that help is needed. Third, rebuilding entails the acceptance of treatment where the victim will begin to recover from the consequences and move on with his or her life.

One of the issues that comes up, however, is that counseling may entail treating both the victim and the abusive caregiver, but in many situations the two must be counseled separately (Sadler, 1994). In the next chapter, primary attention will be given to treating the abuser. Here, attention will be directed toward strategies that have been used to help the victim.

Perhaps the most important step in counseling abuse victims is to make sure that the victim understands that he or she is not to blame for the acts (Teitleman, 1999). At the same time, the caseworker must determine whether abuse actually occurred. As Teitelman (1999) notes, in cases of sexual abuse the APS worker must determine the patient's ability to consent to sexual conduct. This involves determining the elderly person's awareness of the relationship, their ability to avoid exploitation, and their awareness of the risks of sexual activity. Questions that should be asked to determine if sexual activity was consensual or abusive include the following:

1. Is the client aware of who is initiating the sex?
2. Is the behavior consistent with the person's formerly held values and beliefs?
3. Does the client have the capacity to say no?
4. Is the client aware of the risks? (Teitelman, 1999).

In those cases where abuse is substantiated, whether sexual or some other type, counseling can be an effective strategy to help the victim overcome the consequences that were discussed earlier in this chapter. Group therapy for older adults has received a great deal of attention in the counseling and social work literature. Rather than discussing all of the group approaches that have been successful, the following three will be considered: family system's therapy, peer counseling, and discussion therapy groups.

First, family system's therapy treats the entire family from a system's perspective, which emphasizes interrelationships and interdependence between family members (Greene & Soniat, 1991). One of the important assumptions underlying the approach is that blame is not placed on the victim, or the offender for that matter. A problem that sometimes develops is that the elderly victim may be distrustful of the intervention and unwilling to work with family members. In instances such as these, Breckman and Adelman's (1988) staircase approach would be useful. Green and Soniat (1991) see family therapy as being useful in preventing and responding to abuse. They write: "Family therapy can provide an opportunity for members to verbalize and work through the fears, anxieties, anger, and guilt. [It] can also help to clarify roles and deal realistically with emotional stress" (p. 12).

Peer counseling is another approach that has been used to help victims recover from the effects of elder abuse. Burke and Hayes (1986) evaluated a peer counseling program (Peer Counseling for Older Adults Program) to see whether involving elderly persons as peer counselors effectively uses the talents of the elderly volunteers and whether the volunteers were able to help other older citizens deal with their concerns about crime. The program started in 1977 due to the problem of vicarious victimization, which was earlier referred to as interactions about crime (see Yin, 1982). The notion is that just hearing about other victims make elderly persons suffer repercussions of fear, anxiety, and distrust. In the peer counseling program evaluated by Burke and Hayes, thirty-five to forty seniors volunteer to help other seniors. The program led to the development of two programs that are coordinated and administered by the volunteers. First, Operation Senior Security educates elderly persons on ways to minimize their victimization risks. Second, Operation Victim Support trains peer counselors to become counselors to those elderly persons who are victims of crime. Results of the program evaluation suggested that peer counseling helped victims by lowering their anxiety, reducing their risk, and increasing their mobility. Also, elderly volunteers found the program increased their sense of pride.

Third, discussion therapy groups have been shown to be useful in helping older adults deal with their concerns. Waller and Griffin (1984) evaluated discussion therapy groups that were designed to help depressed elderly persons. In particular, they examined the effectiveness of the Special Needs Project for Aurora Seniors. The aims of the project are to prevent depression among elderly persons and to maintain elderly persons' abilities to adapt to their surroundings. Waller and Griffin (1984) suggest that group therapy is effective in responding to perceptions of insecurity. In many cases, these perceptions of insecurities parallel fear of crime and can lead to depression which, as already noted, can have physical and behavioral consequences. The perceptions of insecurity can result from victimization or simply worrying about victimization. Group therapy has been found to be effective in reducing insecurity and thus controlling the depression of the group members.

In one of the few studies on elder abuse support groups, Wolf (2001) interviewed leaders of elder abuse support groups and found that elder abuse support groups housed in domestic violence programs were quite similar to those housed in aging services programs. She also found that resistance to participation was a major barrier to increase the effectiveness of the support groups. Based on her findings, Wolf recommended the following: (1) elder abuse support groups must make sure that the meeting sites are accessible to all elderly persons; (2) funds must be allocated to recruit program participants; (3) program administrators should seek steady funding sources; and (4) program administrators must make efforts to enhance collaborations with other agencies.

Educational Services

Educational and training programs have also been used to intervene in abusive situations. As interventions, these services entail providing the elderly victim, or the caregiver, with information that will assist in resolving conflict. Some refer to these services as "socialization" or "socializing" programs because of the way that individuals' values, beliefs, and behavior patterns are changed as a result of the programs (Sengtock et al., 1989; Salem & Favre, 1993). This training is accomplished through the use of home visitors, adult day care centers, or the services of senior citizen centers (Salem & Favre, 1993).

Educational services are also used in efforts to prevent fraudulent activities. Consider the Retired Senior Volunteer Program (RSVP). In this program, administrators worked with different public and private agencies to staff the National Telemarketing Victim Call Center. Using the services of older volunteers, in its first year, RSVP called 20,000 potential telemarketing fraud victims to alert them about telemarketing fraud (Aziz et al., 2000).

Legal Interventions

Legal intervention refers to a host of procedures that are used to respond to allegations of elder abuse, including police visits, crisis intervention assistance, investigations, prosecution, legal services, guardianships, conservatorships, and protection orders. The goals of legal intervention include the following: (1) stop the criminal behavior, (2) protect the victim and the public, (3) hold the offender accountable and rehabilitate the offender, (4) send a message to society that elder abuse will not be tolerated, and (5) provide victim restitution (Heisler, 1991; Heisler & Quinn, 1995).

Note that these legal interventions exist to both prevent and respond to different kinds of crimes against older persons. In San Francisco, for example, the Volunteer Legal Services Program of Bar Association of San Francisco developed a two-leveled approach to prevent and respond to mortgage fraud against the elderly. These two levels include training and community outreach. In terms of training, a curricula and training tape was developed to train attorneys how to identify mortgage fraud cases. Mortgage fraud attorneys were then asked to volunteer their services to serve as "on call attorneys" for the program. With regard to outreach, participating attorneys "helped raise the awareness of potential victims by participating in panel discussions and community events for seniors and service providers" (Alfonso, 2000).

The way that the criminal and civil justice systems respond to abuse will be considered in detail in the next chapter. For now, it is important to note that some experts are against a great deal of criminal justice involvement because of a belief that the problem would not be solved through a system that is designed to punish. Rather, many continue to see the use of various social services, counseling methods, and educational programs as being particularly useful in responding to elder abuse (Chance, 1987).

Whatever services are provided, whether they are medical, social, therapeutic, educational, or legal, the actors need to recognize the dignity and the competence of the elderly person. Many policies and programs have actually attained this goal. In the next section, positive consequences including recent legislation designed to minimize the consequences of abuse are considered.

POSITIVE CONSEQUENCES OF CRIMES AGAINST ELDERLY VICTIMS

There are positive consequences associated with crimes against elderly persons. These positive consequences equate to what Emile Durkheim (1894) described as functions of crime. In particular, Durkheim argued that crime serves four functions, which are referred to as the warning light syndrome, boundary maintenance, community integration, and social change (Martin, Mutchnick, & Austin, 1990). Each of these can be applied to elder abuse.

First, regarding the warning light syndrome, the occurrence of crime lets society know that a problem is developing. It is not just occurrence, however. Instead, individuals must identify the problem and share the knowledge they have about the problem with others. Recall Stannard's (1973) nursing home study and Baker's (1975) article called "Granny Battering." Upon hearing about these acts, society was able to recognize or be warned that a problem was developing.

Second, boundary maintenance is concerned with the possibility that individuals learn appropriate behavior through hearing about criminal behavior. With regard to elder abuse, if a nurse's aide is abusive toward a patient and is punished for that abuse, then the other nurse's aides will learn that abusive behavior crosses the boundaries of acceptable behavior. Practitioners in the justice system seem to view boundary maintenance as an integral part of the crime and punishment relationship. For example, part of one health care provider's sentence was that as a condition of probation the provider had "to write letters to other [health care providers] warning them of the hazards involved in the violation of Medicaid laws" (*Medicaid Fraud Report,* 1988, p. 11). In a separate case, a judge made the following comment: "The medical profession and other providers should get the clear message that they will go to jail if the situation calls for it" (*Medicaid Fraud Report,* 1987, p. 7). Clearly, in each of these cases, the judges wanted to make sure that a consequence of the offender's behavior was that the boundaries of appropriate behavior were established for others.

Regarding community integration, Durkheim posited that communities will grow closer together when there is evidence of a growing crime problem in a community. On a general level, the way that various groups have formed to respond to crimes against elderly persons can be seen as community integration. These groups likely never would have formed were it not for the elder abuse problem that was developing. For instance, a group referred to as the National Committee for the Prevention of Elder Abuse was formed to increase understanding about elder abuse, improve research on the topic, educate the public and service workers about the topic, and influence legislators in developing legislation in the best interest of the victims (see Box 4.1 Voices from the Field: The National Committee for the Prevention of Elder Abuse) Also, many states formed their own coalitions to come together to battle the problem. Further, some attorneys came together in 1987 to form the National Academy of Elder Law Attorneys (NAELA) to serve as a resource for attorneys and bar organizations who work with elderly clients. This group was "formed to safeguard the rights of elders who are allegedly victims of . . . abuse and are brought into the process of APS" (Meagher, 1993, p. 101). As will be shown in the next chapter, various criminal justice agencies formed units that included members from the community to better understand and respond to crimes against elderly persons. The point is that these individuals, and their communities, were drawn closer together because of the elder abuse problem.

Social change, as a function of crime, is concerned with the way that crime promotes broader changes in society. As far as crimes against elderly persons, changes occurred in educational institutions, nursing homes, and the political arena. The changes in the educational institutions entail greater awareness about the elder abuse problem. Research in the areas, though seen as flawed by some (Macolini, 1995), has increased dramatically in social work and gerontology, and to a lesser degree in sociology and psychology. Journals such as the *Journal of Elder Abuse and Neglect, Elder Law Journal, Journal of Health Politics, Policy, and Law, Kansas Elder Law Network, BIFOCAL* (published by The ABA's Commission on Legal Problems of the Elderly), and the *Journal of Elder Law and Policy* were developed so that an outlet for this research, and a better understanding about legislation related to elderly victims, was available. Also, elder abuse is covered regularly in many college textbooks and college courses. There are even upper level and graduate classes focusing primarily on elder

BOX 4.1. VOICES FROM THE FIELD: THE NATIONAL COMMITTEE FOR THE PREVENTION OF ELDER ABUSE

By Pamela Teaster

". . . our society must address the abuse of the elderly and disabled persons as a critical social problem. The lessons learned in responding to the needs of these individuals may in turn serve as guideposts for advancing the quality of life for all older adults and their families."

Dr. Rosalie S. Wolf, Founder

Chartered in 1988 as a non-profit organization, the National Committee for the Prevention of Elder Abuse (NCPEA) brings together practitioners, administrators, researchers, and educators from both public and private sectors to address the problem of elder mistreatment. NCPEA's members come from a wide variety of fields including adult protective services, aging, social services, health, mental health, law, domestic violence, law enforcement, criminal justice, and public administration (NCPEA, 2003; Wolf, 1999).

The mission of NCPEA is to prevent abuse, neglect, and exploitation of vulnerable adults of any age and older persons through research, advocacy, service, treatment, public and professional awareness, interdisciplinary exchange, and coalition building. NCPEA was founded by the late Dr. Rosalie S. Wolf, of the Institute on Aging, UMass Memorial Health Care in Worcester, Massachusetts. Dr. Wolf was its president until her death in June, 2001.

In 1992, NCPEA embarked on the Affiliate Program, a major national outreach effort to develop linkages with local and state coalitions or task forces interested in the prevention of the abuse of vulnerable adults of any age and older persons. The purpose of the Affiliate Program was to promote collaborative advocacy, information sharing, and professional development. By 1999, NCPEA, with assistance from a grant from the Archstone Foundation, had 17 affiliate groups throughout the United States; included were local community groups, statewide organizations, and multidisciplinary teams. Most of the groups were involved with training, education, public awareness, and legislative action on all aspects of elder mistreatment. In 2004, efforts are underway to re-constitute the Affiliate Program.

NCPEA was a member of the management team of the first National Center on Elder Abuse (NCEA) (1993–1998) and was a partner in NCEA from 1998–2003. Under the sponsorship of NCEA, NCPEA has provided technical assistance, conducted research projects, disseminated information, and carried out education and training programs.

Under the guidance of Dr. Wolf, NCPEA participated in the National Research Council/Institute of Medicine's Committee on the Assessment of Family Violence Intervention, the U.S. National Women's Resource Center's "Issues Forum on Violence and Women Across the Life Cycle," the U.S. Health Resources and Services Administration's "National Family and Intimate Violence

Prevention Initiative," the U.S. Department of Justice Focus Group on Abuse & Victimization of the Elderly, and the U.S. Administration for Children and Families "The Next Millennium Conference Ending Domestic Violence," and the 1995 White House Conferences on Aging.

After Dr. Wolf's death, and continuing as a national organization dedicated to the prevention of elder abuse, members of NCPEA have recently testified at Congressional hearings, participated in many national conferences, focus groups, and committees convened to set national policy on family violence. Specifically, activities include testimony before the Senate Health, Education, Labor and Pensions Committee (2003); the Senate Finance Committee (2002); and the National Summit on Elder Abuse (NCEA-DOJ, AOA) in 2001. In addition, members of NCPEA have presented at several of the joint conferences of the American Society on Aging, National Council on Aging, and several International Conferences on Family Violence. NCPEA leadership also participates in various state and local conferences and serves as a resource to groups.

NCPEA has served as a model for the organization of a similar group in the United Kingdom, *Action on Elder Abuse,* and the Latin American Committee for the Prevention of Elder Abuse, as well as the International Network for the Prevention of Elder Abuse.

Support for NCPEA activities comes from membership dues, donations, and foundation and governmental grants. All members receive a subscription to the international *Journal of Elder Abuse & Neglect.* Celebrating its 17th year in 2004, this quarterly journal provides a forum for the discussion of scientific investigation, program developments, policy initiatives, and personal commentaries about elder abuse, neglect, and exploitation. Enjoying its tenth year, *Nexus,* a publication originally targeted for the Affiliates, is now also a benefit of membership in NCPEA. It features best practice programs and interviews with leaders in the field.

Presently, the NCPEA office is located in Washington, D.C. Robert Blancato, who was NCPEA's First Vice President beginning in 1988, assumed the position of President after Dr. Wolf's death. NCPEA, through the leadership of its officers and Board of Directors, has remained faithful to its original mission and was renewed as a partner of the National Center on Elder Abuse through 2006. NCPEA continues to address the abuse, neglect, and exploitation of the nations' vulnerable younger and older adults. In addition, it has worked to focus and enhance its advocacy work serving as a co-founder of the Elder Justice Coalition working for the enactment of the Elder Justice Act.

References

National Committee for the Prevention of Elder Abuse (NCPEA). (2003, December 17).
About NCPEA. Retrieved from *http://www.preventelderabuse.org/.*
Wolf, R.S. (1999). Retrieved from personal file, NCPEA description.

Pamela B. Teaster earned her doctorate in Public Administration and Public Affairs and the Graduate Certificate in Gerontology from Virginia Polytechnic Institute and State University. She is an Assistant Professor in the University of Kentucky School of Public Health and Ph.D. Program in Gerontology. She serves on the Editorial Board of the *Journal of Applied Gerontology* and is the former editor of the *Journal of Elder Abuse and Neglect*. She is the First Vice President of the National Committee for the Prevention of Elder Abuse, and she serves on the American Bar Association Commission on Law and Aging and the Board of Trustees for the National Guardianship Association. Dr. Teaster has recently published articles in such journals as *Public Administration Review, Journal of Applied Gerontology, Journal of Elder Abuse and Neglect, Journal of Family Relations, Journal of Gerontological Social Work*, and *Journal of Ethics, Law, and Aging*.

abuse that have been developed in various disciplines across the United States. So, the social consequence of elder abuse in the educational arena has been greater attention to and awareness about elder abuse.

In the nursing home industry, changes have occurred in the way employees are recruited, trained, and evaluated. Most states now have abuse registries that list the names of former abusive caregivers that nursing homes can use to determine if applicants should not be hired. Training programs for nurse's aides are beginning to include information about ways to prevent and respond to abuse when it does occur. Also, many nursing homes are developing policies that would result in the dismissal of employees who fail to provide appropriate care to the elderly resident. Glanz (1994) describes one nursing home's response to elder abuse. Specifically, in response to two employees stealing from patients, the Crestview Convalescent Center, with the help of local police, an attorney, and private investigators, developed a program involving screening in hiring, in-depth elder abuse training, and stringent enforcement of mandatory reporting laws. Glanz (1994) points out that the convalescent center now offers rewards, reduces opportunities for theft, and effectively uses state laws to reduce the likelihood of crime in the home. So, the consequence of crime in this nursing home involved changes in the institution's approach to handling elder abuse.

Capezuti and Siegler (1996) have also described how cases of nursing home abuses ultimately led to important changes. In particular, they cite an investigative expose by Gunther as being instrumental in developing programs, passing legislation, and enhancing training programs for those working with elderly persons. The original expose, published in *Philadelphia Magazine* and titled "The Leper Colony," included a "case history of an eighty-year-old nursing home resident with malnutrition, dehydration, and a gangrenous penis" (p. 74). With the effort of ombudsmen, a legal services attorney, and the Pennsylvania attorney general, the case eventually resulted in a successful criminal prosecution, the development of a task force to improve communication, and training programs to increase understanding about elder abuse in neglect.

In the political arena, many politicians became more aware of the elder abuse problem in the eighties and nineties. The result has been an increase in legislation, some seen as positive and some seen as negative, since the late seventies (Anetzberger, Korbin, & Tomita, 1996; Erlich & Antezberger, 1991). The types of legislation that have evolved include protective services legislation, legal services funding legislation, restitution laws, mandatory reporting laws, and penalty enhancement laws. Penalty enhancement laws will be considered in the next chapter in conjunction with a discussion of the sanctions given to offenders convicted of committing crimes against elderly persons. The others will be reviewed in the following paragraphs.

Protective Services Legislation

Experts define protective services legislation differently. In this context, I use the term to refer to those laws that are specifically designed to protect victims of elder absue. Simon (1992) describes four types of laws to protect elder abuse victims. First, protective service laws provide investigative and protective services for older adults. Second, elder abuse laws specifically define elder abuse as illegal and stipulate the criminal sanctions that should be given to the elder abuse offender. Third, domestic violence laws stipulate that domestic violence cases are to be handled certain ways (e.g., mandatory arrest). Fourth, social service laws provide for a host of services to be able to prevent abuse or intervene when the abuse occurs.

Protective services legislation has been around since the fifties, but laws were not widespread until there was the perception in the seventies and eighties that older adults needed protection (Zborowsky, 1985). In the seventies, fourteen states enacted APS laws. These laws then flourished in the eighties as a result of a growing concern about the need to respond to the growing problem of elder abuse. By 1988, every state had APS laws. There is great variation in the laws, although the common theme is that they reflect a "parens patriae" (e.g., in the place of the parent) philosophy characteristic of the orientation of the juvenile justice system (Meagher, 1993). The laws are designed to protect the victim and guard his or her civil rights, and they "integrate that legal and social service aspects of protective services" (Zborowsky, 1985, p. 80).

Another consistent theme in APS laws is that the elderly person, or his or her guardian, usually has to consent to any service delivery provided (Duke, 1997; Ramsey-Klawsnick, 1995). Note, however, that in seven states the laws are written so that service delivery can be administered without the consent of the elderly person, without seeking a court determination (Duke, 1997). Most states, though, agree that APS and police should work together in resolving elder abuse cases (Chermak, 1993).

Much of the protection older adults are afforded legislatively can be traced to the Older Americans Act of 1965, which has assisted older adults with all sorts of activities, including counseling, legal services, and respite care (HHS Press Release, 1998). The Older Americans Act of 1976 (an amended version of the original act) was also instrumental in developing legislation and programs to protect older adults. In particular, the 1976 act established nursing home ombudsmen programs as a response to abuse and neglect of nursing home patients (Lachs & Pillemer, 1995). The amendments stipulated that states had "to establish an ombudsmen program to investigate and resolve problems of residents of nursing homes and other long-term care facilites" (*Aging Magazine,* 1996, p. 117). The Older Americans Act was again amended in 1987 in an effort to force states to take actions to prevent elder abuse. After this amendment, every state "had legislation for the protection of the aged" (Meagher, 1993, p. 92). In all, the nationwide ombudsmen program has about 865 paid full-time employees and 6,750 volunteers. Ombudsmen receive and resolve complaints that affect nursing home residents in an attempt to ensure that residents are protected (Bua, 1997).

A related piece of protective services legislation has to do with abuse registries that states use to keep track of abusive caregivers and allow for a tool that can be used to prevent future abuse. In Michigan, for example, the Department of Health keeps a registry of certified nurse's aides. Those who have been convicted of abuse have their names "flagged." By law, facilities must review the registry before hiring new aides. Those that hire aides who have been convicted of abuse jeopardize losing their Medicaid benefits (*Medicaid Fraud Report,* November, 1992, p. 13).

Restitution Laws

Some states have passed restitution laws that stipulate that a certain amount of restitution will be provided to victims if offenders are convicted of elder abuse or neglect type offenses. Critics see such laws as intruding on judicial discretion, costly to administer, difficult to run, and futile, in that money is sought from offenders who, in many cases, have none (Maveal, 1995). In a related development, some states have passed victim compensation laws to provide for replacement of personal property that is considered essential to victims. These essential items include medical equipment, hearing aids, eyeglasses, and so on (National Center for Victims of Crime, 1995). Unfortunately, reimbursements are often inadequate (Hirschel & Rubin, 1982).

Legal Services Funding Legislation

By law, every state is required to offer funding for some form of free legal services in non-criminal cases to persons available to people over sixty. The free services generally provide consultation and will not be able to solve the elderly client's problem but should be able to guide the elderly person in finding additional resources. Some local bar association and law school clinics also provide free services to elderly persons (Court TV Legal Help, 1999). For instance, the University of Pittsburgh's law school houses a family support clinic which prepares students for subsequent litigation by allowing them to work with cases of family conflict. Elder law is one of the substantive areas that students are educated about in the clinic (Legal Clinics, 1999).

Mandatory Reporting Laws

Recall that mandatory reporting laws were briefly discussed in the first two chapters. Chapter 1 gave a brief overview of the problems critics attribute to mandatory reporting laws. Chapter 2 considered the way mandatory reporting laws were used by legislators to gain political leverage against opponents. At this point, a more in-depth consideration of these laws is warranted.

Mandatory reporting laws exist in forty-two states, with the other eight states having what are referred to as "voluntary" reporting laws (Ehrlich & Anetzberger, 1991). The aims of mandatory reporting laws are to "assure the well-being of older adults and at the same time protect their civil rights" (Zborowsky, 1985). As indicated earlier, the laws were criticized widely by opponents of mandatory reporting legislation. Even before many of the laws were passed, Katz (1979) warned about using the laws as an attempt to solve problems. Drawing parallels to the weaknesses of child abuse mandatory reporting laws, Katz (1979) notes that if much of the abuse was truly caused by stress, as was the widespread belief at that time, then laws should be directed toward preventing the pressures leading to stress. She also argues, as do others, that the laws are ageist because they assume incompetence on the part of the victim. In essence, she warned that more harm than good would come from reporting acts, most of which victims did not want reported. Crystal (1986) points out that people already know the acts are occurring and that reporting would not necessarily stop an abusive situation.

Others are also less than optimistic about mandatory reporting laws as they note that the fact that individuals are not able to agree on what constitutes abuse makes reporting problematic (Anetzberger et al., 1996; Ehrlich & Anetzberger, 1991; Faulkner, 1982). Faulkner (1982) notes that the laws do little to meet the real needs of victims. Further, Ehrlich, and Anetzberger (1991) report that mandatory reporting laws are somewhat ambiguous. In fact, a survey of all states' departments of health conducted by Ehrlich and Anetzberger (1991) revealed that many states had done very little to implement mandatory reporting laws.

A related concern has to do with the fact that some people are uneasy about reporting because the laws are not truly confidential (Burg, 1997; Ehrlich & Anetzberger, 1991; Faulkner, 1982). Reporters are immune from liability so long as the report is made in good faith. If they fail to report, however, they could be held liable under the law. As an example, if a doctor or hospital has reason to suspect abuse but returns the elderly person to a dangerous environment without reporting abuse, then the health care provider could be held accountable (Pavlov & Murov, 1994). At the same time, doctors recognize that harm may come from reporting. The victim might confide in the doctor, asking him or her not to tell anyone. Reporting laws basically supercede confidential communications that have been recognized between patient and physician for centuries (Burg, 1997; Faulkner, 1982). Despite immunity against liability, health care providers still fear defamation suits. It's not that they fear the outcome of the case, as the law is designed to protect them for reporting in good faith; rather, the lawsuit itself could be time consuming and costly to battle (Medical Economics, 1997).

Another important point about the mandatory reporting laws is that they will be effective only to the extent that mandatory reporters choose to report suspected cases of abuse (Ehrlich & Anetzberger, 1991). As written, some argue that the mandatory reporting laws are ineffective either because mandatory reporters do not know they are supposed to report or they disagree with the philosophy of the law (Anetzberger et al., 1993; Tilden et al., 1994).

Another issue is that victims will go out of their way to make sure that signs of abuse cannot be identified. Consider a case in which an older woman was regularly victimized by her grandnephew. He stole her Social Security checks and physically abused her. One incident was so violent that the woman's leg was broken. When seeking medical treatment, rather than explaining what really happened, the woman told medical officials that she fell (Thomas, 2003). If victims are not wanting their victimization recognized, additional barriers to implementation of mandatory reporting laws arise.

These criticisms do not necessarily mean that mandatory reporting legislation should be repealed. Various changes have been suggested to improve reporting. Wolf and Pillemer (1989) note that because the laws were passed without any funding, the laws were destined for failure. They suggest that increased funding to educate about the laws would lead to increases in reporting. A more recent critique of mandatory reporting laws by Moskowitz (1998) calls for a number of programmatic and legislative changes to increase reporting. First, he argues that reporters must be better trained in identifying abuse. Second, he argues that civil penalties need to be imposed more regularly on professionals who fail to report elder abuse. Third, he suggests that institutions that employ professionals who fail to report abuse should be held accountable and sanctioned. Finally, he points out that professional sanctions can be imposed on those who fail to report.

A final criticism that has been levied against the laws is offered by Faulkner (1982): "It is difficult to justify different treatment for those over an arbitrary age" (p. 87). Of course, any time victim rights legislation is passed, it will be met by opposition from groups who perceive such laws as a threat to the rights of criminal defendants. Clark (1994) points out that some see the elder abuse legislation as infringing on offenders' constitutional rights, placing burdens on the justice process and expanding the economic costs of doing justice. Countering these critics, some would argue the elder abuse victim-based legislation is completely justifiable and warranted. For instance, some states have altered the way elder abuse cases are handled in the courts by adapting priority scheduling for elder abuse cases, alternatives to live testimony, accommodations for sensory impairments, and enhanced penalties (National Center for Victims of Crime, 1995). These changes will be discussed in great detail in the next chapter.

CONCLUDING REMARKS

Recall the Vera Dixon case described at the beginning of this chapter. This case led to a study of the way Texas agencies handled elder abuse cases. The study, in turn, "had a pronounced impact on the lawmakers" (Chance, 1987, p. 25). Other isolated incidents have had long-term impacts as far as policy and legislation are concerned. For example, as a result of a case where rural health care providers had problems establishing guardianship for an elderly man who was being abused and neglected by his children, one community "took steps to make it easier to obtain guardianship for older adults whose welfare depends on it" (Dunning, 1994, p. 76). While society should continue to discourage elder abuse, there can be positive consequences arising out of horrific acts committed against seniors.

Indeed, other programs and polices have developed as a result of general concerns about elder abuse. The Coalition of Advocates for the Rights of Infirm Elderly (CARIE), for instance, was created to improve institutionalized adults' lives by taking measures to enhance their care, protect their rights, and ensure their autonomy (Menio, 1996). CARIE established a training program in 1989 that focused on reducing the level of stress caregivers, especially aides, experienced (Keller, 1996). The training entailed an eight-hour program that included educating about abuse, role playing, group work, and case discussion. Material covered included intervention strategies and a consideration of the issues about mandatory reporting laws. Keller reports that an evaluation of 216 aides who took the course showed significant improvements in the aides' perceptions about residents, which would reduce their likelihood of abuse. CARIE was also instrumental in getting a "special ombudsmen" appointed to "troubled nursing homes" in southeastern Pennsylvania (Menio, 1996, p. 67).

Another innovative program was created in 1981 at the Beth Israel Hospital in Boston, Massachusetts. Specifically, a multi-disciplinary hospital assessment team was created to enhance identification and assessment of suspected cases of abuse. The group includes three members—a clinical social worker, a nurse practitioner, and a doctor. Each member has special training in geriatrics and interacts with an advisory group including employees from the emergency department, home care department, and others who would have a high likelihood of encountering cases of elder abuse. The goals of the hospital assessment team are to provide consultation in cases involving elderly persons and to educate the staff about abuse and neglect (Matlaw & Spence, 1994).

Other important changes include innovative programs to reduce elderly persons' risks in their homes. Chatterton and Frenz (1994) describe the use of closed-circuit televisions in fifteen apartment buildings with high numbers of elderly residents as a means of preventing crime and reducing vulnerability. Surveys show that fear decreased among the residents after the closed-circuit televisions were installed.

As well, task forces have developed across the U.S. that include members from various groups such as attorneys, health care providers, police officers, social service employees, APS employees, religious leaders and so on. The task forces that have developed have been instrumental in defining and resolving problems. Also, by bringing members of different groups together, communication between the groups has been enhanced (Wolf, 1992).

The similarity between these programs is that a cooperative effort between various service professionals and seniors ultimately resulted in efforts that would reduce elderly persons' likelihood of victimization as well as minimize the consequences of victimization. Cooperation is certainly the key to the successful resolution of elder abuse cases. The idea of a cooperative effort certainly fits well within the ideals of gero-criminology.

Chapter 5

DETECTING, INVESTIGATING, AND RESPONDING TO CRIMES AGAINST ELDERLY PERSONS: A SYSTEM'S APPROACH

1. What systems are involved in responding to crimes against elderly persons?
2. What is the role of Adult Protective Services (APS) agencies in preventing and responding to elder abuse cases?
3. Compare and contrast the criminal justice system's approach to handling abuse with that of the civil justice system.
4. What is the role of the police in handling crimes against elderly persons?
5. What techniques do the police use to respond to crimes against elderly persons?
6. What is the prosecutor's role in elder abuse cases?
7. What legal obstacles must criminal justice officials overcome in dealing with crimes against elderly persons?
8. Should elder abuse cases be handled exclusively by agents outside of the justice system? Why or why not?

INTRODUCTION

A victim's experiences with those who respond to a criminal event can have a lasting effect on the victim. For example, years ago a woman who was repeatedly abused by her son-in-law told Breckman and Adelman (1988) the following about her victimization:

Well, anyway, an argument started and I went to call the police. My son-in-law went after me and picked me up and threw me in the air. I came flying down

150

and I hit the coffee table. My foot got cut, and it was bleeding a lot. Then he grabbed me by the throat and choked me. Finally I got away from him and I ran down to the corner and called the police. I stood outside until the police car came. (p. 127)

In this case, as in many others (Jerin & Moriarty, 1998), the police were the first contact the victim had with the criminal justice system. In fact, research shows that older victims will call the police more often than they will call any other agency in the family justice network (Lachs et al., 2001). Jerin and Moriarty (1998) note that the way police interact with the victim will often influence the victim's willingness to participate in the criminal justice process. But, the police are not the only agents involved in responding to crimes against elderly persons. In fact, compared to other social service employees, the police spend relatively little time with elder abuse cases. This does not diminish the importance of the role of the police as their impact on the treatment and recovery of the victim can be important and long lasting (Heisler, 1991; Quinn & Tomita, 1997). As Bradley (1996) notes: "There is no correct way of managing elder abuse. It is seldom appropriate for one person or agency to tackle the problem. Effective intervention will probably involve local authority social services, the health authority, and private and voluntary programs" (p. 548). Thus, investigators would include adult protective services (APS) employees, local law enforcement officers, Medicaid Fraud Control Units, and ombudsmen who receive and respond to reports about suspected cases of institutional abuse (Wolf, 1992). It follows that there are a number of systems involved in responding to crimes against elderly persons. These systems include the health care system, the social system, the educational system, the political system, adult protective services, the civil justice system, and the criminal justice system (see Figure 6). The last three will be discussed in great detail because they have the most direct involvement in crimes against elderly persons.

The other systems are significant for many reasons and interact with protective services and the civil and criminal justice systems in various ways. For example, through the passage of various types of legislation, the political system determines what actions will be labeled criminal, establishes sanctions for those acts, and directs funding toward those programs determined to be a priority (Friedrichs, 2003). The legislation that has been developed to protect older adults from abuse can be divided into four categories: (1) Elder Abuse/Adult Protective Services Laws; (2) Institutional Abuse Laws; (3) Long-Term Care Ombudsmen Program Laws; and (4) Criminal Laws. These laws are varied but focus on offering various types of legislative protection for older adults. In fact, a number of states have "made abuse of the elderly . . . a crime by statute" (Mathews, 1988, p. 658). Some of these protective service laws are criticized because they are seen as assuming that elderly victims are "incompetent

Health Care System	Educational System	Political System	Adult Protective Services
– detect	– research	– legislate	– protect victim
– intervene	– training	– establish	– offer support
– treat victim	– increased understanding	penalties	– intervene
		– funding	

Criminal Justice System
 – control crime
 – protect society
 – protect offender's rights

Civil Justice System
 – protect victim's rights
 – guardianship & conservator
 – lawsuits

Probation
 / – punish and treat offender
 /

Police -------------	Prosecutor ---------------	Courts ------------	Corrections ----------	Parole
– protect society	– represent state	– trier of fact	– punish offender	– reintegrate
– maintain order	– determine charges	– determine guilt	– rehabilitate	– treatment
– enforce law	– recommend sent.	– impose sanction	– protect society	

Figure 6. Systems involved in detecting, investigating, and responding to crimes against elderly persons.

Critical Thinking Questions:

1. Discuss how changes in the educational system might influence elder abuse.
2. How do the actions of the police influence the corrections subsystem?

and infantile" due to their age (Mathews, 1988, p. 676). Regarding funding priorities, research and programs directed toward crimes that target older adults (e.g., white-collar crimes) tend to receive less funding than research and programs directed toward other crimes (Friedrichs, 2003; Payne, 1998b).

The health care system responds to crimes against elderly persons in two distinct ways. First, in many states health care providers are required to report suspected cases of abuse to the authorities (Stiegel, 1995). However, research shows that health care providers vary in how they define abuse (Phillips & Rempusheski, 1986). Variation in definitions will lead to variations in the types of acts reported. Second, health care providers are involved in detecting and intervening in cases of elder abuse. As a consequence, members of the health care system are greatly involved in meeting the treatment needs of elderly crime victims.

An elderly victim's social system also responds to cases of elder abuse. On the one hand, the social system may detect and report suspected perpetrators (see Breckman & Adelman, 1988). After the victimization event, the social system can provide support to the elderly victim. The support might be minimal in that assistance is offered but not needed by the victim. In these cases, even low levels of emotional support can be provided for the victim. Or, members of the social system might be involved in counseling the victims, spending time with the victims, transporting them to various social service agencies, or helping them find legal assistance.

The educational system also responds to crimes against elderly persons. This system's response is slightly different than the other systems' responses in that more of an indirect and objective approach is taken in responding to the abuse. That is, members of the educational system who are involved in responding to crimes against elderly persons spend more of their time researching elder abuse-related issues than they do providing direct services to the victim. Indeed, those responding from the educational system generally adhere to a basic set of scientific principles in understanding crimes against elderly persons. The fact that there is less direct contact with victims does not diminish the role of the educational system; rather, increased understanding can lead to better responses, improved training for members of the other systems, and new ways to help older crime victims.

As noted, the adult protective services and the civil and criminal justice systems have more direct contact with elderly victims. In part, this is due to the fact that these systems are specifically designed to handle harmful acts. Though their designs are similar in nature, the purposes of the systems are distinct. Table 12 outlines similarities and differences in the three programs. For instance, the criminal justice system is designed to protect society, safeguard the rights of the accused, prove guilt, and punish offenders convicted of committing criminal acts. The civil justice system is designed as an instrument through which individuals can bring suit against others for harmful acts that may or may not be defined as criminal in a setting where the level of proof is lower and defendants are not afforded the same level of procedural safeguards. Adult protective services is designed to protect older or disabled adults who are in need of protection (Byers & Hendricks, 1993).

In a way, although these are three separate entities, from a system's perspective it is possible that the way that the three agencies interact in handling elder abuse cases represents a relationship that can be perceived as one broader system (see Van Gigch, 1978). According to Van Gigch (1978), a system is "an established arrangement of components that functions together according to plan" (p. 27). Indeed, each system (component) contributes to the other systems (components) with cases being resolved either in one system, two systems, or each of the systems. For example, APS may investigate an allegation, substantiate that the case occurred, and recommend a solution to the abuse without bringing the case to the attention of the other systems.

**TABLE 12. SIMILARITIES AND DIFFERENCES IN SYSTEMS
WITH DIRECT CONTACT WITH ELDERLY PERSONS**

	System		
	Adult Protective Services	*Civil Justice System*	*Criminal Justice System*
Who brings charges	APS worker or Mandatory reporter	Victim	Prosecutor/Gov't
Due process guarantees	Minimal	Medium	Extreme
Purpose	Protect Victim	Resolve private disputes	Punish offender for violating criminal law
Sanctions	Not applicable	Monetary damages	Incarceration, fines, probation, etc.
Primary rationale	Protection	Restitution	Punishment or deterrence
Secondary rationale	Deter crime, restore family	Punish perpetrator	Treatment, reintegration
Focus on elderly victim	Primary	Minimal focus	Minimal focus

Adapted from Stevens and Payne (1999).

Critical Thinking Questions:

1. How do the goals of each system influence the victim's experiences with the system?
2. What is more important–punishment or deterrence? Explain.

Such a closed system approach is actually common in APS agencies (Byers & Hendricks, 1993). Or, APS could investigate and send the case to the civil or criminal justice system, or both (Wolf, 1992).

Before continuing, a few points about process are important. First, there is tremendous variation in the way various states process elder abuse cases. For example, in one-third of the states, law enforcement is given the primary responsibility for investigating allegations of elder abuse. In the other states, the investigative function is performed by a state social service agency (Daniels et al., 1999). Also, each state has its own procedures for the way the elder abuse cases should be handled. The process discussed here is based on a general description that is meant to serve as an ideal type rather than a concrete rule. Further, I will discuss the elder abuse reporting process as if the cases flow from one stage to the next. In reality, there is often overlap in the stages with some occurring simultaneously, some being skipped, and some occurring in an order different than I describe. For purposes of clarity, however, it is important that these stages are noted separately. In general, these stages can be described as: (1) the incident occurs; (2) it is reported to APS; (3) APS investigates; (4) APS makes recommendations; (5) if reported to police, police undertake a prearrest investigation; (6) arrest; (7) booking; (8) intake; (9) arraignment; (10) information or indictment; (11) preliminary hearing; (12) trial; (13) sanction; (14) release to community. Cases that are referred to the civil justice system will follow a slightly different process. What follows is an overview of the three systems that have a great deal of direct contact with elder abuse victims: Adult Protective Services, Criminal Justice System, and Civil Justice System.

ADULT PROTECTIVE SERVICES AND ELDER ABUSE

Every state has legislation giving the state authority to "protect and provide services to vulnerable, incapacitated or disabled adults" (Wolf, 1992, p. 27). Three-fourths of the states use units referred to as "Adult Protective Services" (APS) to receive and screen allegations of abuse. Every other state, except Indiana, gives the department of aging the responsibility of receiving reports. In Indiana, the criminal justice system and the aging department work together in receiving the reports (Wolf, 1992). The Indiana model has been shown to be somewhat effective in promoting cooperation among the various actors (Dolon & Hendricks, 1989). For the other states, the APS or elder abuse programs are generally placed within state human services or social services agencies (Wiehe, 1998). In at least twenty one states, APS workers are also given the responsibility of investigating child abuse cases. One issue that arises in these states is whether knowledge about elder abuse is sacrificed because investigators need to focus much of their attention on child abuse investigations (Jogerst et al., 2001).

The laws of forty-two states stipulate that suspected cases of abuse must be reported to the appropriate authorities, which generally is APS or the equivalent unit. Though there is no universal definition of protective services (Zborowsky, 1985), Mathews (1988) notes that APS involves "a system of services–preventive, supportive, and surrogate–aimed at the elderly or other disabled persons, living in the community to enable them to maintain independent living . . . while at the same time protecting them from abuse and exploitation" (p. 667). The history of APS is traced to 1958 "when the National Council on Aging created an ad hoc committee of social workers" to determine the services older adults needed (Mixson, 1996, p. 14). Mixson (1996) notes that the belief that there was a need for agencies to protect older adults did not catch on until 1975 when Congress stipulated in Title XX of the Social Security Act that states must provide protective services to children, elderly persons, and disabled individuals in order to receive Title XX funds. Not surprisingly, today all states have some form of services available to protect older adults.

APS employees are expected to investigate allegations of abuse, intervene in substantiated cases, and help and support the victim (Harshbarger, 1989). In many ways, the expectations for APS workers mirror the public's expectations for law enforcement officers. Both groups are expected to investigate and substantiate whether wrongful acts occurred. Two differences are noteworthy. First, APS workers are guided by a social casework model while criminal justice employees follow a legal approach (Johnson, Sigler, & Crowley, 1994). Second, and along a related line, APS workers would be involved in investigating a host of different acts, both criminal and non-criminal, while criminal justice officials would direct their efforts towards investigating only those acts which could be legally defined as criminal. Unfortunately, a lack of trust between criminal justice employees and social service employees potentially hinders collaboration and effective responses to elder abuse (Reulbach & Tewksbury, 1994). As Quinn (1985) writes: "Social workers may view attorneys as cold, uncaring, ivory tower people who do not want needy elders to receive services. Attorneys, on the other hand, may see social workers as meddlesome" (p. 23). Sengstock and Barett (1986) appear to agree, writing that lawyers "look to the law to try to solve problems, and social agency personnel try to encourage people to try to change their lifestyle to a more satisfactory one" (p. 58).

As far as the investigation process, APS investigators will receive allegations of abuse from various sources including victims, witnesses, health care providers, social workers, ombudsmen, or any other mandatory reporters (Phillips & Rempusheski, 1986; Lachs, 1995; Wolf, 1992). Cases reported to APS, or the departments of aging, are screened to see if the act is one which should be handled by their agency. Investigations are conducted to substantiate the allegation. Deciding if abuse is present is not an easy task because there is a lingering societal belief that these acts do not occur, and there has been little guidance concerning ways to detect elder abuse cases (Rathbone-McCaun & Voyles, 1982). There are several other constraints that limit detection and subsequent intervention by social service investigators. Phillips and Rempusheski (1986) have identified four of these constraints. First, there are difficulties in proving that abuse occurred. Second, victims and families are often reluctant to participate in the processing of abuse cases. Third, reporters of abuse experience role constraints in that they want to help the victim but realize that in some cases reporting may do more harm than good. Finally, there may indeed be negative consequences as a result of the investigation.

Forrest et al. (1990) describe some of these negative consequences. As an example, the victim might be removed from the home and institutionalized in a nursing home or adult care center, something that the victim could see as worse than the abuse. Others suggest that a fear of institutionalization may keep some victims from reporting cases of abuse (Breckman & Adelman,

1988). Or, if the victim is not removed, the abuse will continue and perhaps get worse if the perpetrator knows he or she has been reported to the authorities. Further, if the caregiver is punished or forced into a treatment program that he or she sees as unfair or punitive, the caregiver may retaliate against on the victim (see Sherman, 1993). Even so, many cases are substantiated and resolved in ways helpful to the victim and the perpetrator.

Sharon (1991) analyzed 2,489 elder abuse cases reported to Wisconsin's Elder Abuse Reporting System in 1988 and 1989 to see what factors contributed to case substantiation. Findings of Sharon's study show that cases that were more likely to result in substantiation were physical and emotional abuse cases, those from rural areas, those referred by criminal justice professionals or human services employees, and ones where victims lived alone or had some high-risk characteristic (e.g., Alzheimer's). Abusers in the substantiated cases tended to be spouses, sons, and other relatives who were also in high-risk categories. Interestingly, those whose cases were substantiated were more likely to refuse services than those whose cases were not substantiated.

While Sharon (1991) examined factors contributing to substantiation, Neale et al. (1997) considered the reasons for case closure in 2,670 cases of elder abuse in Illinois. Six reasons were cited by Neale et al. First, in about a third of the cases, it was determined that the victim was no longer at risk. In about 20 percent of the cases, the victim was placed in a long-term care home or program. Third, the victim moved away in some of the cases. Fourth, some cases were referred to as administrative closures, which entail instances where abuse is not repeated for fifteen months after the initial report. Fifth, the victim refused services in about 12 percent of the cases. Finally, the victim's death was the reason for closure in slightly over 10 percent of the cases.

Shiferaw et al. (1994) found a very low substantiation rate in a rural county in North Carolina. Specifically, of the 123 cases reported and investigated over a three-year time frame, only twenty-three were substantiated as elder abuse. They further point out that the unconfirmed cases "were more likely to reside in a nursing home and/or to be ill" (p. 123). Certainly, illnesses, ailments, and many risk factors make it difficult for the APS worker to establish whether the abuse occurred. Nonetheless, an investigation in and of itself may be enough to stop harmful acts if they are indeed occurring (Heisler, 1991).

Once the case is substantiated, the service worker develops a care plan for the victim. The care plan entails actual decisions about what should be done with the case. The possible outcomes include finding the victim emergency shelter, admitting the victim to the hospital, calling the police, sending the case to the district attorney, or arranging for home care (Wolf, 1992). Caution is taken to find the "least restrictive alternative" so that the victim is not revictimized by the service worker's care plan (Quinn & Tomita, 1997).

It is important to stress that APS investigators are different from police investigators. Police investigators generally investigate for evidence of criminal behavior. APS investigators "investigate for the identification of service needs" (Bergeron, 2000, p. 46). Consequently, different strategies would be used in the two different types of investigations and different results would stem from each as well.

Consider a case in which a daughter tied her mother who had been diagnosed with Alzheimer's to chairs or the bed in order to keep her from roaming around. When an APS worker became aware of this practice, she confronted the caregiver. In the words of the APS worker:

> I informed her that a report would be made to Elderly Protective Services and that a caseworker would be visiting the residence. I also told her that I wasn't making the report because I believed she was intentionally doing anything that would harm her mother, as I honestly didn't. I believed that she and her mother needed assistance. (Ridge, 2002: np)

APS agencies are forced to overcome a number of obstacles in determining the appropriate care plan. For example, they have low budgets and are understaffed with high caseloads (Mixson, 1996). Mixson (1996) also points out that it is often difficult for the service employees to find the right legal assistance needed by the victim. Further, Mixson (1996) argues that social service employees need a great deal of knowledge to effectively communicate with other professionals involved in handling elder abuse cases. These other professionals include doctors, nurses, psychologists, counselors, police officers, prosecutors, judges, defense attorneys, and a host of other actors. APS officials will have to work with police officers, judges, attorneys, and other criminal justice officials in order to criminally or civilly prosecute the elder abuse case.

THE CRIMINAL AND CIVIL JUSTICE SYSTEMS AND ELDER ABUSE

In the early to mid-eighties, cases of elder abuse tended to be handled for the most part within APS agencies (Myers & Shelton, 1987). The "criminalization" of elder abuse began in the late eighties when experts realized that keeping the family together was not always best for the victim (Heisler, 1991; Stiegel, 1995; Wolf, 1992). Thus, it has only been within the last decade or so that the legal system has begun its active involvement in the battle against elder abuse. As Stiegel (1996) writes, "Interest in the pursuit of legal remedies for elder abuse is expanding" (p. 39). Even so, there has been reluctance on the part of victims and social service employees to rely heavily on the justice process for resolving wrongful acts against elderly persons. Several reasons for this reluctance have been suggested in the literature.

First, some point out that elderly victims are ashamed to report the acts because they feel that they have lost control over their lives and that they are somehow to blame for the perpetrator's actions (Burby, 1994; Dolon & Hendricks, 1989; Harshbarger, 1989; Mathews, 1988). Second, victims may fear repercussions or future abuse from the perpetrator (Dolon & Hendricks, 1989; Mathews, 1988; Myers & Shelton, 1987). Third, as Quinn (1990) and Dolon and Hendricks (1989) note, some victims deny that the acts were abusive, or wrong, in nature. Fourth, victims fear that they may be moved into a different, and less suitable, environment (Mathews, 1988; Stiegel, 1995). Moving the older victim is seen as a punishment by the victim, rather than as a solution to the problem (Myers & Shelton, 1987). Fifth, some recognize that they may experience re-victimization at the hands of the justice system (Mathews, 1988). Sixth, many do not want to implicate family members because they fear losing their caregivers and ending up in need of more care (Reulbach & Tewksbury, 1994; Mathews, 1988). Seventh, the physical condition of the victim may make it difficult for him or her to communicate with justice officials (Burby, 1994). Finally, negative attitudes about the criminal justice system keep many victims from using the services offered by the justice system (Stiegel, 1995). What it comes down to is a belief on the part of victims, and some social service providers, that criminal justice intervention will do more harm than good.

Nonetheless, many parts of the legal system have been effective in dealing with crimes against elderly persons, but there certainly is room for improvement. To consider the criminal justice system's response, this discussion will be broken down into three sub-systems: the police, courts, and corrections (Van Gigch, 1978). When discussing the courts and corrections, ideas from both justice systems (e.g., criminal and civil) will be incorporated. Keep in mind that the discussion about process is meant to consider the various phases of the justice process and is not to suggest that the phases occur in isolation, or in a consistent order for that matter. Also realize that once a case enters the justice system, whether an elder abuse case or any other case, it can be dropped out of the justice process at any point for any number of reasons. In most cases, the police are the gatekeepers of the criminal justice process.

THE POLICE AND CRIMES AGAINST ELDERLY PERSONS

Law enforcement officers have an extremely important role in elder abuse cases. As well, with a higher percentage of elderly persons expected in the future, it is expected that police will get more calls to assist elderly individuals

(Chermak, 1993). Their role, in part, is determined by their broader roles as police officers. In particular, James Q. Wilson (1968) has argued that the role of the police entails order maintenance, community service, and law enforcement. He, and others, point out that police officers spend much more of their time maintaining order and providing community service than they do enforcing the law. This is particularly true when crimes against elderly persons are considered. Police will spend much of their time protecting potential elderly victims (e.g., maintaining order) and providing information about ways elderly persons can protect themselves (e.g., community service). Of course, they will spend some of their time enforcing the law, which would include responding to, or searching for, actual allegations of crimes against elderly persons. What follows is an overview of the way that police officers have responded to the needs of elderly persons to respond to or prevent criminal acts. Also included will be some suggestions for improving the way that police officers respond to elder abuse case. (See Box 5.1, Voices in the Field: Policing and the Older Population for a former police officer's views about elder abuse).

19   Police officers become aware of crimes against elderly persons in one of two ways. The first, reactive policing, entails instances where police are told about a crime by a particular source. For crimes against elderly persons, the potential sources include victims, witnesses, APS workers, ombudsmen, other law enforcement officials who may not have jurisdiction over the case, health care providers, private investigators, or any other mandatory reporter. The second way, called proactive policing, entails instance where law enforcement officers actively seek out the criminal acts on their own. Undercover policing is an example of proactive policing and is a method that has been used to detect various crimes against elderly persons.

20   Prior to the late eighties, police were not actively involved in responding to crimes against elderly persons. In fact, a 1988 survey sponsored by the Police Executive Research Forum (PERF) showed that police lacked knowledge about the appropriate response to elder abuse, and that law enforcement officers received very little training in how to detect or respond to elder abuse cases. Based on this, PERF encouraged all police departments "to treat all reports of violence against elderly persons as high-priority criminal activity, without regard to the victims' and abusers' relationships" (Plotkin, 1996, p. 29). By the early nineties, it seemed that PERF's recommendations were being implemented by police departments. In 1994, the National Institute of Justice surveyed criminal justice officials to determine systemic needs and issues. The ensuing report, called the National Assessment Program, showed that eighty-eight of police chiefs and seventy-eight of sheriffs indicated that their departments had taken measures to prevent crimes against elderly persons, with education being the most common measure (*FBI Law Enforcement Bulletin*, 1995).

BOX 5.1. VOICES IN THE FIELD: THE EMOTIONAL IMPLICATIONS OF CALLS INVOLVING OLDER RESIDENTS

These days the number of people over the age of sixty-five is increasing. People are living longer. Due to our highly mobile society, many of these people are living with no family support group in the area. Their children may have re-located to other parts of the country for jobs or the seniors may have moved to a retirement community. Consequently, police officers are going to be encountering more and more seniors without support groups to help them in times of need.

The police can work together with the community to develop programs that will reduce the stress for seniors as well as for the officers handling some of these emotional calls. This approach fits in well with the current emphasis on community policing and in fact many departments have worked to expand their community policing efforts to include the aging population. Understanding the challenges and issues of the aging population will make it easier for officers to effectively handle their calls for service.

My police career was spent in South Florida where there was a high population of seniors. Many calls for service involved these seniors and the dynamics of these calls were often different from the calls involving younger people. Initially, it was difficult to understand the emotions or reactions encountered on "routine" calls. With increased time on the road, I realized that these situations involved more than the "call for service" and I was witnessing emotions related to the aging process brought on by the implications of these calls for the older individual.

Traffic accidents are a good example. I found that at the scene of a fairly minor crash, older residents could be extremely emotional and upset or angry and defensive. Their reactions often seemed totally out of proportion for the nature of the incident. But, I found that older people often interpreted being involved in an accident as a sign of physical deterioration or a lessening of their driving ability, rather than as a mistake or error in judgment. They felt their driving privilege might be at risk. The thought of losing this independence is extremely frightening to seniors. If officers are aware of this, they will understand and anticipate these reactions to a minor accident.

We also frequently responded to unattended death calls involving older residents. We investigated the scene and handled the paperwork and notifications. This often took place with a distraught spouse at the scene and no other family support available. Spouses were reacting not only to the death of their life partner but also perhaps to a loss of identity and lifestyle. What would they do? Where would they live? Would they have to go into a nursing home? These questions ran through their minds as they faced the death of their loved one.

I remember a death I handled that was a natural death of a seventy-five-year-old man. His wife was distraught and worried about where she would live and with whom, as her children all lived up north. Would her children allow her to live alone? Would she have to move up north? Would she be allowed to keep on driving? Would she be able to keep her dog? What about all her friends? Would her children put her in a nursing home? Would she die alone?

Luckily, it was a slow night and I was able to spend time with her. I had notified her children and they were enroute to Florida and her friends in the community were going to stay with her until they arrived. Even though I had made these provisions, it was hard to leave. Every time I tried to leave she jumped up and grabbed my arm and started crying. "Please don't leave me, please don't leave me all alone. I don't know what to do. I need you." It was a difficult situation. But, I eventually had to go back to the street and leave her in the hands of her friends. It was emotionally draining for me and weighed heavily on my heart.

This was not necessarily an unusual case and it can be difficult to understand these emotional outbursts. I think it would help if officers received training in gerontology or the aging process. They would be better equipped to understand the challenges and issues of aging. This knowledge and understanding would help them to be more sensitive to what the older citizens are going through and make the situation less stressful for the officers as they are more prepared and better able to handle the situations.

Linda Forst is a retired Police Captain from Boca Raton Florida. She spent the majority of her career in Road Patrol. She is the author of *The Aging of America: A Handbook for Police Officers,* as well as numerous journal and magazine articles. She earned her doctorate from Florida Atlantic University in Boca Raton, Florida. She is currently a professor of criminal justice at Shoreline Community College in Seattle, Washington.

Around the same time, PERF developed a training curriculum called "Innovative Training Package for Detecting and Aiding Victims of Domestic Elder Abuse." The curriculum included modules designed to enhance law enforcement officers' understanding about the nature of elder abuse, the nature of the aging process, the police role in the social service network, and the legal, ethical, and practical issues that guide decision making in elder abuse cases (Plotkin, 1996). One of the problems police often encounter in elder abuse cases is a lack of evidence (Wiehe, 1998). PERF tries to address this problem through its training curriculum.

To effectively handle crimes against elderly persons, police must be familiar with the different forms of abuse, the identifying factors, the sanctions under laws, and the social services available to the victim and perpetrator (Plotkin, 1996). As such, the police role in elder abuse cases can be characterized as involving *assessment, enforcement,* and *support and referral* (Dolon &

Hendricks, 1989). Each of these areas will affect the outcome of the case. Further, although these are areas that arise in all cases handled by police officers, different tactics are needed, and distinct issues arise, in handling crimes against elderly persons.

Assessment

Assessment entails determining if the abuse occurred, if it is criminal in nature, and who committed the abusive act. In most cases, the police will have to interview the victim to address these questions. Many argue that interviews of elderly victims should be done differently than they would be done with other victims (Quinn & Tomita, 1997; Formby, 1996). For example, Quinn & Tomita (1997) recommend that, where feasible, police should wear plain clothes to interview elderly victims because the police uniform tends to intimidate elderly victims. Other tips have been offered by PERF (1993) to assist in interviewing those who are hearing impaired. PERF's tips include the following:

1. Ask the victim if he or she prefers written communication or an interpreter.
2. Do not stand in front of a window or other source of light.
3. Establish eye contact before speaking.
4. Use a light touch on the arm or shoulder to get the person's attention.
5. Never speak directly into the person's ear.
6. Speak slightly louder than you normally would.
7. Include the victim in all discussions about him or her.
8. Use open-ended questions, not questions that can be answered with yes or no.
9. Use visual aides where appropriate. (Improving the Police Response to Domestic Elder Abuse, 1993, as cited in *Preventing Abusive Behaviors,* 1999)

Formby (1996) also describes interviewing tips that can be used specifically for elderly victims. In particular, he describes what is called the Progressive Interviewing Technique (PRINT). This technique, he suggests, is guided by the following five rules:

1. Use broad questions so answers aren't leading.
2. Less talking by the interviewer results in more talking by the victim.
3. Avoid specific questions.
4. Don't answer interviewees questions because you might share with them what answer is expected and you may lose control of the interview–simply restate the question.
5. Most people won't lie but may not tell the whole truth.

Using these principles as a guide, Formby (1996) points out there are five stages in interviewing. First, he says that police officers must assess the interviewees' non-verbal cues (their facial features, whether they are sweating, etc.). Second, the actual interview is conducted. The third stage entails cultivating the story—trying to get information that has been omitted. The fourth stage is analyzing the story to see if the notions are consistent or inconsistent. He points out, for example, if the suspect refers to the victim as an "old lady," then the suspect probably has little respect for the victim. Finally, the police officer closes the interview in various ways, including eliciting a confession, making an arrest, or trying to get the help for the victim. Closing the interview relates to the next role of police officers in elder abuse cases—enforcement.

Enforcement

Enforcement entails making decisions about whether to report the case to APS (assuming the case was not referred from APS), whether to arrest the offender suspected of committing the abuse, and when to make the arrest. In essence, police use their discretion to make a decision about what should be done with the case.

As far as whether they report the case to APS or not, recent research by Daniels et al. (1999) shows that about half of the officers surveyed reported abuse and neglect and roughly 40 percent reported exploitation cases. Based on their findings, they suggest that mandatory reporting laws are not effective in forcing police officers to share information with APS. Others also note that law enforcement officers do not generally share information about the elder abuse cases they see with APS (Reulbach & Tewksbury, 1994).

There are no figures available that describe the number of cases that result in an arrest as compared to the number of elder abuse cases that police drop out of the criminal justice system. Daniels et al. (1999) point out that the police could not make arrests in all cases of elder abuse because the system, as overcrowded as it is already, would not be able to process all of the cases. Likewise, police must decide if an arrest is in the best interest of the victim who might end up in a nursing home (Plotkin, 1996). So, discretion is used to decide which cases are handled criminally. In financial exploitation cases, for example, some police may see the cases as civil matters "because documents, canceled checks, or contracts are involved" (Mathis, 1994, p. 4). Therefore, they may decide not to arrest in these cases.

Another decision about arrest centers on the timing of the arrest. One nursing home's policy is to request that police arrest suspected perpetrators during shift changes so that maximum exposure is provided to the other employees (Glanz, 1994). Not all nursing homes, however, are this cooperative with the police. Fiesta (1996) describes a case where nurses saw a nurse's aide having sexual intercourse with an eighty-three-year-old woman. The police were not notified until seven hours later and then were notified only at the insistence of the victim's family.

If the police do arrest the perpetrator, police officers will influence the decision as to the type of statute that will be used to prosecute the perpetrator (Daniels et al., 1999). In particular, law enforcement will help decide whether to prosecute under regular criminal statutes, domestic violence statutes, or elder mistreatment statutes. What happens is the "patrol officer becomes a gatekeeper controlling the flow of cases into the social services or the law enforcement system" (Daniels et al., 1999, p. 212). So, whether an arrest is made or not, the police role in elder abuse cases is not completely fulfilled without some sort of support and referral.

Support and Referral

The third area, support and referral, is an area where police are expected to do things they may not do in other crimes. For example, in responding to a robbery, a police officer does not necessarily need to refer the victim to any social services. In an elder abuse case, however, the police officer is expected to find a way to resolve the problem in a way that brings minimal harm to the victim. This may involve finding support and referral services for the victim. Unfortunately, "The victim-police encounter is governed mostly by the needs of the officer, not the victim" (Jerin and Moriarty, 1998, p. 37). Even so, police are expected to do what they can to find help for the elderly victim.

Finding support and offering the right referral is not an easy task. Describing the problems involved, O'Riordan (1990) writes:

> My own experience as a trainer for law enforcement can verify the frustration felt by the police officer trying to find appropriate services for a victim of elder abuse after regular working hours. Few response systems recognize that abuse does not occur between 9AM and 5PM. Abuse is more likely to happen when the abuse has extended contact with the victim, the time spent together after work and on the weekend. (p. 153)

Yet, police are still expected to find the best services for the victims. Research shows that police officers whose responsibility it is to handle only crimes against elderly persons are more effective in meeting this task (Gurnack & Zevitz, 1993). Many states and local police departments have developed and used these "specialized police units" to deal with elder abuse cases. The following provides an overview of some of these police units.

Medicaid Fraud Control Units

Medicaid Fraud Control Units (MFCUs) exist in forty-seven states and are given the duty of detecting, investigating, and prosecuting cases of patient abuse that are committed by providers who receive Medicaid funding (Payne & Cikovic, 1995; Hodge, 1998). As such, they are "the nation's primary law enforcement units responsible for patient abuse investigations and prosecutions" (Hodge, 1998, p. 25).

The federal statutory model for MFCUs was based on New York's appointment of an Independent Special Prosecutor to detect and prosecute nursing home fraud and abuse in 1975. The original office in New York included lawyers, investigators, and auditors who were separate from the Medicaid program (Kuriansky, 1992). MFCUs were then created in 1978 with most units a part of the Office of Attorney General of Chief State's Attorney (Hodge, 1998). In New York alone, where the units originated, the office recovered over 130 million dollars in fines, restitution, and overpayments in its first fifteen years of existence (Kuriansky, 1992). Across the United States, the units have successfully prosecuted over 8,000 cases and have recovered millions as a result of fraud and abuse prosecutions (Hodge, 1998).

MFCUs employ traditional policing techniques to detect and investigate abuse. However, reviewing and analyzing patients' records can be a tedious and complex task (Payne & Cikovic, 1995). To substantiate cases of abuse, some states' fraud control units and attorney generals are beginning to rely more on undercover agents in detecting and prosecuting cases. One unit, for example, placed an undercover nurse in a doctor's office to see if the doctor was overbilling Medicaid (Payne & Berg, 1997). In Arkansas, "undercover operatives kept diaries of their activities and their information was made public to increase awareness of the problems in nursing homes" (Hodge, 1998, p. 36).

Speaks (1995) describes his own experiences as an undercover investigator posing as a nurse's aide in a nursing home in Philadelphia. One of the lessons he learned before he was even hired was that undercover agents' duties are to record and report everything they see or hear. More importantly, he notes that undercover agents should not "pass judgement or form opinions based on [their] observations" (p. 38). Before entering targeted nursing homes, agents must be certified as nurse's aides, or some other health care provider. This includes attending classes and taking written and clinical tests. In some cases, the undercover agent may enter a reputable nursing home so they can gain practical experience in the field. Speaks (1995) did just this and points out that the experience he gained was useful in getting him hired in the targeted nursing home.

In addition to using the reputable home as a reference, the attorney general established a fictitious nursing home as a reference and included a phone number that, if called, would contact the caller directly with the Attorney General's Office. Speaks (1995) was easily hired into the targeted nursing home. One of the interesting role conflicts he experienced is captured in the following statement: "Despite the fact that I was an undercover agent, my first responsibility was to take care of the residents" (p. 40). Nevertheless, by jotting notes and taking pictures with a hidden camera, he was able to substantiate that the nursing home had engaged in serious forms of neglect. He writes:

> In some of the rooms, the air conditioners were not working so I brought in a thermometer to record the temperatures. One room which housed three male residents consistently had readings over 90 degrees. At the beginning of my shift, I frequently discovered these men restrained in bed sweating profusely. I gave them water, got them out of bed, and took them to the air-conditioned lounge. Not long after coming to that unit, an LPN told me one of these men had been taken to the hospital with pneumonia and that the heat had a definite impact on him. (p. 39)

He describes another example of neglect in more graphic terms: "I found a severely contracted black female who was moaning in pain. She was lying in a milky substance which I later learned was the contents of her colon draining out of a decubitus ulcer on her right hip" (Speaks, 1995, p. 44). He followed up on the case and learned that the wounds on the victim were due to "a lack of nourishment and not having been turned properly" (p. 44).

The case against the nursing home eventually ended in a conviction. Without the undercover operation, the evidence needed for conviction likely would have been missing from the case. In addition to the MFCUs and undercover operations used by various attorneys general, other specialized police units have also been successful in responding to crimes against elderly persons.

Triad

The AARP, International Association of Chiefs of Police, and the National Sheriff's Association developed the Triad concept in 1987 (Cantrell, 1994; Harpold, 1994). By the mid-nineties, there were Triad programs in 225 communities and 44 states (Cantrell, 1996). Today, there are over 600 Triad programs nationwide. Triad programs entail local police and sheriffs collaborating with representative elderly persons to deal with crimes against elderly persons. The programs are labeled Triad because of the three pronged effort–sheriffs, police chiefs, and the AARP. The idea is that collaboration will make the groups stronger, increase resources available to help elderly crime victims, and provide the groups with greater credibility in responding to the needs of elderly persons (Cantrell, 1994).

Once an agreement is formed between police, sheriffs, and elderly representatives, SALT (Seniors and Lawmen Working Together) councils are formed. Members might include individuals from senior centers, the health department, the department of aging, and APS employees. After having members attend a training session, surveys are conducted in the local community to determine the needs of elderly persons in that community (Cantrell, 1996). Surveys are a key component of the Triad/SALT effort because they use seniors from the community to alert law enforcement to ways that police can assist in meeting elderly persons' needs (Harpold, 1994). SALT programs vary from community to community. Some communities have established adopt-a-senior programs where deputies regularly visit certain elderly persons. Others have focused their efforts toward improving conditions in nursing homes (Cantrell, 1996). Stanus (1999) notes the initiatives of some other SALT programs:

1. Senior shoppers wanted more patrols in parking lots (Ohio).
2. Security gates around neighborhoods where a high percentage of elder persons lived were requested (Washington)
3. Low cost emergency lights were wanted in various places (New Jersey).
4. Seniors wanted emergency identification of inclement weather (Charlottesville).

The point is that every community's needs are different and the Triad/SALT initiative responds to those differences.

Another important focus of Triad is that the programs are designed to educate elderly persons, law enforcement officers, and businesses in a way to prevent crimes against elderly persons (Cantrell, 1994). For instance, Triad would encourage local banks to train their employees how to spot instances of financial exploitation against elderly persons more quickly. Likewise, the Triad concept is included in courses offered at the FBI Academy in Quantico, Virginia (Harpold, 1994). Related to the notion of education is the sub-discipline of law enforcement gerontology.

Law Enforcement Gerontology

According to Rykert (1994), law enforcement gerontology "is a branch of law enforcement science designed for addressing the particular crime-related problems of the aged" (p. 5). He describes three important functions performed by law enforcement gerontologists. First, law enforcement gerontologists work with seniors from the community to learn of their concerns and develop mechanisms and policies to address their concerns. Second, law enforcement gerontologists alert seniors about on-going scams that are targeting elderly persons. Third, they try to get elderly persons from the community involved in volunteer projects.

Rykert (1994) points out that training available to law enforcement gerontologists has increased in the nineties. In March, 1993, Illinois was the first state to train officers to specialize in this area. He also points out that the AARP offers various training programs to increase officers' understanding about elderly crime victims. Finally, he notes that the National Crime Prevention Institute in Louisville, Kentucky, offers a course to train law enforcement gerontologists. The course addresses demographics, myths of aging, abuse, fraud, and con games.

Local, Private, and Volunteer Efforts

Hundreds, if not thousands, of other specific local, private, and volunteer law enforcement efforts have been developed across the United States to assist elderly crime victims. A sampling of these efforts include *Rhode Island's Senior Citizen's Police Advocate Program, Norfolk's CARE Program, Los Angeles' Elder Person's Estate Unit, Senior Crime Stoppers,* and *volunteer programs*. There are plenty of other "senior crime units," but for brevity only these will be considered here.

First, the East Providence Rhode Island Police Department established the *Senior Citizen's Police Advocate Program* to deal with increases in the number of service calls from elderly persons. The program altered the way that police deal with elderly offenders and elderly victims (Gilfillan, 1994). The Senior Citizen Police Advocate acts as a liaison between the senior and the relevant social service agencies, in part because many calls police received were to deal with social problems confronting elderly residents. Advocates are able to collaborate with senior service employees to enhance service delivery to seniors (Cantrell, 1994). The advocate also spends time developing and presenting crime prevention programs, interacting with older persons, and educating them about ways to avoid being scammed. When initially implemented, the program was viewed as a win-win situation. Calls for police were reduced and elderly persons received better assistance (Gilfillan, 1994). After the development of this program, every department in Rhode Island was required to have a police advocate for seniors.

In Los Angeles, the LAPD developed the *Elder Person's Estate Unit (EPEU)* to investigate embezzlement of the elderly person's assets. The EPEU works with the Fiduciary Abuse Specialist Team (FAST). Together individuals representing the following groups work to investigate the fraud: APS, the Office of the Public Guardian, ombudsmen, law enforcement, district attorneys office, real estate brokers, and mental health professionals. The unit meets monthly and is involved in training others how to recognize and investigate abuse. Within a short period of time, the unit was instrumental in recovering over $30 million worth of stolen goods (Bruce, 1996). FAST, as a separate unit, "offers expert consultation to protective service workers on financial abuse cases" (Price & Fox, 1997, p. 69). FAST was created because APS workers were unable to effectively investigate and resolve complaints involving financial abuse. The unit serves as an investigation team and a deterrent (Aziz, 2000; Malks et al., 2002).

Senior Crime Stoppers is a private security program developed by Sedgwick. The program protects seniors against patient abuse, neglect, and other offenses that could occur in institutions. The program is designed to make seniors and their families feel safer, to reduce crime, and to lower lawsuits against institutions (*Risk Management,* 1998). The institutions pay a monthly fee to be a part of the program. If an incident occurs, Senior Crime Stoppers gets involved in investigating the incident through interviews and offers of financial rewards for tips leading to a substantiated case (*Risk Management,* 1998).

Volunteer programs are also used in some places to assist in detecting and investigating crimes against elderly persons. For example, a recent program instituted by the Health Care Financing Administration offers seniors awards of up to $1,000 for reporting suspected cases of fraud. Initial results suggest that the reporters are not concerned with the reward but simply want to help eliminate fraud in the Medicare system (Haugh, 1999). A related program in the Department of Health and Human Services trains retired professionals how to detect fraudulent billings submitted to either Medicaid or Medicare. The goal of the program is to get the trainees to share information with other seniors. The program was successful in recovering over $67 million for Medicare and $73 million in civil fines in its first year of implementation (Blecher, 1997).

A great deal of attention has been given to these "specialized senior police units." Evidence suggests that specialized units better meet the needs of elderly persons. For example, Gurnack and Zevitz (1993) surveyed elderly individuals who received services from a specialized police unit (n = 112) and elderly individuals who received services from traditional police officers (n = 112). They found that the first group had their needs met to a greater degree, received better care, and they were also more likely to see their neighborhood as safe. Though very little research has examined other specialized police units, logic suggests that being empathetic in handling older victims, as specialized police units would do, would certainly improve police-victim relations. This is particularly important because the way the victim perceives the police will influence whether the victim cooperates with actors in the courts.

THE COURTS AND CRIMES AGAINST ELDERLY PERSONS

In considering the courts and elderly victims, attention will be given to both criminal and civil courts. As noted earlier, cases can be heard in criminal courts, civil courts, or both. As well, law enforcement officials may officially refer the case to the prosecutor for criminal prosecution, or the police, with input from the elder's care team, may recommend that the victim seek restitution in civil court. In either case, the actors involved will fulfill various roles in the pursuit of case resolution. In criminal cases, the prosecutor is a central figure in directing the case through the criminal courts.

The Role of the Criminal Prosecutor

Prosecutors are often referred to as the chief law enforcement officer of a community. They are either elected or appointed, depending on state laws. Regardless, the position is political in nature and the successful resolution of criminal cases will result in reelection or reappointment. Losing too many cases, alternatively, sets the prosecutor up for losing the next election or not being reappointed once the current term expires. Prosecutors have the authority to select which cases to prosecute. Therefore, prosecutors tend to select cases in which they have a stronger likelihood of getting a conviction (Gottfredson & Gottfredson, 1988).

Successful prosecutions of elder abuse cases are also beneficial to others. As an example, successful convictions can lead to improved care provided by long-term care providers (Costen, 1996). Unfortunately, several barriers make it difficult to prosecute elder abuse cases. For instance, in many financial exploitation and theft cases, prosecutors must rely on a complex paper chase to substantiate their cases (Zuzga, 1996). Proving intent is difficult. Complicating matters even more are offenders' claims that the property was given to them by the victim (Quinn & Tomita, 1997).

Biggs et al. (1995) sees other barriers limiting elder abuse prosecutions. First, they point out that abuse, as conceptualized in APS and the literature, is not defined in legal terms. Second, they note that criminal justice officials, including some prosecutors, see the abuser (e.g., caregiver) as a victim of stress caused by the care the elderly person needed from the caregiver. Because some prosecutors see the caregiver as the victim, they choose not to prosecute the case. Third, they argue that a lack of training for both criminal justice professionals and social workers has limited the groups' abilities to work together in prosecuting elder abuse cases. Hodge (1998) agrees, pointing out that local prosecutors have little knowledge about elder abuse cases and subsequently give a low priority to these cases.

Zuzga (1996) describes additional barriers. For instance, she notes that the victim may die before the case (either financial exploitation or abuse) is detected. Without the victim, the prosecutor's case is more difficult to prove. Further, Zuzga (1996) points out that the prosecutor has to establish who the caregiver is in neglect cases. The parent may be suffering the consequences of the neglect, but who is the caregiver—the parent, who in many cases has a higher income, or the child, who has always relied on the parent? Also, she points out that it is hard to establish a cause and effect relationship between the crime and the consequences of victimization. This is an area that limits prosecutions in many types of white-collar crimes, not just those involving elderly persons (Friedrichs, 2003). But since the elderly are more likely to experience various physical ailments than younger persons, it is more difficult for prosecutors to show that the consequence was caused by an abusive act, be it physical abuse or exploitation (Zuzga, 1996). After all, injuries suffered by older adults could be caused by many events other than abuse.

Zuzga (1996) points out that prosecutors will face witness problems during the trial. It is difficult, for instance, to find expert witnesses willing to testify in elder abuse cases. Also, some victims may get confused and agree with everything the prosecutor and the defense attorney says. Memory problems resulting from the natural aging process, and from medications they may be taking, may also limit the witnesses' testimony. Further, elderly persons may be vague in their recollections, giving defense attorneys the opportunity to poke holes in their testimony. Zuzga (1996) also argues that elderly persons with communication problems may need special accommodations in testifying. As well, victims may be unwilling to face the defendant in court (Heisler, 1991). This unwillingness to be a witness results in a weak case for the prosecutor, who again may lose his or her job if too many cases result in an acquittal. Or, if prosecuted, there is a chance that the victim will be revictimized.

Heisler (1991) believes that the prosecutor can prosecute the case without re-victimizing the elderly victim. The key, she argues, is that professionals work with victims to make sure the victims are aware of the resources available to them, as well as the policies designed to protect them. These resources include:

1. Placing responsibilities of arrest, prosecution, and sentencing within the respective agencies;
2. Informing victims about support service;

3. Using special procedures for the elderly;
4. Using a vertical manner to prosecute the elder abuse cases–have the same prosecutor handle the case from beginning to end;
5. Provide the court with a range of sentencing alternatives; and,
6. Use protective orders to protect the victim.

Heisler (1991) and Quinn and Tomita (1997) further argue that the victim should not be given the burden of deciding if a case should be prosecuted. Heisler (1991) writes, "When the criminal justice system takes the responsibility for prosecuting the case for the victim, society makes it clear that the conduct is a public concern, not a mere private, family affair" (p. 7). As will be seen, the courts, both criminal and civil, have recently instituted various measures to try to limit the revictimization experienced by elderly victims.

Criminal Court Versus Civil Court

The word "court" refers to so many different things (Waldron et al., 1989). On the one hand, it is a building or a structure (e.g., the courthouse or the courtroom). On the other hand, the word refers to an actual part of the justice process (the court is in session). It may also refer to a person or a group of people (the court decided. . . .). Complicating it even more is the fact that every state has its own court system, and those state court systems are completely separate from the federal courts. In fact, we have a dual court system in the United States with independent judicial systems at the state level and the federal level. Important in the area of elder abuse cases, however, is the distinction between criminal and civil courts.

As far as process is concerned, the two courts are similar. Cases are argued in front of a judge or jury with rules and restrictions governing procedures in both criminal and civil courts. They take place in the same physical structure (e.g., "the courthouse") but have very different orientations and outcomes. For example, in criminal court cases, the local, state, or federal prosecutor brings the charges against the offender. In civil court cases, the victim, referred to as the plaintiff, brings the charges against the defendant. Also, due process procedural guarantees are more extensive in criminal cases, with civil cases being designed more to resolve private disputes. The sanctions are also different. A criminal court can impose sanctions such as incarceration, fines, and probation. The civil court most often awards monetary damages but can make decisions about competency, guardianship, and other elder abuse-related matters. Finally, the purpose of the criminal court is to punish offenders and deter future misconduct, whereas the primary purpose of civil courts is to make restitution to the victim (Stevens & Payne, 1999).

Historically, the courts have not had a great deal of experience in elder abuse cases (Stiegel, 1995). Nonetheless, theoretically, elder abuse cases could be handled in both courts. In fact, Quinn and Tomita (1997) predict that "more cases of elder maltreatment will be simultaneously handled by both systems as civil and criminal agencies work more cooperatively" (p. 140). Presently, judges will hear the following kinds of elder abuse cases: (1) criminal assault, battery, rape, or theft; (2) civil fraud or conversion matters; (3) personal injury cases; (4) guardianship or conservatorship; (5) mental health commitment; (6) special protective proceedings initiated through APS; (7) cases deciding about health care for incapacitated adults; and (8) criminal or civil cases about institution's care in the nursing homes or other places (Stiegel, 1995).

#32   Variations in state law in elder abuse cases exist with differences in whether the court with jurisdiction is established by law, whether the case can continue after a victim's death, and whether traditional videotape or hearsay rules are relaxed (Stiegel, 1995). In California, court dates are expedited for elderly victims, and if the victim dies, the case, by law, can continue (Heisler, 1991). The next state to implement such a law was Arizona where the State Supreme Court ruled that families of abused elderly persons can recover damages for pain and suffering even after the death of the elderly person. Prior to this ruling, if the victim passed away, the pain and suffering no longer existed and damages could not be awarded on this claim (Cassens, 1998). In South Carolina, videotaped testimony is permissible for older or disabled victims and witnesses in lieu of their actual presence in court (Stiegel, 1995).

Various issues continue to influence the way elder maltreatment cases are handled in the courts. For example, Hankin (1996) notes that in exploitation cases, it is difficult to establish that the victim is incompetent and that the perpetrator took advantage of that incompetence. Quinn and Tomita (1997) point out that "the search for a commonly accepted definition of competence can be likened to the search for the Holy Grail" (p. 138). Further, Hankin (1996) notes the level of proof in criminal cases (beyond a reasonable doubt) is too high for the amount of evidence actually present in cases involving nursing homes and other health care providers. Quinn and Tomita (1997) build on these ideas, suggesting that judges and juries tend to blame the victim and see caregiver stress and allegations of undue burdens on the caregiver as somehow justifying the abusive act. At the same time, however, juries tend to be empathetic toward elderly victims, seeing quality of life as an important component of elderly persons' needs (Brienza, 1995).

Hodge (1998) notes a number of other barriers that limit the effectiveness of the courts in handling elder abuse cases. In particular, he describes the following obstacles:

1. Judges are not interested in elder abuse cases and give lenient sanctions.
2. Judges and juries do not believe the prosecutor's evidence making cases difficult to prove beyond a reasonable doubt.
3. State agencies won't report information to prosecutors because they fear they are violating patient confidentiality.
4. Local prosecutors give a low priority to elder abuse cases. (p. 33)

Elder abuse cases are also difficult to litigate in civil court. As Eisenberg (1991) notes, many of these cases are not clear-cut, the victim is not enthusiastic about participating in the lawsuit, the litigation can be costly, and the abuser is seen as more credible than the victim. These factors have caused many attorneys to recommend that victims not file lawsuits against the perpetrators.

Along with the criminalization of elder abuse in the late eighties and early nineties came an increase in the number of lawsuits filed against elder abuse perpetrators (Brienza, 1995; Higgins, 1998). The increase came, in part, because of legislation making it more practical for attorneys to sue abusive caregivers. Hankin (1996) describes California's Elder Abuse and Dependent Adult Civil Protection Act of 1992, which was designed to make civil courts more accessible in cases of abuse, neglect, and financial exploitation. Prior to this act, if the patient died, the case would end. Thus, perpetrators were better off if the victim was old and frail. Defense attorneys could drag cases out hoping for the victim's inevitable death. If the victim died, the plaintiff's attorney would not get paid for his or her time. Making it even more troublesome was that the abusers would use the victims' finances to pay for their own legal expenses. These issues were addressed by California's law, which allowed cases to continue after the victim's death, and stipulated that the plaintiff's attorney fees would be paid by the perpetrator if serious abuse is substantiated (Hankin, 1996).

The fact that the attorneys would be rewarded financially for their efforts in elder abuse cases likely contributed to the increase in elder abuse lawsuits. Their participation in these cases is needed for successful case resolution, and the cases require a great deal of time and energy. Eisenberg (1991) describes five things plaintiff's attorneys must do in elder abuse cases. First, the attorney must make sure the client understands the consequences of the caregiver's actions. Second, the alternatives available to the victim must be addressed by the attorney. Third, the attorney should file suit only after the victim understands the acts. Fourth, the attorney must protect the victim's rights. Finally, the attorney must take action to stop the abuse.

Thus far, attention has been directed toward cases argued in general trial courts in the criminal and civil justice systems. As far as the appellate courts are concerned, all that can really be said is that they have been inactive when elder abuse and neglect cases are considered. In fact, a study by Pollack (1995) reveals that between 1981 and 1993, only ten elder abuse cases "were appealed to a higher court" (p. 13). Cases that were appealed concerned questions about attorney fees, elder abuse registries, guardianship, the definition of an older person, the duty to care for an older person, and penalty enhancement. States vary in their approach to each of these matters.

One central premise of the states' recent initiatives, however, is that measures must be taken to protect elderly victims. Measures that have been used by the courts to protect elderly persons include *restraining and protective orders, guardianships,* and *the appointment of conservators. Restraining* and *protective orders* are examples of civil remedies used by victims of domestic violence (Mathews, 1988). But there are limits as to how these can be used. Even so, there are two types of protection orders–temporary and permanent. Temporary protection orders are also known as emergency protection orders and last for a short period of time (usually around fourteen days). They are granted in those instances where practical constraints limit the possibility of a full hearing on the matter. Permanent restraining orders are also known as "civil protection orders" and are not forever, as the name suggests, but last anywhere from a few months to years, depending on the time frame assigned by the court (Plotkin, 1996).

Conservatorships and *guardianships* are used by the courts to prevent the financial abuse of elderly persons' assets. Conservators "handle a client's estate" while guardians "handle a client's personal affairs" (Quinn & Tomita, 1997). Guardianship is traced to Roman law when "surrogates were appointed to manage the property, but not the personal affairs of the mentally impaired" (Schimer & Anetzberger, 1999, p. 20). Wiehe (1998) describes the policies in the following manner: "A legal guardian generally is responsible for the complete care of a person who is totally incompetent and unable to manage personal and financial affairs. A conservator generally provides business and property affairs for a person who is coherent and competent, but not able to manage their affairs" (p. 161).

The underlying assumption of guardianship is that the state has a duty to protect those who are unable to protect themselves (Schimer & Anetzberger, 1999). Guardians are appointed to limit the possibility of financial exploitation. Whether guardianship is awarded is determined by the individual's ability to understand his or her situation, and the consequences of the situation (Wilber, 1990). To award guardianship, the court must find the patient to be incompetent and/or incapacitated and in need of "a surrogate decision-maker to manage [their] personal and/or financial affairs" (Pavlov & Murov, 1994, p. 250). Courts typically grant them when the need arises, with anywhere from 400,000 to 500,000 Americans having their decisions made by legal guardians (Quinn & Tomita, 1997; Wiehe, 1998).

Volunteer Court Programs, Legal Aid Societies, and Crimes Against Elderly Persons

As with the law enforcement response to elder abuse, various programs, volunteer and non-profit, have been developed to assist the courts in handling crimes against elderly persons. A few in particular include *law school-based legal clinics, utilizing the services of retired and semi-retired attorneys,* and *legal aid societies.*

As an example of a *law school-based legal clinic,* since 1981, Southern Illinois University's Legal Clinic has provided services to elderly persons (Eisenberg, 1991). The clinic provides the following civil legal services to persons aged sixty and over: drafting of simple wills, powers of attorney, assistance securing public benefits, family law matters, public utilities problems, and guardianship. Services are not provided for criminal cases or cases where the attorney's fee is stipulated by the recovered amount of penalties. The services that are provided are at no charge to the elderly person (Legal Services to Older Persons, 1999). On the clinic's world-wide-web homepage, comments from clients show an appreciation for the services:

1. The hours that the legal clinic has spent on my case with the positive results make a difference in our lives. The difference between getting by and having enough income to do something like home repairs.
2. [They] made me feel like I was talking to a close friend about legal matters. I felt at ease with all of them.
3. It is a wonderful service for senior citizens, especially to people like us whose funds are limited. We really appreciated the fact they came to our home since my husband is ill.

In another volunteer program *utilizing the services of retired and semi-retired attorneys,* the Brooklyn District Attorney's Office has retired volunteers assist in investigating and prosecuting crimes against elderly persons. Initiated in 1992, one of the strengths of the program is that older attorneys may be more sensitive to the needs of older victims. Former judges, legislators, prosecutors, and defense attorneys are among thse lawyers who have become involved in the volunteer effort. They are particularly successful in guiding victims through the criminal justice process (Fried, 1997).

Legal aid societies are also used to provide legal services to elderly persons at no cost. Sengstock and Barrett (1986) analyzed reports filed by a legal aid agency in Detroit that specialized in assisting senior citizens with legal matters. Nearly all of the cases that they saw were for financial abuse. They point out that workers expected this given the fact that legal measures would be needed to recover stolen property. Activities the lawyers were involved in were described as court actions, non-court legal actions, non-legal actions (referrals), and, to a less degree, counseling. Sengstock and Barrett (1986) note that other agencies take more indirect actions, such as "counseling or referral of the victim and/or family of the victim to another agency" (p. 58).

Improving the Court Response to Crimes Against Seniors

Stiegel (1995) surveyed 398 participants in a delphi study to see how the courts could better handle elder abuse cases. Based on the results of her study, she developed twenty-nine specific recommendations for improving the courts' handling of elder abuse cases. The recommendations include better training, accommodating the needs of the disabled, expediting cases, and so on. The major emphasis she notes, however, should be directed toward training. Elsewhere, Stiegel (1996) writes, "Training judges about elder abuse, with the input of others whose disciplines involve elder abuse, would enhance the courts' ability to handle these cases" (p. 41). The aim is to enhance judges' understanding about elder abuse so that they effectively use the courts, and the corrections programs, to respond to crimes against elderly persons.

CORRECTIONS AND CRIMES AGAINST ELDERLY PERSONS

The methods of sanctioning behavior vary in the criminal and civil justice systems. In the criminal justice system, corrections departments are generally responsible for administering the sanctions imposed by judges. In the civil justice system, usually fines are assessed on the defendant with little interaction with treatment or punishment programs. Attention will be given to both the criminal sanction and civil sanctions given to offenders who commit crimes against elderly persons.

Criminal Sanctions

Criminal court judges have many sanctions at their disposal in elder abuse cases. As Harshbarger (1989) writes, "Prosecution does not necessarily mean the offender will go to jail; other types of criminal sanctions are also available and may well be more appropriate than incarceration in a particular case" (p. 10). Before sentencing occurs, the probation office will conduct a pre-sentence investigation and develop a pre-sentence report that will guide the judge in determining the sentence given to offenders. In a study of patient abuse offenders, Payne and Cikovic (1995) found that incarceration was one of the least used sentencing alternatives. Indeed, all of the traditional sanctions used in regular criminal cases can be applied to elder abuse offenders. These sanctions include: (1) incarceration; (2) probation; (3) house arrest; (4) electronic monitoring; (5) fines; (6) community service; (7) restitution, and (8) participation in a counseling or treatment program (Chermak, 1993; Heisler, 1991; Heisler & Quinn, 1995). Other sanctions are also assessed in various places. For example, individuals might have their names placed on an elder abuse registry. In a similar vein, sex offenders' identities may be placed on a registry that members of the public could easily access.

The 1994 Crime Control Act stipulated that federal authorities had jurisdiction over crimes targeting elderly persons and made the penalties stiffer for offenders who target elderly persons (Blake, 1996). States also passed laws making penalties for elder abuse offenders more harsh than they were in the past. In Louisiana, a law was passed requiring that offenders who commit violent crimes against elderly persons receive a five-year mandatory minimum sentence with no chance of parole. In Nevada, offenders who victimize elderly persons could be given a prison sentence twice as long as the sentence that would be given to offenders who committed the same offense against younger victims (National Center for Victims of Crime, 1995).

In applying sanctions to elder abuse perpetrators, there is argument about whether the sanction should be more severe, equal to, or less severe than sanctions imposed for other offenses. On the one hand, as already noted, some states have enhanced penalties and harsher sentences for those convicted of certain crimes against elderly persons (Harshbarger, 1991; Hodge, 1998; Stiegel, 1995). The basis for the more severe sentences centers on the violation of trust that perpetrators commit against victims and society (Mathis, 1994). On the other hand, there are those who stress the need to use "the least restrictive alternative" in sanctioning these cases. The grounds for lenient sanctions are that sanctions that are too severe will ultimately hurt the victim who may be placed in a nursing home (Sadler, 1994) and that the elder abuse problem "will not be solved by sending people to jail" (Chance, 1987, p. 25). Quinn and Tomita (1997) note that the ideal of the least restrictive alternative is not easily applied to elder abuse cases. Somewhere in the middle are those who argue that traditional sanctions should be given to these offenders to protect defendants' rights and at the same time make sure the victim is not revictimized by the justice process. Tied in to this mix is the question of whether those who commit crimes against elderly persons can be successfully treated.

Not all agree on the effectiveness of rehabilitation programs. Johnson et al. (1994) surveyed social service employees and criminal justice officials and found that social service employees held treatment in a more favorable light than criminal justice officials. Alternatively, recent research shows that police chiefs hold more punitive attitudes towards elder abuse cases than do nursing home professionals and other social services professionals (Payne & Berg, 2003; Payne, 2003; Payne, Berg & James, 2001).

Regardless of professionals' attitudes, treatment approaches have been used to try to stop abusive situations. Some treatment approaches focus on providing services that will reduce the stress felt by the caregiver (meals on wheels, respite care, etc.) (Myers & Shelton, 1987). In a related manner, Wolf (1992) cites three treatment approaches that are based on common theoretical models used to explain the existence of elder abuse. First, the situational model sees caregiver stress as causing abuse and suggests that assistance in daily routines, such as those noted by Myers and Shelton (1987), are needed to lower caregivers' stress, which may lower their propensity for violence. Next, the environmental press model suggests that strain between the caregiver's abilities and the elderly person's needs presents a situation where abuse is likely. Intervention approaches focus on raising the caregiver's competence and lowering the elderly person's needs "through greater stimulation and socialization" (p. 273). Third, the social exchange model sees the dependency of the abuser on the elderly person as the cause of abuse and suggests that treatment approaches encourage independence for the caregiver. This independence would be achieved through counseling, drug treatment, financial support, or other changes that would reduce the extent to which the caregiver relies on the elderly person. If these changes don't help, this model recommends incarceration for offenders to raise the costs of their abusive behavior.

Wiehe (1998) agrees that treatment programs should be based on the actual causes of the abusive behavior and notes that vocational counseling, housing placement, drug treatment, family therapy, and financial support to reduce dependency are a few programs that have shown some success in handling abusive caregivers. Forrest et al. (1990) report on a program where at-risk caregivers were given "training through mental health centers on biopsychosocial issues in aging, problem solving, stress, and anger management, and utilization of community resources" (p. 74). As compared to non-participants, participants' levels of psychological distress and caregiving burden decreased. They recommend treating other abusers with similar programs. But, as Myers and Shelton (1987) note, the offender and victim may need to be separated during the treatment. This would entail having the perpetrator live on his or her own or finding protective placement for the victim for temporary relief. Once again, the victim may see removal from the home as a less than ideal alternative.

Another issue that arises is that sometimes the sanctions given to elder abusers are questionable, especially when the abusers suffer from some mental illness or related dementia. Recall from Chapter 3 that older sex offenders are sometimes sent to long-term-care settings because the criminal justice system is not seen as a viable option. This sort of questionable sentencing is not limited to elder sexual abusers. For example, a forty-nine-year-old, mentally ill man who plead guilty to cases of elder abuse was "sentenced to probation and ordered to live at a board and care facility" (Jones, 2003: B-3).

Civil Sanctions

Civil lawsuits against abusive caregivers and institutions became common in the nineties with six-figure awards being the norm, though "multi-million dollar awards are common" (Brienza, 1995, p. 65). In California, a woman was awarded $95 million after breaking her hip in a nursing home. In Florida, the family of a man who drowned after wandering from his nursing home was awarded $6.3 million (Thompson, 1998). The belief is that the assessment of punitive damages makes filing the lawsuits in the best interest of victims and attorneys (Eisenberg, 1991). Federal prosecutors are also suing nursing homes under the False Claims Act, which states that caregivers who file Medicaid/Medicare claims for services they never provided can be held liable. Successful suits bring in $10,000 per claim and triple the amount lost for damages (e.g., the amount of harm experienced by the victim) (Higgins, 1998). Nursing home litigation increases have been compared to the high level of medical malpractice and product liability suits twenty-five years ago (Brienza, 1995).

There are restrictions limiting the use of civil sanctions. When elder abuse cases go to civil court, typically claims focus on "pain and suffering" that the elderly person experiences. Generally, elderly persons have no claims for "lost earnings, diminution of earnings, or medical expenses not covered by insurance" (Cassens, 1998, p. 39). Also, elderly persons who use federal funds to pay for their care must "exhaust administrative remedies before they can sue" (Higgins, 1998, p. 28). Some states also limit the amount of punitive damages that can be awarded to victims. Often, large punitive damages are justified on the idea that they will prevent future misconduct. The deterrent value of these large awards is debatable. There is no evidence that others hear about the awards, that sanctions are applied swiftly enough for deterrence, or that the sanctions truly are severe to the defendant (Stevens & Payne, 1999).

A Note about the Justice System and Institutional Abuse

Much of the attention about the way the system investigates and prosecutes crimes against elderly victims has centered on cases where individual offenders commit crimes against victims. Similar, yet different, principles guide the way the system responds to institutional abuse, or what some refer to as corporate deviance (Ermann & Lundman, 1982). Granted, the Speaks' (1995) undercover investigation, discussed earlier, was an example of an investigation concerning corporate deviance by a nursing home. Also, nursing homes that fail to provide adequate care can be charged with involuntary manslaughter if the inadequate care can be shown as the cause of death (Capezuti & Sigler, 1996). But, more often than not, our system relies more on compliance strategies rather than deterrence strategies to ensure that nursing homes are providing appropriate care to the residents (Braithewaite, 1993).

40

Compliance strategies are those that limit the use of sanctions and provide incentives for abiding by state regulations (Friedrichs, 2003). According to Grubbs and Urban (1995), effective compliance programs include the following elements: (1) compliance standards and procedures; (2) overall compliance program oversight; (3) due care in the delegation of activity; (4) employee training; (5) consistent enforcement and discipline; (6) monitoring and auditing systems; and (7) responsive and corrective actions (pp. 40–41).

Braithewaite (1993) has described the way that compliance strategies are used in nursing homes. Basically, nursing homes are inspected at various times throughout the year. Nursing home inspections average 156 hours and involve a team of three to five inspectors who interview residents and inspect the building. Considerable time is spent reviewing patients' records and charts. Of the violations that are found, over 90 percent are resolved through "lodging a satisfactory plan of correction without any law enforcement action being taken" (p. 23). Resolution without punishment is an implicit goal of compliance programs.

For those cases where sanctions are applied, administrative sanctions such as fines are quite popular alternatives. License revocation and Medicaid decertification are available options but are rarely used because they ultimately equate to a death penalty for the nursing home. Without Medicaid support, or without a license, the nursing home would have to close (Braithewaite, 1993). Once again, many elderly victims would be revictimized because they would have no where to live.

Long-term-care ombudsmen are also involved in ensuring that long-term care settings are complying to the regulations set forth. The concept "ombudsman" is a Swedish word meaning "a public official appointed to investigate citizens" (Administration on Aging 1999). As initially conceived, ombudsmen programs would use paid employees and unpaid volunteers to receive and handle suspected allegations of nursing home abuse (Paton, Huber & Netting, 1994; Lachs & Pillemer, 1995). In 1997, 880 paid employees and 6,800 certified volunteers handled 191,000 complaints and shared information with 200,000 citizens (Administration on Aging, 1999). Ombudsmen are in a particularly important position because they are front-line advocates for nursing home residents. Their duties include investigating complaints, reviewing nursing home licenses, and protecting the rights of nursing home residents (Netting et al., 1992; Vladeck & Feuerberg, 1995). Surveys on 633 ombudsmen show that the factors that influenced volunteers' decisions to file complaints include their identification with advocacy roles, negative work experiences, and minimal informal contact with nursing home staff (Keith, 2001).

CONCLUDING REMARKS

Think back to the story at the beginning of this chapter about the woman who waited for the police to come after her son-in-law abused her in her home. The police alone did not successfully resolve this case. Instead, it took a cooperative effort on the part of counselors, APS employees, and the police to finally help the victim. This is not an isolated case when crimes against elderly persons are considered. Mathews (1988) points out that "the criminal justice system alone is clearly not the solution to the problem of elder abuse" (p. 659). In fact, cooperation and open communication between the various groups will increase the likelihood of providing useful services to the victim.

The idea of cooperation fits in well with the assumptions of gerocriminology–that crimes against elderly persons can be best understood by integrating notions from various disciplines. The problem, however, is that those who need to work together in resolving elder abuse cases often know very little about those with whom they should be cooperating. For instance, criminal justice officials note that they know very little about elder abuse. Lack of knowledge for law enforcement results in problems recognizing and gathering evidence. At the same time, APS workers lack law enforcement knowledge, making collaboration more difficult. Further, prosecutors who are not familiar with elder abuse issues may choose not to prosecute (Stiegel, 1996).

The knowledge the various groups have about one another is not only scant, it may be wrong. Indeed, criminal justice employees and APS employees have barriers limiting their cooperation. Describing these barriers, Harshbarger (1989) writes, "both sides must work to eradicate the barriers that have arisen because of these misperceptions" (p. 5). As it is, those working with elderly persons likely have had little exposure to the criminal justice system. Alternatively, those who work in the justice system have had little contact with those who work with elderly persons (Heisler & Quinn, 1995).

Another barrier that exists is goal confusion. Basically, different agencies involved in the response to elder abuse cases may have different goals. For APS investigators, the goal is case resolution, while for criminal justice investigators, the goal is often a successful prosecution. To combine these goals, some researchers point out that the goal of reduction of future risk should be the most appropriate indicator of success in elder abuse cases (Wolf & Pillemer, 2000). To efficiently reduce risk, it is necessary that all parties involved in the case cooperate.

The key to increasing cooperation is education. Educating various actors involved in the battle against elder abuse is of paramount importance (Capezuti & Siegler, 1996). Many believe that the various agencies can work together. Of course, there may be instances where cooperation is not needed. Or, if one agency cannot help the elderly victim, others potentially can (Dolon & Hendricks, 1989; Reulbach & Tewksbury, 1994). Members from these agencies working together are referred to as "multi-disciplinary teams" (Quinn & Tomita, 1997). They include members from "mental health, law enforcement, religious, legal, and financial services" (Wolf, 1992). These sorts of teams are mandated in Illinois for areas with more than 7,200 people where they meet monthly to address the needs of elderly residents in the community (Wolf, 1992).

The multi-disciplinary teams are certainly examples of the cooperative effort that I have stressed as important throughout this text. As well, the use of multi-disciplinary teams fits well within the assumptions of a gero-criminological response to elder abuse. When individuals from different backgrounds come together and use the varied strengths to address a problem, the likelihood of resolving the problem increases greatly. Illinois and other states have recognized this need by developing these teams. As the elderly population continues to grow, it is hoped that other states will follow suit.

Chapter 6

UNDERSTANDING AND EXPLAINING CRIMES AGAINST SENIORS: ELDER ABUSE AND CRIMINOLOGICAL THEORIES

1. Why is it important to understand the causes of crime?
2. What principles do researchers follow in trying to explain crimes against seniors?
3. What is meant by intra-individual explanations?
4. What does dependency have to do with elder abuse?
5. Compare and contrast transgenerational explanations with caregiver stress explanations.
6. How does strain theory explain crimes against elderly adults?
7. What does social disorganization have to do with elder abuse?
8. Compare and contrast the way routine activities theory addresses crimes against seniors with the way control theory addresses crimes against seniors.

INTRODUCTION

Research I was working on a few years ago considers the reasons ombudsmen believe elder abuse occurs (Payne & Gray, 2002). Long-term-care ombudsmen receive and handle complaints of nursing home abuses. Surveys were mailed to 405 ombudsmen, and 205 usable surveys were returned. In addition to several other questions, ombudsmen were asked the following: "Why do you think elder abuse occurs?" Their responses are telling and reflect many of the theories considered throughout this chapter. Consider the following responses from four different ombudsmen:

1. Elders are and are seen by others as vulnerable both physically and cognitively. They are easy prey unfortunately. Where family members are the exploiters, often the elderly "victim" won't press charges or admit a problem for fear that they don't have anyone to love or take care of them. This is a more serious issue than aides or strangers exploiting them.

2. Elder abuse occurs because society does not value the elderly. Media attention given to the elderly is minimal, and they are portrayed as weak, sick individuals who are defenseless. Families are spread out and children often have little valuable interactions with family elders.

3. I believe it stems from the old problem of captives being powerless and thus easy marks for sadistic behavior. It is really very akin to child abuse.

4. The elderly, like children and disabled people, are not valued because they don't work, don't spend lots of money, and don't vote. People take their frustrations out on them because they are easy targets. People in nursing homes are totally dependent on the staff for their care. Overworked staff blame residents and abuse can result. (Payne & Gray, 2002)

On the surface, one might argue that it does not matter what ombudsmen believe the causes of elder abuse are. After all, it would seem more important that attention be given to the actual causes of elder abuse as opposed to what certain individuals believe the causes to be. Alternatively, it is reasonable to suggest that their beliefs about the causes of elder abuse will influence their reactions to the problem. For instance, if individuals believe elder abuse is caused by stress that the caregiver feels as a result of providing assistance to older persons, they would likely recommend programs to reduce the stress on the caregivers. Alternatively, if individuals believe that abuse occurs because elderly persons are targeted for certain offenses, then programs that would protect elderly persons from victimization would be recommended. To fully understand the causes of elder abuse, it is important that attention be given to the role of theory in promoting understanding about the problem.

THE ROLE OF THEORY IN UNDERSTANDING
ELDER ABUSE

A theory is different from an explanation. The four quotes from ombudsmen provided in the beginning of this chapter could be best seen as explanations. Explanations are simply plausible reasons that behaviors occur. A theory, on the other hand, is a set of empirically testable propositions that attempt to explain behavior, whether it is criminal behavior or non-criminal behavior. Some elder abuse researchers have attempted to develop and test theories explaining elder abuse, while others have investigated the various risk factors that might help explain why elder abuse occurs. Both types of research (e.g., elder abuse theory development and elder abuse risk factors research) are important because they each enhance our understanding of the potential explanations of elder abuse.

Understanding explanations of abuse is important for five reasons. First, explanations of abuse will play a role in attempts to stop elder abuse. Describing the role of theory in potentially reducing crime, Alston (1986) writes, "Reductions in crime ultimately benefit everyone, from those who would have become victims to the general public which underwrites insurance premiums and supports police, courts, and prisons with its taxes" (p. 245). The point is that if we can figure out why people commit crimes against elderly persons, we can prevent these offenses from occurring in the future. Such prevention efforts would benefit all of society, not just crime victims.

Second, policies are developed that are based on the assumptions about the causes of abuse. As will be shown in this chapter, a majority of politicians and researchers originally believed that elder abuse was caused by caregiver stress experienced as a result of attempts to provide assistance to burdensome, and dependent, elderly family members. Policies therefore originally focused on providing respite care and other forms of assistance to overburdened caregivers (Wolf, 1992). Research by Pillemer (1986) questioned the caregiver stress ideology and suggested that in some cases the abuser was actually dependent on the victim, contrary to what others believed. Pillemer (1986) therefore recommended policies that would help reduce the caregiver's dependency on the victim as a strategy to prevent elder abuse. Based on this same line of thinking, Folkenberg (1989) writes, "caregiver support groups or in-home assistance may not be the most helpful long term solutions" (p. 87).

Third, as already suggested, a practitioner's beliefs about the causes of abuse will influence the way he or she responds to abuse. If someone believes people are abusive because of abuse they experienced as children, then the treatment provided by that person to offenders would be substantially different from the response of one who believes that all offenders are rational actors who deserve punishment in order to deter their future misconduct. Because many case workers see elder abuse resulting from factors relating to characteristics of the individual (e.g. the offender or the victim), they orient their services toward fixing individual problems. As Sadler (1994) notes, most elder abuse interventions in the U.S. "focus on individualistic casework with elder abuse victims and abusers, consistent with theories explaining abuse in terms of individual characteristics and familial interactions" (p. 3).

※2   Fourth, theory will guide the formulation of research questions aimed at better understanding elder abuse. Anetzberger (1987), for instance, interviewed adult children who abused their elderly parents in order to determine the appropriateness of the following explanations of elder abuse: abuse socialization, pathology of the offender, stress, social isolation, exchange theory, and vulnerability. These explanations helped her frame the questions addressed in her study, and likely influenced the types of questions she asked of the respondents.

✳2   Fifth, past explanations of elder abuse will be used to interpret research findings. For example, Harris and Benson (1996) surveyed nursing home professionals to learn more about theft in nursing homes. Harris and Benson (1996) then used the following explanations to guide their understanding of the respondents' comments: exchange theory; rationalization theory; lack of responsibility on the part of administrators; and elderly persons are seen as easy prey. Each of these theories and explanations will be considered in more detail later in this chapter. For now, it is important to stress that the role of theory in responding to elder abuse cannot be understated. (See Box 6.1 for more on the importance of understanding the causes of elder abuse.)

Before discussing these explanations, some background about the relationship between theory development and the scientific method is needed. In developing theories and explanations of elder abuse, theorists and researchers are guided by what Bierstedt refers to as "principles of science." In particular, Bierstedt (1970) describes seven principles of science he saw as relating to sociology in general. Later, Fitzgerald and Cox (1988) expanded on these principles and applied them to research. More recently, Payne and King (1995) showed how these principles are followed by both educators and criminal justice practitioners. The principles originally considered by Bierstedt (1970) were the following: *ethical neutrality, objectivity, parsimony, relativism, empiricism, determinism,* and *skepticism.* A brief review of these principles and the way they relate criminological theory construction and attempts to explain why elder abuse occurs is warranted.

Ethical neutrality and *objectivity* are similar principles that are concerned with whether social scientists (or practitioners for that matter) will allow past experiences, beliefs, and values to influence their explanations. For example, if one were recently a victim a home repair fraud, this could influence the way one would explain crime. Taken together, the principles of ethical neutrality and objectivity suggest that individuals must set aside their own experiences to explain the experiences of others. The phrase *verstehen,* meaning value-free, refers to these attempts to keep one's experiences separate from one's interpretations of human behavior. Of course, researchers and theorists are not completely value-free in their research or theory development. But, being as value-free as possible will increase the likelihood that theories or explanations

BOX 6.1. VOICES FROM THE FIELD: THE IMPORTANCE OF UNDERSTANDING THE CAUSES OF ELDER ABUSE

By Georgia J. Anetzberger, Ph.D.

Suppose your car fails to run and you take it to an automotive center. You ask the service representative there to do whatever is necessary to have the car run again. The center has at least three options in responding to your request. First, it can determine the cause of the problem and then make repair specific to the identified cause. Second, it can analogize your car's situation to that of comparable vehicles, and assume that the problem may have similar cause and remedy. Finally, the automotive center can do a complete overhaul of your car, hoping in the process to correct the problem and perhaps prevent others as well.

You would be appalled if the automotive center approached your car's problem using other than the first option. Afterall, only the first option is empirically based and relevant. Only it is likely to be both effective and efficient in its remedy. Analogy can be imprecise, resulting in erroneous conclusion. Complete overhaul can be extravagant, diverting resources in directions where no problem exists.

Yet, we have remained somewhat complacent and allowed the options of complete overhaul and analogy to dominate our unraveling of elder abuse etiology. Certainly the earliest writings on the subject proposed laundry lists of possible causes. Later elder abuse etiology was based on analogy with other abused populations, first analogy with child abuse and hence an emphasis on caregiver stress as the major underlying cause, and then analogy with domestic violence and hence an emphasis on power and control as fostering abuse occurrence. Even now, false assumption and folk belief often provide the basis for our discussions on elder abuse etiology and underlie many public policies, treatment modalities, and training programs aimed at the problem.

There are many reasons for the dominance of a "shotgun" approach and use of analogy instead of empirical research in explaining elder abuse. Among them are the following:

- The complexity of the problem itself, making it likely that each form, setting, or category of victim/perpetrator relationship has a somewhat different etiology
- The difficulty of accessing victims and perpetrators for the purpose of conducting research
- The ease of using established explanatory models and the appeal of using politically correct or popular oness

However, without clearly identifying the etiology of elder abuse, the field is severely hampered. If we fail to understand the root causes of the problem, we cannot know how to properly respond to it. Etiology is key to accurate case finding. Knowing the origins of elder abuse increases the likelihood that victims who need protection are recognized and receive it. It also increases the likelihood that persons in contact with elders but who are not abusive will not be falsely accused. Moreover, etiology is key to the development of effective public policy and clinical practice. Intervention design is meaningful only to the extent that it reflects an understanding of problem origins. At best, inappropriate, and therefore ineffective, policy and practice are wasteful, absorbing scarce resources, reducing support for innovation. At worst, they can victimize further the very people they are intended to help.

Most public policies and clinical practices in elder abuse were established during the late 1970s or 1980s, before much scientific inquiry into problem etiology. As research explaining elder abuse evolves, it will be instructive to see whether or not policy and practice evolve similarly. Will institutions and professionals faced with change hunker down and resist, or will they lead the charge for reform? Will we find that the field of elder abuse is littered with true believers, or lined with pure advocates? For elder abuse victims, the answers to these questions will make all the difference.

Georgia J. Anetzberger, PhD, ACSW, LISW, is a consultant in private practice, Research Associate with the Visiting Nurse Association Healthcare Partners of Ohio, Adjunct Assistant Professor of Medicine at Case Western Reserve University, University Graduate Faculty in Health Care Administration at Cleveland State University, and Fellow in the Gerontological Society of America. She has spent over twenty-five years addressing the problem of elder abuse, initially as an adult protective services worker and most recently as a researcher, administrator, and educator concerned with the dynamics of elder abuse situations. She has authored more than thirty publications on elder abuse or related interventions, including those which have appeared in such journals as *The Gerontologist, Violence Against Women, Generations,* and *Journal of Cross-Cultural Gerontology.*

accurately portray reality. Given the horrific nature of many elder abuse cases, it is particularly important that elder abuse researchers attempt to remain objective in conducting their research, whether it is exploratory research or explanatory research testing specific theories about the causes of this behavior.

Parsimony suggests that theories and explanations should be kept as simple as possible. They cannot be too simple because they will exclude important variables, nor can they be too complex lest they risk not being communicated beyond the immediate scientific community finding interest in the particular theory or explanation. Fitzgerald and Cox (1988) write, "whatever the scope of the phenomenon being studied, the simplest explanation with the most empirical support is preferred" (p. 23). When I talk about parsimony in my classes, I often use music as an analogy. I ask students what songs bring them the most joy, and I ask any musicians in the class to share what they know about those songs. Inevitably, the songs that students like the most are those that the musicians report as being among the easiest to play. These songs are communicated easily to the public, but they are not *too* simple.

One of my colleagues, Randy Gainey, uses the example of road maps to explain the importance of keeping theories simple. On a road map, you may want to have every road, turn off, and street sign. You might also want elevation gain, detours, and bumps in the road. But notice, as you get more specific (less parsimonious), the map gets bigger and bigger until it is the size of the actual region (area) you are traveling. In the end, with too much detail, the map would be totally useless. Explanations of elder abuse are similar. Basically, theories and explanations of elder abuse must also be easy to understand and follow in order to be accepted by the academic and professional communities.

Empiricism means that social scientists can only theorize about those things that are real to the senses and stresses that social scientists will make scientific observations to test theories. Social science theory and research cannot explain phenomenon that may exist beyond this world. This principle is indirectly relevant to definitions of elder abuse. The way elder abuse is empirically defined will certainly determine the subsequent explanations of elder abuse. If elder abuse researchers define psychological abuse as a crime, then their explanations of these acts will be different from those who see psychological abuse as non-criminal. Thus, theory development and explanations of elder abuse will be influenced by the way researchers define various elder abuse concepts and themes.

Relativism means that all things are related and implies that changes in one area will lead to changes in other areas. The principle is concerned with (1) the numerous influences that broader changes have on society, and (2) the way that groups vary in their perceptions about issues such as elder abuse. Regarding theory development and explanations of elder abuse, relativism is important because changes in society will influence our understanding of these offenses. For example, many used to see caregiver stress as a primary cause of elder abuse. Now, after society has changed, and understanding has increased, some experts see the role of caregiver stress in elder abuse cases as overstated and oversimplified (Baron & Welty, 1996; Korbin, Anetzberger, & Austin, 1995). As well, cross-cultural differences influence individuals' decisions to define actions as abusive. Two people from completely different cultures could look at the same act and interpret the act differently. One might define it as deviant and the other might define the act as normal. As the saying goes, "it's all relative."

Determinism as a principle of science suggests that behavior is influenced by preceding events. Many social scientists tend to believe that behavior is caused by preceding events. This principle is central to the development of explanations about the causes of elder abuse. Imagine if someone asked experts why they believed offenders committed elder abuse, and the experts said "just because." In contrast to the notion of determinism is the principle of free-will, which suggests that actors rationally think about possible outcomes and freely choose their actions. Proponents of free-will would argue that actions are not dictated by preceding events. However, in keeping with the deterministic principle, many of the most avid supporters of the free-will approach support the use of sanctions to keep offenders from abusing in the future. Thus, they see punishment as determining future behavior. So even free-will advocates are guided by notions of determinism; they simply see different causes of behavior.

Skepticism as a principle of science means that theorists should question and requestion everything. It further suggests that there is no such thing as "the perfect theory" or "completely accurate explanation." Rather, researchers will test theories to see if the available evidence supports or refutes them. This point is particularly important for lay persons to remember in order to avoid getting caught up in believing that a certain explanation is 100 percent accurate in all cases. One would hope if we really knew why crimes were committed against elderly persons, then actions would have already been taken so elderly persons would not be victimized. The fact that crimes continue to occur against older adults means that we don't know for sure why all of these offenses occur. Instead, experts have developed "plausible explanations of reality" that will guide our understanding of crimes against elderly persons. So, the reader must avoid accepting any of the following explanations as "the truth." The fact that the explanations are not perfect does not diminish their relevance. Rather, theories and explanations of elder abuse will continue to guide policies, research, and actions by practitioners.

THEORIES EXPLAINING CRIMES AGAINST ELDERLY PERSONS

In keeping with each of these principles, several different theories and explanations for elder abuse have been addressed in the literature. Table 13 provides an overview of some of the explanations that have been addressed in the past. As shown in the table, most elder abuse researchers seem to agree that there is no single explanation or theory that would account for all types of elder abuse (Bennett & Kingston, 1992; Comijs et al., 1998; Fulmer, 1990; Korbin, Anetzberger & Eckert, 1990; Myers & Shelton, 1987; Lang, 1993; Pedrick-Cornell & Gelles, 1982; Phillips, 1983; Sayles-Cross, 1989; Wolf, 1996b). In fact, some elder abuse researchers contend that different types of abuse require different explanations because no single factor has been able to explain all of the various types of elder abuse. For instance, some say that

TABLE 13. EXPLANATIONS AND RISK FACTORS FOR ELDER ABUSE CONSIDERED IN PAST RESEARCH*

Author	Explanation/Risk Factor	Abuse Type**	Publication
Davidson (1979)	Economic and population changes Changes in older parent's life Changes in adult child's life Family relations Parents living with adult child	Elder abuse	Chapter in Block/Sinnot's *Battered Elder Syndrome*
Fulmer et al. (1984)	Impairment theory Individual pathology of abuser Theory of internal family dynamics Internal stress theory External stress theory	Elder abuse	Journal article
Wolf, Godkin, & Pillemer (1984)	Intra-individual dynamics External stress Intergenerational transmission of violence Dependency and exchange relations Social isolation	Elder abuse	Research report
Phillips (1986)	Situational model Social exchange theory Symbolic interactionism	Elder abuse	Book chapter
Anetzberger (1987)	Abuse socialization Pathology Stress Social isolation Exchange theory Vulnerability	Elder abuse	Book based on author's dissertation
Myers & Shelton (1987)	Personal factors Interpersonal factors Situational factors Sociocultural factors	Elder abuse	Journal article
Steinmetz (1988)	Social/emotional dependency Mobility dependency Emotional problems Financial problems Household dependency Cycle of violence	Elder abuse	Book
Tomita (1990)	Situational model Social exchange Symbolic interactionism Social learning Pscyhopathology Privacy of the family Techniques of neutralization	Elder abuse	Journal article

(*continued*)

TABLE 13. (CONTINUED)

Author	Explanation/Risk Factor	Abuse Type**	Publication
Pillemer & Moore (1990)	Stress and burnout Patient conflict Patient aggression toward staff	Physical abuse in nursing homes	Journal article
Pillemer & Bachman (1991)	Institutional characteristics – size, profit/non-profit, fees Staff characteristics – occupational position, education Situational characteristics – level of conflict, stress, alcohol	Physical abuse in nursing homes	Journal article
Fulmer (1991)	Dependency Caregiver burden Transgenerational violence Non-normal caregivers Isolation	Elder abuse	Journal article
Paris et al. (1995)	History of mental illness Substance abuse Family history of violence Isolation	Elder abuse	Journal article
Payne & Cikovic (1995)	Gender interactions Job pressures Training	Physical abuse in nursing homes	Journal article
Baron & Welty (1996)	Dependency of the victim Dependency of abuser Abuser psychopathology Transgenerational family violence Environmental pressures Caregiver stress	Elder abuse	Journal article
Bradley (1996)	Deteriorating family relations History of abuse Isolation Psychopathology Imbalance of power	Elder abuse	Journal article
Coyne et al. (1996)	Dementia Violence by Alzhiemer's patients History of violence Caregiver burden/depression	Elder abuse	Journal article
Harris & Benson (1996)	Exchange theory Rationalization Easy prey Lack of responsibility	Theft in nursing homes	Book chapter
Harris (1996)	Intra-interpersonal – psychopathology – psychiatric illnesses – substance abuse	Elder spouse abuse	Journal article

TABLE 13. (CONTINUED)

Author	Explanation/Risk Factor	Abuse Type**	Publication
	Social theories – learning – subculture of violence – social stress model		
Jerin & Moriarty (1998)	Personality disorder Social learning theory Social exchange theory Conflict theory Symbolic interactionism Role theory Situational theory Functionalism	Elder abuse	Chapter in Victimology text
Doener & Lab (1998)	Intraindividual explanations Situational aspects Symbolic interactionism Social exchange Social attitudes	Elder abuse	Chapter in Victimology text
Payne (1998a)	Training Lack of enforcement Structural influences Victim vulnerability	Elder abuse & Medicare fraud	Journal article
Rosoff et al. (2003)	Societal causes Organizational causes Institutional causes	White-collar crime	White-collar text
Wiehe (1998)	Aggression as instinct or drive Aggression as result of frustration Aggression as learned behavior Aggression as power and control	Family violence	Family violence text
Shaw (1998)	Multiple stressors Substance abuse History of domestic violence Lack of pay and appreciation	Physical abuse in nursing homes	Journal article
Harris (1999)	Situational theory Vulnerability theory Exchange theory Routine activities General theory of crime	Theft in nursing homes	Journal article

*The fact that these are considered by an author(s) does not mean the author(s) supports the approach. It simply means the author(s) discussed the approach.
**Unless otherwise specified, elder abuse generally refers to physical abuse and neglect by family members.

Critical Thinking Questions:

1. Is it possible to determine the cause of behavior? Explain.
2. Why is it important to understand one's own beliefs about causality?

financial abuse is caused by dependency while physical abuse is caused by a history of violence in the offender's life (Sadler, 1994). Another model cited by Wolf (1996a) suggests that financial abuse occurs because greedy offenders target isolated victims, and that physical abuse occurs because of offenders' psychopathological problems. Of course, some argue that there may be several valid explanations for elder abuse (Pedrick-Cornell & Gelles, 1982). After all, elder abuse is seen as "a complex syndrome whose dynamics vary widely among cultural groups, types of abuse, and whether the abuser is a spouse or adult child" (Lang, 1993, p. 30).

Another important point concerning these past explanations is that elder abuse explanations have, until recently, ignored traditional explanations of criminal behavior (see Harris, 1999). Or, criminological theories have been noticeably scarce in the elder abuse literature. This is likely due in part to the fact that criminologists have generally ignored crimes against elderly persons, and have directed their efforts more towards explaining youthful offenses (see Chapter 2). What has happened is that elder abuse theories have been separated from criminological theories. Describing the separation of family violence research and criminological endeavors, Ohlin and Tonry (1989) write:

> This fragmentation of family violence research and the divide between family violence studies and criminological studies was regrettable because it balkanized knowledge and policy-relevant insights, but it was doubly regrettable because it *impoverished theory and generated fundamentally incomplete accounts of different forms of antisocial behavior.* (p. 3)

I believe, as do others (see Braithwaite, 1993; Harris & Benson, 1998; Harris, 1999), that some criminological theories can be useful in understanding crimes against elderly persons. To establish this point, I will first consider the explanations that elder abuse researchers have addressed in the past. Then, I will suggest ways that criminological theories can be useful in increasing our understanding about elder abuse. In the end, the reader should not be surprised when I recommend integrating elder abuse explanations and criminological theories to expand our understanding of elder abuse. This sort of theoretical integration fits well within the ideals of a gero-criminological approach.

ELDER ABUSE EXPLANATIONS

Early on in the development of elder abuse as a social problem, Pedrick-Cornell and Gelles (1982) point out that initial explanations of elder abuse were primarily speculative, relying on intuitive analysis based on studies of other types of family violence such as spouse abuse and child abuse. These early speculations saw the sources of elder abuse as being stress, physical and mental impairment of the victims, and beliefs about a cycle of violence. They called for empirical research to test these original speculations. Some of these original beliefs have been dispelled, others have been supported, and others remain speculative. The explanations for elder abuse in the family that have been addressed in the literature include the following: *intra-individual explanations, stress, dependency, transgenerational violence, symbolic interactionism, isolation, rationalizations by abusers,* and *patriarchy theory* (Anetzberger, 1987; Coyne, Potenza, & Berbig, 1996; Fulmer et al., 1984; Fulmer, 1990; Steinmetz, 1988; Tomita, 1990; Wolf et al., 1984). Explanations for abuse in nursing homes include *institutional factors, staff characteristics, situational characteristics, educational influences,* and *vulnerability* (Harris & Benson, 1996; Payne, 1998a; Pillemer & Bachman, 1991; Pillemer & Moore, 1990). After reviewing each of these explanations, the way that criminological theories can be used to explain elder abuse will be considered.

Intra-individual Explanations

#6 Intra-individual explanations are concerned with the cognitive, behavioral, and emotional characteristics of offenders or victims that may contribute to the abuse. These explanations are similar to what some refer to as inter- or intra-personal explanations (Harris, 1996; Myers & Shelton, 1987), impairment theory (Fulmer et al., 1984), and pathology or psychopathology (Anetzberger, 1987; Bradley, 1996; Tomita, 1990). The assumption underlying intra-individual approaches is that behavior is based on something within the offender or victim (Doerner & Lab, 1998). What these explanations tend to focus on are the following: *alcohol abuse problems of offenders and victims, emotional problems of offenders,* and *impairments of offenders and victims.*

#7 Many intra-individual explanations are critiqued on the grounds that they have not withstood the test of sound empirical research. *Alcohol abuse* is one intra-individual explanation that has been supported by empirical research (Pillemer, 1986; Anetzberger, Korbin, & Austin, 1994). Indeed, not only has alcohol been implicated in cases of elder abuse, it has been found to be a factor in many types of crimes. By some estimates, at least one-half of all arrested offenders were under the influence of alcohol when they committed their crimes (Stimmel, 1991). Not surprisingly, alcohol is seen as a contributing factor in half of all U.S. murders and is reported to be a risk factor in domestic assaults (Block & Christakos, 1995; Siegel, 1998). Kinney (2000) estimates that alcohol is abused by 72 percent of perpetrators and 79 percent of victims and reports that two-thirds of family violence cases involve alcohol abuse. Thus, alcohol abuse by either victims or offenders is seen as a contributing factor in elder abuse cases (Paris et al., 1995).

Some point out that the diminished inhibitions resulting from alcohol use may provide a setting where the likelihood of abuse increases (Pillemer, 1986). The belief is that drugs, such as alcohol, may have a "disinhibiting effect" causing the abuser to do things he or she otherwise would not do (Bradley, 1996). As well, alcohol leads to biochemical changes that ultimately may lead to violence or abusive behavior (Pringle, 1997; Wiehe, 1998). Along this line, alcohol abuse has also been implicated in cases of physical abuse in nursing homes. Shaw (1998) notes that alcohol and drug abuse by nursing home staff "impairs their impulse control and resistance to aggression by residents" (p. 12). Pillemer (1986), however, points out that alcohol may simply be used as a convenient excuse by abusers who wish to explain away their transgressions and deny responsibility for their actions.

Not considered in great detail in the literature is the role that alcohol plays in cases of neglect. In the alcohol literature, a common and accepted claim is that alcohol abuse will affect the alcoholics' spouses and their children (Ackerman, 1987; Royce, 1981). An underlying assumption is that children and spouses will be neglected as a result of the alcoholic's addictive behavior. Regarding elder neglect, caregivers with alcohol problems would seem to be less likely to provide appropriate care to elderly persons. Elderly parents of alcoholics could then be at a higher risk of experiencing physical, social, emotional, or financial neglect. It is important that the role of alcohol in contributing to cases of abuse and neglect is not overstated. Alcohol is not the primary cause of violent behavior (Goode, 1999). However, substance abuse is the contributing factor that adult protective services workers report encountering most often (Jones, 1996).

A related intra-individual explanation centers on *emotional problems of the offender.* Elder abusers have been found to have personality disorders, low self-esteems, and related psychological problems (Chen et al., 1981; Godkin, Wolf, & Pillemer, 1989). Though not specifically applied to elder abuse, two theories that would address how emotional problems contribute to elder abuse in the family are *Maslow's hierarchy of needs* and *Ellis' rational emotive theory.*

Abraham Maslow argued that all individuals have certain needs that can be organized into a hierarchy of most basic needs to higher level needs. He described five levels of needs: physiological needs, security needs, belonging needs, self-esteem needs, and self-actualization. The central premise underlying Maslow's approach is that individuals will direct their behavior toward fulfilling specific needs, until those needs are met, at which point they will direct their behavior toward needs at the next level.

Physiological needs involve the need for food, air, water, and other matter which are essential for survival. Security needs entail the need to feel safe and secure in one's environment. Belonging needs are concerned with the need to be a part of a group. Self-esteem needs entail the desire to feel good about one's self. Self-actualization is defined as "the need to be one's best self" (Hafen & Brog, 1983, p. 12). According to Maslow, all individuals strive for self-actualization, but few reach it.

As far as the relationship between Maslow's hierarchy of needs and elder abuse, it is important to recall that elder abusers have been found to have low self-esteems (Chen et al., 1981). Advocates of Maslow's approach would argue that abusers commit various types of abuse as a result of the low self-esteem. Further, if circumstances change in individuals' lives, they may be forced to direct their behavior toward fulfilling needs that were previously fulfilled. For example, imagine an individual with a relatively high self-esteem who encounters emotional and social problems while having to provide to care an elderly parent. That individual would not necessarily direct his or her behavior toward maintaining a high self-esteem. On a similar line, imagine individuals who encounter unexpected financial hardships and commit financial abuse against elderly persons to deal with their financial problem. From Maslow's perspective, elder abuse occurs because offenders have problems meeting certain needs, and behavior is "directed toward . . . frustrated, or unmet needs" (Hafen & Brog, 1983, p. 12).

Ellis's (1958) rational emotive theory also looks at the psychological problems of individuals to explain their behavior but sees the root of abusive behavior as being an irrational belief system. Rarely applied to elder abuse scenarios, the approach has more often been directed toward understanding discord in domestic relationships (see Ellis et al., 1989). Even so, the approach, which is intricately tied to rational-emotive therapy (RET), can be used to understand how emotional and psychological problems of abusers can lead to elder abuse.

Rational emotive theory is often explained with the ABC model (Ellis et al., 1989). The ABC model breaks behavior down into the following pattern:

(A) Activating event occurs.
(B) Belief system kicks in.
(C) Consequence of belief system.

As an example of how this model would explain elder abuse, consider a situation where a caregiver (or a spouse) perceives an elderly person's comments as verbally abusive (e.g., the activating event). The caregiver's beliefs (B) are that the elderly person is not appreciative of the caregiver's services, and the caregiver feels that all the person does is complain. The consequence (C) of these beliefs could be physical, psychological, or emotional abuse. To prevent the abuse, Ellis suggests that individuals must dispute (D) their beliefs in order to eliminate irrational beliefs. Once individuals dispute their beliefs, a new effect (E) should be forthcoming. Thus, in the preceding case, if the caregiver changes his or her belief system to see how the elderly person actually appreciates the caregiver's efforts, then the caregiver would be less likely to respond abusively in a particular situation.

Basically, Ellis believes that irrational thinking leads to distress, which can result in abhorrent behavior such as elder abuse. Ellis et al. (1989) describe five types of irrational thinking. Although they did not apply their typology to elder abuse, the parallels between Ellis et al.'s typology and abusive scenarios are striking. The first type of irrational thinking is *demandingness,* which entails instances where individuals require (as opposed to prefer) things from others. Cases where a caregiver demands certain responses from elderly persons surely could lead to abuse. Second, *neediness* entails circumstances where individuals need certain things to be happy. The way that many abusers are dependent on victims (discussed below) is an example of this type of irrational thinking. Third, *low frustration tolerance* as a type of irrational thinking is clearly related to cases of elder abuse where abusers get easily frustrated and abuse their parents or relatives. Fourth, *awfulizing* is blowing things out of proportion, which could also lead to abuse. Finally, *damning of oneself or others* involves situations where individuals place negative labels on themselves or others. Recall from Chapter 5 that police officers listen for labels such as the "old lady" or other stereotypical terms to determine whether a suspect actually abused the elderly victim. It is important to stress that these five types of irrational thinking will, according to Ellis, lead to negative consequences such as elder abuse.

Though she was not discussing rational-emotive theory, a quote from Harris (1996) shows how rational-emotive theory and the ABC model would address spousal elder abuse cases: "name calling, nagging, or other types of abuse from a partner can cause a loss of control and abusive behavior from a person who has learned spousal aggression from his/her family" (p. 4). In essence, the name calling or nagging is the activating event (A), the belief (B) is that it is appropriate to be aggressive toward one's spouse, and the consequence (C) is the loss of control. Taking this a step further, advocates of Ellis' approach would argue that abusers needs to dispute (D) their beliefs about the appropriateness of violence in order to see a new effect (E).

Another intra-individual explanation has to do with *impairments of the offenders or victims.* Referred to as impairment theory, this type of intra-individual explanation suggests that offenders or victims with physical or mental impairments have higher rates of crime (in the case of offenders), or are at a higher risk of elder abuse (in the case of victims) (Fulmer et al., 1984). As an example of the relationship between physical impairment and the offender, consider that chemical imbalances and low levels of seratonin have been attributed to various types of family violence, including elder abuse (Arbetter, 1995).

As far as the relationship between victim impairments and elder abuse, research suggests that elderly victims are more likely to have cognitive and functional impairments than non-victims (Godkin et al., 1989). As an example, persons with Alzheimer's are "2.25 times at greater risk for a physically abusive episode than an older person living in the community" (Paveza et al., 1992, p. 497). Coyne et al. (1996) build on this idea and suggest that "aggressive, combative, or violent behavior seen in Alzheimer's disease and other dementias plays a role in triggering abuse from caregivers" (p. 95). Even though victim impairments have been found to be related to victimization risks, the caregiver's characteristics are generally seen as more important in explaining elder abuse than the victim's characteristics are (Conlin, 1995; Pillemer, 1985). That is, to fully understand why abuse occurs, we should focus on offenders' characteristics, rather than looking at victims' characteristics, which risks falling into the trap of blaming the victim for the abuse. As well, note that recent research suggests that the importance of cognitive impairment in explaining maltreatment may be overstated (Phillips, de Ardon, & Briones, 2000).

Intra-individual explanations tend to look within the individual to see the source of elder abuse. These explanations are critiqued because, with the exception of rational-emotive theory, they often ignore specific situations or timing factors that may precipitate abuse (Anetzberger, 1987). Even so, the fact that caseworkers and criminal justice officials will encounter so many offenders and victims with substance problems, psychological disorders, and impairments makes it necessary to consider these explanations in attempting to explain crimes against elderly persons.

Stress

Stress has also been seen as a source of elder abuse. The two types of stress are external stress and internal stress. The distinction has to do with the origin of the stress. External stressors include accidents, income, employment status, financial problems, relationship problems, work-related problems, loss of job, limited educational resources, divorce, and death of a loved-one (Arbetter, 1995; Baron & Welty, 1996; Fulmer et al., 1984; Godkin et al., 1989; Harris, 1996; Paris et al., 1995; Vinton, 1991). Internal stressors are those that originate within the individual and include "anxiety, headaches, insomnia, and depression" (Fulmer et al., 1984, p. 132).

The two types of stress are not mutually exclusive, meaning that external stress may lead to internal stress, or vise versa. For instance, job problems may lead to anxiety, headaches, or illnesses. Or, anxiety may lead to work-related problems. Also, both types of stress have been seen as precipitating events, but not necessarily causes, in cases of nursing home violence (Harris & Benson, 1996; Payne & Cikovic, 1995), and cases of elder abuse by caregivers (Bendik, 1992). The interaction between external stresses and internal stresses in the caregiving context has been referred to as caregiver stress. Caregiver stress refers to the stress caregivers experience as a result of the burden they encounter from providing care to the dependent elderly victim (Fulmer et al., 1984).

Caregiver stress was one of the first explanations used to address why elder abuse occurs (Greenberg, McKibben, & Raymond, 1990). The caregiving stress explanation sees three primary sources of stress arising out of the interactions between the external and internal stressors. These three sources include the following:

1. Physical, financial, and emotional problems from caring for impaired elderly persons;
2. A lack of "regular" caregiver assistance from community programs; and,
3. Subordination of the caregiver's private time to take care of the elderly person's needs (Griffin & Williams, 1992, p. 25).

The underlying assumption is that caregiver burden arises out of attempts to deal with the elderly person's impairments, and that abuse results from the stress (Powell & Berg, 1987). Stress is believed to contribute more to physical and emotional abuse than to financial abuse (Sabato, 1993). To determine the role of stress in elder abuse cases, Coyne, Reichman, and Berbig (1993) surveyed 342 caregivers "who called a telephone help line specializing in dementia" (p. 643). Their results suggest that the psychological and physical demands that are a part of caring for relatives with dementia contribute to an increased likelihood of abuse.

Bendik (1992) surveyed 110 caregivers to see what factors precipitated abuse. She found that mood disturbance was the strongest predictor of abuse. However, she argues that the potential for abuse is not caused by a stressful situation. Rather, the following factors were suggested to be the most important factors: income inadequacy, poor emotional health, a low level of social support, and an external locus of control orientation.

The caregiver stress explanation is critiqued on the grounds that many people experience stress without abusing others (Anetzberger, 1987; Tomita, 1990). Also, many believe that the stress itself is not the cause of abuse; rather, the way the caregiver responds to the stress is seen as the significant factor (Arbetter, 1995; Baron & Welty, 1996; Bendik, 1992). Steinmetz (1988) writes, "[A]n *individual's perceptions* of the stress and feeling of burden–subjective measures–are far stronger predictors of abuse than the more objective factors" (emphasis added) (p. 218). So, it is not the stress itself that causes stress, but how individuals handle stress. It is not surprising, then, that some point out that stress, combined with a lack of training, can be a contributing factor in cases where elderly persons suffer from dementia (Jones, 1996). It is also important to note that some see the role of caregiving stress in leading to abuse as overrated (Baron & Welty, 1996), and some view the stress explanation as an "oversimplification" (Korbin, Anetzberger & Eckert, p. 7).

Indeed, some experts argue that an over reliance on the caregiver stress explanation has resulted in laws, policies, and practices that fit this "oversimplified" assumption (Bergeron, 2001). According to Bergeron (2001), elder abuse policies should be guided by domestic violence theories. Changing the policies, Bergeron argues, would theoretically result in more appropriate interventions and case assessments. Essentially, many elder abuse victims are family violence victims first and foremost, and in order to serve them, the responses should be couched within domestic violence interventions rather than child abuse interventions.

Dependency

Dependency has also been seen as a source of elder abuse. Fulmer (1991) notes that a natural result of the aging process is that older persons may need assistance with daily activities. Thus, they may become more dependent on others for care. Dependency can then provide a situation where the offender uses the dependency to control and abuse the elderly person. Of course, the notion of dependency is a vague concept, meaning far different things to all of those who attribute elder abuse to "dependency" (Fulmer, 1990). Also, Fulmer (1990) notes that the use of different types of populations and research samples will influence the relevance of dependency. For instance, different findings would be expected depending on the caregiving needs of the elderly person (e.g., those with dementia may need more attention than those without, therefore they would be at a higher risk for abuse). Not surprisingly, there is disagreement about the types of dependency, and the direction of the dependency.

For example, Steinmetz (1988) describes six different types of dependency: household dependency, personal grooming/health dependency, financial dependency, mobility dependency, mental health dependency, and social/emotional dependency. She uses the concepts of generational inversion to refer to the process by which parents become dependent on adult children. Central to the dependency thesis is the belief that the dependency leads to stress, which leads to abuse (Pillemer, 1985). The belief originally was that the elderly person's dependence on the caregiver leads to abuse. Today, experts use the concept of dependency to refer to the "unhealthy dependency of the perpetrator on the victim and vise versa" (Wolf, 1996b, p. 6). Thus, dependency is seen as a two way street–the offender may be dependent on the victim or the victim may be dependent on the offender.

The shift in seeing the dependence of the offender on the victim was considered by Pillemer (1985) who argued that the abusers' dependence on victims made them feel powerless. The powerlessness, he hypothesized, resulted in violence to regain the power in the relationship. To test this relationship, Pillemer (1985) interviewed forty-two physically abused elderly persons and forty-two non-abused elderly persons. He found that the abuse group was *less* dependent on the caregiver group than the non-abused group was. Also, there was no difference in the functional impairments between the groups. He suggests that the notion that the victim is abused because he or she is dependent "must be called seriously into question" (p. 151). He further found that caregivers from the abused group were more likely than the other caregivers to be financially dependent on the abuser. But, he notes that it is not just the perpetrator's dependency in and of itself that leads to elder abuse. Rather, he finds that mental illness may also play a role.

To further test the direction of the dependency relationship, Pillemer and Finkelhor (1989) interviewed sixty-one elder abuse and neglect victims and 251 randomly selected elderly persons who acted as a control group. As with Pillemer's earlier research, "the abusers were . . . found to be substantially more dependent on the elderly they victimized than were the comparison relatives" (p. 184). Other studies have also suggested that an offender's dependency on the victim was more important than the victim's dependency on the offender explaining many cases of abuse (Anetzberger, 1987; Conlin, 1995; Wolf, Strugnell, & Godkin, 1982). Lang (1993) writes that abusers are more likely "to be dependent on the elderly person for housing, money, and transportation than relatives who don't abuse" (p. 30).

Some have addressed why dependency contributes to abuse. Finkelhor (1983) points out that abusive acts could be "carried out by abusers to compensate for their perceived lack or loss of power" (p. 19). Baron and Welty (1996) appear to agree, writing that dependency "results in compensatory abusive behavior" (p. 41). Others, however, have examined the relationship between dependency and other characteristics of the offenders. For instance, Greenberg et al. (1990) analyzed 204 substantiated cases of elder abuse by adult children in Wisconsin and found that financially dependent adult children often had drug or alcohol problems, lived with the victim, and were typically less than forty years old. They also found that a small group of offenders "were dependent because of problems related to mental illness" (p. 73).

Some have used social exchange theory to explain how dependency contributes to elder abuse (Pillemer, 1985; Wolf et al., 1984; Tomita, 1990). Social exchange theory looks at the interdependency between the offender and the victim and is particularly useful in explaining the way that an abuser's economic dependence on the elderly victim contributes to elder abuse (Tomita, 1990). The theory "holds that individuals attempt to maximize their rewards and minimize their costs in a relationship" (Vinton, 1991, p. 12). Godkin et al. (1989) see the elderly person and the caregiver as becoming more interdependent because of a "loss of other family members, increased social isolation, and the increased financial dependency of the perpetrator on the elderly person" (p. 207). Individuals will continue in their relationship as long as they think they are reaping benefits from the relationship. When a member thinks he or she is "losing" power in the relationship, he or she may engage in physical, financial, or verbal abuse to gain benefits in the relationship (Harris & Benson, 1996). To offset the possibility of abuse, experts suggest increases in the rewards of reduced dependency and increases in the costs of offensive behavior (Wolf, 1992).

Transgenerational Violence

The notion of transgenerational violence refers to the possibility that abusers learned how to be abusive from their parents or other role models. Also referred to as a "cycle of violence" (Steinmetz, 1988) and the "theory of internal family dynamics" (Fulmer et al., 1984), the transgenerational violence approach is an example of a social learning theory and is based on the process of modeling (Wiehe, 1998). The concept of transgenerational violence refers to "violence that has been passed along from generation to generation" (Jerin & Moriarty, 1998, p. 115). This approach was promoted because many cases of elder abuse occurred in homes where there was a history of violence and abusive acts (Myers & Shelton, 1987).

Korbin et al. (1990) report that the cycle of violence is "the most commonly reported causal factor in the child abuse literature" (p. 10). This means that children who are abused are more likely to become parents who abuse their children. Applying the approach to elder abuse requires a shift in orientation. In essence, when looking at elder abuse this perspective suggests the following: "If the adult child was treated violently as a child, he or she is much more likely to respond to parents with similar retaliative measures" (Pierce & Trotta, 1986, p. 104). Along a similar line, Pillemer (1986) notes that the transgenerational violence approach to explaining elder abuse is an approach "with elements of retaliation as well as imitation" (p. 243). The argument is that unresolved conflict may cause the child victim to want to get back at his or her abusive parents (Sayles-Cross, 1988). This approach has garnered widespread attention despite the fact that little empirical research has supported the transgenerational violence perspective (Korbin et al., 1995; Pillemer, 1986).

To assess the relevance of this approach in the area of elder abuse, Korbin et al. (1995) surveyed twenty-three elder abusers and twenty-one child abusers. Though the two groups' experiences with "overall" violence were not different, they found that child abusers were more likely to have experienced "severe violence" than were elder abusers. Based on this, they suggest that the transgenerational cycle of violence is more useful in understanding child abuse than elder abuse.

There has been limited and indirect support for the transgenerational approach for some categories of elder abusers. For instance, Coyne et al. (1996) report that that "a history of family violence prior to the onset of dementia appears to be associated with a greater likelihood of abuse between caregivers and patients" (p. 95). Also, moderate support for the cycle of violence has been found in spouse abuse cases among older persons (Harris, 1996). In particular, Harris (1996) found that "respondents who had witnessed parental violence as a teen were more likely than others to report violence in the couple relationship" (p. 18). Further, it is important to note that this approach, if valid at all, would explain physical and psychological abuse but would not be useful in explaining financial abuse or neglect (Sadler, 1994).

Despite its widespread popularity, a great deal of literature shows little support for the relationship between transgenerational violence and elder abuse (Godkin et al., 1989; Korbin et al., 1995; Pillemer, 1986; Tomita, 1990; Wolf, 1996b). Another criticism of the approach is that not everyone who has been exposed to crime in their childhood commits criminal acts later in their lives (Tomita, 1990). Conversely, there are individuals who commit elder abuse but were never abused as children. Along a related line, with any type of learning theory, there is always a question of origin (Martin et al., 1990). That is, someone had to be the first person to learn to be violent. Where did they learn it from? It is analogous to the chick and egg argument. Which one came first—the chicken or the egg? What came first—elder abuse or the learning of elder abuse?

Symbolic Interactionism

Symbolic interactionists look at the interactions between the victim and the caregiver and pay particular attention to the meaning they attach to the behavior (Doerner & Lab, 1998). Phillips (1983) sees symbolic interactionism as the theory that best explains the relationship between the offender and the elder abuse victim. The central focus of this approach is on the way the two parties interact with one another. Implicit within this perspective is the idea that conflict may arise out of the meanings participants give to various behaviors and interactions.

As an example, a study by Goodridge, Johnston, and Thomson (1996) reveals that nursing assistants in one facility they examined were "physically assaulted by residents 9.3 times per month and verbally assaulted 11.3 times per month" (p. 49). A symbolic interactionist would ask how nursing assistants, or other caregivers, might respond to being abused. The situation in and of itself has no meaning. After all, as Berg (1998) notes, "Meaning is conferred on [the situation] by and through human interaction" (p. 9). If the caregivers define the abuse as a personal attack, they would be more likely to respond to abuse with abuse. If, on the other hand, they define the abuse as an unfortunate part of their job, they would be less likely to be abusive when they are physically or verbally assaulted. In a survey of caregivers providing support to those with dementia, Coyne et al. (1993) found that caregivers "who were physically abused by patients were more likely than those who were not to have directed abuse toward patients in their care" (p. 645). From a symbolic interactionist perspective, this "abuse response to abuse" occurs because of the meaning actors give to the initial abusive act.

Isolation

Isolation has been found to be higher among elderly victims. Therefore, some may argue that abuse occurs because elderly victims are isolated. Tomita (1990) refers to isolation as "the privacy of the family unit" (p. 174). She points out that industrialized societies have made nuclear families even more isolated than they were in the past. The result is that abuse is more likely to be unnoticed. Not surprisingly, then, research by Phillips (1983) shows that abused elders reported less contact with friends (e.g., phone calls, correspondences, and calls in times of trouble) than non-abused elderly. Phillips also found that abused elderly victims perceived "less overall support from the individuals involved in their social network" (p. 391).

Some argue that isolation might also be a consequence of abuse in that elderly victims tend to withdraw after abusive acts (Pillemer, 1986; Baron & Welty, 1996). Isolation may also occur as a result of a fear of victimization (Iutcovich & Cox, 1990; Wilber & Reynolds, 1996). Watson (1991) refers to this type of isolation as "self-imposed house arrest" (p. 54). According to Watson, this sort of self-confinement, rather than reducing the risks of victimization, actually increases an elderly person's risks of abuse inside the home. The end result is that it is difficult to determine if isolation is the cause of abuse and neglect or a consequence of abuse and neglect (Godkin et al., 1989).

Rationalizations by Abusers

One approach to explaining elder abuse that has relied on a traditional criminological theory is Tomita's (1990). In particular, Tomita (1990) used Sykes and Matza's (1957) neutralization theory to address the way that offenders rationalized their actions to justify their abusive behavior. She considered Sykes and Matza's (1957) five original neutralization techniques (denial of responsibility, denial of injury, denial of victim, condemnation of condemners, appeal to higher loyalties) and two neutralization techniques attributed to Minor (1980). The basic assumption of neutralization theory is that offenders will rationalize their actions before committing a criminal or deviant act and that the rationalization provides the offender the motivation to commit the act.

Denial of responsibility is concerned with ways that offenders will deny culpability for their actions by suggesting that their behavior is beyond their own control. Tomita (1990) points out that the use of stress as an excuse for elder abuse is an example of denying responsibility. *Denial of injury* refers to situations where the abusers justify their actions on the grounds that nobody was hurt. Instances where nursing home professionals suggest that the victim will not miss stolen items are just one example of this neutralization. Another example would be situations where caregivers justify physical abuse by suggesting that occasional abuse is not harmful. Third, *denial of victim* includes situations where the offender contends that the victim deserves to be injured. Caregivers may justify their actions on the grounds that they were provoked by an aggressive elderly person (Payne & Cikovic, 1995). Fourth, *condemnation of condemners* is concerned with instances where offenders allege that everybody does things that are wrong, particularly those who are likely to find fault with the offenders. Tomita (1990) points out that offenders may view adult protective service (APS) workers as "snoopy" (p. 178). Fifth, *appeal to higher loyalties* refers to instances where individuals' actions are justified on the grounds that they met the needs of a larger group of which the individual is a part. Tomita (1990) provides the example of abusers feeling that they need to be abusive in order to be considered powerful by others. She also notes that instances where victims refuse to report the abusive situation, because the offender appeals to the victim's remorse, are examples of this neutralization technique. So, the offender appeals to the victim for forgiveness, and the victim does not report the abuse for fear of being removed from the group and subsequently institutionalized in a nursing home.

Sykes and Matza (1957) developed the previous neutralizations, while Minor (1980) conceived the next two. *Defense of necessity* involves claims where abusers allege that the actions were needed. Adult children might justify stealing by saying that it is the only way to keep their parents from wasting their money (Tomita, 1990). *Metaphor of the ledger* refers to beliefs than an occasional transgression is permissible, as long as one has generally engaged in law-abiding behavior. Caregivers may argue that they have done an awful lot for the victim, and that an occasional act of abuse does not compare to all of the good the caregiver has done for the victim.

Tomita (1990) applied these neutralizations to elder abuse situations where caregivers, in most cases family members or relatives, are responsible for the abuse. Note, however, that these neutralizations also have been applied to white-collar crimes, many which target older persons (Rosoff et al., 2003). For instance, one who is defrauding elderly persons might argue that they are not responsible for their actions (e.g., denial of responsibility), or that they need the money to help their family survive (e.g., appeal to higher loyalties). In fact, because rationalizations have been seen as so common among white-collar offenders, criminologists have added several other rationalizations to Sykes and Matza's and Minor's original lists. These other rationalizations include the following: denial of laws, defense of entitlement, borrowing claims (Coleman, 1998), and claims that everybody is doing it (Friedrichs, 2003). Like the neutralization techniques considered by Tomita (1990), these additional neutralizations could explain all of the types of offenses committed against elderly persons. That is, they could explain elder abuse by caregivers, abuses in nursing homes, white-collar crimes that target elderly persons, and any of the other crimes involving elderly victims.

Denial of the law entails instances where offenders claim that the rules and regulations guiding their behavior are unfair. Situations where health care providers commit fraudulent acts on the grounds that the insurance rules are too rigid are an example of this rationalization.

Defense of entitlement includes justifications where the offenders argue that they deserve whatever they are getting from the abusive act. Instances where adult children steal from their parents on the grounds that they are entitled to the money because they will receive it eventually is an example of an entitlement claim. In other financial exploitation cases, the inability of victims to testify results in offenders making claims that they were entitled to the money, either because it was given to them or they were borrowing it.

In addition to financial abuse by family members and known caregivers in the community, interviews with nursing home employees by Harris and Benson (1996) also reveal that aides will rationalize their financially abusive behavior by stating that they are underpaid, overworked, and underappreciated. Certainly one can see claims of entitlement arising out of these beliefs.

Borrowing is a rationalization where offenders rationalize their behavior by claiming they intend to return the stolen property. Coleman cites Cressey's (1953) *Other People's Money,* which suggests that fraudulent bank clerks justified their actions by suggesting that they intended to return the stolen property. It is equally plausible that caregivers will convince themselves that they can steal (e.g., borrow) from elderly victims as long as they return the stolen (e.g., borrowed) property. In all likelihood, they will not return the property.

Finally, *claims that everybody is doing it* involve justifications where offenders argue that their actions are the norm. An example would be adult children who steal from their parents because they believe their siblings are stealing their parent's property. If their brothers and sisters are doing it, why shouldn't they?

Patriarchal Theory

Elder abuse researchers and criminologists have used patriarchal theory to understand various types of family violence (Crichton et al., 1999; Moyer, 1992a; Vinton, 1991). Patriarchal theory looks at the power differences between men and women (Moyer, 1992a; Wiehe, 1998). Wiehe (1998) notes that there are two different types of power focused on by patriarchal theorists. First, personal power is analogous to the physical power that comes from one's inner self. Second, structural power refers to the power individuals receive from society. The power that comes from society is derived from societal norms and expectations (Vinton, 1991). In a patriarchal society, more structural power is given to males than to females. Patriarchal theorists argue that these power differences contribute to the abuses committed against females.

Support for patriarchal theory has been found in the literature. For instance, Crichton et al. (1999) examined 185 elder abuse cases and found that women were more likely to be victims of elder abuse while men were more likely to be the offenders. The authors suggest that the socialization of males plays a role in fostering attitudes that would promote the use of violence to control females. They also note that elderly women face a double-edged sword in that they are discriminated on the basis of their age and gender. This is similar to what one criminologist refers to as "unequal gender power" and "unequal generational power" (see Moyer, 1992b). In particular, males have more physical and structural power than females, and caregivers (generally younger than elderly persons) have more structural and physical power than elderly persons. This is not a finding limited to the United States. Cross-cultural research on cultures dominated by a male ideology demonstrates a relationship between patriarchal beliefs and marital violence in elderly couples (Kim & Sung, 2001).

Note that patriarchal theory can be seen as a type of conflict theory. The underlying assumption of conflict theory is that individuals with power use their resources and political leverage to control powerless individuals. Along this line of thinking, Jerin and Moriarty (1998) write: "Elderly persons often have few resources, wealth, power, or prestige. As a result, they are abused by those who must take care of them" (p. 115). Thus, conflict theory suggests that those with power do things to powerless individuals in order to maintain or even strengthen the power they have over powerless individuals. Patriarchal theory, as a type of conflict theory, suggests that the power is given to males as a result of the way structural factors influence the socialization process.

EXPLAINING ABUSE IN NURSING HOMES

Some of the above explanations can be applied to the various types of abuse committed in nursing homes. For example, abusers might rationalize their abusive acts before committing the offense. Or, some might argue that the aides have irrational belief systems, giving rise to unacceptable behavior. Still others might suggest that the interactions and the meanings residents and staff give to the interactions contribute to violent behavior. However, a set of different explanations has arisen to deal specifically with abuse in nursing homes. These other explanations can be referred to as institutional factors, staff characteristics, situational characteristics, educational influences, and patient vulnerability (Harris, 1999; Pillemer & Finkelhor, 1991; Pillemer & Moore, 1990).

Institutional factors are concerned with characteristics of the institution and whether general factors at the institutional level may foster abuse. These factors include the size of the institution, whether the institution is private or public, and the rates charged for the institution's services (Pillemer & Bachman, 1991). Based on interviews with nursing directors and an analysis of the inspection reports of 410 nursing homes in Australia, Jenkins and Braithewaite (1993) report that neglect and abuse of residents is higher in for-profit homes than it is in non-profit homes. They argue, "[P]ressure for lawbreaking comes from the top down and from profits" (p. 221). Alternatively, surveys of 577 nurse's aides and licensed practical nurses found that facility characteristics were not contributing factors in cases of physical abuse (Pillemer and Moore, 1991). So, facility characteristics might influence neglect and quality of care, but probably do not contribute to cases of physical abuse where employees physically assault residents.

Staff characteristics are concerned with the characteristics of employees working in nursing homes (Pillemer & Bachman, 1991). These characteristics include age, gender, level of pay, education, occupational position, and attitudes toward patients. Research by Harris and Benson (1998), for instance, finds that nursing home staff with negative attitudes toward patients are more likely to commit theft in nursing homes than those with positive attitudes toward patients are. They also found that job dissatisfaction contributed to theft. Further, nurse's aides have been found to be the group implicated most often in cases of financial abuse and physical abuse (Harris & Benson, 1996; Payne & Cikovic, 1995). The low salaries of nurse's aides have also been implicated in nursing home theft and physical abuse cases (Shaw, 1998; Harris & Benson, 1996). Further, males have been found to be overrepresented in cases of physical abuse and nursing home theft (Harris & Benson, 1996; Payne & Cikovic, 1995). Even though staff characteristics have been shown to be significant, other research argues that situational characteristics are the most important predictors of physical and psychological abuse (Pillemer & Bachman, 1991; Pillemer & Moore, 1990).

Situational characteristics refer to factors such as the level of conflict, the presence of alcohol use, stress, burnout, and responses to aggression. Evidence of the importance of these factors was found in a telephone survey of 577 nurse's aides and licensed practical nurses described by Pillemer and Moore (1989, 1990). Results of the interviews showed that stress, patient conflicts, and patient aggression toward staff were factors contributing to the physical abuse of residents. Regarding stress, the authors suggest that the respondents felt "burned out" because they did not have enough time to perform their expected duties. Patient conflict entailed conflicts over eating habits, hygiene, toileting, and unwillingness to dress. Describing the potential for conflict, Keller (1996) writes, "[R]esidents' behavioral problems and communication deficits may trigger negative reactions by caregivers" (p. 110). Only 20 percent of the respondents indicated no conflicts with the residents. Regarding aggression, the authors found that "only 11 percent of the staff had not been insulted or sworn at during the preceding year" and only 13 percent were not pushed, grabbed, or pinched in the previous year. Based on their findings, Pillemer and Moore (1989) report that the relationship between patient and staff may be the most important factor determining the type of care patients receive.

Using the same data, Pillemer and Bachman (1991) used multivariate regression techniques to determine whether facility characteristics, staff characteristics, and situational characteristics predicted the existence of elder abuse. Their findings indicate that situational characteristics such as burnout and level of patient-staff conflict were the most important predictors of abuse. Recall, however, that they focused only on physical and psychological abuse, and that explanations of financial abuse and neglect may be different.

Educational influences, or the lack of training, has been cited as a contributing factor in cases of nursing home abuse (Myers & Shelton, 1987; Payne, 1998a; Payne & Cikovic, 1995; Pillemer & Bachman, 1991), and for other situations where caregivers abuse those in need of care (Coyne et al., 1996). Goodridge et al. (1996) write, "[Many] nursing assistants who work with the elderly receive virtually no training on the interpersonal care and often limited education on the technical aspects" (p. 64). Certainly training on how to deal with potential violent situations would go a long way toward lowering the risk of abuse (Payne & Cikovic, 1995; Pillemer & Moore, 1991). In addition to the lack of training, the lack of effective criminal background checks has been seen as potentially increasing the risk of physical, psychological, and financial abuse in nursing homes (Schwartz, 1998).

Vulnerability is another factor that may contribute to abuse in nursing homes (Harris, 1999; Payne & Cikovic, 1995). Basically, because of the way that residents are isolated from society, various abuses can occur without being detected by authorities, or anyone for that matter. The belief is that these actions occur because there is often very little to stop them from occurring. Further, most of the cases of abuse in nursing homes occur without witnesses (Payne & Cikovic, 1995). Without witnesses, patient abuse "remains hidden from sight like an iceberg" (Sundram, 1986, p. 21). Compounding the problem even more are negative perceptions or overexaggerated beliefs about the vulnerability of the residents (Harris, 1999). As a group, elderly persons are not as vulnerable as they are made out to be. However, if abusers define them as vulnerable, abusers will attempt to take advantage of that perceived vulnerability and prey on elderly victims.

With the exception of Maslow's hierarchy of needs and Ellis's rational emotive theory, the previous explanations are those that have been offered in the literature to explain elder abuse. Maslow and Ellis's theories were included to demonstrate how intra-individual explanations of elder abuse would explain various abuses against elderly persons. Oddly, missing from many of the elder abuse explanations are the criminological theories that criminologists have used to try to explain why crime in general occurs. To be sure, some elder abuse researchers have used criminological theories such as neutralization theory and patriarchal theory to explain the mistreatment of elderly persons. Also, recent literature examining crimes in nursing homes used criminological theories to explain institutional mistreatment (Harris & Benson, 1996; Harris, 1999; Jenkins & Braithewaite, 1993; Van Wyk, Benson, & Harris, 1998). Moreover, the way elder abuse researchers talk about transgenerational violence is similar to how criminologists address the way offenders learn criminal behavior. Even so, a large body of criminological theory is missing from the elder abuse research that addresses the causes of elder mistreatment.

CRIMINOLOGICAL EXPLANATIONS

Criminological theories generally rely on input from sociological and psychological perspectives to address the existence of crime. Because criminology is seen by many as a sub-discipline of sociology (Gibbons, 1994), it is not surprising that many of the theories criminologists have claimed, tested, and developed have their roots in sociology. What is surprising is the fact that many of the theories criminologists hold central to their discipline have not been used to address elder abuse. To fill this void, I will consider six criminological theories and show how these theories could be used to explain elder abuse. The theories I will consider are deterrence theory, strain theory, differential association, control theory, routine activities theory, and social disorganization theory.

Deterrence Theory

Deterrence theory is traced to Cesare Beccaria's (1764) *Essays on Crime and Punishment.* Beccaria's theory was based on the assumption that human beings are rational actors who will weigh the positives and negatives before acting. To deal with crime, he suggested that society must take measures so that potential offenders would see more negatives associated with the criminal acts than positives. In developing these notions, he considered both specific and general deterrence. Specific deterrence ideals are fulfilled when actions are oriented toward keeping the individual offender from committing future offenses. General deterrence ideals are fulfilled when actions are oriented toward keeping the rest of society from committing future offenses.

Using ideas that many suggest are related to social learning theory, Beccaria advocated that that surest way to deter crime was through punishment of offenders. Effective punishment, however, has to be part of a three-pronged formula: (1) it has to be swift enough so that offenders would link the concepts of crime and punishment in their minds; (2) it has to be certain enough so that rational offenders would know ahead of time that their actions would result in punishment; and (3) it has to be just severe enough to outweigh the pleasure offenders would get from the criminal acts. Today, many sentencing policies are based on deterrence ideals as discussed by Beccaria (Martin et al., 1990).

A more modern version of deterrence theory is known as rational choice theory (Cornish & Clarke, 1986). This perspective suggests that offenders are rational actors who will rationally consider their needs, abilities, and situational factors before deciding to commit a crime. If the crime fits the offender's needs, and the criminal has the ability to commit the crime with a minimal risk of punishment and detection, the criminal will be more likely to commit the act. Not surprisingly, some have advocated that stronger law enforcement responses combined with stiffer sanctions for offenders are needed (Wilson, 1983).

Indeed, many sentencing policies handling elder abuse offenders are based on deterrence ideals (Alston, 1986). Recall that some states have enacted stiffer penalties for offenders who target elderly persons (Stiegel, 1995). Enhanced civil penalties for civil litigants are another example of deterrence ideals. The belief is that a severe monetary sanction will keep offenders, in these cases usually businesses such as nursing homes, from abusing or neglecting elderly persons. The reality is that stiff civil sanctions likely do little to reduce abuse because the sanctions are (1) applied inconsistently (e.g., they are not certain), (2) not enforced until long after the commission of the act (e.g., they are not swift), and (3) often disproportionate to the actual harm experienced by the victims (e.g., they may actually be too severe) (Stevens & Payne, 1999). In some cases, the punitive sanction awarded by the jury may be so high that the sanction is reduced or set aside by an appellate judge. In other cases, the offending business may simply close and declare bankruptcy, in which case the victim would never receive the monetary award. The end result is that a small group of civil offenders are given stiff sanctions with others not becoming aware of the sanction, thus limiting the deterrent value of the sanction.

Strain Theory

Modern criminological strain theory can be traced to Robert Merton's "Social Structure and Anomie" (1938). Merton argued that society creates goals for individuals and proscribes legitimate means to attain goals. For instance, in a capitalist society, individuals' goals are generally oriented toward financial success. Individuals also learn that the legitimate means to attain financial success include working hard, going to college, and abiding by society's rules. What happens, according to Merton, is that strain may develop between the goals and the means. Or, something may block individuals' opportunities to attain their goals. If this strain occurs, individuals are forced to adapt to the blocked opportunities.

Merton uses the phrase "modes of adaptation" to refer to the various ways that individuals respond to strain. The way he presented his typology is provided in Table 14. As shown in the table, Merton considered five modes of adaptation. First, the conformist is the individual who accepts the goals of society and the means to attain the goals. This mode of adaptation is the one followed by most individuals. Second, the innovator is the individual who accepts the goals of society but replaces legitimate means with illegitimate methods (e.g., property offenders, financial white-collar crimes, etc.). Third, the ritualist is a person who rejects the goals of society, but continues to abide by the rules. Fourth, the retreatist is the individual who rejects the goals and the means proscribed by society. Merton suggests that substance abusers fit into this category. Finally, the rebel is the individual who rejects the goals and

TABLE 14. MERTON'S MODES OF ADAPTATION

Adaptation Mode	Goals	Means
Conformist	Accept	Accept
Innovator	Accept	Reject
Ritualist	Reject	Accept
Retreatist	Reject	Reject
Rebel	Reject/Replace	Reject/Replace

Critical Thinking Questions:

1. Which mode best describes your behaviors?
2. What other modes of adaptation do you think exist?

means of society, and replaces the goals and means with his or her own goals and means (e.g., cults, gangs, etc.).

Merton's theory has yet to be applied to elder abuse. His modes of adaptation, however, certainly describe responses elderly caregivers may follow in responding to blocked opportunities. First, most nursing home professionals never abuse their clients (Shaw, 1998). Thus, the majority of nursing home professionals are conformists. Second, an example of the innovator mode would be instances where caregivers financially abuse their relatives in an effort to achieve financial success, or where fraudulent telemarketers defraud elderly persons of their life savings. Third, one might contend that caregivers who give up on their own goals but continue to provide care to the elderly persons are ritualists. Fourth, substance abusers who abuse and neglect elderly persons could be regarded as retrseatists. Fifth, Merton describes the rebel adaptation as occurring when "the reigning standards, due to frustration or to marginalist perspectives, leads to the attempt to introduce a new social order" (p. 676). On a societal level, this adaptation is not easily applied to elder abuse. However, on an individual level, it is plausible to argue that some caregivers, particularly children who physically abuse their parents in an effort to reach their own goals, fit into the rebel category.

Merton's theory is critiqued on a number of grounds. As already noted, a lot of people get frustrated, but not everyone resorts to offensive behavior to deal with their frustrations (Tomita, 1990). Another point some authors make is that traditionally strain was measured in terms of an individual's ability to attain financial goals. More recently, Agnew (1992) broadened the concept of strain to refer to "negative affective states–most notably anger and related emotions–that often result from negative relationships" (p. 49). This seems to suggest that stress could be a source of strain. Recall the earlier consideration of the relationship between stress and elder abuse. Though the role of caregiver stress may be overstated, other types of strain might contribute to abusive acts against elderly persons. What follows is an overview of the way that Agnew's general strain theory could be used to better understand elder abuse.

According to Agnew (1992), strain theory focuses "explicitly on negative relationships with others; relationships in which the individual is not treated as he or she wants to be treated" (p. 60). Within these negative relationships, individuals could experience strain. Agnew (1992) cites three sources of strain: (1) failing or expecting to fail at positively valued goals; (2) removal or expected removal of positively valued stimuli; and (3) confronting or expecting to confront negative stimuli.

As far as the first source of strain is concerned, it is possible that caregivers experience external stresses that would cause them to either fail at their goals or believe they will fail at their goals. Theoretically, "life crises can create stress and serve as a trigger for violence" (Chen et al., 1981, p. 5). These external pressures (job problems, financial stresses, etc.) could lead to problems in the caregiving relationship. So, it may not be the caregiving situation that creates the stress. Instead, the response to stress may simply be manifested during the caregiving relationship.

Caregivers might also experience strain due to the loss, or the fear of losing, positively valued stimuli. It is plausible that caregivers fear they are losing independence while caring for elderly persons. Note again that they may not be losing independence because the elderly person is becoming dependent on them; rather, the caregivers may be the ones losing independence and subsequently becoming more dependent on the elderly person (Pillemer, 1985). Perceiving the loss of independence could be a source of strain. As well, caregivers may perceive that they are losing their free time or other positively valued stimuli. These perceptions would also lead to frustration.

Caregivers might also confront or expect to confront negatively valued stimuli. Fear of medical bills is one example of expecting to confront negatively valued stimuli. Caregivers might worry about other financial costs associated with caregiving. Death is certainly another example of a negatively valued stimulus. When caregivers must care for their elderly parents, they are forced to confront the fact that they and their parents are mortals. Questioning one's own mortality could lead to strain in an individual's life.

It is important to emphasize that it is not the caregiving situation that creates stress but the individual's perceptions of the situation. Thus, stress and frustration are seen as setting the stage for many of the abusive acts committed against elderly persons (Pierce & Trotta, 1986). It is not just physical abuse that necessarily results from frustration. Harris and Benson (1998) surveyed 284 nursing home employees and found that dissatisfied (e.g., frustrated) employees are more likely to steal from their patients than satisfied employees are. It is plausible, then, to suggest that strain can lead to a host of reactions including physical abuse, financial abuse, verbal abuse, psychological abuse, and so on.

Differential Association

Differential association is a social learning theory developed by Edwin Sutherland. The theory is a dominant criminological approach that some see as pioneering modern criminology (Martin et al., 1990). Sutherland presented his theory in a series of nine propositions. The thrust of his theory is found in his first four propositions:

1. Criminal behavior is learned.
2. Criminal behavior is learned in interaction with other persons in a process of communication.

3. The principal part of the learning of criminal behavior occurs within intimate personal groups.
4. When criminal behavior is learned, the learning includes (a) techniques of committing the crime, which are sometimes very complicated, sometimes very simple; (b) the specific direction of motives, drives, rationalizations, and attitudes. (Sutherland & Cressey, 1970, pp. 77–79)

Some may see Sutherland's theory as suggesting that criminals become criminals from being around other criminals. This sort of thinking oversimplifies differential association theory. Rather, Sutherland's theory suggests that individuals become criminals from learning definitions favorable to criminal behavior.

His theory is further explained in the remaining propositions where he outlines the way that the learning process influences criminal behavior. Briefly, he suggests that individuals who learn more definitions favorable to law violation (as opposed to definitions unfavorable to law violation) are more likely to commit criminal acts. He further suggests that criminal behavior is learned through the same learning process that any type of behavior is learned. For instance, my dad used to teach my brother and sister and me how to change and rotate the tires on his automobile. He told us how to do it (e.g., the techniques–loosen the lug nuts, place the jack under the car, etc.) and why to do it (e.g., the motivations–to keep the tires from becoming prematurely worn). Sutherland concluded his propositions suggesting that criminal behavior, though an expression of general needs and values, is not caused by those general needs and values because non-criminal behavior is also an expression of those same general needs and values. In essence, according to Sutherland, all behavior is an expression of general needs and values. Therefore, we cannot say that criminal behavior is caused by general needs and values.

Like the other criminological theories, differential association is not found in the elder abuse literature. However, other types of social learning theories have been used to explain elder abuse. Also, comments from various elder abuse researchers indirectly suggest that differential association may apply to some cases of elder abuse. For instance, according to Shaw (1998), nursing home staff must develop immunity to external stressors to avoid becoming abusive. This suggests that staff must learn definitions unfavorable to law violations, rather than definitions favorable to law violations. Shaw recommends improved training programs as a method to increase this immunity. Training goes hand in hand with Sutherland's theory.

Others have argued that peer support groups will be effective in educating caregivers and subsequently reducing the likelihood of violence (Pillemer & Suitor, 1992). The underlying implication is that the caregivers will learn appropriate definitions of behavior in small groups (recall that Sutherland noted that behavior was learned in "intimate personal groups"). In fact, a policy implication of Sutherland's theory is that programs "could use the concept of associating with role models who provide conventional definitions of behavior" to reduce crime (Williams & McShane, 1994, p. 81).

Along a similar line, research by Kilburn (1996) shows that caregivers who have a social network of peers with experience providing care to Alzheimer's patients will be less likely to be violent. Kilburn writes, "having a higher number of associates with experience as caregivers is clearly related to the absence of caregiver's violent feelings" (p. 79). Again, the implication is that caregivers would learn more definitions unfavorable to elder abuse if they are around those who provide support for conventional definitions of behavior.

Sutherland's theory is not perfect. Some say that its ambiguity makes it untestable (Gibbons, 1994). Others point out that the origin of learning is not specified, e.g., from whom did the first offender learn criminal behavior (Williams & McShane, 1994). And others say that the theory oversimplifies the learning process (Martin et al., 1990). Nonetheless, the theory is cited as "one of the enduring classics in criminology" (Cullen & Agnew, 1999, p. 82). The theory of differential association certainly could be used as a guide in researching and understanding elder abuse.

Control Theory

Rather than asking why do people commit crime, control theory, also known as social bonding theory, posits "Why don't people commit crime?" (Hirschi, 1969). Applying this to elder abuse, control theorists would ask, "Why don't the majority of caregivers, nursing home professionals, or others abuse elderly persons?" The answer, according to control theory, is that individuals do not commit crime because they have strong bonds with society. Those with weak bonds are those who are more likely to abuse elderly persons.

Hirschi's (1969) *Causes of Delinquency* is perhaps the foundation of modern control theory. In this work, Hirschi argued that the bond individuals have with society is made up of four elements—attachment, belief, involvement, and commitment. Attachment refers to the degree to which individuals are attached to their family or institutions whose standards are in line with conventional standards. Belief is concerned with whether individuals believe in the rules of society. Commitment refers to the degree to which individuals are committed to conventional societal goals. Finally, involvement refers to whether individuals are involved in activities that would keep them out of trouble. The premise of Hirchi's control theory is that individuals will refrain from criminal behavior as long as these elements remain strong. If an element of the bond becomes weak, an individual's likelihood of criminal behavior increases. So, if caregivers are bonded to society, they are less likely to commit offenses against elderly persons. If their bond is weakened, they will be more likely to be abusive.

More recently, Gottfredson and Hirschi (1990) published *A General Theory of Crime* in which they argue that an individual's level of self-control, combined with the opportunity to commit crime, is the cause of criminal behavior. In particular, they argue that those with a lower self-control are more likely to be involved in criminal acts. Self-control, they contend, comes from the lack of appropriate parenting received during one's childhood. They further suggest that one's self-control is stable throughout one's life and that when confronted with opportunities, those with a lower self-control are more likely to commit criminal acts than those with a higher self-control.

As far as why self-control affects crime, Gottfredson and Hirschi (1990) argue that those with a low self-control are more likely to be "impulsive, insensitive, physical (as opposed to mental) risk taking, short-sighted, and non-verbal" (p. 90). In addition, Gottfredson and Hirschi (1990) also believe that this theory explains street crimes as well as white-collar crimes. In fact, they argue that low self-control can explain all offenses, including those against elderly persons (e.g., physical abuse, psychological abuse, financial abuse, white-collar crime, etc.).

One author has noted that nursing home employees' self-control levels may contribute to nursing home offenses (Harris, 1999). It is equally plausible that elder abusers in domestic settings may lack self-control. For instance, basing her description of the abuser on past literature, Conlin (1995) describes elder abusers as having (1) psychopathological problems, (2) dependency on elderly persons for financial support and housing, (3) difficulties with the law, (4) drug and alcohol problems, (5) hospitalizations for psychiatric illnesses, (6) poor social skills, (7) poor communication skills, (8) a history of anti-social behavior, and (9) an unstable lifestyle. Others also note that elder abusers have personality disorders, low levels of tolerance, low self-esteems, financial troubles, and substance abuse problems (Chen et al., 1981). Gottredson and Hirschi (1990) would argue that many if not all of these problems are indicators of a low self-control. An elder abuser's low self-control would not automatically result in criminal behavior. Rather, the individual with a low self-control must be presented with the opportunity to commit the offense.

Routine Activities Theory

Opportunity is also a central element of routine activities theory. This is a relatively recent approach that is related to the rational choice perspective. Routine activities theory was developed by Cohen and Felson (1979) who argue that the three elements of crime are (1) a motivated offender, (2) a suitable target, and (3) the absence of a capable guardian. Cohen and Felson further argue that the lack of any of these elements is enough to stop a crime from occurring. For example, if a motivated offender finds an individual with a great deal of cash, but the individual is a uniformed police officer, then the third element would be missing and the likelihood of crime would be reduced if not eliminated altogether. Alternatively, if a motivated offender such as a caregiver finds cash hidden in an elderly person's nightstand, and there is no one to catch the offender stealing the cash, then all three elements are present and the likelihood of the crime occurring increases. The underlying assumption of routine activities theory is that crime is best explained by considering "the manner in which the spatio-temporal organization of social activities helps people to translate their criminal inclinations into action" (Cohen & Felson, 1979, p. 588). Thus, the routine activities (e.g., common social activities) that offenders and victims engage in will contribute to crime.

To a limited degree, routine activities theory has been applied to crimes against seniors. Often it is used to explain why elderly persons are less likely to be criminally victimized than younger persons. That is, elderly persons spend less time engaging in activities that would result in street crime victimization; therefore, they are less likely to find themselves in a situation where they would be suitable targets. Researchers have also used rational activities theory to examine elderly homicide victims. This research suggests that the fact that elderly persons are more likely to be killed at or near their homes is consistent with routine activities theory (Messner & Tardiff, 1985; Kennedy & Silverman, 1990). Messner and Tardiff (1985) write: "those persons who lead lives that are centered around the home are precisely those who are most likely to be victimized at home and to be killed by family members" (p. 262).

Kennedy and Silverman (1990) tested the efficacy of routine activities theory as it relates to elderly homicide victims in Canada by analyzing murders in Canada between 1961 and 1983. They found that routine activities theory explained homicides against elderly persons that are committed by family members. Not directly consistent with routine activities theory, they also found that many of the crime-based homicides were committed by strangers. This is inconsistent with routine activities theory, which would suggest that homicides would be committed more often by caregivers or family members with whom the victims would have routine contacts. The authors reconcile this discrepancy by suggesting a modified version of the theory that suggests that older persons who live alone are vulnerable to theft and fatal injuries. They write, "their isolation, coupled with the offender's motivation to burglarize . . . creates a potential homicide situation" (p. 317).

Consistent with routine activities theory, a recent study of 1,797 independently living elderly persons in the Netherlands shows that individuals who live with others are more likely to be physically and verbally abused, whereas those who live alone are more likely to be financially abused (Comijs et al., 1998). Comijs et al. (1998) never specifically mention routine activities theory, but their findings are nonetheless consistent with the theory. Those elderly persons who live with others would be expected to be physically victimized by their relatives more often than those who live alone because there would be more interactions between (1) motivated offenders, (2) suitable targets, and (3) the absence of capable guardians to stop the physical abuse. Like Kennedy and Silverman (1990), Comijs et al. (1998) also report that property offenses are more likely to be targeted toward elderly persons who live alone. From a routine activities perspective, those elderly persons who live alone would be suitable targets for financial offenses because capable guardians are more likely to be absent—thus giving motivated offenders the opportunity to steal.

When considering the risk factors for elder abuse in nursing homes, assumptions of routine activities theory are borne out. Specifically, one author cites the following risk factors as increasing the likelihood of elder abuse in long-term-care settings: (1) low staffing levels, (2) little staff development, (3) poor supervision, (4) lack of incident reporting, and (5) a closed/inward looking culture (Kmietowicz, 2003). The first two factors describe motivated offenders; the third and fourth refer to a lack of capable guardians; and the final one refers to what Cohen and Felson meant by vulnerable targets.

Routine activities theory has been used to address thefts occurring in nursing homes (Harris, 1999). Describing how this approach would address nursing home thefts, Harris states the following:

> Unfortunately, the nursing home environment is one in which suitable targets and motivated offenders are likely to converge under conditions of low or non-existent guardianship. Most nursing home patients keep personal items, such as jewelry, money, and clothing in their rooms. Small, easy to hide, and valuable, these items make attractive targets. Because of age, health, and cognitive disabilities, many patients lack the ability to protect their belongings and hence, can provide little surveillance. (p. 146)

Elsewhere, Harris and Benson (1996) write, "theft is everywhere in some nursing homes because the administration ignores it" (p. 183). This comment parallels "the absence of a capable guardian" as considered by Cohen and Felson (1979).

The way that the government regulates nursing homes also parallels routine activities theory. In the mid-nineties, a group of Republicans wanted to repeal the federal standards overseeing nursing home regulation that were passed in 1987. Their argument was that states could do a better job regulating their own nursing homes (Carlson, 1995). Carlson (1995) points out that states failed to regulate in the eighties, making it necessary for the federal government to pass legislation giving the Centers for Medicare and Medicaid Services (CMS) authority to investigate and enforce standards. In essence, the CMS became a capable guardian. From a routine activities perspective, removing the CMS's authority would increase the likelihood of mistreatment in nursing homes.

Routine activities theory could also be used to explain why elderly persons are more likely to be victims of white-collar crimes such as fraud than are younger persons. O'Neill and Flanagan (1998) note that elderly persons have more money in their checking accounts, and more assets, than younger persons. They also note that elderly persons may rely on others for help in managing their finances, thus increasing the likelihood they will be targeted for financial abuse. Along a similar line, Harris (1995) argues that older persons are targets of fraud for four reasons: (1) they have more assets than ever; (2) they have leisure time; (3) they are isolated; and (4) they have anxiety about the future. Green and Fogel (1996) cite an AARP study of 745 elderly telemarketing fraud victims that found that older victims "often believe the scams they hear and can not distinguish real claims from false ones" (p. 9). Taken together, the money and assets make them suitable targets, while the isolation reduces the likelihood that a capable guardian will stop the offense. Once a motivated offender enters the scene, the likelihood of fraud increases.

Though criminologists have used routine activities theory to address crimes against elderly persons, few elder abuse researchers have tested the approach, or used it as a guide for that matter. Many findings and claims in the elder abuse literature are actually quite similar to assumptions underlying routine activities theory. For instance, Fulmer (1991) writes, "isolated elders are at risk for mistreatment because they lack gatekeepers who can report mistreatment" (p. 30). This comment is similar to what Cohen and Felson (1979) refer to as "absence of a capable guardian." Warren and Bennett (1997) report that elderly individuals who are in need of more care are more likely to be abused than those who rely less on caregivers. It could be that they are more likely to encounter motivated offenders than those who do not rely on as much care. Sabato (1993) suggests that vulnerability combined with an offender's "lack of resources and support" provides a setting where the likelihood of financial abuse increases (p. 22). In essence, Sabato is alluding to the motivated offender (one who lacks resources and support) and to the suitable target (e.g., the vulnerable victim).

The notion of situational crime prevention is an ideology that parallels routine activities theory. Basically, situational crime prevention sees crime as resulting from situations and opportunities (Clarke, 1992). The goal of situational crime prevention is to "find practical ways to prevent crime" (Felson, 1998, p. 167). Harris (1999) lists the following things that nursing homes can do as examples of situational crime prevention:

1. Make targets less accessible to offenders.
2. Limit access of visitors and employees.
3. Use surveillance systems.
4. Develop property identification systems.
5. Do background checks on employees (p. 148).

She cites several other practices that can be followed to reduce the likelihood of crimes in nursing homes. Alston (1986) does not refer to the concept of situational crime prevention, but suggests certain measures to reduce an elderly person's vulnerability to victimization. These other measures include implementing (1) escort services for elderly persons, (2) neighborhood patrols, (3) programs making it easier to find companions, and (4) modifications in the environment so elderly persons have more control over their immediate resources. Clearly, there are a great number of policies and activities oriented toward protecting elderly persons that fit within the framework of situational crime prevention. In the end, situational crime prevention is less concerned with theory and more concerned with finding practical ways to prevent crime (Felson, 1998).

Social Disorganization Theory

At the most general level, social disorganization theory suggests that crime exists in certain parts of a city or community where disorganization is the highest. Disorganization is measured by a number of factors including the level of poverty, number of rental properties, amount of transition, and proportion of single parent families in a neighborhood. Traced to writings of Park and Burgess (1921), recent tests of the theory suggest that social disorganization theory among the more popular current explanations of crime offered by criminologists. To be sure, these recent empirical investigations suggest that social disorganization offers a viable explanation of criminal behavior.

Although the relationship between elder abuse and social disorganization has not yet been tested, findings from a few past studies and on-going research indirectly support the importance of the theory in explaining some types of elder abuse. In one study examining ninety-nine counties in Iowa, for example, researchers found that county demographics were risk factors for both reported and substantiated cases of elder abuse (Jogerst et al., 2000). This suggests that something at the community level may be fostering abuse.

On-going research by Payne and Gainey (2004) is testing the role of social disorganization theory in explaining elder abuse in neighborhoods from three different cities. Based on the assumption that sufficient evidence exists suggesting that the caregiving experience is influenced by neighborhood characteristics, Payne and Gainey (2004) point to research that finds that differences between rural and urban communities influence the Alzheimer's caregiving experience (Turyn, 2001). It is equally plausible that differences between certain neighborhoods within the same community may influence the caregiving experience. These differences between neighborhoods may impact *service utilization, burden,* and *maltreatment.*

Although no research has considered whether Alzheimer's caregivers from different neighborhoods have different levels of *service utilization,* variation between neighborhoods is likely to exist. A number of neighborhood characteristics may make it more difficult for individuals to seek formal caregiving assistance. For example, from the criminological literature, we find that disadvantaged communities are less apt to place a great deal of trust in government agencies. Perceived legitimacy is important, and less trust generally means less service utilization (see Sun, Triplett, & Gainey, 2003). Consider also access to transportation. In socially disorganized communities, restraints on public transportation may increase an older person's isolation. Isolation increases vulnerability, which increases risk (Redd, 2003).

Research shows that service utilization is not fully determined by caregiver need (Rudin, 1994; Toseland et al., 2002). Logically one should ask why those who need services do not seek them. A lack of trust in public agencies or an inability to access services would certainly be reasons to avoid utilization of services.

Age composition and the percent of elderly persons in a neighborhood may also be seen as influencing service utilization. Neighborhoods with fewer elderly persons may have fewer Alzheimer's patients. Caregivers in neighborhoods with fewer Alzheimer's patients may find it more difficult to find social support from their peers. Further, if cases are geographically isolated, as in many rural areas, information regarding potential services may not be shared. The combination of a lack of support at the private level and little access to formal social support may increase the difficulties inherent in caring for Alzheimer's patients.

Though never examined in past research, neighborhood characteristics also likely influence the way Alzheimer's caregivers experience *burden.* Differences between affluent and disadvantaged communities are especially significant in terms of caregiver burden. In more affluent communities, less external community stressors exist. This is not to suggest that caregiving does not present a burden in these settings; instead, we simply suggest that external community stresses do not compound caregiver burden in the same way that we would expect it to do so in disadvantaged communities. In affluent communities, members generally have opportunities available to them to reduce stress. In disadvantaged communities, not only are opportunities lacking, the existence of external stresses work to compound the stress experienced by Alzheimer's caregivers. Higher crime and unemployment rates, greater isolation among caregivers, transportation problems, lower incomes, and a number of other qualities of disadvantaged communities serve only to increase the burdens already experienced by Alzheimer's caregivers in these communities.

Neighborhood characteristics could also influence the *maltreatment* of Alzheimer's patients. According to some criminologists, social disorganization inhibits social control in communities, which is conducive to crime. Social disorganization is measured by a number of variables including racial heterogeneity, single parent families, poverty, vacant and rental properties in the neighborhood, and population turnover or instability. There is strong empirical evidence in the criminological literature that measures of social disorganization are related to crime (see Triplett, Gainey, & Sun, forthcoming, for a comprehensive review).

In terms of maltreatment of Alzheimer's patients, research suggests that they are at a higher risk of elder abuse. Unfortunately, research has not considered whether Alzheimer's patients living in certain neighborhoods are more susceptible to maltreatment than those living in other neighborhoods. However, according to Payne and Gainey (2004), there is certainly theoretical reason and anecdotal evidence to suggest that those living in disadvantaged and disorganized neighborhoods would be at higher risk of maltreatment.

The impact of neighborhood characteristics on the caregiving experience cannot be ignored. It is likely that these characteristics work together to set off a chain of events in the caregiving experience. For instance, if those living in disadvantaged communities are less apt to seek services, then those caregivers will be more burdened by the caregiving experience. The caregiver burdens are compounded by the community burdens placed on the caregiver. External and internal burdens occurring in socially disorganized communities exacerbate the likelihood of maltreatment.

CONCLUDING REMARKS

In the beginning of this chapter, I shared quotes from ombudsmen who were addressing why they believed elder abuse occurs. Their quotes are telling because they reflect many of the theories considered throughout this chapter. As I have already indicated, one's beliefs about the causes of behavior will likely influence one's reactions to criminal behavior. More important is the fact that the quotes from the ombudsmen suggest that there are numerous factors contributing to elder abuse, and that explanations can cross disciplines. That is, the ombudsmen used ideas from past elder abuse explanations and from the criminological literature to explain elder abuse.

The task at hand is for researchers to do the same thing. Indeed, integration of elder abuse theories and criminological theories can go a long way toward better understanding the mistreatment of elderly persons. Some of the approaches appear to be easily integrated. Elder abuse researchers have long considered the role of stress in leading to abuse. Stress explanations are similar to what criminologists refer to as strain theory. Also, the way that elder abuse explanations center on intra-individual dynamics closely relates to Gottfredson and Hirschi's (1990) ideas about individuals' self-control levels. The notion of transgenerational violence is similar to social learning theory and Sutherland's differential association. As well, the way that some elder abuse researchers talk about the role of isolation is similar to the way that criminologists talk about routine activities theory. So, the stage is already set for integration of criminological and elder abuse explanations.

Note that I have not considered all of the criminological theories, or all of the elder abuse explanations for that matter. The elder abuse explanations I selected are those that seem to have been given the most attention in the elder abuse literature. The criminological theories I discussed were selected because they are the ones that were the simplest to apply to crimes against elderly persons. This certainly does not mean that the other criminological theories and elder abuse explanations are not useful in understanding the victimization of elderly persons. Rather, it is my hope that the reader will see that criminological theories and elder abuse explanations can be used to address crimes against elderly persons, and that integration of the two schools of thought is possible.

Chapter 7

PREVENTING ELDER ABUSE: AN INTEGRATED APPROACH

1. How can older individuals and their loved ones prevent abuse?
2. How are traditional crime prevention strategies related to elder abuse prevention strategies?
3. What can be done to limit abuse in long-term-care settings?
4. What roles do social services and health care professionals have in prevention?
5. How effective are legislative remedies in preventing elder abuse?
6. What is your role in preventing elder abuse?

INTRODUCTION

A few months ago, I was driving down a busy road near my university when I saw an elderly man with a walker crossing about six lanes of traffic. Just one day before, our area had received a few inches of snow, something which is crippling to a southeastern city. The snow banks made it difficult for the man to maneuver through his customary path and seemingly made the act of crossing the road appear to be quite dangerous. While watching this, I noticed a police officer turn on his overhead lights and pull his car into three lanes of traffic so that no one would be able to drive near the older pedestrian. In effect, the officer had prevented harm from occurring.

The thing about prevention is that it is difficult to determine how much harmful activity is truly prevented by different measures. The lack of research on prevention has resulted in the use of crime prevention strategies that are based on intuition rather than any sound empirical basis. The Los Angeles County Sheriff's department, for instance, uses SkunkShot (a gel with an aw-

228

ful odor) to keep people out of abandoned buildings. It makes sense, doesn't it? Why would trespassers hang out in a smelly building. A creative and intuitive approach was developed to deal with a problem (Dixon, 2003).

While SkunkShot may not be needed to prevent elder abuse, similar creativity and intuition would go a long way towards preventing harm. Would this man have been harmed had the officer not blocked traffic? Maybe not. But the officer's forward thinking offered safety and ensured that harm would not fall upon the man. In considering the prevention of elder abuse, there are several things that individuals can do that potentially minimize the possibility of abuse.

This chapter will focus on strategies to prevent (1) elder abuse and fraud in the community and (2) resident abuse in nursing homes. Strategies will be categorized into five areas: (1) individual strategies, (2) provider strategies, (3) institutional strategies, (4) criminal justice and social services strategies, and (5) legislative strategies. These five areas capture the integrated response to elder abuse in that they involve activities that several different parties can conduct in an effort to prevent elder abuse.

INDIVIDUAL STRATEGIES TO PREVENT ELDER ABUSE AND FRAUD

In this context, individual strategies refers to things that individuals can do themselves to prevent victimization against themselves or their loved ones. In terms of elder abuse, there are certain things seniors can do to prevent victimization and there are things that their familial caregivers–including spouses, adult offspring, and so on–can do to prevent victimization.

Empowering Seniors to Prevent Victimization

Individuals themselves can do a number of things to reduce their likelihood of victimization. More often than not, however, crime prevention strategies are aimed at keeping strangers from hurting us. Individuals will do a number of things to protect themselves from strangers. Among other things, we will buy burglar alarms, avoid dangerous areas, train our dogs to scare off strangers, trim our hedges away from our houses, and form neighborhood watch groups. To be sure, these strategies are likely effective in preventing stranger victimization. The paradox, however, that arises is that older persons are more likely to be hurt by someone they know than by a stranger. In effect, the typical crime prevention strategies may do very little to prevent the kind of victimization that is most likely to occur against seniors.

Authors have recognized this paradox and suggest a number of possible things seniors can do to prevent victimization by known acquaintances. Mack and Jones (2003) cite five actions that will reduce the likelihood of different types of abuse. In particular, they recommend that seniors (1) be encouraged to join organizations, (2) remain active, (3) stay organized, (4) send and open their own mail where feasible, and (5) use direct deposit for the Social Security and retirement checks.

Note that some strategies will prevent physical abuse, others will reduce financial abuse, and others will reduce both types of abuse. More recently, attention has been given to ways to reduce financial abuse. San Diego Deputy District Attorney Paul Greenwood advises that seniors should do the following:

1. Inventory and document all of their jewelry
2. Provide photos of the jewelry to a trusted family member or attorney
3. Provide a trusted acquaintance with duplicate copies of bank statements so they can monitor transactions
4. Be cautious about any bargains
5. Conduct occasional credit checks on one's self (Sherman, 2003).

MacDonald (2003) adds that elderly parents should refrain from bailing their adult offspring out of financial problems, especially in those situations where the adult offspring seem to always be financially irresponsible. Encouraging them to solve their own financial problems will benefit both the parent and the adult offspring in the long run.

One common element between each of the above abuse prevention strategies is that they call for the empowerment of seniors. Empowerment itself is believed to have prohibitive qualities in terms of abuse. However, sometimes empowerment must be encouraged by acquaintances of the elderly person. Family members are one group that can call for the empowerment of their aging parents. As will be shown in the next section, they can do a number of other things to protect their elderly relatives from abuse.

Familial Caregivers and Elder Maltreatment Prevention

Family members are in a prime position to reduce the likelihood of victimization against their elderly relatives. Unfortunately, very little guidance has been provided to family members other than the typical recommendations that individuals should follow in protecting against stranger victimization. Despite the lack of attention in this area, several steps can be taken by family members to help reduce the likelihood that their older relatives will be victimized. In the following section, four recommendations that could help family members protect their loved ones are discussed.

RECOMMENDATION NUMBER ONE–FAMILY CAREGIVERS SHOULD SEEK OUT STRESS REDUCING ACTIVITIES. Caregivers must be encouraged to seek out stress reducing activities. This is especially important for adult offspring providing care to their aging parents as more and more research is beginning to show that familial caregivers are the group most often involved in cases of abuse. As noted earlier, the role of stress is not clear. Everyone gets stressed. Healthy living habits (eating well and exercising) have been found to help reduce stress. As well, seeking out and joining caregiver support groups can help to reduce the amount of stress experienced by caregivers.

The importance of support groups cannot be overstated. Citing work by Toseland (1995), Bergeron and Gray 2003 describe eight ways that support groups should help to control or reduce stress. In particular, support groups provide the following: (1) respite for the caregiver, (2) reductions in isolation, (3) a safe place to vent, (4) a place to be validated, (5) a place where they are appreciated for their caregiving efforts, (6) education about aging, (7) education about coping strategies, and (8) the development of action plans to reduce stress. In the end, being around others in like situations shows caregivers that they are not alone in the obstacles and barriers they confront while providing care to their loved ones.

RECOMMENDATION NUMBER TWO–FAMILY MEMBERS SHOULD DO THEIR RESEARCH IN PROVIDING CARE FOR, AND SEEKING SERVICES FOR, THEIR LOVED ONES. Family members assisting in providing care to their loved ones must do their research and educate themselves about the caregiving experience. When individuals find themselves in the position of caregiver for their older relatives, they are typically in a place in their life course where they have had no exposure to such a type of caregiving (Payne & Gainey, 2002). Not knowing how to provide care, many may fall into the trap of relying on their instincts or their experiences as a parent providing care to their children.

Such a step is shortsighted and destined for problems. Recall that many cases of neglect are cases of passive, or unintentional, neglect. Not knowing how to provide appropriate care can indeed result in harm to the care recipient. In addition, it is important to realize that the type of caregiving older adults need is significantly different from the type of care children need. As such, the caregiving demands will also be different. Learning about the caregiving experience through research will prepare caregivers for the demands they are sure to face. For example, it may be difficult to cope with an elderly person's actions that are caused by some form of dementia. When caregivers learn the true source of these unintentional actions, they will be better able to cope with the stresses of caregiving.

Family members should also "do their research" when they are helping to decide the kinds of services or care their older relative needs. Doing research is something most of us have done since we were old enough to start asking questions. Before making major decisions in our lives, we generally do our research. When buying a new car, we do our research. When we buy a new house, we do our research. Decisions about services for our older relatives, especially those who are vulnerable, require that we do our research.

A number of strategies can be followed in learning about service providers. The Internet, for example, has become an extremely valuable source for learning about the quality of different service providers. Most states have websites that provide information about different professionals' (including health care providers, contractors, and others) licensing status. Also, the Center for Medicare and Medicaid Services provides information about the results of nursing home inspections for all long-term-care providers receiving some form of federal funding in the United States. This information is readily available at www.medicare.gov/nhcompare. Doing the search is easy and provides a wealth of information. There are also private websites that provide information about different occupations. For example, one can go to www.contractor.com to read how different contractors have performed their jobs. Clients of contractors provide information to the site administrator who in turn publishes that information.

While the Internet can be a valuable tool in researching service providers, it is not the only tool. Family members should interview care or service providers if the older person is unable to. Questions to be asked vary according to the type of professional being interviewed. For instance, when interviewing contractors, the following questions should be asked:

1. How long have you been in business?
2. Are you licensed and registered with the city? Do you have a contractor's license?
3. How many projects like mine have you completed in the last year?
4. Will my project require a permit?
5. May I have a list of your references?
6. Will you be using subcontractors on this project?
7. What types of insurance do you carry? (*Working for Justice in Indiana*, 2004, http://www.in.gov/attorneygeneral/ncpw/home_improvement.htm).

Alternatively, when hiring a home health care providers, the following questions are appropriate:

1. Do they have employees to provide the type of care needed?

2. Do they have on call availability during all hours?
3. Is care available on weekends?
4. Is the agency accredited by the Joint Commission on the Accreditation of Healthcare Organization (JCAHO) or the Community Health Accreditation Program?
5. What are the credentials of the staff?
6. How are staff supervised?
7. What are the costs? (Madigan, 1997).

Without a doubt, important decisions about care must be thoroughly researched using all available means before any decisions are made.

RECOMMENDATION NUMBER THREE–FAMILIAL CAREGIVERS MUST BE PREPARED TO COMMUNICATE OPENLY ABOUT THE POSSIBILITIES OF MALTREATMENT WITH THEIR OLDER RELATIVES. The experience of maltreatment is extremely devastating to victims. Perhaps because individuals feel shame about the experience of abuse, there is a tendency for individuals to not even talk about the likelihood or possibility of maltreatment. This sort of denial increases the risk of maltreatment. Adult offspring should speak openly with their older parents about any concerns of abuse. Opening the lines of communication should reduce the older person's isolation and vulnerability.

Questions about the possibility of maltreatment should be asked in a non-threatening manner. It is not just about asking questions, however. Instead, it is important that the adult offspring actively listen to the concerns of their parents or grandparents. In effect, communication involves both asking questions and watching for signs of maltreatment (discussed in more detail below). Effective communication requires asking questions, listening to individuals' concerns, and observing.

RECOMMENDATION NUMBER FOUR–ENCOURAGE ADULT FAMILY MEMBERS OUT OF A JOB TO SEEK EMPLOYMENT COUNSELING. As noted earlier, a misguided belief is that older persons are victimized because they are dependent on their children or grandchildren for care. Though this may be the case in some instances, many elder abuse cases, financial abuse in particular, occur because the offender is financially or emotionally dependent on the older person. Financial dependence usually arises when the adult offspring has no source of income other than his or her parents.

To minimize the likelihood that unemployed family members will be abusive towards their parents, concerned relatives should encourage that family member to do whatever he or she can to find a job. Finding a job in and of itself would not necessarily eliminate the risk of abuse, but it should theoretically reduce the risk for four reasons:

1. Individuals feel better about themselves when they are employed.

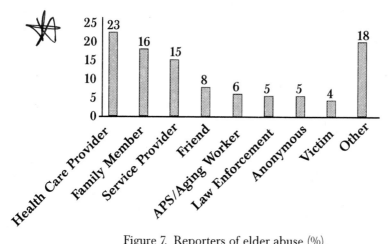

Figure 7. Reporters of elder abuse (%).
Source: National Center on Elder Abuse, 2004.

Applied Critical Thinking Questions:

1. Why do you think health care providers are the most common reporters of elder abuse?
2. Why are victims so rarely the reporters?

2. Building one's own income reduces the likelihood that one would be financially dependent on relatives.
3. The sheer fact that they would be spending more time at work and less time with their parents reduces the degree of opportunity for victimization.
4. When individuals hold a job, they generally don't want to do things that would risk losing the job. Committing criminal conduct, whether at home or other places, would risk losing the job.

Of course, finding a job is no easy task. However, most communities have employment counselors whose sole purpose is to help individuals seek employment. The importance of employment cannot be underestimated.

PROVIDER STRATEGIES TO PREVENT ELDER MISTREATMENT

Health care and social services providers are also in a prime position to prevent elder mistreatment. Indeed, year after year, these groups combined account for approximately 38 percent of the reports of suspected elder abuse cases (see Figure 7 for an overview of the proportion of reports made by different professions). This suggests that they are encountering cases of elder mistreatment on a regular basis. As such, these providers must do four things in efforts to prevent elder mistreatment. Specifically, they must:

- Be aware of the possibility of mistreatment
- Watch for signs of mistreatment
- Effectively document signs of mistreatment
- Share information about experiences with abuse victims
- Make use of available legislation

Awareness about the Possibility of Elder Mistreatment

In terms of awareness about the possibility of mistreatment, health care and social services professionals are steps ahead of other professions in recognizing that elder abuse is a problem. However, strides still need to be taken to make sure that all professionals in these respective groups recognize elder mistreatment for the problem that it is. Currently, most medical schools, universities, colleges, and other training programs offer very little, if any, formal training about elder abuse. The exposure many of these professionals have to elder mistreatment likely comes from seeking out knowledge on their own, either by attending courses for continuing education credits, participating in elder abuse conferences, reading scholarly articles on their own, or seeking advice from fellow professionals.

Watching for Signs of Mistreatment

TABLE 15. WARNING SIGNS FOR DIFFERENT TYPES OF ELDER MALTREATMENT

	Abuse Types				
Physical Abuse	*Sexual Abuse*	*Financial Exploitation*	*Emotional Abuse*	*Neglect*	*Self-Neglect*
Cuts	Bruising	Unusual	Withdrawn	Rashes	Changing
Bruises	around	banking	Depressed	Sores	intellectual
Fractures	private areas	Unpaid	Reduced	Malnourished	ability
Sudden	Unexplained	bills	eye contact	Untreated	Suicide
weight loss	STDS	Lack of	Helpless	health	attempts
Poor skin	Torn/stained	amenities	Unusual	problems	
condition	clothes	Missing	behavior	Health/safety	
		property		hazards	

Source: Adapted from Mack and Jones (2003).

Not only must health care providers be aware of the possibility of elder mistreatment, they must also actively search for signs of mistreatment. The warning signs of different types of mistreatment were addressed in Chapter 4. Table 15 further illustrates these warning signs. Note that different signs of abuse vary according to abuse types. A problem that arises is that "many diseases and changes from normal aging can mimic the signs and symptoms of abuse" (Lachs, 2002: 155). The mere appearance of symptoms is not enough to substantiate abuse or neglect.

Because one cannot determine mistreatment simply by how a person looks, the AMA encourages health care providers to ask patients the following questions when mistreatment is suspected:

- Does anyone hit you?
- Are you afraid of anyone at home?
- Does anyone take things that belong to you without asking?
- Has anyone ever touched you without your consent?
- Are you alone a lot?
- Does anyone yell at you or threaten you? (Gray-Vickrey, 2000).

Caution should be taken in relying on patients' explanations of injuries that appear to direct blame away from caregivers. Butler (1999, p. 3) advises, "Abuse must also be suspected when injuries are unexplainable, when the explanation is inconsistent with medical findings, or when contradictory explanations are given by the patient and the caregiver." Young (2000, n.p.) expands on this advice writing:

> With all physical and sexual abuse suspicions, it is important to look for a pattern of unexplainable injuries. If a long-time patient recently was forced to move in with a relative and them suddenly appears with multiple bruises on the arms and legs, abuse is a serious possibility. Placing your fingers on the bruises to see if they match the size and shape of fingers or thumbs can help determine whether abuse may be involved. Likewise, look for handprints or linear markings on the buttocks or back. Unusual bruising, such as large areas of it on the lower extremities or buttocks, warrant further investigation. If neither the patient nor the caregiver can adequately explain the physical signs, you are obliged to report your suspicion of physical abuse.

Also, health care providers must recognize that victims may not define acts as abusive or neglectful (Marshall et al., 2000). They must further recognize that mistreatment is more likely to occur in an individual's home than in a long-term care setting (Gray-Vickrey, 2001). Still, taken together, responses to questions such as these and signs of mistreatment form a solid base from which providers can decide whether suspected cases of mistreatment warrant attention from adult protective services.

Effectively Documenting Suspected Mistreatment

In attempting to prevent future mistreatment to the patient, health care providers must take measures to ensure that the mistreatment is appropriately documented. Such documentation can go a long way in stopping future harm against the patient. The American Medical Association suggests that the following should be included in patients' charts:

- Chief complaint, history (in patient's words), and information about the perpetrator
- A complete medical history and relevant social history
- Physical examination with information about injuries—number, size, and location and their consistency with patient's explanation of injury
- Photographs and body charts may be used to enhance written information
- The health care provider's opinion about whether the patient adequately explained the injuries
- Name of caller if appointments are repeatedly canceled
- If police are contacted, name of person taking the report and any actions taken (Fisher & Dyer, 2003; Pavlov & Murov, 1994).

Oftentimes, defense attorneys will raise a number of issues trying to keep the victim's medical records out of court. Many of the issues they bring up center around the wording found in the medical records. Legal experts suggest a number of strategies to make sure that medical charts will be useful in court. These strategies include the following:

- Photograph injuries believed to be a consequence of mistreatment.
- Write information clearly. Where possible, use computers to overcome illegible handwriting.
- Use quotation marks to set off the patient's own words or use phrases such as "patient states" or "patient reports" to indicate that the information on the document reflects the patient's own words.
- Avoid phrases such as "patient claims" and "patient alleges."
- Use medical terms rather than legal terms (e.g, alleged perpetrator, assailant, and assault).
- Try not to summarize a patient's report of abuse in conclusive terms.

238   *Crime and Elder Abuse: An Integrated Perspective*

- Do not place the term "domestic violence" or related concepts in the diagnosis of a medical record. These are not medical terms.
- Include a description of the patient's demeanor. For example, describe whether the patient was crying or seemed agitated, upset, calm, or happy. Also describe whether his or her demeanor is inconsistent with what would be expected.
- Record the time of day the examination occurred. If possible, include the amount of time that has passed since the abuse occurred (e.g., "Patient states that her daughter hit her early this morning") (Isaac & Enos, 2001).

By structuring medical charts in a manner which increases the likelihood that the charts will be usable in court, it is believed that health care providers are protecting elder abuse victims and potentially preventing future harm to that specific patient.

INSTITUTIONAL STRATEGIES TO PREVENT ABUSE

A recent survey I conducted with one of my graduate students (see Payne & Fletcher, 2004) asked nursing home directors how they responded to allegations of elder abuse. Among other things, this study considered prevention strategies the nursing home directors reporting utilized. In considering prevention, the following four themes arose:

- Facility-based themes
- Education
- Community outreach
- Building security

Facility-based themes referred to policies and procedures that the home followed in an effort to reduce the likelihood of mistreatment. These policies included strategies such as doing background checks, conducting drug screens, doing reference checks, ensuring adequate staffing, and allowing frequent rounds by quality assurance teams. To date, in most states, there are no regulations that force nursing homes to do any of these activities. So, when they are part of the home's overall policies, they can be seen as facility-based themes. The ability of strategies such as background checks to effectively prevent abuse is discussed below. (Box 7.1 includes a discussion from a former nursing home ombudsmen about preventing elder abuse.)

With regard to education, our research found that nursing home directors

BOX. 7.1. VOICES FROM THE FIELD: HOW APPROACH AND COOPERATION IN THE FIELD AFFECT ABUSE, NEGLECT, EXPLOITATION OF THE LONG-TERM CARE RECIPIENT

By Margaret Roston, RN, BSN, BA, LTC Ombudsman

The working definitions of "abuse," "neglect," and "exploitation" are generally the same for the agencies which work most closely with the long-term care ombudsman. The frustrations arise as to where the limits are set as to what each agency can actually do. When a complaint is received regarding a resident of a long-term care facility, the adult protective services (APS) worker will specifically devise ways to protect that individual.

Once that individual is determined to be safe, the APS case is generally considered closed. Consider this example. A person is alleged to have been neglected at a facility and is currently in the hospital, even possibly due to the alleged neglect. While the resident is in the hospital and if the resident does not return to the allegedly neglecting facility, the APS worker does not necessarily investigate the complaint farther than to assure that the individual is safe. The APS worker might assist in relocating the resident to another facility. If the adult is competent and says he does not want APS to interfere in his behalf, then APS must close the case. Technically, any allegation of neglect should be forwarded to the licensing agent for that facility for further follow-up, but this does not happen as often as is necessary to monitor the level of care in facilities.

When ombudsmen learn of this situation, they are likely to be frustrated because of the need to have a signed authorization of a waiver of confidentiality to pursue this case at the facility. This may be difficult to obtain from the alleged victims or their guardians. Without this waiver, ombudsmen have no right to investigate the case on their own. They cannot even specifically discuss the case with the facility, unless the facility asks to consult the ombudsman on the issue. If the APS worker chooses and is involved in an active investigation, he or she could allow the ombudsman to view the records. However, due to time constraints, APS workers generally do not have the time to investigate cases which they do not have to investigate more deeply. Once they have determined that the alleged victim is safe from the alleged situation, then they may not even have the right to peruse the victim's records. It would now fall to the police to determine whether or not alleged criminal neglect, abuse or exploitation occurred. Rarely are these cases followed by the police because there is generally insufficient concrete evidence presented to definitely prove that the case is worth considering.

The APS workers are not required to alert the ombudsman to the complaint they have received, but the ombudsman is required, in the state of Virginia, to alert APS to any complaints of abuse, neglect, or exploitation. In practice, APS workers will tell complainants to call the ombudsman if the complaint is one that is more regarding residents' rights than issues of abuse, neglect, and exploitation. The complainant may or may not call the ombudsman. If the APS workers and ombudsmen have a good working relationship and are in frequent contact, the complaint might be mentioned. This is not a reliable system. If the ombudsman is not alerted to the issues reported to other agencies, the ombudsman does not know to monitor them.

It takes much courage for a complainant to call and report a facility where they or a loved one is vulnerable. Complainants fear reprisals. Most people do not report what they know. Even fewer report to more than one agency. People should not have to muster their courage more than once to report their concerns. Also, complainants have a right to expect that once they tell someone, the "system" should work to protect them or the person about whom they are concerned.

If the police are approached by anyone, they must have more than just hearsay evidence to prove a crime has been committed. APS workers, licensing authorities, ombudsmen, etc. rarely decide to spend the time pursuing court action when a long-term care resident has been allegedly wronged. The cases are usually not "winnable." Facilities may claim they do not have the funds to provide adequate care, but most seem to find the money to pay attorneys' fees and other costs to defend the facility. Facilities fight any blemishes to their records. The district attorneys know that to win a case against a long-term care facility, they must have indisputable evidence.

Since most cases will not go to trial, it is even more important that the recipients of long-term care are well served by the regulatory and protective agencies. Cooperation amongst all the various regulatory and protective agencies involved in long-term care could be enhanced by a more consistent sharing, amongst them, of received complaints. If this were done, those that could pursue an issue more completely would know of its existence. Another very important aspect of this follow-up should be increased funding to encourage experienced professionals in these fields to remain in their positions and not seek employment elsewhere. No one has the time to read old files each time a complaint comes in; so much is in the memory of the individual intake workers and investigators. It takes much time to "learn" the dynamics of the community and the facilities being monitored.

Also, it is important that the various licensing and regulatory agencies endeavor to develop and maintain a working relationship with the facilities as well as amongst themselves. If the relationship is always seen as adversarial, then not much cooperation will occur and changes will be harder to make and information more difficult to get. Also, occasionally requests must be made of the facilities. For example, if the facility feels comfortable with people such as the APS workers, then it will be easier for emergency admissions to be granted by the facility. The ideal relationship is one of mutual respect and assistance where the facility expects the regulators and inspectors to be fair in their appraisal of the situation, considering the facility's perspective equally with the complainant's.

Increasingly frequently, the people in the field are constrained, in how they can act or respond, by their respective superiors, in their corporate or agency headquarters. Each person on all sides of these encounters, with experience, develops his or her own way of relating to the others' individual approaches and circumstances. The interpersonal relationships and cooperation often make a big difference in how successfully situations are resolved.

The development of national databases of information regarding elder abusers, facilities, long-term care management and ownership corporations, etc. would also be extremely useful. Complaints recorded in a way that information could be cross-referenced nationally via computers by various regulatory and protective agencies would also be very useful. This would make it possible to recognize patterns. If patterns are recognized, then educational, as well as disciplinary, programs could be implemented. Often the problems in long-term care facilities are not cases of criminal neglect, abuse, or exploitation, but rather the results of flaws in the educational or organizational systems within and outside the facilities. With more efficient sharing of information, the vulnerable elderly and disabled would be more able to live in safety and with far less fear.

Margaret Coston is a former long-term-care ombudsmen and as a founding member of Informed Citizens Action Network, she assisted people in receiving information on multiple sides of issues of local concern on the premise that the more people understood others' perspectives, the more likely a long-term resolution to issues could be found. She was hired as the local long-term ombudsman in her community due to proven tenacity and effectiveness at working toward minimizing the roots of problems. Her ideas have found their way to local, state, regional, and national committees. In addition, her nursing career gave her experience in long-term care, family practice, burn and critical care, outpatient surgery, and caring for family members.

believed that three groups need to be better educated about elder mistreatment. First, staff need to be educated so they won't commit abusive or neglectful acts. As it is, training is believed to be insufficient in this area. Second, residents need to be educated about safe reporting mechanisms so they will not be afraid to report inappropriate acts by long-term-care employees. Third, family members need to be made aware of what to expect in terms of the type of care their loved ones will receive in the facility. Family members should also learn how useful their visits can be. According to one author team, frequent visits by family members reduces the possibility of abuse (Mack & Jones, 2003). Developing relationships with staff is seen as an added measure to protect nursing home residents. In addition, visits place family members in a position where they could identify a case of abuse if they were aware of the relevant warning signs.

27 Community outreach themes involve strategies that would reduce the isolation of long-term-care setting residents. Efforts to connect residents to the community are seen as a win-win strategy because they help residents and they improve the perception that the community has of the long-term-care setting. In addition, allowing crime prevention and safety programs taught by local law enforcement authorities connects residents with law enforcement officials and subsequently reduces their isolation.

Building security themes centered on structural changes can be used to prevent harm. Strategies such as locking doors, having security guards, placing closed-circuit television in hallways, locking up residents' valuables, and placing electronic devices on cognitively impaired residents are a few examples. The idea underlying building security strategies is that simple changes to the physical environment can improve the safety of the long-term-care setting.

Other researchers have also considered strategies to prevent elder abuse in nursing homes. For example, Harris (1999) describes the following seven strategies nursing homes use to prevent theft in nursing homes:

- Target hardening
- Access control
- Exit screening
- Formal surveillance
- Surveillance by employees
- Target Removal
- Property identification

28 *Target hardening* refers to a host of strategies that are designed to make it more difficult to steal certain items. Examples of target hardening include locking closets and drawers, using ring guards to protect one's jewelry, and fastening down valuable property such as televisions and video casette recorders. Theoretically, making it more difficult to obtain these items unlawfully would prevent thefts from occurring (Harris, 1999).

Access control entails activities that control how one can enter and leave a nursing home's premises. Requiring visitors to sign-in and wear badges are examples. Also, having visitors enter by security staff or another nursing home employee are examples of access control (Harris, 1999). Think of shopping at a retail store where a greeter stands at the entrance and says hello to all shoppers entering the establishment. It may seem as if they are there to be friendly; rather, their presence is designed to deter theft. Individuals who are seen entering a location will, in theory, be less likely to commit a crime in that location.

Exit screening refers to practices that monitor the items actually leaving the nursing home. Harris (1999, p. 148) provides the examples of using clear trash bags to prevent employees from using dark colored bags to hide stolen items and having "female employees carry clear plastic purses." In implementing such measures, administrators must take into account the effect that the strategies might have on staff morale.

Formal surveillance strategies include commonly used, structured security actions. Installing security alarms is an example of a formal surveillance strategy. Other examples include using closed-circuit television systems, installing hidden cameras, and calling on crime prevention officers to examine a building's security measures (Harris, 1999).

Surveillance by employees involves encouraging employees to actively watch for and report suspects cases of theft. Some administrators may simply tell employees about instances where property is believed to be missing, but Harris (1999) recommends nursing homes actually develop an "in-house" hotline to report unusual activity. She also suggests that employees should work in pairs if feasible. Of course, the costs of doing business may make it difficult to have nursing home workers work in teams. To offset this problem, another author team suggests that volunteers may be used as the team member who can watch for signs of misconduct (Payne & Cikovic, 1995). Indeed, the presence of volunteers in nursing homes has been found to significantly reduce the number of deficiencies found by regulators (Filinson, 2001). Lachs (2003, p. 156) adds that nursing homes should "organize an advocacy council with concerned family members of residents."

Target removal strategies involve an assortment of activities that aim to get rid of any potential item that may be attractive to thieves. Wearing fake jewelry and placing valuable items in a safe are a few examples (Harris, 1999). If the items are removed from a potential thief's presence, then theft has been prevented.

CRIMINAL JUSTICE/SOCIAL SERVICES STRATEGIES

Criminal justice and social services agencies also play a role in preventing elder mistreatment. Their prevention role is performed through four overlapping activities: (1) education, (2) community service, (3) investigation/enforcement, and (4) empowerment. While there is overlap between each activity, they are discussed separately below.

Education as a Criminal Justice/Social Service Strategy

In terms of education, those working with elderly victims and potential elderly victims need to increase awareness among at least four different groups about elder mistreatment. First, professionals who are familiar with offenses against elderly persons need to educate older persons about ways to prevent elder abuse. Second, they must educate family members and caregivers about ways to watch for, identify, and report suspected cases of elder abuse. Third, they must educate fellow professionals (e.g., law enforcement officials, prosecutors, lawyers, protective services workers, and others involved in the family justice network) about the strategies they have found successful in controlling misconduct against seniors. Finally, where feasible, they must educate policy makers about the seriousness of elder mistreatment.

Most often, these crime prevention education strategies tend to focus on ways to keep strangers from getting into the elderly person's home. However, the educational strategy needs to be broadened to include a focus on preventing cases of elder mistreatment which would include all types of harm perpetrated against older persons. One way to encourage this broader educational strategy would be to have both criminal justice and protective services workers work together to educate elderly persons about the crimes they may confront. Criminal justice officials would have more background regarding stranger offenses while protective services workers would have more to offer about elder mistreatment. Such a strategy certainly fits within an integrated approach to responding to elder mistreatment.

Community Service Strategies to Prevent Elder Abuse

Criminal justice and social services professionals can also work towards preventing elder mistreatment through performing various community service activities. To be sure, educating the public is a form of community service. But, there are other community service activities professionals advocating for the protection of the elderly can carry out. Creating or joining interdisciplinary groups that aim to prevent crimes against seniors would be one example. Developing programs to help the elderly keep track of their assets would be another example.

The number of community service programs to prevent elder abuse pales in comparison to the number of service programs designed to prevent other types of family violence. This is not to suggest that there are too many of these other programs; rather, my intent is to suggest that more programs need to be developed for the elderly population.

The experience of some agencies shows that these prevention programs can be created. In Norfolk, Virginia, for example, the sheriff's department has a program called *CARE (Check and Respond Everyday)* that uses technology to protect vulnerable seniors. Basically, a computerized software system calls participating elderly persons several times a day at designated times. If no one responds after repeated calls, an officer will visit the residence (Stanus, 1999). The strategy can prevent crime because potential offenders know that the older person has a "watch guard" who is checking in on him or her.

Investigation/Enforcement as a Crime Prevention Strategy

Criminal justice and social services professionals also fulfill elder mistreatment prevention ideals through investigating suspected offenses and applying laws and regulations as needed. In effect, just by doing their job as they have agreed to should help to control elder mistreatment. Recall the discussion on deterrence theory and routine activities theory from Chapter 6. Many offenders will think about whether they can get away with an offense without getting caught before engaging in a harmful act. The presence of professionals whose aim is to protect elderly persons ought to dissuade some individuals from misconduct.

Empowerment as a Crime Prevention Strategy

Empowerment is a fourth strategy that criminal justice and social services professionals can aspire to in an effort to prevent crimes against seniors. This simply means allowing seniors to play a role in the crime prevention process. Cases where seniors are involved in serving as undercover investigators, attorneys, and counselors have been shown to be effective for the victim as well as the senior volunteer. They should also be involved in developing prevention and recreation programs in nursing homes (Hall & Bocksnick, 1995). In fact, one author calls for "the empowered and paid participation of older adults" in responding to elder abuse (Harbison, 1999, p. 14). Such a response certainly makes sense.

Older persons should also be involved in determining what the goals of elder abuse investigations should be. Older victims often want to keep the family intact. Facing options of punishing a loved one, even in the face of serious victimization, prohibits many victims from reporting victimization to the police in the first place. Attention needs to be given to strategies to meet older victims' desires with the justice system's goals (Bergeron, 2002).

TABLE 16. VIRGINIA'S MANDATORY REPORTING LAW

§ 62.1–55.2. Protection of aged or incapacitated adults; physicians, nurses, etc., to report abuse, neglect or exploitation of adults; complaint by others; penalty for failure to report.

A. Matters giving reason to suspect the abuse, neglect or exploitation of adults shall be reported by any person licensed to practice medicine or any of the healing arts, any hospital resident or intern, any person employed in the nursing profession, any person employed by a public or private agency or facility and working with adults, any person providing full-time or part-time care to adults for pay on a regularly scheduled basis, any person employed as a social worker, any mental health professional and any law enforcement officer, in his professional or official capacity, who has reason to suspect that an adult is an abused, neglected or exploited adult. The report shall be made immediately to the local department of the county or city wherein the adult resides or wherein the abuse, neglect or exploitation is believed to have occurred. If neither locality is known, then the report shall be made to the local department of the county or city where the abuse, neglect, or exploitation was discovered. If the information is received by a staff member, resident, intern or nurse in the course of professional services in a hospital or similar institution, such person may, in place of the report, immediately notify the person in charge of the institution or department, or his designee, who shall make such report forthwith. Any person required to make the report or notification required by this subsection shall do so either orally or in writing and shall disclose all information that is the basis for the suspicion of abuse, neglect or exploitation of the adult. Upon request, any person required to make the report shall make available to the adult protective services worker and the local department investigating the reported case of abuse, neglect or exploitation any information, records or reports which document the basis for the report. All persons required to report suspected abuse, neglect or exploitation who maintain a record of a person who is the subject of such a report shall cooperate with the investigating adult protective services worker of a local department and shall make information, records and reports which are relevant to the investigation available to such worker to the extent permitted by state and federal law.

B. The report required by subsection A shall be reduced to writing within seventy-two hours by the director of the local department on a form prescribed by the State Board of Social Services.

C. Any person required to make a report pursuant to subsection A who has reason to suspect that an adult has been sexually abused as that term is defined in § 18.2–67.10, and any person in charge of a hospital or similar institution, or a department thereof, who receives such information from a staff member, resident, intern or nurse, also shall immediately report the matter, either orally or in writing, to the local law-enforcement agency where the adult resides or the sexual abuse is believed to have occurred, or if neither locality is known, then where the abuse was discovered. The person making the report shall disclose and, upon request, make available to the law-enforcement agency all information forming the basis of the report.

D. Any financial institution that suspects that an adult customer has been exploited financially may report such suspected exploitation to the local department of the county or city wherein the adult resides or wherein the exploitation is believed to have occurred. Such a complaint may be oral or in writing. For purposes of this section, a financial institution means any bank, savings institution, credit union, securities firm or insurance company.

TABLE 16. (CONTINUED)

E. Any person other than those specified in subsection A who suspects that an adult is an abused, neglected or exploited adult may report the matter to the local department of the county or city wherein the adult resides or wherein the abuse, neglect or exploitation is believed to have occurred. Such a complaint may be oral or in writing.

F. Any person who makes a report or provides records or information pursuant to subsection A, D or E of this section or who testifies in any judicial proceeding arising from such report, records or information shall be immune from any civil or criminal liability on account of such report, records, information or testimony, unless such person acted in bad faith or with a malicious purpose.

G. All law-enforcement departments and other state and local departments, agencies, authorities and institutions shall cooperate with each adult protective services worker of a local department in the detection and prevention of abuse, neglect or exploitation of adults.

H. Any person who is found guilty of failing to make a required report or notification pursuant to subsection A or C of this section, within 24 hours of having the reason to suspect abuse shall be fined not more than $500 for the first failure and not less than $100 nor more than $1,000 for any subsequent failures.

Applied Critical Thinking Questions:

1. What changes, if any, would you make in this law? Explain.
2. Do you think mandatory reporting laws threaten an individual's autonomy? Explain.

LEGISLATIVE STRATEGIES

Legislative strategies that are designed to prevent elder mistreatment involve laws and policies passed at the state level to direct the activities of professionals encountering cases of elder mistreatment. These strategies are not concerned with the laws prohibiting specific offenses; rather, they are concerned with general policies that are seen as having preventive qualities for all types of elder mistreatment. In considering legislative strategies, four areas will be addressed: (1) mandatory reporting laws, (2) penalty enhancement statutes, (3) criminal background checks, and (4) the Elder Justice Act.

Mandatory Reporting Laws

Mandatory reporting laws are laws that state that certain professionals must report suspected cases of elder mistreatment to appropriate authorities. Forty-two states have mandatory reporting laws. State laws vary in their definitions of abuse and categories of mandatory reporters. States that have mandatory reporting laws generally list (1) the professionals who must report, (2) where

TABLE 17. PENALTIES FOR FAILING TO REPORT ELDER ABUSE

State	Misdemeanor	Incarceration	Fine	Civil Liability	Report to Licensing
Alabama	+	+	+		
Alaska			+		
Arizona	+				
Arkansas	+				
California	+	+	+		
Colorado					
Connecticut			+		
Delaware			+		
D.C.	+	+			
Florida	+				
Georgia	+				
Hawaii	+				
Idaho	+				
Illinois					
Indiana					
Iowa	+			+	
Kansas	+				
Kentucky	+				+
Louisiana		+	+		
Maine					
Maryland			+		
Massachusetts			+		
Michigan			+	+	
Minnesota	+			+	
Mississippi	+		+		
Missouri	+				
Montana	+				
Nebraska	+				
Nevada	+				
New Hampshire	+				
New Jersey			+		
New Mexico	+				
New York					
North Carolina					
North Dakota					
Ohio					
Oklahoma	+				
Oregon			+		
Pennsylvania					
Rhode Island	+		+		
South Carolina	+	+	+		+
South Dakota					
Tennessee	+				
Texas	+				
Utah					

35

TABLE 17. (CONTINUED)

State	Misdemeanor	Incarceration	Fine	Civil Liability	Report to Licensing
Vermont		+	+		
Virginia			+		
Washington					
West Virginia		+	+		
Wisconsin					
Wyoming					

Source: American Bar Association Home Page. "Facts about Law and the Elderly–Table 2. State-by-State Mandatory Reporting Requirements–Sanctions for Failure to Report. Available online at www.abanet .org/media/factbooks/eldt2.html. Accessed May 5, 2004.

Applied Critical Thinking Questions:

1. Do you think more severe punishments will increase the likelihood that mandatory reporters will report suspected cases of elder mistreatment? Explain.
2. Does the fact that a particular state has harsher punishments for violations of mandatory reporting laws mean that that particular state takes the legislation more seriously?

reports should be filed, (3) an assurance of immunity for reports made in good faith, and (4) criminal and civil penalties for failing to report. Table 16 shows the Commonwealth of Virginia's mandatory reporting law.

As far as the professionals who are supposed to report suspected cases of abuse, generally those who are cited as mandatory reporters include health care professionals, criminal justice officials, and long-term-care professionals. A recent trend has seen a call for listing bank employees as mandatory reporters of elder abuse. Including bank employees is justified on the grounds that they are in a perfect position to identify cases of financial abuse.

In terms of who receives the reports, in most states, the adult protective services agency or its equivalent entity is responsible for receiving complaints of elder mistreatment, not that these are just complaints. It is up to protective services officials, then, to determine is mistreatment can be substantiated.

As noted in chapter 4, mandatory reporting laws also include an assurance of immunity for those who make reports in good faith. This simply means that individuals cannot be held liable for reporting cases of mistreatment that prove to be false so long as the reporter did not make the report maliciously. The immunity clause of the legislation serves to increase the likelihood that individuals will report suspected cases of abuse.

The penalties for failing to report vary across the United States. Table 17 outlines how different states' laws recommend punishing those who fail to report suspected cases of mistreatment. As shown in the table, a number of states recommend incarcerating those who fail to report mistreatment, while most have less severe sanctions. While strict penalties exist, in reality, it is extremely rare that they are applied.

Mandatory reporting laws are criticized on a number of grounds. Prior literature cites at least eight criticisms of these laws. Specifically, it is believed that the laws:

- don't really help victims
- impinge on confidentiality between professionals and victims
- are based on vague definitions of elder abuse
- raise concerns about professional liability
- are too punitive
- may harm the victim by removing him or her from the home
- will not uncover the truly serious cases of elder abuse
- are not based on research (Payne & Gainey, 2002).

The lack of research on mandatory reporting laws likely contributes to these criticisms. Indeed, a lack of understanding about the consequences of mandatory reporting laws adds fuel to the arguments presented by opponents of these laws. One recent study, however, finds some usefulness in the laws. In particular, Payne and Gainey (2004a) examined whether states that had mandatory reporting laws for nursing home employees experienced different rates and types of nursing home violations. While the rate of violations was not influenced by the presence of the laws, their research showed that those states with mandatory reporting laws had less severe violations than those did not have the laws. In effect, the laws may not stop wrongdoing, but they may minimize it.

Others have argued that the laws can be useful if they are designed and implemented appropriately. According to Daniels et al. (1989), in order for mandatory reporting policies to be effective, six criteria must be met:

- The policy must be explicit about the population that is being protected.
- Abusive behaviors must be clearly defined.
- The policy must clearly establish who the mandated reporters are.
- The policy should justify why that group is a mandated reporter.
- Immunity against lawsuits for unintentional false allegations must be assured to the reporters.
- Confidentiality must be promised to reporters.

A number of questions that need to be addressed in future research remain about the usefulness of mandatory reporting laws.

TABLE 18. NEVADA'S PENALTY ENHANCEMENT
STATUTE FOR OLDER CRIME VICTIMS

NRS 193.167 Additional penalty: Certain crimes committed against person 60 years of age or older.

    1. Except as otherwise provided in NRS 193.169, any person who commits the crime of:

        (a) Murder;

        (b) Attempted murder;

        (c) Assault;

        (d) Battery;

        (e) Kidnapping;

        (f) Robbery;

        (g) Sexual assault;

        (h) Embezzlement of money or property of a value of $250 or more;

        (i) Obtaining money or property of a value of $250 or more by false pretenses; or

        (j) Taking money or property from the person of another, against any person who is 60 years of age or older shall be punished by imprisonment in the county jail or state prison, whichever applies, for a term equal to and in addition to the term of imprisonment prescribed by statute for the crime. The sentence prescribed by this subsection must run consecutively with the sentence prescribed by statute for the crime.

    2. Except as otherwise provided in NRS 193.169, any person who commits a criminal violation of the provisions of chapter 90 or 91 of NRS against any person who is 60 years of age or older shall be punished by imprisonment in the county jail or state prison, whichever applies, for a term equal to and in addition to the term of imprisonment prescribed by statute for the criminal violation. The sentence prescribed by this subsection must run consecutively with the sentence prescribed by statute for the criminal violation.

    3. This section does not create any separate offense but provides an additional penalty for the primary offense, whose imposition is contingent upon the finding of the prescribed fact.

Applied Critical Thinking Questions:

1. What are the advantages of stiffer sentences for elder abusers?
2. What are some of the problems you see with penalty enhancement statutes?

Penalty Enhancement Statutes

    Penalty enhancement statutes are laws that allow or call for more serious sentences for certain types of crimes. Based on deterrence theory ideals, the notion is that stricter sanctions will prevent misconduct. Applauding these statutes, one criminal justice official working with elder abuse victims made the following comments:

Delaware's enhanced penalties for crimes against the elderly are very effective in these cases. Assaults or thefts that are generally misdemeanors are elevated to felonies when they involve elderly victims. Separate charges exist for abuse/ neglect of a patient, endangering the welfare of an incompetent person and exploitation of an infirm adult. . . . After conviction, it is almost always a condition of the sentence that the offender is excluded from working in direct-care health care. (Payne 2003).

States vary in the types of penalty enhancement statutes they have developed. Some are simply a part of a particular state's set of aggravating factors. Aggravating factors are factors that allow a judge to impose penalties more serious than usual. In Illinois, for example, the penal code states that certain "factors shall be accorded weight in favor of imposing a term of imprisonment or may be considered by the court as reasons to impose a more severe sentence." One of those factors listed is whether "the defendant committed the offense against a person 60 years of age or older or such person's property." (§730 ILCS 5/5-5-3.2). Other states may list a specific statute that specifically designates the abuse of vulnerable adults as a special category of crime for which offenders could receive a more severe punishment. Table 18 shows Nevada's penalty enhancement statutes for cases involving older victims.

A recent study by Payne and Gainey (2004b) calls into question the effectiveness of these laws. Examining the sentences given to patient abusers across the United States, Payne and Gainey found that states with elder abuse penalty enhancement statutes actually meted out less severe sanctions than those states that did not have the statutes. One explanation for this discrepancy is that prosecutors may be using the enhancement statutes as leverage to gain guilty pleas, which would carry less severe sanctions than convictions by trial would.

Criminal Background Checks

Criminal background checks are also seen as a strategy to prevent elder mistreatment, namely those committed by employees such as home health care providers and employees in long-term-care settings. Background checks are routinely conducted in a number of different professions and one recent survey found that "91 percent of workers approve of background checks for criminal records" (*Risk Management,* 2003: 8). Criminal background checks are justified on the grounds that they technically prevent crime, quicken the hiring process, and make the workplace safer. Despite this appeal of criminal background checks, their use to prevent elder mistreatment is not widespread.

While few studies have empirically tested the usefulness of criminal background checks, the implications of a few studies suggest that there is some merit to implementing background checks as crime prevention strategy. A recent study by Payne and Gainey (2004b), for instance, examined 801 cases of patient abuse investigated by Medicaid Fraud Control Units across the

United. The authors characterized the offenders into three categories: stressed abusers, pathological abusers, and serial abusers. Serial abusers were those who committed offenses in the past. At least 25 percent of the abusers were characterized as serial abusers, and some of them had documented cases of past offenses in nursing homes in neighboring states. Looking thoroughly into the backgrounds of potential employees should reduce the number of serial abusers in nursing homes. Of course, background checks would not eliminate offending, but the policies should reduce it.

One of the biggest criticisms of background checks is cost. One expert estimates that for every dollar spent on background checks, businesses actually save fifteen dollars by reducing employee offending (*Risk Management,* 2003). Still, the concern about cost persists as one of the most commonly cited problems in instituting criminal background check programs.

To offset this concern about cost, on December 8th, 2003, President George W. Bush signed into law the Medicare Reform Law. Among other provisions, this law called for a "10-state pilot program that would start free criminal background checks of potential [nursing home] employees" (Killian, 2004: 1). While the program would be free for nursing homes, the law budgeted $25 million to do the background checks between 2004 and 2005. The goal of the pilot program is to eventually develop a national criminal background check program.

The Elder Justice Act

The Elder Justice Act is another legislative strategy aimed at preventing and effectively responding to elder abuse. The act was introduced in 2002 as Senate Bill 2933 in the 107th Congress by Senators John Breux of Louisiana and Orrin Hatch of Utah. It was reintroduced by Senator Breux in 2003 as Bill 333. At press time, the act had not yet been voted on. Among other things, the most recent version of the act calls for the following:

- Five Centers of Excellence that would prevent elder abuse through research and information sharing.
- Mandatory reports to law enforcement for nursing home offenses.
- Increased nursing home security.
- Criminal background checks for federally funded health care providers serving elderly persons.
- Coordinated responses by federal, state, and local governments to elder abuse.
- New programs for victims.
- Education and training grants to increase professionals' understanding about elder abuse.

The Elder Justice Act is seen as "historic" because of the following three reasons: (1) it is the most comprehensive approach the federal government has ever considered in its response to elder abuse; (2) it redefines the federal government's role in elder abuse cases; and (3) it emphasizes a coordinated approach between government agencies and levels of government (Teaster & Anetzberger, 2002). Robert Blancato (2002: 182), president of the National Commitee for the Prevention of Elder Abuse, hails the act as "the most comprehensive bill ever proposed in the more than 25 years of federal involvement in the fight against elder abuse." This coordinated response has received a favorable response from a number of different professionals representing the different agencies that get involved in the response to elder abuse (see Johnson, 2002; Mixson, 2002; Paveza, 2002; Thomas, 2002). To date, several dozen U.S. Senators have signed on as sponsors of the bill. Whether it will be passed by the Senate and House of Representatives remains to be seen.

CONCLUDING REMARKS

This chapter has considered several different strategies to prevent elder abuse. One theme permeates throughout the chapter—the best way to prevent elder abuse is through a coordinated or integrated effort in which all individuals involved in elder abuse cases work together to limit the likelihood of abuse. This integrated effort includes the efforts of seniors and their family members or loved ones, paid caregivers, protective services officials, social services providers, health care providers, criminal justice officials, researchers, legislators, and any other group that either directly or indirectly gets involved in elder abuse cases. To be sure, the problem will never go away; however, with intensive and coordinated efforts, the extent of elder abuse can be minimized.

Chapter 8

RECOMMENDATIONS FOR FUTURE POLICY AND RESEARCH

1. How will cooperation influence the response to elder abuse?
2. Should elder abuse be criminalized? Explain.
3. What role do citizens have in responding to crimes against elderly persons?
4. How does funding influence the response to elder abuse?
5. How would cross-cultural research be useful in understanding offenses against elderly persons?
6. Should social service employees be given special training on how to interact with elderly crime victims? Explain.
7. What role do you play in the response to elder abuse?

INTRODUCTION

One day a few years ago, I was riding my bike when I noticed my neighbors, a married couple who are each in their early eighties, appearing to dance in their automobile to a Beastie Boys song. The lyrics I heard were "You've got to fight for your right to party." From what I could see at first glance, the couple was swaying their upper body in unison with the music. On second glance, I noticed that the music was actually coming from the car next to my neighbor's, and that my neighbors were actually rolling up their windows so they would not have to hear the music. The elder abuse problem is similar as far as perceptions are concerned. At first glance, many think that the problem is not that significant. I would argue that a second glance would be more telling for those who believe that crimes against elderly persons are not significant.

It is my hope that the reader will by now appreciate that crime is a very important phenomena in the lives of older adults. They may not be victims of street crime in the same magnitude as younger persons, but this does not mean that crime is irrelevant to elderly persons. In fact, as established in Chapter 1, and throughout the remainder of this text, elderly persons are at a higher risk for different offenses than younger persons are. In Chapter 2, the reasons that some social scientists (primarily criminologists) ignore crimes against seniors were considered. Recall that magnitude issues, conceptual problems, political issues, and methodological constraints were seen as those factors limiting research into this area.

Chapter 3 considered the types of offenses committed against elderly persons. Clearly, elderly persons can be victims of a host of different types of offenses. The consequences of their victimization were considered in Chapter 4, which looked at victimization experiences and losses. Chapter 5 focused on the way that various systems get involved in responding to elder abuse. Particular attention was given to the way that the criminal justice system responds to offenses against elderly persons. Chapter 6 considered the explanations that elder abuse researchers have given for the existence of elder abuse. The way that criminological theories would address crimes against elderly persons was also considered.

Without a doubt, special attention needs to be given to elderly crime victims because of the different experiences of older crime victims, the different needs they require from those responding to the offenses, and the multiple causal factors associated with offenses against elderly persons. The theme throughout the text is that attention that is needed is best accomplished through an integrated effort that I have referred to as gero-criminology. This effort links assumptions and ideas from various disciplines (e.g., gerontology, sociology, criminology, social work, etc.) and various occupations (e.g., social workers, case workers, police officers, lawyers, etc.) in an effort to promote increased understanding of (1) the victimization experiences of older adults, (2) victims' needs, and (3) explanations of crimes against elderly persons. Based on this perspective and past elder abuse and criminological literature, a number of recommendations can be made.

Recommendation 1—More rigorous research is needed. One of the most cited criticisms of early elder abuse research is that the studies lacked rigor and were often unscientific. Since then, the study of elder abuse has increased dramatically and we have witnessed drastic increases in the quality of elder abuse research published in various professional and scholarly journals. Indeed, it has been a very exciting time for elder abuse researchers. It is not time, however, for those who have been involved in promoting or conducting better research to rest on their laurels. Rather, there is a long way to go in increasing our understanding of the victimization experiences of elderly persons.

In particular, criminologists need to get more involved in this relatively recent wave of research examining the victimization of elderly persons. Also, the research that has been done has tended to focus on acts the fit nicely under the heading of elder abuse (e.g., physical abuse of elderly persons; psychological abuse; financial abuse by caregivers, etc.). Missing from much of this research are examinations of white-collar offenses (medical fraud, telemarketing fraud, institutional fraud, etc.) that are directed toward elderly persons. Criminologists who do study elder abuse tend to focus more on institutional abuse than individual abuse. Focusing on institutional abuses is important because these actions were ignored in the past, and they could certainly lead to individual abuse (Viano, 1983; Pritchard, 1996b). Logically, if an institution's actions and policies are abusive to residents, it is plausible that the institution is also hurting the employees who, in turn, may take out their frustrations on residents. It is imperative that those studying offenses against elderly persons recognize that there are numerous offenses that target elderly persons, and that these offenses are interrelated. Likewise, research efforts must be broadened to include a focus on those types of offenses that have been overlooked in past studies.

Recommendation 2–An integrated effort among academics from various disciplines is needed. To accomplish the broadening of research, it will be necessary that social scientists from various disciplines come together to study crimes against elderly persons. As Anetzberger (1995) notes, "A problem as complex as elder abuse requires the involvement of multiple disciplines and perspectives" (p. 14). This sort of academic integration has already happened to a degree. For instance, a quick glance at the editorial board of the *Journal of Elder Abuse and Neglect* shows that scholars from the following disciplines have expertise in the area of elder abuse: social work, human services, gerontology, medicine, nursing, human development, family studies, and law. Also, both those working in the field and those researching the problem in academic settings are included on the editorial board. This suggests that integration has already started.

I would argue that there is room for more integration and cooperation among social scientists. For instance, there are many individuals within each of the disciplines noted above who continue to see elder abuse as insignificant. This suggests the need for increased understanding of victimization experiences among those doing research in these various fields. Second, noticeably scarce in the elder abuse literature are studies by criminologists. Likewise, elder abuse studies are scarce in the criminological literature. This suggests that criminologists need to get more involved in studying the victimization of elderly persons.

In their defense, there have been some studies by criminologists who have considered various elder abuse issues. Their efforts, unfortunately, generally exclude input from traditional elder abuse researchers. In the end, the result of fragmentation or lack of cooperation is that victims do not receive the services they need (Perttu, 1996). Note, of course, that a few criminologists have been greatly involved in studying elder abuse, and even more have considered elderly offenders (see Forsyth & Shover, 1986; Newman & Newman, 1982). More criminologists, however, need to get involved in studying offenses against elderly persons.

This integrated research effort should produce integrated explanations of elder abuse. Summarizing the risk factors related to elder abuse, Kosberg (1988) writes that elder abuse "results from the dynamic interaction between personal, family, social and cultural values, priorities, and goals" (p. 49). Also recall all of the risk factors cited in Chapter 6. With risk factors that relate to all of the disciplines within the social sciences, it is imperative that scholars from all of the social science disciplines get involved in examining the causes of abuse. Ideally, and more importantly, this sort of theoretical integration would tell us what measures would be most effective in preventing crimes against elderly persons.

Recommendation 3–An integrated effort among practitioners, policy makers, citizens, and scholars is needed. Generally, when integrated efforts are considered, the focus is oriented at specific occupations. For example, some would argue, justifiably I might add, that APS employees, police officers, health care workers, caseworkers, and others must work together to respond to elder abuse (see Recommendation 4). In addition to those working directly with elderly victims working with one another, it is imperative that those scholars researching elder abuse become involved in working with citizens, practitioners, and policy makers to prevent elder abuse.

Researching the topic is the most obvious way that scholars can get involved in the fight against elder abuse. However, as Rogers (1991) writes, "[T]he scholarly, ordered world of social research seems far removed from the emotional, chaotic world of politics of government. . . . Researchers on crime . . . need to do a better job of climbing out of the tower and getting into the fray" (Rogers, 1991, p. 282). Thus, the research must be shared in such a way that it comes to the attention of policy makers, citizens, and the practitioners who are directly working with elderly crime victims. Sharing is not simply publishing in a scholarly journal, but writing letters to members of congress, speaking to community organizations, and interacting with practitioners who deal with older victims as part of their occupational routine.

Recommendation 4–An integrated effort among practitioners or the use of teams to prevent and respond to elder abuse is needed in more jurisdictions. Various professionals from vastly different occupations will encounter cases of elder abuse. Of course, some will encounter more cases than others will. Those who might encounter cases of elder abuse include, but are not limited to, protective services workers, social service providers, nurses, health aides, agency homemakers, physicians, public-welfare caseworkers, police officers, clergy, lawyers, and nursing home professionals (Blakely & Dolon, 1991). With elder abuse potentially confronting so many different occupations, the cooperation of these groups is necessary in order to effectively prevent and respond to elder abuse. One way that cooperation has been promoted is through the use of teams.

In a more recent study, Blakely and Dolon (2000) surveyed 395 adult protective services workers to assess the quality of relationships they reported having with criminal justice officials. The protective services workers indicated that criminal justice officials were most helpful in: (1) providing escorts to victim's homes, (2) investigating elder abuse, (3) assisting victims, (4) arresting perpetrators, (5) providing protective orders, (6) protecting perpetrators, (7) providing guardians, (8) providing restraining orders, (9) reporting elder abuse, and (10) enforcing involuntary commitments. Although these were the areas that protective services workers believed criminal justice professionals *could* help, there was not universal agreement that criminal justice professionals *did* help. Fully 149 of the respondents, for instance, indicated it was difficult to get the criminal justice system to prosecute offenders. Still, this research suggested that many occupations became more effective in successfully handling elder abuse cases (Blakely & Dolon, 2001).

In Chapter 5, examples of teams who respond to crimes against seniors were considered. Unfortunately, these teams do not exist everywhere. Indeed, there needs to be more widespread reliance on the use of teams to serve elderly victims. Teams have also been used in hospitals to address the needs of elderly clients. Dyer et al. (1999) describe the Interdisciplinary Geriatric Assessment and Intervention Team (IGAIT), which is a part of the geriatric program at Baylor College of Medicine. The team consists of two board-certified geriatricians, three board certified internists, three geriatric nurse practitioners, three master's prepared social workers, a chaplain, physical and occupational therapists, and a nurse care manager. The team develops interdisciplinary plans for elderly persons and helps APS workers confront medical issues about which the APS worker may know very little. Describing other teams, Matlaw and Spence (1994) point out that the teams "help to increase awareness about elder abuse and can present an organized approach in offering education and consultation to the staff" (p. 36).

Note that it takes a team of diverse individuals to meet an elderly person's medical needs. It follows that criminal justice officials should not be expected to meet the victims' needs on their own. In some places, a team approach is being used, even if the approach is not referred to as such. For instance, one of the major functions of APS workers is to "work with law enforcement authorities and the courts" (Bergeron, 1999, p. 91). In those cases where APS employees and criminal justice officials are truly working together, it can be said that a team approach is being used. Indeed, a problem as complex as elder abuse requires a team approach to effectively deal with the problem.

Of course, not all are working together. The perceived nature of social service work (e.g., to protect, help, and offer services) is different from the perceived nature of criminal justice work (to detect, control, and punish) (Reulbach & Tewksbury, 1995). According to Harshbarger (1989), criminal justice employees and protective services employees "have many misperceptions about each other" (p. 5). Others also note philosophical differences between the groups (Johnson et al., 1994; Payne et al., 1999). To see whether police officers and social service providers had different beliefs about the factors contributing to elder abuse, Dolon and Hendricks (1989) surveyed fifty-one police officers and fifty-five social service professionals. They found that police officers believed family conflict was more important than social service workers did, and that social service workers saw other factors (physical dependency, economic dependency, stress, mental health, and lack of resources) as being more important than the police officers did. They also found that police did not rank social service providers as useful, but social service providers saw police as useful in elder abuse cases.

Barriers clearly exist that limit cooperation between the groups responding to elder abuse. Blakely and Dolon (1991) cite the following five barriers: (1) training deficiencies, (2) communication problems, (3) excessive workloads, (4) funding problems, and, (5) ageism. The end result of these barriers is that elderly victims are re-victimized by a process where their needs are not met.

While there are examples of a lack of cooperation between groups, Massachusetts provides a good model of how law enforcement and social service professionals can work together (Reulbach & Tewksbury, 1994). For instance, Harshbarger and Morse (1998) describe a training program made available in Massachusetts that shows cooperative effort between providers and prosecutors. The groups have convened two conferences and several regional workshops to study abuse in long-term care settings. They also developed a training program and video, *Keeping Nursing Facility Residents Safe,* which educates employees about abuse in institutions. The cooperation has led to a 20 percent decrease in cases of reported patient abuse. So, while lack of cooperation may present obstacles, the obstacles can be overcome.

Recommendation 5–More funding is needed to study and to respond to crimes against elderly persons. As noted in Chapter 2, research on elderly crime victims seems to be at the bottom of the "research funding ladder." Studies focusing on topics such as drugs, juvenile delinquency, and street crime are more likely to be funded than studies focusing on victims. In turn, research focusing on younger victims is more likely to be funded than research focusing on older victims. The justification for the funding disparity would likely be that there are so few elderly crime victims as compared to juvenile victims and offenders. I have already established that crime is a relative concept, and that elderly persons may not be victims of street crime as often as younger persons, but they are certainly overrepresented in cases of fraud, white-collar crime, and institutional abuse. Further, with more elderly persons in the future, there is a possibility that there will be more elderly crime victims (see Covey & Menard, 1988). It is imperative that more research be funded to address the characteristics, consequences, and causes of elder abuse.

Increased funding is also needed to more effectively respond to offenses against elder abuse. Police chiefs, for instance, report more funding is needed to effectively respond to crimes against elderly persons (Payne, Gainey, & Flores, 2000). A recent survey of Medicaid Fraud Control Unit directors found that the majority of directors faced budget problems that limited their capacity to respond to offenses (Payne & Berg, 1997). It is not only law enforcement officers who need more funding.

For example, Stiegel (1995) surveyed various criminal justice officials involved in responding to elder abuse and made numerous recommendations concerning methods to improve the justice system's response to elder abuse. Among those recommendations, she focused on improving the administration of justice and case management and recommended the following:

1. Courts should accommodate persons with physical and cognitive deficiencies, and hold hearings, if necessary, in settings that best accommodate the elder abuse victim.
2. Elder abuse cases should be expedited on the court calendar.
3. Courts should recognize that elderly persons' capacities change (e.g., with time of day or medications) and should schedule hearings at times that accommodate the elder abuse victim (p. 8).

Though she never mentions the need for increased funding, these recommendations would require at least slight increases in funding in order to effectively meet victims' needs. Indeed, in order to help elderly crime victims, resources must be devoted to developing the programs that would most meet their needs.

Of course, there are some who would argue that state budgets already dedicate enough resources to elderly person's needs. Cohen (1994) refutes this assumption and suggests that funding in general is more often directed toward issues more relevant to the younger population. According to Cohen, 15 percent of Arizona's population is over the sixty-five, but only 11 percent of state funds are directed toward programs for the elderly. Cohen also notes that slightly over 13 percent of Wisconsin's population is over sixty-five, but less than 4 percent of the state budget is dedicated to services for older people. Other states show similar figures. The point is that enough is not being spent on programs for elderly persons. In particular, programs for older crime victims are underfunded. In fact, funding has been described as "the greatest challenge" faced by these programs (Wolf & Pillemer, 1994, p. 129). This is particularly problematic since the programs that do exist have been found to be extremely useful for addressing the needs of elderly victims.

Recommendation 6–Special programs focusing only on crimes against seniors are needed. Various programs that have been successful in helping elderly crime victims were highlighted throughout this book. Research on these programs generally shows that the programs are useful in meeting elderly persons' needs. Successful programs have been found to share three characteristics: (1) they have low start-up and maintenance costs; (2) they are flexible in nature and could operate within many different agencies; and (3) they are able to provide technical assistance (Wolf & Pillemer, 1994). Also implied in past research is the need for programs in areas where there are currently no special services available for older victims.

Program development can be a difficult process. Wolf and Pillemer (1994) note that successful programs must rely on available research and information in developing the program's policies, aims, and strategies. For example, program developers must not fall into the trap of offering services for only one type of victim. Consider programs that define elder abuse as abusive activities committed by an adult child against an elderly parent. Sengstock (1991) notes that this approach would exclude the vast number of older spouse abuse victims. It would also exclude a large number of fraud and white-collar crime victims.

As indicated earlier, several successful elder abuse programs have been developed. Personal affairs management programs have helped elderly persons maintain their independence through teaching money management techniques (Tokarek, 1996). This, in turn, reduces their risks of financial exploitation.

Another program designed to eliminate, or at the very least reduce financial exploitation, is the Massachusetts Bank Reporting Project, which was created in 1996 by Massachusetts bankers and legislators. Price and Fox (1997) point out that over two-thirds of the banks that were members of the Massachusetts Bankers Association allowed a total of one thousand employees to participate in the project. The main part of the project entailed training employees to (1) recognize financial exploitation and (2) understand what procedures should be followed to report suspected cases of exploitation. Price and Fox point out that the number of financial exploitation cases reported by bank employees increased from ten in the previous twelve months to fifty-seven in the first six months of the program's existence.

Special law enforcement programs have also been developed to address concerns about elderly victimization. Some of these programs were addressed in Chapter 5. Another one that reflects that nature of these programs is the Senior Victim Assistance Team (SVAT), which is a part of the Colorado Springs Police Department (Bliss, 1996). The SVAT provides specialized assistance to elderly victims. SVAT members attend training programs where they learn about crisis intervention and the referral process. The team is headed by a caseworker coordinator who oversees the volunteers. Volunteers, so far twenty-five in all, come from senior groups, families of police officers, and referrals from the police department (Bliss, 1996). Bliss suggests that the program has helped police become more efficient and, more importantly, has met seniors' needs. Bliss further argues that other police departments can develop similar volunteer programs with limited resources.

Prevention programs can also be developed to protect seniors. Fattah (1986) argues that prevention programs for elderly persons should (1) harden targets, (2) create protective environments, (3) strengthen elderly persons' social networks, (4) educate seniors about prevention and risks, and (5) encourage seniors to avoid unnecessary risks. Not all programs will be successful. Wolf and Pillemer (1994) note that programs are more likely to succeed in urban areas where agencies have support of the local APS system, and where cooperation between the human services agencies is already occurring.

Recommendation 7–Criminal definitions of elder abuse must be agreed on by practitioners, scholars, and policy makers. Using a social harm approach, I have argued throughout the text that elder abuse is a crime. This does not necessarily mean that all cases of elder abuse are, or should be for that matter, criminally illegal. The justice system is already overburdened as it is, and full prosecution of all elder abuse cases would be impossible. As well, regulatory laws giving adult protective services employees the authority to respond to elder abuse can be instrumental in offering a process through which some elder abuse cases can flow (Formby, 1992). However, when criminal definitions are considered, it is safe to suggest that disparity in definitions has hampered efforts to respond to offenses against seniors (Hugman, 1995; Valentine & Cash, 1986; Vinton, 1991).

The reason this disparity is problematic centers on the relatively recent entrance of criminal justice officials into the fight against elder abuse. Describing this trend, Wolf (1992) states the following:

> The inclusion of law enforcement and criminal justice personnel as part of the organizational network serving abused and neglected elders represents a shift in approach to intervention. The knowledge that many of the cases involve

spouses, that victims are not necessarily disabled, and that perpetrators may be dependent on their victims suggests that those interventions preferred for victims of domestic violence may be more appropriate than supplying home care services intended to relieve overburdened caregivers. These strategies should be evaluated before further 'criminalization of elder abuse takes place' (p. 275).

Unfortunately, the criminalization has taken place with little thought given to the most appropriate criminal definitions of abuse and neglect, or the other offenses that target seniors (e.g., fraud, health care crimes, etc.). The criminalization likely occurred due to the belief that increased law enforcement presence and legal assistance would deter many instances of elder abuse (see Bower, 1989; Heisler, 1991; Pillemer & Finkelhor, 1989). While criminalization has occurred, one of the oversights regarding the definition of elder abuse has been the exclusion of victims' perspectives. Not surprisingly, with vague crime definitions and limited funding, the criminalization has not yet been successful. A quote from Mathews in Chapter 5 is worth repeating: "the criminal justice system alone is clearly not the solution to the problem of elder abuse" (p. 659). Rather, the integrated effort described throughout this text is the one experts see as the most feasible response to elder abuse.

Nonetheless, given the criminalization trend that has occurred, it seems logical that a criminological definition of elder abuse be developed. A criminological definition must integrate elder abuse themes and crime-related themes. Payne et al. (1999) developed an integrated definition of elder abuse that was based on input from nursing home employees, police chiefs, and criminal justice and sociology students. The definition of elder abuse offered by Payne et al. is "any criminal, physical, or emotional harm or unethical taking advantage that negatively affects the physical, financial, or general well being of an elderly person" (p. 81). Note that instances of institutional abuse, fraud, white-collar crime, and street crime are captured in this definition. Indeed, for criminologists to get more involved in the study of elder abuse, those acts that are typically studied by criminologists (e.g., street crimes, white-collar crimes, etc.) must be included in a criminological definition of elder abuse.

Recommendation 8–Comparative research focusing on crimes against elderly persons in other cultures should continue. Understanding the way other cultures respond to elder abuse with formal response systems will broaden our understanding of human behavior (Brammer, 1996; Kosberg & Garcia, 1995; Saveman, Hallberg, & Norberg, 1996; Saveman & Hallberg, 1997; Sijuwade, 1995). To attain this increased understanding, the characteristics and consequences of elder abuse have been examined in places such as Canada (Vida, 1994), India (Shah, Veedon, & Vasi, 1995), Ireland (Horkan, 1995), Norway (Johns & Hydle, 1995), Finland (Perttu, 1996), Poland (Halicka, 1995), and South Africa (Eckley & Vilakazi, 1995). Among other things, elder abuse researchers in one country can learn from the way that researchers in other countries assess the extent of elder abuse (McCreadie & Hancock, 1997; McCreadie, Bennett, & Tinker, 1998; Sharon & Zoabi, 1997).

Understanding how other cultures confront and respond to elder abuse will also tell us about elder abuse issues that arise in various minority populations in a country as diverse as the United States. As evidence, researchers have considered the way that elder abuse influences or is influenced by Hispanic communities (Montoya, 1997), Vietnamese families (Le, 1997), Filipino women (Pablo & Braun, 1997), Asian Indians (Nagpaul, 1997), and Native American elders (Brown, 1989).

Cross-cultural research will also show how cultural attitudes, traditions, and belief systems play a role in the types of elder abuse found in a society (Anetzberger, Korbin, & Tomita, 1996). For example, research by Sharon and Zoabi (1997) finds that psychological abuse is the most common form of abuse in Arab countries, whereas neglect, material abuse, and physical abuse are the most common forms of abuse in Western nations. The authors suggest that psychological abuse is higher in Arab countries because of "strong controls in Arab communities which suppress the most overtly unacceptable behaviors such as physical abuse and neglect" (p. 53). Note that in addition to influencing types of elder abuse, cultural beliefs also play a role in preventing, contributing to, and responding to abuse (Le, 1997; Montoya, 1997; Tomita, 1998).

The use of the culturagram to aid in detecting abuse is just one example of the way that cultural influences are important factors in preventing and responding to abuse. The culturagram is described as "an assessment tool that was developed to improve practitioners' understanding and ability to empower culturally diverse families" (Brownell, 1997, p. 20). Brownell further states that the culturagram "lends itself to a sensitive evaluation of risk factors for elder abuse within immigrant families from diverse cultures" (p. 21). The culturagram is useful in determining risk of abuse because it assesses various dimensions including, but not limited to:

1. reasons for immigration;
2. age at immigration;
3. language spoken at home and in the community;
4. health beliefs; and
5. values about family, unemployment, and education disparity (Brownell, 1997).

Looking at the cultural influences can help caseworkers determine whether an individual is at risk of abuse, and what services should be provided for those who have already been abused. Those working with older victims need to consider differences between ethnic groups in order to determine the appropriate treatment (Tomita, 2000).

Recommendation 9–Seniors should be given more opportunities to be involved in responding to offenses that target elderly persons. In various parts of this text, I addressed ways that elderly persons have, or could, become more involved in responding to elder abuse. From assisting in developing performance measurement systems in the research arena (see Chapter 2) to being actively involved in law enforcement efforts, elderly persons need to be given the opportunity to get more involved in responding to elder abuse. All available evidence suggests that empowerment is an achievable and worthwhile goal. As illustrated in Chapter 7, several different programs have been implemented based on this empowerment ideal.

Recommendation 10–Those who will encounter cases of elder abuse need to receive more training on how to detect and respond to cases of elder abuse. It is certainly imperative that those who will encounter cases of elder abuse be trained how to intervene in and respond to suspected cases of elder abuse. After all, the training one receives will influence one's decisions in handling cases of elder abuse (Bergeron, 1999). Those who need increases in training include police officers, court officials, health care providers, and nursing homes employees (Braun et al., 1997; Payne, 1998a; Stiegel, 1995).

Increased training for police officers is needed simply because many have received very little training in how to interact with elderly crime victims (Stock, 1995). Mathis (1994) recognizes that law enforcement departments are overburdened, understaffed, and underbudgeted. Nonetheless, he argues, as would I, that protection and prevention of crimes against older adults must be made a priority. To attain this end, he, and others, argue that education of new and current officers must increase. He writes, "Officers need to realize that not all criminal activity is violent, that not all property is stolen in the night, and that documents need not confuse, but may incriminate and convict guilty exploiters" (p. 4).

There have been some advances in training. The Police Executive Research Foundation (PERF) developed a training package (*Innovated Training Package for Detecting and Aiding Victims of Domestic Elder Abuse*) that is useful in training police officers and protective services employees how to detect and respond to elder abuse. In addition, the National Association of Medicaid Fraud Control Units has been instrumental in enhancing training for law enforcement officers (Hodge, 1998). Still, a survey of criminal justice professionals by Stiegel (1996) found that professionals reported knowing very little about elder abuse. Stiegel points out that lack of knowledge for police officers equates to problems recognizing abuse, gathering evidence, and interacting with victims. Until all officers are better trained in how to assist elderly victims, elderly victims will be underserved.

Court officials also need to be trained how to better respond to elder abuse cases (Stiegel, 1995). Given the changing policies and laws governing elder abuse, court officials must be prepared to effectively implement the policies and enforce the laws. Stiegel recommends that judges and court staff should be better prepared to understand the following topics: (1) elder abuse and family violence dynamics, (2) the types of elder abuse, (3) capacity issues, (4) state laws relating to elder abuse, (5) the APS structure, (6) case management problems, (7) procedural changes, (8) effective resolutions to elder abuse cases, and (9) ways to gather data about elder abuse cases (p. 7). Indeed, with all of the changes in the eighties and nineties, court officials need to be made aware of the way that elder abuse cases are most effectively handled.

Increased training for medical professionals is also needed. In particular, health care providers need to become aware of the ways that they can become involved in the fight against elder abuse (Lachs, 1995; Lang, 1995; McGreevy, 1993; Ritter, 1992; Rosenblatt, 1996; Saveman et al., 1996). Recall that medical professionals are in positions where they are likely the first to see the physical consequences of abusive actions. They need to be aware of ways to identify abuse, who to report it to, and how to prevent it. Indeed, medical professionals are often the "gatekeepers" who receive information and pass it on to APS, hospital teams, or other social service professionals (Warren & Bennett, 1997). They are also in positions where they must provide patients with medical care to offset the consequences of elder abuse (Rosenblatt, 1996). It is not surprising, then, that Demoss (1993) argues that "doctors should insist on 'private time' with their elderly patients" (p. 1223). Unfortunately, a 1994 Association of American Medical College survey, cited by Boxer (1995), found that 60 percent of medical students viewed the amount of time given to instruction about domestic violence as inadequate. Certainly, there is room for increased training of medical professionals in the area of elder abuse.

Nursing home professionals need to be trained in similar ways. Recent research shows that education increases nursing home managers' abilities to respond to elder abuse (Richardson et al., 2002). All professionals working in long-term-care settings need to be trained how not to be abusive on the job (Payne & Cikovic, 1995; Pillemer & Moore, 1989). Employees also need to be aware of assessment tools, intervention strategies, and laws governing the reporting of elder abuse (Pettee, 1997). Further, a common theme in the past elder abuse literature is that situational factors contribute to physical abuse in nursing homes. If these factors actually contribute to abuse, nursing home professionals can be trained in what to look for in order to avoid abusive actions. The Virginia Coalition for the Prevention of Elder Abuse (VCPEA) sponsors training programs each year to do just this.

To effectively train about elder abuse, Braun et al. (1997) recommend active learning strategies such as role playing and small group discussions because they are more likely to be interesting, and thus informative, than traditional lecture-styled programs—which nurse's aides would find rather boring.

Braun et al. further point out that the training costs can be quite high but note that the "cost may be reduced by entering into partnerships with college programs" (p. 10). Also, if elder abuse is an interagency problem, it would seem that interagency training would be useful. Unfortunately, different education and interest levels of employees from different agencies makes integrated training difficult (Weiner, 1991).

Recommendation 11–More attention needs to be given to offenses occurring in nursing homes and other long-term-care settings. Certainly the effects of abuse in nursing homes go far beyond those immediate physical, financial, and emotional consequences experienced by victims. For instance, abuse in institutions makes individuals in the community afraid of staying in institutions (Burger, 1996). Initially, attention was primarily directed toward elder abuse cases within the family. Research that considered elder abuse in nursing homes initially was oriented toward understanding cases of physical and psychological abuse. Only recently have researchers begun to focus on financial offenses committed in nursing homes (Harris & Benson, 1996; Harris, 1999). The organizational offenses committed by the administration need to also be understood (Braithewaite, 1993). Taken together, there are several different offenses that could be committed in long-term-care settings. As it is, relatively little is known about the criminal acts committed in these settings.

Recommendation 12–Citizens need to be more educated about crimes committed against elderly persons. If citizens were more aware of the problems facing elderly crime victims, then policy makers, who answer to the citizens, would be forced to take measures that would be in the best interest of elderly crime victims. Indeed, citizen support can go a long way toward helping elder abuse victims, and elderly persons who are victims of other offenses as well (Blakely & Dolon, 1998; Burger, 1996; Filinson, 1995). Encouraging political support is just one way that citizens can get involved in the battle against elder abuse. Members of the public also need to be educated about the warning signs of elder abuse, how to report it, and what the consequences of abuse are (Blakely & Dolon, 1998; Kaye & Darling, 2000). As potential victims, older adults need to become aware of the criminal justice system's role in elder abuse cases and should understand that the system can prosecute without the victim's consent (Stiegel, 1996). According to Stiegel, if older citizens understood this, the burden they would feel about being blamed for deciding, or not deciding, to prosecute the offender would be minimized.

Citizens should also be proactive in attempts to battle elder abuse. Consider the case of Helen Karr. Tired of hearing about horrific cases of elder abuse, the sixty-nine-year-old woman enrolled in San Francisco Law School. She took night classes for four years and eventually became licensed to practice law in California. Her motivation was to "donate her services to seniors through the elder abuse unit of the San Francisco district attorney's office" (Johnson, 2003: 2). She focuses her energies specifically on financial abuse.

CONCLUDING REMARKS

A number of advances in the area of elder abuse have been made since practitioners, scholars, and policy makers first discussed the issue over two decades ago. One recent development was the creation of coalitions to prevent elder abuse. In 1993, the National Committee for the Prevention of Elder Abuse provided funding for five states (Idaho, Montana, Tennessee, Texas, and Virginia) to establish statewide coalitions to prevent elder abuse. Members of the coalitions include those individuals from those areas that are most likely to encounter cases of elder abuse. As such, the coalitions are interdisciplinary in focus.

In Virginia, the VCPEA educates the public about elder abuse, offers training programs for those working with elderly persons, and serves as an advocate for policies protecting elderly persons residing in the Commonwealth. The coalition has established curricula for law enforcement officers and nurse's aides. In addition, the coalition was successful in lobbying for funds targeted directly at APS, and worked with attorneys to establish an elder abuse newsletter (VCPEA, 1999). Part of the success of the coalition has been its involvement in preventing crimes against elderly person. Typically, programs and services are aimed at reacting to victimization, rather than offering measures that would reduce victimization (Kinderknecht, 1986). The coalition acts rather than reacts. Though the coalition has been effective, it must continue to work to prevent crimes against elderly persons. Also, thought should be given to creating similar coalitions in other states. After all, elder abuse is not limited to these five states.

In the end, when considering crimes against elderly persons, a host of different questions arises. Political questions focus on the way that politicians have responded to offenses against elderly persons. Legal questions center on the way that laws have been developed to legislate against elder abuse. Medical questions center on the need to understand what the physical and emotional consequences of elder abuse are. Sociological questions focus on the role of society in contributing to and responding to elder abuse. Theoretical questions address the actual causes of abusive behavior. Criminological questions center on whether these acts should be defined and treated as criminal. Ethical questions ask whether these laws and responses are appropriate.

Anetzberger, Dayton, and McMonagle (1997) note that the best way to respond to ethical questions is to consider the way that various perspectives would address the ethical issues. A similar case could be made for all of the other questions as well. That is, to be best address the political, legal, medical, sociological, theoretical, and criminological questions surrounding elder abuse, one should consider the way that other perspectives would address the issue. Addressing the questions in this manner is what I mean by the gero-criminological approach.

REFERENCES

Ackerman, R. (1987). *Children of alcoholics* (2nd Ed.). New York: Simon and Schuster.

Adams, G.R., & Schvaneveldt, J.D. (1985). *Understanding research methods*. New York: Longman.

Adams, M.H. (1998). Florida auto agency owner banned for life. *National Underwriter, 102, 36,* 51.

Aging Magazine. (1996). Study calls for strengthening the nursing home ombudsmen program. 367, 117–118.

Agnew, R. (1992). Foundation for a general strain theory of crime. *Criminology, 30,* 47–87.

Akers, R.L., La Greca, A.J., Sellers, C., & Cochran, J. (1987). Fear of crime and victimization of the elderly in different types of communities. *Criminology, 25*(3), 487–505.

Alfonso, H. (2000). Mortgage fraud prevention program. *Journal of Elder Abuse and Neglect, 12*(2), 75–80.

Allen, J.V. (2000). Financed abuse of elderly and dependent adults. *Journal of Elder Abuse and Neglect, 12*(2), 85–91.

All, A.C. (1994). A literature review: Assessment and intervention in elder abuse. *Journal of Gerontological Nursing,* July, 25–32.

Alston, L.T. (1986). *Crime and older Americans*. Springfield, IL: Charles C Thomas.

American Association of Retired Persons. (1998). Consumer fraud. www.aarp.org/fraud/home.htm.

American College of Emergency Physicians. (1999). Elderly abandonment. www.acep.org/public/TP009804.htm.

Anderson, E.G. (1997). Osteoporosis: Epidemic of the 21st century? *Geriatrics, 52*(6), 76–77.

Anetzberger, G. (1987). *The etiology of elder abuse by adult offspring*. Springfield, IL: Charles C Thomas.

Anetzberger, G.J., Lachs, M.S., O'Brien, Js.G., Pillemer, K.A., & Tomita, S.K. (1993). Elder mistreatment: A call for help. *Patient Care, 27*(11), 93–111.

Anetzberger, G.J., Korbin, J.E., & Austin, C. (1994). Alcoholism and elder abuse. *Journal of Interpersonal Violence, 9*(2), 184–193.

Anetzberger, G. (1995). Commentary on preaching to the unconverted. *Journal of Elder Abuse & Neglect, 7*(4), 13–16.

Anetzberger, G.J., Korbin, J.E., & Tomita, S.K. (1996). Defining elder mistreatment in four ethnic groups across two generations. *Journal of Cross-Cultural Gerontology, 11,* 187–212.

Anetzberger, G.J., Dayton, C., & McMonagle, P. (1997). A community dialogue series on ethics and elder abuse: Guidelines for decision-making. *Journal of Elder Abuse & Neglect, 9*(1), 33–50.

Arbetter, S.R. (1995). Family violence. *Current Health, 22,* 6–12.

Aviv, J. (1995). Presbycusis (The inner ear). *The Columbia University College of Physicians and Surgeons complete home medical guide* (3rd Ed.). Columbia, MA: Crown.

Aziz, S.J. (2000). The National Telemarketing Victim Call Center. *Journal of Elder Abuse and Neglect, 12*(2), 93–98.

Aziz, S. (2000). Los Angeles County Fiduciary Abuse Specialist Team. *Journal of Elder Abuse and Neglect, 12*(2), 79–83.

Bachman, R. (1992). *Crime victimization in city, suburban, and rural areas.* National Crime Victimization Survey Report. Washington, DC: U.S. Bureau of Justice Statistics.

Bachman, R. (1998). The factors related to rape reporting and behavior and arrest: New evidence from the national crime victimization survey. *Criminal Justice and Behavior, 25*(1), 8–29.

Bachman, R., & Taylor, B.M. (1994). The measurement of family violence and rape by the redesigned national crime victimization survey. *Justice Quarterly, 11*(3), 499–512.

Bachman, R., Dillaway, H., & Lachs, M.S. (1998). Violence against the elderly. *Research on Aging, 20*(2), 183–198.

Baker, A.A. (1975). Granny battering. *Modern Geriatrics, 8,* 20–24.

Baker, L.C. (1999). Association of managed care market share and health expenditures for fee-for-service Medicare patients. *Journal of the American Medical Association, 281*(5), 432–437.

Baldassare, M. (1986). The Elderly and fear of crime. *Sociology and Social Research, 70*(3), 218–221.

Barker, J.F. (1993). Consumer protection telemarketing hearing. Testimony before U.S. House of Representatives, February 17, Washington, DC: GPO.

Baron, S., & Welty, A. (1996). Chapter IV: Elder abuse. *Journal of Gerontological Social Work, 25*(1–2), 33–57.

Beccaria, C. (1764). Essays on Crime and Punishment. Trans. Henry Paolucci. Indianapolis, IN: Bobbs-Merrill (Reprinted 1963).

Beck, M., & Gordon, J. (1991, December 23). A dumping ground for granny. *Newsweek, 118*(26), 64.

Beebe, D.K. (1991). Emergency management of the adult female rape victim. *American Family Physician, 43*(6), 2041–2046.

Bendik, M.F. (1992). Reaching the breaking point: Dangers of mistreatment in elder caregiving situations. *Journal of Elder Abuse & Neglect, 4*(3), 39–59.

Bennett, G., & Kingston, P. (1992). *Elder abuse: Concepts, theories, and interventions.* London: Chapman and Hall.

Belyea, M.J., & Zingraff, M.T. (1988). Fear of crime and residential location. *Rural Sociology, 53*(4), 473–486.

Berg, B. (1998). *Qualitative research methods for the social sciences* (3rd Ed.). Boston: Allyn and Bacon.

Bergeron, L.R. (1999). Decision-making and adult protective services workers: Identifying critical factors. *Journal of Elder Abuse & Neglect, 10*(3/4), 87–114.

Bergeron, L.R. (2000). Servicing the needs of elder abuse victims. *Policy and Practice of Public Human Services, 58*(3), 40.

Bergeron, L.R. (2001). An elder abuse case study. *Journal of Gerontological Social Work, 34*(4), 47–57.

Bergeron, L.R. (2002). Family preparation: An unidentified approach in elder abuse protection *Families in Society,* December, 547–556.

Bergeron, L.R., & Gray, B. (2003). Ethical dilemmas of reporting suspected elder abuse. *Social Work, 48*(1), 96–105.

Berliner, H. (2001). Abuse of older adults. Clinical Reference Systems. 2001: 19.

Besleme, K., & Mullin, M. (1997). Community indicators and healthy communities. *National Civic Review, 86*(1), 43–53.

Bierstedt, R. (1970). *The social order.* New York: McGraw-Hill.

Biggs, S., Phillipson, C., & Kingston, P. (1995). *Elder abuse in perspective.* Buckingham: Open University Press.

Blake, K. (1996). Phone scam update: Seniors beware. *Consumer's Research Magazine, 79*(2), 23–27.

Blakely, B.E., & Dolon, R. (1991). The relative contributions of occupation groups in the discovery of elder abuse and neglect. *Journal of Gerontological Social Work, 17,* 183–199.

Blakely, B.E., & Dolon, R. (1998). A test of public reactions to alleged elder abuse. *Journal of Elder Abuse & Neglect, 9*(4), 43–66.

Blakely, B.E., & Dolon, R. (2000). Perceptions of adult protective service workers of the support provided by criminal justice professionals in a case of elder abuse. *Journal of Elder Abuse & Neglect, 12*(3/4), 71–94.

Blakely, B.E., & Dolon, R. (2001). Another look at the helplessness of occupational groups in the discovery of elder abuse and neglect. *Journal of Elder Abuse & Neglect, 13*(3), 1–24.

Blancato, R.B. (2002). The Elder Justice Act: A landmark policy initiative. *Journal of Elder Abuse & Neglect, 14*(2/3), 181–185.

Blecher, M.B. (1997). Senior sleuths. *Hospitals and Health Networks, 71*(22), 43.

Bliss, L. (1996). Police practice: Assisting senior victims. *The FBI Law Enforcement Bulletin, 65,* 6–9.

Block, C.R., & Christakos, A. (1995). Intimate partner homicide in Chicago over 29 years. *Crime and Delinquency, 41,* 496–526.

Block, M., & Sinnot, J.D. (1979). *The battered elder syndrome.* College Park, MD: Center on Aging, University of Maryland.

Blunt, A.P. (1993). Financial exploitation of the incapacitated: Investigation and remedies. *Journal of Elder Abuse & Neglect, 5*(1), 19–32.

Bowen, C. (1998). Weird medicine reports. *Editor and Publisher, 131*(22), 29.

Bower, B. (1989). Relative downfalls behind elder abuse. *Science News, 135*(18), 276–277.

Bowers, K.E., & Thomas, P. (1995). Handle with care. *Harvard Health Letter, 20*(10), 6–7.

Bowker, A.L. (1999). Investigative planning: Creating a strong foundation for white-collar crime cases. *FBI Law Enforcement Bulletin, 68*(6), 22–25.

Box, S., Hale, C., & Andrews, G. (1988). Explaining fear of crime. *British Journal of Criminology, 28*(3), 340–356.

Boxer, B. (1995, April 6). Statement on introduced bills and joint resolutions. *Congressional Record,* S5404–5452.

Boyd, J.H. (1982). The increasing rate of suicide by firearms. *The New England Journal of Medicine, 308*(15), 872–874.

Bradley, M. (1996). Elder abuse: Caring for older people. *British Medical Journal, 313*(7056), 548–550.

Braithwaite, J. (1989). Criminological theory and organizational crime. *Justice Quarterly, 6,* 333–358.

Braithwaite, J., Makkai, T., Braithewaite, D.G., & Ermann, D. (1990). *The contribution of the standards monitoring process to the quality of nursing home life: A preliminary report.* Canberra: Department of Community Services and Health.

Braithwaite, J. (1993). The nursing home industry. In M. Tonry & A.J. Reiss (Eds.), *Beyond the law: Crime in complex organizations* (pp. 11–54). Chicago: University of Chicago Press.

Brammer, A. (1996). Elder abuse in the UK: A new jurisdiction? *Journal of Elder Abuse & Neglect, 8*(2), 33–48.

Brandl, B., & Horan, D.L. (2002). Domestic violence in later life: An overview for healthcare providers *Women Health,* February, 41–53.

Braun, K.L., Suzuki, K.M., Cusick, S.E., & Howard-Carhart, K. (1997). Developing and testing training materials on elder abuse and neglect for nurses aides. *Journal of Elder Abuse & Neglect, 9*(1), 1–15.

Breckman, R.S., & Adelman, R.D. (1988). *Strategies for helping victims of elder mistreatment.* Newbury Park, CA: Sage.

Brewer, J., & Hunter, A. (1989). *Multimethod research: A synthesis of styles.* Newbury Park, CA: Sage.

Brienza, J. (1995). Elder abuse cases hit home with jurors. *Trial, 31*(12), 65–66.

Broidy, L., & Agnew, R. (1997). Gender and crime: A general strain theory perspective. *Journal of Research in Crime and Delinquency, 34*(3), 275–306.

Brown University Long-Term Care Quality Letter. (1996). Characteristics of residents with contractures. 8(7), 1.

Brown, E.W. (1989). A brighter world for cataract patients. *Medical Update, 22*(9), 2.

Browne, K.D., & Hamilton, C.E. (1998). Physical violence between young adults and their parents: Associations with a history of maltreatment. *Journal of Family Violence, 13*(1), 59–80.

Brownell, P. (1997). The application of the culturagram in cross-cultural practice with elder abuse victims. *Journal of Elder Abuse & Neglect, 9*(2), 19–34.

Bruce, C.H. (1994). Elder abuse. *Journal of the American Academy of Physician Assistants,* 7(3), 170–174.

Bruce, J. (1996). Swindlers lose license to steal in L.A. *Aging Magazine, 367,* 74–75.

Bua, R.N. (1997). *The inside guide to America's nursing homes.* New York: Warner Books.

Burby, L.N. (1994, January 2). Doctors and lawyers on long island are being alerted to watch out for financial abuse of elderly. *New York Times,* Section 14, 4.

Bureau of Justice Statistics. (1994). *Elderly crime victims: National crime survey.* Washington, DC: U.S. Department of Justice.

Bureau of Justice Statistics. (1998). *Criminal victimization in the United States, 1995,* NCJ-171129, Washington, DC: U.S. Department of Justice.

Bureau of Justice Statistics. (1999). *Victim characteristics: An information sheet.* Washington DC: U.S. Department of Justice.

Burg, B. (1997). When to report abuse–and when not to. *Medical Economics, 74*(12), 78–91.

Burger, S.G. (1996). Consumer views on assuring quality of care: Lessons from 'The Corporation' case. *Journal of Elder Abuse & Neglect, 8*(3), 87–90.

Burke, M.J., & Hayes, R.L. (1986). Peer counseling for elderly victims of crime and violence. *Journal for Specialists in Group Work, 11*(2), 107–113.

Business Wire. (2003). Union Bank of California accepts financial watch program. January, 28.

Butler, R.N. (1969). Ageism: Another form of bigotry. *The Gerontologist, 9,* 243–246.

Butler, R.N. (1987). Ageism. In G. Maddox (Ed.), *The encyclopedia of aging.* New York: Springer.

Butler, R. (1999). Warning sings of elder abuse. *Geriatrics. 54*(3), 3–4.

Byers, B., & Hendricks, J.E. (1993). *Adult protective services: Research and practice.* Springfield, IL: Charles C Thomas.

Byers, B., & Lamanna, R.A. (1993). Adult protective services and elder self endangering behavior. In B. Byers & J.E. Hendricks (Eds.), *Adult protective services: Research and practice* (pp. 61–86). Springfield, IL: Charles C Thomas.

Calavita, K., Pontell, H.N., & Tillman, R.H. (1997). *Big money crime: Fraud and politics in the savings and loan crisis.* Berkeley, CA: University of California Press.

Calvan, B.C. (1998, September 26). Phony roofers con woman out of $4,000. *The Virginian-Pilot,* p. B3.

Campbell, D.A. (1988). The needless death of Cassandra Life. *50 Plus, 28,* 18–19.

Cantrell, B. (1994). Triad: Reducing victimization risk. *FBI Law Enforcement Bulletin, 62*(2), 19–23.

Cantrell, B. (1996). Sheriffs: Seniors sheriffs, and police chiefs join to fight crime in 225 communities. *Aging Magazine, 367,* 36–37.

Capezuti, E., & Siegler, E. (1996). Educating health and social service professionals in the detection and management of mistreated nursing home residents. *Journal of Elder Abuse & Neglect, 8*(3), 73–86.

Carlson, M.B. (1995, October 30). Back to the dark ages. *Time,* 63.

Cartwright, P.S., & Moore, R.A. (1989). The elderly victim of rape. *Southern Medical Journal, 82*(8), 988–989.

Cassens, D. (1998). Expanded damages in elder abuse cases. *ABA Journal, 84,* 39.

Chalk, R., & King, P.A. (1998). Facing up to family violence. *Issues in Science and Technology, 15*(2), 39–47.

Chance, P. (1987). Attacking elderly abuse. *Psychology Today,* November, 24–25.

Chatterton, M.R., & Frenz, S.J. (1994). Closed circuit television: Its role in reducing burglaries and the fear of crime in sheltered accommodations for the elderly. *Security Journal, 5*(3), 133–139.

Chen, P.N., Bell, S.L., Dolinsky, D.L., Doyle, J., & Dunn, M. (1981). Elderly abuse in domestic settings: A pilot study. *Journal of Gerontological Social Work, 4*(1), 3–17.

Chermak, S. (1993). Adult protective services and the criminal justice system. In B. Byers & J.E. Hendricks (Eds.), *Adult protective services: Research and practice* (pp. 109–136). Springfield, IL: Charles C Thomas.

Childs, H.W., Hayslip, B., Radika, L.M., & Reinberg, J.A. (2000). Young and middle aged adults' perceptions. *Gerontologist.* 40(1), 78–85.

Childress, D.J. (2003). 10 warning signs of abuse. *Segunda Juventud.* Available online.

Choi, N.G., Kulick, D.B., & Mayer, J. (1999). Financial exploitation of elders: Analysis of risk factors based on county adult protective services data. *Journal of Elder Abuse & Neglect, 10*(3/4), 39–61.

Church, G.J. (1997, August 25). Elderscam: Reach out and bilk someone. *Time,* 54–57.

Clark, C.S. (1994). Crime victim's rights: Do victims need new laws and protections? *CQ Researcher, 4*(27), 627–642.

Clarke, R.V., Ekblom, P., Hough, M., & Mayhew, P. (1985). Elderly victims of crime and exposure to risk. *Howard Journal of Criminal Justice, 24*(1), 1–9.

Clarke, R.V., & Jones, P.R. (1989). Suicide and increased availability of handguns in the United States. *Social Science and Medicine, 28*(8), 805–809.

Clarke, R.V. (Ed.). (1992). *Situational crime prevention.* New York: Harrow and Heston.

Clayton, C. (1999, March 16). Helping elderly people play it safe. *The Virginian Pilot,* B3.

Clinard, M.B., & Yeager, P.C. (1980). *Corporate crime.* New York: Free Press.

Clemente, F., & Kleiman, M.B. (1976). Fear of crime and age. *Geronotologist, 16*(3), 207–10.

Cobb, R.W., & Elder, C.D. (1983). *Participation in American politics.* Baltimore: Johns Hopkins Press.

Cohen, G.D. (1994). Journalistic elder abuse: It's time to get down to the facts. *The Gerontologist, 34*(3), 399–401.

Cohen, L.E., & Felson, M. (1979). Social change and crime rate trends: A routine activities approach. *American Sociological Review, 44,* 588–607.

Cohen, M.A., & Miller, T.R. (1998). The cost of mental health care for victims of crime. *Journal of Interpersonal Violence, 13*(1), 93–110.

Cohen, W.S. (1996). *Keeping fraudulent providers out of Medicare and Medicaid. Hearing.* Washington, DC: Government Printing Office.

Coker, J., & Little, B. (1997). Investing in the future: Protecting the elderly from financial abuse. *FBI Law Enforcement Bulletin, 66*(12), 1–5.

Coleman, J. (1998). *The criminal elite: Understanding white-collar crime.* New York: St. Martin's Press.

Comijs, H.C., Smit, J.H., Pot, A.M., Bouter, L.M., & Jonker, C. (1998). Risk indicators of elder abuse in the community. *Journal of Elder Abuse & Neglect, 9*(4), 67–76.

Conlin, M.M. (1995). Silent suffering: A case study of elder abuse and neglect. *Journal of the American Geriatrics Society, 43,* 1303–1308.

Connolly, M.J. (1996). Obstructive airways disease: A hidden disability in the aged. *Age and Aging, 25*(4), 265–267.

Consalvo, M. (1998). Hegemony, domestic violence, and 'cops': A critique of concordance. *Journal of Popular Film and Television, 26*(2), 62–70.

Consumer's Research Magazine. (1996). Beware the pitch. 79, 23–27.

Consumer Rights and the Elderly. (1999). www.state.me.us/ag/clg21.htm.

Contractor. (1993). Florida 'hvac cont'rs' indicted in $2.3 million scam on elderly. 40(5), 1–2.

Cornish, D.B., & Clarke, R.V. (Eds.). (1986). *The reasoning criminal: Rational choice perspectives on offending.* New York: Springer-Verlag.

Costen, R.W. (1996). The criminal prosecutor's roles in assuring quality care in health care settings. *Journal of Elder Abuse & Neglect, 8*(3), 21–36.

Court TV Legal Help. (1999). www.courttv.com/legalhelp/elder.

Covey, H.C., & Menard, S. (1988). Trends in elderly criminal victimization from 1973 to 1984. *Research on Aging, 10,* 329–341.

Coyne, A., Reichman, W.E., & Berbig, L.J. (1993). The relationship between dementia and elder abuse. *American Journal of Psychiatry, 159*(4), 643–646.

Coyne, A., Potenza, M., & Berbig, L. (1996). Abuse in families coping with dementia. *Aging, 367,* 92–5.

Craig, B.M. (1991). Emergency rooms. *Aging, 362,* 29–30.

Cressey, D.R. (1953). *Other people's money.* New York: Free Press.

Crichton, S.J., Bond, J.B., Harvey, C.D.H., & Ristock, J. (1999). Elder abuse: Feminist and ageist perspectives. *Journal of Elder Abuse & Neglect, 10*(3/4), 115–130.

Cromwell, J., Adamache, K.W., Khandker, R.K., & Ammering, C. (1997). Programmatic, economic and demographic forces underlying Medicaid enrollment trends. *Medical Care Research and Review, 54*(2), 150–175.

Crumb, D.J., & Jennings, K. (1998). Incidents of patient abuse in health care facilities are becoming more and more commonplace. *Dispute Resolution Journal,* February, 37–43.

Crystal, S. (1986). Social policy and elder abuse. In K.A. Pillemer & R.S. Wolf (Eds.), *Conflict in the family* (pp. 331–340). Dover, MA: Auburn House.

Crystal, S. (1987). Elder abuse: The latest crisis. *Public Interest, 88,* 56–66.

Cullen, F.T., & Agnew, R. (1999). Criminological theory: Past to present. Los Angeles: Roxbury.

Curry, B.S., Johnson, I.M., & Sigler, R.T. (1994). Elder abuse: Justice problem, social problem, or research problem? *Free Inquiry in Creative Sociology, 22*(1), 65–71.

Dabney, D., & Berg, B. (1994). Perceptions of drug and supply diversion among nurses. *Free Inquiry in Creative Sociology, 22*(1), 13–21.

Daly, J., & Jogerst, G. (2001). Statute definitions of elder abuse. *Journal of Elder Abuse and Neglect, 13*(4), 39–52.

Daniels, R.S., Baumhover, L.A., & Clarke-Daniels, C.L. (1989). Physician's mandatory reporting of elder abuse. *The Geronologist, 29*(3), 321–327.

Daniels, R.S., Baumhover, L.A., Formby, W.A., & Clark-Daniels, C.L. (1999). Police discretion and elder mistreatment. *Journal of Criminal Justice, 27*(3), 209–226.

Danis, F.S. (2003). Domestic violence and crime victim compensation. *Violence Against Women, 9*(3): 374–390.

Davidson, J.L. (1979). Elder abuse. In M.R. Block & J.D. Sinnot (Eds.), *The battered elder syndrome: An exploratory study* (pp. 40–56). College Park, MD: Center on Aging, University of Maryland.

Deem, D.L. (2000). Notes from the field: Observations in working with the forgotten victims of personal financial crimes. *Journal of Elder Abuse & Neglect, 12*(2), 33–48.

Dembner, A. (2003). Doctor files suit for under medicating. *Boston Globe.* November 4, C1.

Demoss, B.C. (1993). The physician's role in preventing elder abuse. *American Family Physician, 48*(7), 1223.

Derfel, A. (2003). Inquiry into abuse works. *The Gazette.* November 28, A6.

Dessoff, A.L. (1999). No relief? *Contemporary Long Term Care, 22*(5), 7.

de Pommereau, I. (1998). Florida fraud squads protect seniors from Medicare scams. *Christian Science Monitor, 90*(33), 3.

Direct Marketing. (1997). Seniors scammed out of $1 million. 59(12), 10.

Dixon, C. (2003). What's that skunky smell? *New York Times.* A40.

Doerner, W.G., & Lab, S.P. (1998). *Victimology.* Cincinnati, OH: Anderson.

Dolon, R., & Hendricks, J.E. (1989). An exploratory study comparing attitudes and practices of police officers and social service providers in elder abuse and neglect cases. *Journal of Elder Abuse & Neglect, 1*(1), 75–90.

Donegan, C. (1996). Preventing juvenile crime: Is tougher punishment the answer? *CQ Researcher, 6*(10), 219–237.

Drowns, R.W., & Hess, K.M. (1990). *Juvenile justice.* New York: West.

Duke, J. (1997). A national study of involuntary protective services to adult protective services clients. *Journal of Elder Abuse & Neglect, 9*(1), 51–68.

Dunlop, B.D., Rothman, M.B., Gordon, K.M., Hebert, K.S., & Martinez, I.C. (2000). Elder abuse: Risk factors and use of case data to improve policy and practice. *Journal of Elder Abuse & Neglect, 12*(3/4), 95–122.

Dunning, S. (1994). Elder abuse is our fight, too. *RN,* August, 76.

Durkheim, E. (1897). *The rules of the sociological method.* (J.A. Solovay & G. Simpson, Trans.) Chicago: University of Chicago Press, 1938.

Dyer, C.B., Barth, J., Portal, B., Hyman, D.J., Pavlik, V.N., Murphy, K., & Gleason, M.S. (1999). A case series of abused or neglected elders treated by an interdisciplinary geriatric team. *Journal of Elder Abuse & Neglect, 10*(3/4), 131–139.

Eckley, S.C.A., & Vilakazi, P.A.C. (1995). Elder abuse in South Africa. In J.I. Kosberg & J.L. Garcia (Eds.), *Elder abuse: International and cross-cultural perspectives* (pp. 171–182). Binghamton, NY: Haworth.

Ehrlich, P., & Anetzberger, G. (1991). Survey of state public health departments on procedures for reporting elder abuse. *Public Health Reports, 106*(2), 151–154.

Eisenberg, H. (1991). Combating elder abuse through the legal process. *Journal of Elder Abuse & Neglect, 3*(1), 65–96.

Eleazer, G.P. (1995). Elder abuse. *Journal of the South Carolina Medical Association, 91*(10), 431–34.

Ellis, A. (1958). Rational psychotherapy. *Journal of General Psychology, 59*, 35–49.

Ellis, A., Sichel, J.L., Yeager, R.J., DiMattia, D.J., & DiGiuseppe, R. (1989). *Rational-emotive couples therapy.* New York: Pergamon Press.

Ellis, R.M. (1998). Access to emergency services and care in Florida. *Florida Bar Journal, 72*(1), 26–33.

Eve, S.B. (1985). Criminal victimization and fear of crime among the non-institutionalized elderly in the United States. *Victimology, 10*, 397–408.

Ermann, D., & Lundman, R. (1982). *Corporate deviance.* New York: Holt, Rinehart, and Winston.

Fashimpar, G.A., & Phemister, S. (1984). Criminal victimization and its effects upon elderly residents of public housing. *Journal of Housing for the Elderly, 2*(2), 3–15.

Fattah, E.A. (1986). The role of senior citizens in crime prevention. *Ageing and Society, 6*, 471–480.

Faulkner, L. (1982). Mandating the reporting of suspected cases of elder abuse. *Family Law Quarterly, 15*(1), 69–91.

FBI Law Enforcement Bulletin. (1995). National assessment program: 1994 survey results. 64(10), 22–27.

Feder, L. (1998). Police handling of domestic and nondomestic calls: Is there a case for discrimination? *Crime and Delinquency, 44*(2), 335–349.

Federal Bureau of Investigation. (1996). *Summary of uniform crime reporting program.* Washington, DC: U.S. Government Printing Office.

Federal Bureau of Investigation. (1999). *Uniform crime reporting handbook.* Washington, DC: U.S. Government Printing Office.

Federal Bureau of Investigation's Supplementary Homicide Reports. (1999). *Sourcebook of Criminal Justice Statistics Online.* U.S. Department of Justice: Bureau of Justice Statistics.

Felson, M. (1998). *Crime and everyday life* (2nd Ed.). Thousand Oaks, CA: Sage.

Ferraro, K.F. (1995). *Fear of crime: Interpreting victimization risk.* Albany, NY: State University of New York Press.

Fiesta, J. (1999). No dumping: Emergency department transfer risk. *Nursing Management, 30*(1), 10–11.

Fiesta, J. (1996). Legal issues in long-term care–Part II. *Nursing Management, 27*(2), 18.

Filinson, R. (1995). A survey of grass roots advocacy organizations for nursing home residents. *Journal of Elder Abuse & Neglect, 7*(4), 75–91.

Filosa, G. (2003). DNA evidence undercut confession. *The Times Picayune,* May 7, p. 1.

Finkelhor, D. (1983). Common features of family abuse. In D. Finkelhor, R.J. Gelles, G. Hotalins, & M. Straus (Eds.), *The dark side of families: Current family violence research* (pp. 17–26). Beverly Hills, CA: Sage.

Fitzgerald, J.D., & Cox, S.M. (1988). *Research methods in criminal justice: An introduction.* Chicago: Nelson-Hall.

Folkenberg, J. (1989). Elder abuse. *American Health, 8,* 87.

Fisher, J.W., & Dyer, C.B. (2003). Physicians can help patients surmount intimate family violence. *Post Graduate Medicine, 113*(4), np.

Ford, J. (1992). Health care fraud: The silent bandit. *FBI Law Enforcement Bulletin, 61,* 2–7.

Formby, W.A. (1992). Should elder abuse be decriminalized? A justice system perspective. *Journal of Elder Abuse & Neglect, 4*(4), 121–130.

Formby, W.A. (1996). Getting more information from elder abuse interviews. *Aging Magazine, 367,* 38–40.

Forrest, S., Beall, C., Bynum, J., Stephens, G., Grote, N.P., Baumhouver, L.A., & Bolland, J.M. (1990). Training for abusive caregivers: An unconventional approach to an intervention dilemma. *Journal of Elder Abuse & Neglect, 1*(4), 73–86.

Forsyth, C.J., & Shover, N. (1986). No rest for the weary . . . Constructing a problem of elderly crime. *Sociological Focus, 19*(4), 375–386.

Fox, J.A., & Levin, J. (1991). Homicide against the elderly: A research note. *Criminology, 29*(2), 317–327.

Fogel, B.S. (1995). Contractures apparent result of Alzheimer's disease. *The Brown University Long-Term Care Quality Letter, 7*(16), 8–9.

Fried, J.P. (1997, May 25). Prosecutors who still haven't rested. *New York Times,* 30.

Friedman, M. (1992). Confidence swindles of older consumers. *Journal of Consumer Affairs, 26*(1), 20–46.

Friedman, M. (1998). Coping with consumer fraud: The need for a paradigm shift. *Journal of Consumer Affairs, 32*(1), 1–11.

Friedrichs, D.O. (2003). *Trusted criminals: White-collar crime in contemporary society* (2nd Ed.). Belmont, CA: Wadsworth.

Fulmer, T., Street, S., & Carr, K. (1984). Abuse of the elderly: Screening and detection. *Journal of Emergency Nursing, 10,* 131–140.

Fulmer, T. (1990). The debate over dependency as a relevant predisposing factor in elder abuse and neglect. *Journal of Elder Abuse & Neglect, 2*(1/2), 51–57.

Fulmer, T. (1991). Elder mistreatment: Progress in community detection and intervention. *Family and Community Health, 14*(2), 26–34.

Fulmer, T., McMahon, D.J., Baer-Hines, M., & Forget, B. (1992). Abuse, neglect, abandonment, violence, and exploitation: An analysis of all elderly patients seen in one emergency department during a six-month period. *Journal of Emergency Nursing, 18*(6), 505–510.

Fundraising Management. (1999). Telemarketing fraud under the gun. 29(12), 7–8.

Gantz, B.J., Schindler, R.A., & Snow, J.B. Jr. (1995). Adult hearing loss: Some tips and pearls. *Patient Care, 29*(14), 77–84.

Gardner, J. (1996). Study: Medicare risk HMO overpaid. *Modern Healthcare, 26*(34), 8.

Garrett, A.W. (1996). Cosmetic dermatology. *Drug and Cosmetic Industry, 158*(2), 10–11.

Garvin, R.M., & Burger, R.E. (1968). *Where they go to die: The tragedy of America's aged.* New York: Delacorte Press.

Gates, G.A., & Rees, T.S. (1997). Hear ye? Hear ye! Successful auditory aging. *The Western Journal of Medicine, 167*(4), 247–252.

Geis, G. (1976). Defrauding the elderly. In J. Goldsmith & S. Goldsmith (Eds.), *Crime and the elderly* (pp. 7–19). Lexington, MA: D.C. Heath.

Geis, G., Jesilow, P., Pontell, H., & O'Brien, H. (1985). Fraud and abuse of government medical benefit programs by psychiatrists. *American Journal of Psychiatry, 142,* 231–234.

Gemignani, J. (1999). Feds take another stab at patient dumping. *Business and Health, 17*(1), 8.

Gibbons, D.C. (1994). *Talking about crime and criminals: Problems and issues in theory development in criminology.* Englewood Cliffs, NJ: Prentice-Hall.

Gilfillan, C.J. (1994). Senior citizen's police advocates. *The FBI Law Enforcement Bulletin, 63*(6), 14–15.

Gilliland, N., & Jimenez, S. (1996). Elder abuse in developed and developing societies: The U.S. and Costa Rica. *Journal of Developing Societies, 12,* 88–100.

Gilman, L. (1993). Elder abuse. *American Health, 12,* 84.

Ginsberg, Y. (1985). Fear of crime among elderly Jews in Boston and London. *International Journal of Aging and Human Development, 20*(4), 257–268.

Gitner, D.M. (1995). Nursing the problem: Responding to patient abuse in New York state. *Columbia Journal of Law and Social Problems, 28,* 559–607.

Glanz, J. (1994). One nursing home's 'get tough' approach to crime. *Nursing Homes, 43*(5), 20.

Godkin, M.A., Wolf, R.S., & Pillemer, K.A. (1989). A case-comparison analysis of elder abuse and neglect. *International Journal of Aging and Human Development, 28*(3), 207–225.

Goffman, E. (1961). *Asylums.* New York: Doubleday.

Goldstein, M.Z. (1995). Practical geriatrics: Maltreatment of elderly persons. *Psychiatric Services, 46*(12), 1219–1225.

Goode, E. (1999). *Drugs in American society* (5th Ed.). Boston: McGraw-Hill.

Goodridge, D.M., Johnston, P., & Thomson, M. (1996). Conflict and aggression as stressors in the work environment. *Journal of Elder Abuse & Neglect, 8*(1), 49–67.

Gordon, M.L., & Hecker, M.S. (1997). Care of the skin at midlife: Diagnosis of pigmented lesions. *Geriatrics, 52*(8), 56–60.

Gottfredson, M.R., & Gottfredson, D.M. (1988). *Decision making in criminal justice.* Cambridge, MA: Ballinger.

Gottfreson, M.R., & Hirschi, T. (1990). *A general theory of crime.* Stanford, CA: Stanford University Press.

Gray-Vickery, P. (2001). Protecting the older Adult. *Nursing Management, 32*(10), 37–41.

Green, G. (1990). *Occupational crime.* Chicago: Nelson-Hall.

Green, M.W., & Fogel, J.A. (1996). Telemarketing fraud: Seniors beware. *Rural Telecommunications, 15*(2), 9.

Greenberg, J.R., McKibben, M., & Raymond, J. (1990). Dependent adult children and elder abuse. *Journal of Elder Abuse & Neglect, 2*(1), 73–86.

Greene, J. (1998). Muddled miracles. *Hospitals and Health Networks, 72*(23/24), 68.

Greene, R.R., & Soniat, B. (1991). Clinical interventions with older adults in need of protection: A family systems perspective. *Journal of Family Psychotherapy, 2*(1), 1–15.

Greenspan, S. (1999). A seventy-three-year old woman with osteoporosis. *Journal of the American Medical Association, 281*(16), 153.

Grier, C. (1999, June 21). Adult-care homes: A pattern of neglect. *Virginian Pilot,* A1+.

Griffin, L.W., & Williams, O.J. (1992). Abuse among African-American elderly. *Journal of Family Violence, 7*(1), 19–35.

Griffin, L.W. (1994). Elder maltreatment among rural African Americans. *Journal of Elder Abuse & Neglect, 6,* 1–27.

Gross, B.M., & Straussman, J. (1974). The social indicators movement. *Social Policy,* September, 43–44.

Grubbs, J.M., & Urban, C.R. (1995). Federal fraud laws target health care professionals. *Indianapolis Business Journal, 16*(15), 38–41.

Gurnack, A.M., & Zevitz, R.G. (1993). Components of variation in elderly crime victims' perceptions of neighborhood safety. *Police Safety, 16,* 20–27.

Hafen, B., & Brog, M. (1983). *Alcohol* (2nd Ed.). New York: West.

Halika, M. (1995). Elder abuse and neglect in Poland. In J.I. Kosberg & J.L. Garcia (Eds.), *Elder abuse: International and cross-cultural perspectives* (pp. 157–170). Binghamton, NY: Haworth.

Hall, B.L., & Bocksnick, J.G. (1995). Therapeutic recreation for the institutionalized elderly: Choice or abuse. *Journal of Elder Abuse & Neglect, 7*(4), 49–60.

Hall, P.A. (1987). Minority elder maltreatment: Ethnicity, gender, age and poverty. *Journal of Gerontological Social Work, 9*(4), 53–72.

Hall, P.A. (1989). Elder maltreatment items, subgroups, and types: Policy and practice implications. *International Journal on Aging and Human Development, 28*(3), 191–205.

Hankin, M.B. (1996). Making the perpetrators pay: Collecting damages for elder abuse, neglect, and exploitation. *Aging Magazine, 367,* 66–70.

Hanna, C. (1998). The paradox of hope: The crime and punishment of domestic violence. *William and Mary Law Review, 39*(5), 1505–1584.

Harbison, J. (1999). Models of intervention for elder abuse and neglect: A Canadian perspective on ageism, participation, and empowerment. *Journal of Elder Abuse & Neglect, 10*(3/4), 1–18.

Harpold, J.A. (1994). The FBI and the elderly. *The FBI Law Enforcement Bulletin, 63*(2), 10–11.

Harris, D.K., & Benson, M.L. (1996). Theft in nursing homes: An overlooked form of elder abuse. In L.B. Cebik, G.C. Graber & F.H. Marsh (Eds.), *Advances in bioethics: Violence, neglect, and the elderly* (pp. 171–178). Greenwich, CT: JAI Press.

Harris, D.K., & Benson, M.L. (1998). Nursing home theft: The hidden problem. *Journal of Aging Studies, 12*(1), 57–67.

Harris, D.K. (1999). Elder abuse in nursing homes: The theft of patients' possessions. *Journal of Elder Abuse & Neglect, 10*(3/4), 141–151.

Harris, L. (1975). *The myth and reality of aging in America.* Washington, DC: The National Council on Aging.

Harris, M. (1995). Elder fraud. *Money, 24*(11), 144–147.

Harris, S.B. (1996). For better or for worse: Spouse abuse grown old. *Journal of Elder Abuse & Neglect, 8*(1), 1–33.

Harshbarger, S. (1989). A prosecutor's perspective on protecting older Americans: Keynote address. *Journal of Elder Abuse & Neglect, 1*(3), 5–15.

Harshbarger, S. (1993). From protection to prevention: A proactive approach. *Journal of Elder Abuse & Neglect, 5*(1), 41–55.

Harshbarger, S., & Morse, N. (1998). Confronting elder abuse and neglect. *Nursing Homes, 47*(4), 34–36.

Haugh, R. (1999). Fraud busters. *Hospitals and Health Networks, 73*(1), 16.

Hashimoto, M. (1987). The minimum wage law and youth crimes: Time series evidence. *Journal of Law and Economics, 30,* 443–464.

Heisler, C. (1991). The role of the criminal justice system in elder abuse cases. *Journal of Elder Abuse & Neglect, 3*(1), 5–30.

Heisler, C., & Quinn, M.J. (1995). A legal perspective. *Journal of Elder Abuse & Neglect, 7*(2/3), 31–156.

HHS Press Release: HHS Announces New National Center on Elder Abuse. (1998). HHS Press Office, October 8.

Hickey, T., & Douglass, R.L. (1981). Mistreatment of the elderly in a domestic setting. *American Journal of Public Health, 71*(5), 500–507.

Higgins, M. (1998). Getting sued by seniors. *ABA Journal, 84,* 28–29.

Hirschel, J.D., & Rubin, K.B. (1982). Special problems faced by the elderly victims of crime. *Journal of Sociology and Social Welfare, 9*(2), 357–374.

Hirschi, T. (1969). *Causes of delinquency.* Berkely, CA: University of California Press.

Hoberok, B. (1997, December 14). Steps help prevent elderly abuse. *Tulsa World,* A1.

Hodge, P.D. (1998). National law enforcement programs to prevent, detect, investigate, and prosecute elder abuse and neglect in health care facilities. *Journal of Elder Abuse & Neglect, 9*(4), 23–41.

Holt, M. (1993). Elder sexual abuse in Britain: Preliminary findings. *Journal of Elder Abuse & Neglect, 5*(2), 63–71.

Horkan, E.M. (1995). Elder abuse in the Republic of Ireland. In J.I. Kosberg & J.L. Garcia (Eds.), *Elder abuse: International and cross-cultural perspectives* (pp. 119–138). Binghamton, NY: Haworth.

Hospital Home Health. (2002). Spotting Patient Abuse. August 2, NP.

Hudson, M. (1991). Elder mistreatment: A taxonomy with definitions by delphi. *Journal of Elder Abuse & Neglect, 3*(2), 1–20.

Hudson, M. (1992). Loan scams that prey on the poor. *Business and Society Review, 1992,* 11–15.

Hudson, M. (1994). Elder abuse: Its meaning to middle-aged and older adults-part II: Pilot results. *Journal of Elder Abuse & Neglect, 6*(1), 55–81.

Hugman, R. (1995). The implications of the term elder abuse for problem definition and response in health and social welfare. *Journal of Social Policy, 24*(4), 493–507.

Hyatt, L. (1999). Post-acute consult: A new and dangerous game. *Nursing Homes, 48*(5), 14–15.

Hylton, M.B. (1992). The economics and politics of emergency health care for the poor. *Brigham Young Law Review, 4,* 971.

Improving the police response to domestic elder abuse. (1993). Edison, NJ: Police Executive Research Forum.

Inciardi, J. (1999). *Criminal justice* (6th Ed.). New York: Harcourt Brace.

Isaac, N.E., & Enos, V.P. (2001). *Documenting domestic violence.* Washington DC: U.S. Department of Justice.

Iutcovich, J.M., & Cox, H. (1990). Fear of crime among the elderly: Is it justified? *Journal of Applied Sociology, 7,* 63–76.

Jackson-Lee, S. (1996, May 7). Crimes against children and elderly persons increased punishment act. *Congressional Record, 142*(62), H4467–4493.

Jenkins, A., & Braithewaite, J. (1993). Profits, pressures, and corporate lawbreaking. *Crime, Law and Social Change, 20,* 221–232.

Jerin, R.A., & Moriarty, L.J. (1998). *Victims of crime.* Chicago: Nelson-Hall.

Jesilow, P., Pontell, H., & Geis, G. (1985). Medical criminals: Physicians and white-collar criminals. *Justice Quarterly, 2*(2), 149–165.

Jesilow, P., Pontell, H., & Geis, G. (1993). *Prescription for profit: How doctors defraud Medicaid.* CA: University of California Press.

Jesilow, P., Geis, G., & Harris, J. (1995). Doomed to repeat our errors: Fraud in the emerging health care systems. *Social Justice, 22*(2), 128–138.

Jogerst., G.J., Dawson, J.D., Hartz, A.J., Ely, J.W., & Schweitzer, L.A. (2000). Community characteristics associated with elder abuse. *Journal of the American Geriatrics Society, 48*(5), 513–518.

Jogerst, G., Daly, G.M., & Ingram, J. (2001). National elder abuse questionnaire: Summary of adult protective service investigator responses. *Journal of Elder Abuse & Neglect, 13*(4), 59–72.

Johns, S., & Hydle, I. (1995). Norway: Weakness in welfare. In J.I. Kosberg & J.L. Garcia (Eds.), *Elder abuse: International and cross-cultural perspectives* (pp. 139–156). Binghamton, NY: Haworth.

Johnson, A. (2002). Geriatric education for the field of elder abuse. *Journal of Elder Abuse & Neglect, 14*(2/3), 185–192.

Johnson, A. (2003). Advocate is committed to fighting elder abuse. *Los Angeles Times.* August 1, p. 2.

Johnson, I.M., Sigler, R.T., & Crowley, J. (1994). Domestic violence: A comparative study of perceptions and attitudes toward domestic abuse cases among social service and criminal justice professionals. *Journal of Criminal Justice, 22*(3), 237–248.

Johnson, I.M. (1995). Family members' perceptions and attitudes toward elder abuse. *Families in Society, 76*(4), 220–230.

Jolin, A., & Morse, C.A. (1997). Evaluating a domestic violence program in a community policing environment. *Crime and Delinquency, 43*(3), 279–298.

Jones, G.M. (1987). Elderly people and domestic crime. *British Journal of Criminology, 27*(2), 191–201.

Jones, J.H. (2003). Transient gets probation for attacking a woman, 76. *San Diego Tribune,* July 15, B3.

Jones, P. (1996). Adult protection work: The stories behind the statistics. *Aging Magazine, 367,* 19–24.

Jorgenson, J.E. (1993). An intervention program for dentists to detect elder abuse and neglect. *Public Health Reports, 108*(2), 171–172.

Kalish, R.A. (1979). The new ageism and the failure models: A polemic. *The Gerontologist, 19,* 398–402.

Kalter, J. (1995). I trusted him. *New Choices for Retirement Living, 35,* 66–69.

Katz, K.D. (1979). Elder abuse. *Journal of Family Law, 18*(4), 695–722.

Kaye, A.P., & Darling, G. (2000). Oregon's efforts to reduce elder financial exploitation. *Journal of Elder Abuse & Neglect, 12*(2), 99–104.

Keith, P. (2001). Correlates of reported complaints by volunteers in an ombudsman program in nursing facilities. *Journal of Elder Abuse & Neglect, 13*(3), 43–60.

Keller, B.H. (1996). Training course reduces abuse in nursing homes. *Aging Magazine, 367,* 110–112.

Kennedy, L.W., & Silverman, R.A. (1985). Significant others and fear of crime among the elderly. *International Journal of Aging and Human Development, 20*(4), 241–256.

Kennedy, L.W., & Silverman, R.A. (1990). The elderly victim of homicide: An application of routine activities approach. *The Sociological Quarterly, 31*(2), 307–319.

Kerr, J., Dening, T., & Lawton, C. (1994). Elder abuse and the community psychiatric team. *Psychiatric Bulletin, 18,* 730–732.

Kim, J.Y., & Sung, J-T. (2001). Marital violence among Korean elderly couples: A cultural residue. *Journal of Elder Abuse & Neglect, 13*(4), 73–89.

Kilburn, J.C. (1996). Network effects in caregiver to care-recipient violence. *Journal of Elder Abuse & Neglect, 8*(1), 69–80.

Kinderknecht, C.H. (1986). In home social work with abused or neglected elderly: An experiential guide to assessment and treatment. *Journal of Gerontological Social Work, 9*(3), 29–42.

King, M. (2003). Kirkland case signals tougher stand against elder neglect. *Seattle Times.* August 5, p.A1.

Kinney, J. (2000). *Loosening the grip: A handbook of alcohol information* (6th Ed.). Boston: McGraw-Hill.

Kmietowicz, Z. (2003). Bullying and harassment in Manchester unit. *British Medical Journal, 327*(7417), 697.

Korbin, J.E., Anetzberger, G.J., & Eckert, J.K. (1990). Elder abuse and child abuse: A consideration of similarities and differences in intergenerational family violence. *Journal of Elder Abuse & Neglect, 1*(4), 1–14.

Korbin, J.E., Anetzberger, G., & Austin, C. (1995). The intergenerational cycle of violence in child and elder abuse. *Journal of Elder Abuse & Neglect, 7*(1), 1–15.

Kosberg, J.I. (1988). Preventing elder abuse: Identification of high risk factors prior to placement decisions. *The Gerontologist, 28*(1), 43–50.

Kosberg, J.I., & Garcia, J.L. (Eds.) (1995). *Elder abuse: International and cross-cultural perspectives.* Binghamton, NY: Haworth.

Kosberg, J.I. (1998). The abuse of elderly men. *Journal of Elder Abuse & Neglect, 9*(3), 69–78.

Koss, L. (1992). Preventing hotel crime. *Hotel and Hotel Management, 207*(120), 15–16.

Koss, M.P. et al. (1991). Deleterious effects of criminal victimization on women's health and medical utilization. *Journal of the American Medical Association, 265*(22), 2952.

Kuriansky, E.J. (1992). Health care fraud and waste (part 1). Hearing. *U.S. House Committee on Energy and Commerce.* Washington DC: Government Printing Office.

Kurrle, S.E., Sadler, P.M., & Cameron, I.D. (1992). Patterns of elder abuse. *Medical Journal of Australia 157,* 673–676.

La Rocco, S.A. (1985). A case of patient abuse. *American Journal of Nursing, 1985,* 1233–1234.

Lachs, M.S. (1995). Preaching to the unconverted: Educating physicians about elder abuse. *Journal of Elder Abuse & Neglect, 7*(4), 1–12.

Lachs, M.S., & Pillemer, K. (1995). Abuse and neglect of elderly persons. *New England Journal of Medicine, 332*(7), 437.

Lachs, M.S., Williams, C., O'Brien, S., Hurst, L., & Horowitz, R. (1996). Older adults: An 11-year longitudinal study of adult protective service use. *Archives of Internal Medicine, 156*(4), 449–553.

Lachs, M.S., Williams, C.S., O'Brien, S., Pillemer, K.A., & Charison, M.E. (1998). The mortality of elder mistreatment. *Journal of the American Medical Association, 280*(5), 428A(1).

Lachs, M.S., Bove, C., Wearing, M., Williams, C., Bachman, R., & Cooney, L. (2001). The Clinical Epidemiology of Crime Victimization in older adults: A multidisciplinary study. *Journal of Elder Abuse & Neglect, 13*(3), 79–90.

Lang, S. (1993). Findings refute traditional views on elder abuse. *Human Ecology Forum, 21*(3), 30.

Lang, S. (1995). Physicians need to act on elder abuse. *Human Ecology Forum, 23,* 23–24.

Lash, C., & Rotstein, G. (2003). Atrium, NH, chief to be charged. *Pittsburgh Post Gazette.* October 22. Available online.

Le, Q.K. (1997). Mistreatment of Vietnamese elderly by their families in the United States. *Journal of Elder Abuse & Neglect, 9*(2), 51–62.

Lee, G.R. (1982). Residential location and fear of crime among the elderly. *Rural Sociology, 47*(4), 655–669.

Leenars, A.A., & Lester, D. (1990). Suicide in adolescents: A comparison of Canada and the United States. *Psychological Reports, 67*(3), 867–873.

Legal clinics: University of Pittsburgh Law School. (1999). www.law.pitt.edu/clinhome.htm.

Legal services to older persons. (1999). Southern Illinois University Law School. www.siu.edu/~lawsch/clinic/elderly/public.htm.

Lester, D., & Murrell, M.E. (1986). The influence of gun control laws on personal violence. *Journal of Community Psychology, 14*(3), 315–318.

Lindquist, J.H., & Duke, J.M. (1982). The elderly victim at risk: Explaining the fear of crime paradox. *Criminology, 20*(1), 115–126.

Littwin, S. (1995). A call for help! The untold story of elder abuse today. *New Choices of Retirement Living, 35*(7), 3.

Lofland, J. (1971). *Analyzing social settings.* Belmont, CA: Wadsworth.

Longman, P.J. (1997, August 11). Who is the victim? *U.S. News and World Report, 123*(6), 18–20.

Longmire, D.R. (1982). The new criminologist's access to research support: Open areas or closed doors? In H.E. Pepinsky (Ed.), *Rethinking criminology* (pp. 19–34).

Beverly Hills, CA: Sage.

Luchs, C.M. (1998). When insurer's make 'wrong mistakes.' *Best's Review–Property-Casualty Insurance Edition, 98*(9), 61.

Lynch, J.P. (1996). Clarifying the divergent estimates of rape from two national surveys. *Public Opinion Quarterly, 60*(3), 410–431.

Macdonald, K. (2003). Weighing your options: Financial abuse. Daily Telegraph. September 23, p. 31.

Mack, B.N., & Jones, K. (2003). Elder abuse: Identification and prevention. *ASHA Leader, 8*(14), 10–11.

Macolini, R.M. (1995). Elder abuse policy: Considerations in research and legislation. *Behavioral Sciences and the Law, 13,* 349–363.

Males, M. (1991). Teen suicide and changing cause of death certification. *Suicide and Life Threatening Behavior, 21*(3), 245–259.

Malks, B., Schmidt, C.M., & Austin, M.J. (2002). Elder abuse prevention: A case study of the Santa Clara County Financial Abuse Specialist Team (FAST) Program. *Journal of Gerontological Social Work, 39*(3), 23–40.

Marshall, C.E., Benton, D., & Brazier, M. (2000). Using clinical tools to identify clues of mistreatment. *Geriatrics, 55*(2), 42.

Martin, R., Mutchnick, R., & Austin, W.T. (1990). *Pioneers in criminological thought.* New York: Macmillan.

Mathews, D.P. (1988). The not-so-golden years: The legal response to elder abuse. *Pepperdine Law Review, 15*(4), 653–676.

Matthias, R.E., & Benjamin, A.E. (2003). Abuse and neglect of clients in agency-based and consumer-directed home care. *Health and Social Work, 28*(3), 174–184.

Mathis, E. (1994). Policing the guardians: Combating guardianship and power of attorney fraud. *FBI Law Enforcement Bulletin, 62*(2), 1–5.

Matlaw, J.R., & Spence, D.M. (1994). The hospital assessment team: A protocol for suspected cases of elder abuse and neglect. *Journal of Elder Abuse & Neglect, 6*(2), 23–37.

Maveal, G.M. (1995). Victim restitution will tie courts into knots. *National Law Journal, 18*(1), A21.

Maxfield, M.G., & Widom, C. (1996). The cycle of violence: Revisited six years later. *Archvies of Pediatrics and Adolescent Medicine, 150,* 390–395.

Mawby, R.I. (1986). Fear of crime and concern over the crime problem among the elderly. *Journal of Community Psychology, 14*(3), 306–318.

McCabe, K.A., & Gregory, S.S. (1998). Elderly victimization: An examination beyond the FBI's index crimes. *Research on Aging, 20*(3), 363–372.

McCord, J. (2003). Cures that harm: Unanticipated outcomes of crime prevention programs. *The Annals of the American Academy of Political and Social Science.* May, 16–30.

McCreadie, C., & Hancock, R. (1997). Elder abuse: Can the British OPCS surveys throw any light? *Journal of Elder Abuse & Neglect, 8*(4), 31–42.

McCreadie, C., Bennett, G., & Tinker, A. (1998). Investigating British general practitioners' knowledge and experience of elder abuse: Report of a research study in an inner London borough. *Journal of Elder Abuse & Neglect, 9*(3), 23–40.

McGreevy, J.C. (1993). Preventing elder abuse takes physician awareness. *Pennsylva-*

nia Medicine, 96(2), 20–22.

McIntosh, J.L. (1991). Middle age suicide: A literature review and epidemiological study. *Death Studies, 15*(1), 21–37.

Meagher, M.S. (1993). Legal and legislative dimensions. In B. Byers & J.E. Hendricks (Eds.), *Adult protective services: Research and practice* (pp. 87–108). Springfield, IL: Charles C Thomas.

Meddaugh, D.J. (1993). Covert elder abuse in the nursing home. *Journal of Elder Abuse & Neglect, 5*(3), 21–37.

Medicaid Fraud Report. (1987–1993). Washington, DC: National Association of Attorneys General.

Medical Economics. (1997). How can you protect yourself against defamation suits? 74(12), 82.

Melone, K. (2003). Judge says repay woman. *Hartford Courant.* October 8, p 3.

Menio, D.A. (1996). Advocating for the rights of vulnerable nursing home residents: Creative strategies. *Journal of Elder Abuse & Neglect, 8*(3), 59–72.

Merton, R. (1938). Social structure and anomie. *American Sociological Review, 3,* 672–682.

Messner, S.F., & Tardiff, K. (1985). The social ecology of urban homicide: An application of the 'routine activities' approach. *Criminology, 23*(2), 241–267.

Michalowski, R.J., & Pfuhl, E.H. (1991). Technology, property, and the law: The case of computer crime. *Crime, Law, and Social Change, 15*(3), 255–276.

Mickish, J.E. (1993). Abuse and neglect: The adult and elder. In B. Byers & J.E. Hendricks (Eds.), *Adult protective services: Research and practice* (pp. 33–60). Springfield, IL: Charles C Thomas.

Miller, T.R., Cohen, M.A., & Wiersma, B. (1996). *Victim costs and consequences: A new look.* National Institute of Justice Report. Washington, DC: U.S. Department of Justice.

Mills, L.G. (1998). Mandatory arrest and prosecution policies for domestic violence. *Criminal Justice and Behavior, 25*(3), 306–318.

Minaker, K., & Frishman, R. (1995). Elder abuse: Love gone wrong. *Harvard Health Letter, October,* 9–12.

Minor, M.W. (1980). The neutralization of criminal offenses. *Criminology, 18,* 103–120.

Mion, L.C., Minnick, A., Palmer, R., Kapp, M.B., & Lamb, K. (1996). Physical restraint use in the hospital. *The Milbank Quarterly, 74*(3), 411–433.

Mitchell, B. (2003). Caregiver worked for woman, 90. Seniors relatives advised to be Alert. *Toronto Star.* December 5, E05.

Mitchell, B. (2003). Police allege credit card fraud by housekeeper. *Toronto Star.* December 5, E05.

Mitchell, C.A., & Smyth, C. (1994). A case study of an abused older woman. *Health Care Women International, 15*(6), 521–535.

Mixson, P.M. (1996). How adult protective services evolved and obstacles to ethical casework. *Aging Magazine, 367,* 14–17.

Mixson, P.M. (2002). Taking a leap forward: Adult protective services and the Elder Justice Act. *Journal of Elder Abuse & Neglect, 14*(2/3), 193–198.

Monnette, D.R., Sullivan, T.J., & Dejong, C.R. (1989). *Applied social research* (2nd Ed.).

Orlando, FL: Holt.

Montoya, V. (1997). Understanding and combating elder abuse in Hispanic communities. *Journal of Elder Abuse & Neglect, 9*(2), 5–18.

Moore, E., & Mills, M. (1990). The neglected victims and unexamined costs of white-collar crime. *Crime and Delinquency, 36*(3), 408–418.

Morris, M.R. (1998). Elder abuse: What the law requires. *RN, 61*(8), 52–53.

Moskowitz, S. (1998). Private enforcement of criminal mandatory reporting laws. *Journal of Elder Abuse & Neglect, 9*(3), 1–22.

Motor Age. (2003). Smog shop charged with elder abuse. 122(4): 78–79.

Moyer, I. (1992a). *The changing roles of women in the criminal justice system.* Prospect Heights, IL: Waveland.

Moyer, I. (1992b). Changing conceptualization of child sexual abuse: Impact on the prosecution of cases. *Justice Professional, 7*(1), 69–92.

Mungin, L. (2002). Rape, assault case may be related. *Atlanta Journal Constitution.* December 27, P1 JJ.

Munro, J. (1977). *Administrative behavior and police organization.* Cincinnati, OH: Anderson.

Muram, D., Miller, K., & Cutler, A. (1992). Sexual assault of the elderly victim. *Journal of Interpersonal Violence, 7*(1), 70–76.

Myers, J.E., & Shelton, B. (1987). Abuse and older persons. *Journal of Counseling and Development, 65,* 376–380.

Nachmiash, D., & Reis, M. (2000). Most successful intervention strategies for abused older adults. *Journal of Elder Abuse & Neglect, 12*(3/4), 53–70.

Nagpaul, K. (1997). Elder abuse among Asian Indians: Traditional versus modern perspectives. *Journal of Elder Abuse & Neglect, 9*(2), 77–92.

Nandlal, J.M., & Wood, L.A. (1997). Older people's understandings of verbal abuse. *Journal of Elder Abuse & Neglect, 9*(1), 17–32.

National Association of Attorneys General. (1997). Telephone scams: Recent crimes and crackdowns. www.naag.org/tele1197.htm.

National Association of Attorneys General. (1998). Protect yourself and your home from home repair fraud. www.naag.org/hr1298.htm.

National Center on Elder Abuse. (1996). *Understanding the nature and extent of elder abuse in domestic settings.* Washington, DC: National Center on Elder Abuse.

National Center on Elder Abuse. (1997). *Domestic elder abuse information series #1: Types and number of domestic elder abuse cases.* Washington, DC: National Center on Elder Abuse.

National Center for Victims of Crime. (1995). *Elder abuse legislation.* Washington, DC: National Center for Victims of Crime.

National Citizen's Coalition for Nursing Home Reform. (1999). *Fact sheets.* www.ncccnhr.org/factsheet.htm.

National Consumer's League. (1997). They can't hang up: Help for elderly people targeted by fraud. National Consumer's League: Washington, DC.

Neale, V., Hwalek, M.A., Goodrich, C.S., & Quinn, K. (1997). Reason for case closure among substantiated reports of elder abuse. *Journal of Applied Gerontology, 16*(4), 442–459.

Nelesen, D. (2003). Violence in the home–unwanted guest. *San Diego Union Tribune.* August 30, ES.

Nerenberg, L. (2000). Forgotten victims of financial crime and abuse: Facing the challenge. *Journal of Elder Abuse & Neglect, 12*(2), 49–62.

Newman, D., & Newman, E. (1982). Senior citizen crime. *The Justice Reporter, 2*(5), 1–7.

Nieves, E. (1995, December 12). Victim of scam heaps guilt on her loneliness. *New York Times,* p. B5+.

Norton, L. (1982). Crime prevention education for elderly citizens, fear of crime, and security conscious behavior. *Criminal Justice Review, 7*(2), 9–15.

Nursing home compare. (1999). Health Care Financing Administration. www.medicare .gov/nursing.

Oakar, M.R. (1991, January 3). Honor thy father and mother. *Congressional Record, Daily Edition,* p. E39.

O'Brien, M.E. (1994). Elder abuse: How to spot it–how to help. *North Carolina Medical Journal, 55*(9), 409–411.

O'Neill, P.O., & Flanagan, E.A. (1998). Elderly customers are a significant market–but may need special protection. *Journal of Retail Banking Services, 20*(1), 25–33.

O'Riordan, A. (1990). Review of a time for dignity. *Journal of Elder Abuse & Neglect, 2*(1/2), 151–154.

O'Sullivan, M. (2003). Elderly preyed on by sales staff. *Dominion Post.* November 19, 3.

Ohlin, L., & Tonry, M. (1989). Family violence in perspective. *Crime and Justice: A Review of Research, 11,* 1–18.

Ogg, J., & Munn-Giddings, C. (1993). Researching elder abuse. *Aging and Society 13*(3), 389–414.

Otis, L.H. (1996). Three new states enact elder abuse victim protections. *National Underwriter, 100*(18), 4.

Otis, L.H. (1997). Abuse victim protection model eyed. *National Underwriter, 101*(1), 4, 26.

Pablo, S., & Braun, K.L. (1997). Perceptions of elder abuse and neglect and help-seeking patterns among Filipino and Korean elderly women in Honolulu. *Journal of Elder Abuse & Neglect, 9*(2), 63–76.

Pain, R.H. (1995). Elderly women and fear of violent crime. *British Journal of Criminology, 35*(4), 584–598.

Paris, B.W., Meier, D.E., Goldstein, T., Weiss, M., & Fein, E. (1995). Elder abuse and neglect: How to recognize the warning signs and intervene. *Geriatrics, 50*(4), 47–51.

Parmalee, P.A., Katz, I.R., & Lawton, M.P. (1991). The relation of pain to depression among institutionalized aged. *Journals of Gerontology, 46*(1), 15–21.

Patient Care. (1993). Categories of abuse and neglect. 27(11), 16.

Patterson, A.H. (1985). Fear of crime and other barriers to use of public transportation by the elderly. *Journal of Architectural and Planning Research, 2*(4), 277–288.

Paulson, M.C., & Blum, A. (1989). You have definitely won a prize! Oh yeah? *Changing*

Times, 43(8), 34–38.

Paveza, G.J., Cohen, D., Eisdorfer, C., Freels, S., Semla, T., Ashford, J.W., Gorelick, P., Hirschman, R., Luchins, D., & Levy, P. (1992). Severe family violence and Alzheimer's disease: Prevalence and risk factors. *The Gerontologist, 32*(4), 493–497.

Paveza, G.J. (2002). The Elder Justice Bill's impact on research. *Journal of Elder Abuse & Neglect, 14*(2/3), 199–204.

Pavlov, H., & Murov, K.L. (1994). Legislative update: Elder abuse–Part II. *Contemporary Orthopaedics, 29*(4), 249–250.

Payne, B.K., & Cikovic, R. (1995). An empirical examination of the characteristics, consequences, and causes of elder abuse in nursing homes. *Journal of Elder Abuse & Neglect, 7*(4), 61–74.

Payne, B.K., & King, T. (1995). The principles of science and the introductory criminal justice student. *Journal of the American Criminal Justice Association,* 1995: 15–20.

Payne, B.K., & Berg, B.L. (1997). Looking for fraud in all the wrong places. *The Police Journal,* July, 220–230.

Payne, B.K., & Dabney, D. (1997). Prescription fraud: Characteristics, consequences, and influences. *Journal of Drug Issues, 27*(4), 807–820.

Payne, B.K. (1998a). Conceptualizing the impact of health care crimes on the poor. *Free Inquiry in Creative Sociology, 26*(2), 159–168.

Payne, B.K. (1998b). White-collar crimes against elderly persons. A paper presented at the annual meeting of the American Society of Criminology. November, Washington, DC.

Payne, B.K., & Berg, B. (2003). Perceptions about the criminalization of elder abuse. *Crime and Delinquency, 49*(3), 39–60.

Payne, B.K., Berg, B., & Byers, K. (1999). A qualitative examination of the similarities and differences of elder abuse definitions among four groups: Nursing home directors, nursing home employees, police chiefs and students. *Journal of Elder Abuse & Neglect, 10*(3/4), 63–86.

Payne, B.K., Berg, B., & James, L. (2001). Attitudes about sanctioning elder abuse. *International Journal of Offender Therapy and Comparative Criminology, 45*(3), 363–382.

Payne, B.K., & Fletcher, L. (2004). Elder abuse prevention strategies in nursing homes. *Journal of Criminal Justice,* in press.

Payne, B.K., & Gainey, R. (2004a) Social altruism and patient abuse. *Journal of Crime and Justice.* (in press).

Payne, B.K., & Gainey, R. (2004b). Routine activities and patient abuse. Unpublished manuscript.

Payne, B.K., & Gray, C. (2001). Fraud by home health care workers. *Criminal Justice Review, 26,* 207–232.

Payne, B.K., & Gray, C. (2002). Theoretical orientation and response to abuse among ombudsmen. *Journal of Social Work in Long-Term Care, 2*(1): 33–54.

Payne, B.K. (2001). Understanding differences in opinion and 'facts' between ombudsmen, police chiefs and nursing home directors. *Journal of Elder Abuse & Neglect, 13*(3), 61–80.

Payne, B.K. (2003). *Crime in the home health care field.* Springfield, IL: Charles C Thomas.

Pediatrics. (1996). Adolescent assault victim needs: A review of the issues and a model protocol. 98(5), 991–1001.

Pedrick-Cornell, C., & Gelles, R. (1982). Elder abuse: The status of current knowledge. *Family Relations, 31*(3), 457–465.

Perhale, B., & Parker, J. (2000). *Elder abuse practitioner's guide.* Birmingham, England: Venture Press.

Perkins, C. (1997). *Age patterns of victims of serious violent crime.* Bureau of Justice Statistics, U.S. Department of Justice.

Perttu, S. (1996). Abuse of the elderly: Services provided for victims in a Finnish nursing home–1992–1993. *Journal of Elder Abuse & Neglect, 8*(2), 23–32.

Pettee, E. (1997). Elder abuse: Implications for staff development. *Journal of Nursing Staff Development, 13*(1), 7–12.

Phillips, L.R. (1983). Abuse and neglect of the frail elderly: An exploration of theoretical relationships. *Journal of Advanced Nursing, 8,* 379–392.

Phillips, L.R. (1986). Theoretical explanations of elder abuse. In K.A. Pillemer & R.S. Wolf (Eds.), *Elder abuse: Conflict in the family* (pp. 197–217). Dover, MA: Auburn House.

Phillips, L.R., & Rempusheski, V.F. (1986). Making decisions about elder abuse. *Journal of Contemporary Social Work, 67*(3), 131–140.

Phillips, L.R., de Ardon, E., & Briones, G. (2000). Abuse of female caregivers by care recipients: Another form of elder abuse. *Journal of Elder Abuse & Neglect, 12*(3/4), 123–140.

Pierce, R., & Trotta, R. (1986). Abused parents: A hidden family problem. *Journal of Family Violence, 1*(1), 99–110.

Pillemer, K. (1985). The dangers of dependency: New findings on domestic violence against the elderly. *Social Problems, 33*(2), 146–158.

Pillemer, K. (1986). Risk factors in elder abuse: Results from a case-control study. In K.A. Pillemer & R.S. Wolf (Eds.), *Elder abuse: Conflict in the family* (pp. 239–263). Dover, MA: Auburn House.

Pillemer, K.A., & Wolf, R.S. (Eds.). (1986). *Elder abuse: Conflict in the family.* Dover, MA: Auburn House.

Pillemer, K., & Finkelhor, D. (1988). Prevalence of elder abuse: A random sample survey. *Gerontologist, 28*(1), 51–57.

Pillemer, K., & Finkelhor, D. (1989). Causes of elder abuse: Caregiver stress versus problem relatives. *American Journal of Orthopsychiatry, 59*(2), 179–187.

Pillemer, K., & Moore, D.W. (1989). Abuse of patients in nursing homes: Findings from a survey of staff. *The Gerontologist, 29*(3), 314–320.

Pillemer, K., & Moore, D.W. (1990). Highlights from a study of abuse of patients in nursing homes. *Journal of Elder Abuse & Neglect, 2,* 5–29.

Pillemer, K., & Bachman-Prehn, R. (1991). Helping and hurting: Predictors of maltreatment of patients in nursing homes. *Research on Aging, 13*(1), 74–95.

Pillemer, K.A., & Suitor, J.J. (1992). Violence and violent feelings: What causes them among family caregivers? *The Gerontologist, 28,* 51–57.

Plotkin, M.R. (1996). Improving the police response to domestic elder abuse victims. *Aging Magazine, 367,* 28–33.

Poertner, J. (1986). Estimating the incidence of abused older persons. *Journal of Gerontological Social Work, 9*(3), 3–15.

Pollack, D. (1995). Elder abuse and neglect cases reviewed by appellate courts. *Journal of Family Violence, 10*(4), 413–424.

Pontell, H., Jesilow, P., & Geis, G. (1982). Policing physicians: Practitioner fraud and abuse in a government medical program. *Social Problems, 30*(1), 117–126.

Powell, S., & Berg, R.C. (1987). When the elderly are abused: Characteristics and intervention. *Educational Gerontology, 13,* 71–83.

Preventing abusive behaviors: A curriculum designed to train aides in nursing homes, adult care residents, and home care programs. (1999). A training program presented at the annual meeting of the Virginia Coalition for the Prevention of Elder Abuse.

Price, G., & Fox, C. (1997). The Massachusetts bank reporting project. *Journal of Elder Abuse & Neglect, 8*(4), 59–72.

Pringle, L.P. (1997). *Drinking: A risky business.* New York: Morrow Junior Books.

Pritchard, J. (1996a). Darkness visible. *Nursing Times, 92*(42), 27–31.

Pritchard, J. (1996b). *Working with elder abuse: A training manual for home care, residential and day care staff.* London: Jessica Kingsley.

Pullen, R. (1998, October 1). The race is on. *Best's review–Life-health insurance edition,* 52.

Quinn, M.J. (1985). Elder abuse and neglect raise new dilemmas. *Generations: The Journal of the Western Gerontological Society, 10*(2), 22–25.

Quinn, M.J., & Tomita, S. (1997). *Elder abuse and neglect: Causes diagnosis and intervention strategies* (2nd Ed.). New York: Springer.

Rachlin, J. (1987, July 20). Poison lures at the end of the line. *U.S. News and World Report, 103,* 47–48.

Ramsey-Klawsnik, H. (1991). Elder sexual abuse: Preliminary findings. *Journal of Elder Abuse & Neglect, 3*(3), 73–90.

Ramsey-Klawsnik, H. (1995). Investigating suspected elder maltreatment. *Journal of Elder Abuse & Neglect, 7*(1), 41–67.

Ramsey-Klawsnik, H. (1999). Elder sexual abuse: Workshop handouts. Presented at the annual meeting of the Virginia Coalition for the Prevention of Elder Abuse, June 10.

Rand, M. (1998). *Criminal victimization 1997, Changes 1996–1997 with trends 1993–1997.* Bureau of Justice Statistics: Washington, DC.

Rathbone-McCaun, E., & Voyles, R. (1982). Case detection of abused elderly parents. *American Journal of Psychiatry, 139*(2), 189–192.

Redd, C. (2003). Some elders suffering in silence. *The Boston Globe.* November 9, p. 1.

Reiboldt, W., & Vogel, R.E. (2001). A critical analysis of telemarketing fraud in a gated senior community. *Journal of Elder Abuse & Neglect, 13*(4), 21–38.

Reidy, A., Minassian, D.C., Vafidis, G., Joseph, J., Farrow, S., Wu, J., Desai, P., & Connolly, A. (1998). Prevalence of serious eye disease and visual impairment in a north London population. *British Medical Journal, 316*(7145), 1643–1646.

Reiman, J. (1995). *The rich get richer and the poor get prison* (4th Ed.). Boston: Allyn and Bacon.

Report on the AARP forum: Abused elders or older battered women? (1993). American Association of Retired People: Washington, DC.

Reulbach, D., & Tewsbury, J. (1994). Collaboration between adult protective services and law enforcement: The Massachusetts model. *Journal of Elder Abuse & Neglect, 6*(2), 9–21.

Richardson, B., Kitchen, G., & Livingston, G. (2002). The effect of education on knowledge and management of elder abuse. *Age and Aging, 31*(5), 335–341.

Riedel, M. (1990). Nationwide homicide data sets: An evaluation of the uniform crime reports and national center for health statistics Data. In D.L. Mackenzie, P.J. Baunach, & R.R. Roberg (Eds.), *Measuring crime: Large scale, long range efforts* (pp. 175–208). Albany, NY: State University of New York Press.

Ridge, L. (2002). Strategies when you suspect elder abuse. *ED Nursing,* March.

Risk Management. (1998). Resting easy. 45(2), 8.

Risk Management. (2003). Employee crime prevention. 50(10), 8.

Ritter, M. (1992, November 24). Doctors should ask aged about abuse. *Ann Arbor News,* A8.

Roby, J., & Sullivan. (2000). Adult Protective Services Laws. *Journal of Elder Abuse & Neglect, 12*(3/4), 17–34.

Roethlisberger, F.J., & Dickenson, W.J. (1939). *Management and the worker.* Cambridge, MA: Harvard University Press.

Rogers, J.L. (1991). Missed opportunities: Politics, research, and public policy. *International Journal of Offender Therapy and Comparative Criminology, 35,* 279–282.

Roomi, J., Johnson, M.M., Waters, K., Yohannes, A., Helm, A., & Connolly, M.J. (1996). Respiratory rehabilitation, exercise capacity, and quality of life in chronic airways disease in old age. *Age and Ageing, 25*(1), 12–16.

Rosado, L. (1991, July 29). Who's caring for grandma: The growing problem of elder abuse. *Newsweek,* p. 47.

Rosenblatt, D. (1996). Elder abuse: What can physicians do? *Archives of Family Medicine, 5*(2), 88–90.

Rosoff, S.M., Pontell, H.N., & Tillman, R. (2003). *Profit without honor: White-collar crime and the looting of America.* Upper Saddle River, NJ: Prentice-Hall.

Rotstein, G., & Lash, L. (2003). Cases of elder neglect, abuse. *Pittsburgh Post Gazette.* October 26, B1.

Rounds, D. (1996). Victimization of individuals with legal blindness: Nature and forms of victimization. *Behavioral Sciences and the Law, 14,* 29–40.

Royce, J.E. (1981). *Alcohol problems and alcoholism: A comprehensive survey.* New York: Free Press.

Rozek, D. (2003). Prosecutors say heirs starved woman. *Chicago Sun Tribune.* October 22, 54.

Rykert, W.L. (1994). Law enforcement gerontology. *FBI Law Enforcement Bulletin, 62*(2), 5–8.

Sabato, A.E. (1993). Preventing elder abuse: An issue that can affect all families. *BusinessWest, 10*(3), 22.

Sacks, D. (1996). Prevention of financial abuse, focus of new institute at Brookdale Center on Aging. *Aging Magazine, 367,* 86–89.

Sadler, P. (1994). What helps? Elder abuse interventions and research. *Australian Journal of Social Work, 47*(4), 27–36.

Salem, S.R., & Favre, B.C. (1993). Providing protective services to special populations. In B. Byers & J.E. Hendricks (Eds.), *Adult protective services: Research and practice* (pp. 167–190). Springfield, IL: Charles C Thomas.

Sanchez, Y.M. (1996). Distinguishing cultural expectations in assessment of financial exploitation. *Journal of Elder Abuse & Neglect, 8*(2), 49–60.

Saveman, B., Hallberg, I., & Norberg, A. (1996). Narratives by district nurses about elder abuse within families. *Clinical Nursing Research, 5*(2), 220–236.

Saveman, B., & Hallberg, I.R. (1997). Intervention in hypothetical elder abuse situations suggested by Swedish formal carers. *Journal of Elder Abuse & Neglect, 8*(4), 1–20.

Sayles-Cross, S. (1988). Profile of familial elder abuse: A selected review of literature. *Journal of Community Health Nursing, 5*(4), 209–219.

Scalzi, C.C., Zinn, J.S., Guilfoyle, M.J., & Perdue, S.T. (1994). Growth and decline in the supply of providers of medicare-covered home health services in the 80's: National and regional experience. *Home Health Care Services Quarterly, 15*(1), 3–17.

Scandlen, M. (2003). Surrogate accused of exploitation. *Tampa Tribune.* October, 49, 12.

Schiff, L. (2001). Jury finds that under law pain equals elder abuse. *RN, 64*(10), 14.

Schneider, H. (1997, August 24). Telemarketing scams reach across borders. *Washington Post,* p. A21.

Schimer, M.R., & Anetzberger, G.J. (1999). Examining the gray zones in guardianship and involuntary protective services laws. *Journal of Elder Abuse & Neglect, 10*(3/4), 19–38.

Schneiderman, H., & Ramakrishnan, N. (1995). Elderly man with bent fingers. *Consultant, 35*(5), 673–674.

Schulhofer, S.J. (1995). The feminist challenge in criminal law. *University of Pennsylvania Law Review, 143*(6), 2151–2207.

Schupbacj, A. (1998). Report on sweepstakes fraud causes backlash. *Direct Marketing, 61*(5), 6–7.

Schwartz, B. (1974). Waiting, exchange, and power. *American Journal of Sociology, 79,* 841–871.

Schwartz, R.M. (1998). Background checks: Consistency lacking. *Nursing Homes, 47*(11), 11.

Seaver, C. (1996). Muted lives: Older battered women. *Journal of Elder Abuse & Neglect, 8*(2), 3–22.

Seeman, B.T. (1993, July 8). Swindlers target lonely, unwary seniors. *Miami Herald,* 1BR+.

Sengstock, M.C., & Barrett, S. (1986). Elderly victims of family abuse, neglect, and maltreatment: Can legal assistance help? *Journal of Gerontological Social Work, 9*(3), 43–61.

Sengstock, M.C., Hwalek, M., & Petrone, S. (1989). Services for aged abuse victims: Service types and related factors. *Journal of Elder Abuse & Neglect, 1*(4), 37–56.

Sengstock, M.C. (1991). Sex and gender implications in cases of elder abuse. *Journal of Women and Aging, 3*(2), 25.

Serafini, M.W. (1997). Medicare crooks. *National Journal, 29*(29), 1458–1460.

Shah, G., Veedon, R., & Vasi, S. (1995). Elder abuse in India. In J.I. Kosberg & J.L. Garcia (Eds.), *Elder abuse: International and cross-cultural perspectives* (pp. 101–118). Binghamton, NY: Haworth.

Shapiro, J.P. (1992, January 13). The elderly are not children. *U.S. News and World Report, 112,* 26+.

Sharon, N. (1991). Elder abuse and neglect substantiations: What they tell us about the problem. *Journal of Elder Abuse & Neglect, 3*(3), 19–43.

Sharon, N., & Zoabi, S. (1997). Elder abuse in a land of transition: The case of Israel's Arabs. *Journal of Elder Abuse & Neglect, 8*(4), 43–58.

Shaw, M. (1998). Nursing home resident abuse by staff. *Journal of Elder Abuse & Neglect, 9*(4), 1–22.

Sherman, C. (2003). Seminar offers advice on avoiding abuse. San Diego Tribune. November 6, page NC-3.

Sherman, L.W. (1993). Defiance, deterrence, and irrelevance: A theory of the criminal sanction. *Journal of Research in Crime and Delinquency, 30,* 445–473.

Shiferaw, B., Mittelmark, M.B., Wofford, J.L., & Anderson, R.T. (1994). The investigation and outcome of reported cases of elder abuse: The Forsyth County aging study. *Gerontologist, 34*(1), 123–125.

Siegel, L.J. (1998). *Criminology* (6th Ed.). Belmont, CA: West/Wadsworth.

Sijuwade, P.O. (1995). Cross-cultural perspectives on elder abuse as a family dilemma. *Social Behavior and Personality, 23*(3), 247–252.

Simmons, K.L. (1993). *67 ways to protect seniors from crime.* New York: Holt.

Simon, D.R., & Hagan, F.E. (1999). *White-collar deviance.* Boston: Allyn and Bacon.

Simon, M.L. (1992). *An exploratory study of adult protective services programs' repeat elder abuse clients.* Washington, DC: AARP.

Sklar, J. (2000). Elder and dependent adult fraud. *Journal of Elder Abuse & Neglect, 12*(2), 19–321.

Skogan, W.G., & Maxfield, M.G. (1981). *Coping with crime: Individual and neighborhood reactions.* Beverly Hills, CA: Sage.

Slotter, K. (1998). Hidden faces: Combating telemarketing fraud. *FBI Law Enforcement Bulletin, 67*(3), 9–17.

Smith, D.W.E. (1998). Nosology and vital statistics of dementing conditions of elderly people. *Journal of Geriatric Psychiatry and Neurology, 11*(1), 25–28.

Sobel, C. (2003). To video or not to video. *Progressive Grocer, 82*(7), 113.

Speaks, G. (1995). Documenting inadequate care in the nursing home: The story of an undercover agent. *Journal of Elder Abuse & Neglect, 8*(3), 37–45.

Spencer, H. (1873). *The study of sociology.* London: NLB.

Spencer, K., & Anderson, J. (2003). Decade old case gets hot. *Omaha World Herald.* April 18, 1B.

Stannard, C. (1973). Old folks and dirty work: The social conditions for patient abuse in a nursing home. *Social Problems, 20*(3), 329–342.

Stanus, J.C. (1999, March 16). Norfolk to launch its Triad program. *The Virginian Pilot,* B3.

Steffensmeier, D., & Harer, M. (1991). Did crime rise or fall during the Reagan Administration? The effects of an 'aging' U.S. Population on the nation's crime rate. *Journal of Research in Crime and Delinquency, 28,* 330–339.

Steffensmeier, D., & Allan, E. (1996). Gender and crime: Toward a general theory of female offending. *Annual Review of Sociology, 22,* 459–487.

Stein, K.F. (1991). A national agenda for elder abuse and neglect research: Issues and recommendations. *Journal of Elder Abuse & Neglect, 3*(3), 9–108.

Steinmetz, S.K. (1988). *Duty bound: Elder abuse and family care.* Newbury Park, CA: Sage.

Stevens, E., & Payne, B.K. (1999). Applying deterrence theory in the context of corporate wrongdoing. *Journal of Criminal Justice, 27*(3), 195–208.

Stiegel, L.A. (1995). *Recommended guidelines for state courts handling cases involving elder abuse.* Washington DC: American Bar Association.

Stiegel, L. (1996). What can courts do about elder abuse? *The Judges Journal, 35*(4), 38–47.

Stimmel, B. (1991). *The facts about drug use: Coping with drugs and alcohol in your family, at work, and in your community.* Yonkers, NY: Consumer Reports Books.

Stock, R.W. (1995, August 10). Senior class: Humanizing the law's forbidden face. *New York Times,* C8.

St. Petersburg Times. (2003). Caregiver admits to abuse of elderly patients. August 3, 6B.

St. Petersburg Times. (2003). Caregiver admits to abusing elderly patients. October 16, p. 3.

Straus, M.A. (1987). State and regional differences in U.S. homicide rates in relation to sociocultural characteristics of the states. *Behavioral Sciences and the Law, 5*(1), 61–75.

Sullivan, S.F. (1997). Florida insurance agency gets tough on fraud. *Life Association News, 92*(10), 29–30.

Sundram, C.J. (1986). Strategies to prevent patient abuse in public institutions. *New England Journal of Human Services, 6*(2), 20–25.

Sutherland, E. (1949). *White-collar crime.* Holt, Rinehart, and Wilson.

Sutherland, E., & Cressey, D. (1970). *Principles of criminology.* Philadelphia: Lippincott.

Sykes, G., & Matza, D. (1957). Techniques of neutralization: A theory of delinquency. *American Sociological Review, 22,* 664–670.

Taira, F., & Taira, D. (1991). Patient dumping of poor families. *Families in Society, 72*(7), 409–415.

Tanne, J.H. (1992). Granny dumping in the United States. *British Medical Journal, 304*(6823), 333–334.

Tatara, T. (1993). Understanding the nature and scope of domestic elder abuse with the use of state aggregate data: Summaries of the key findings of a national survey of state APS and aging agencies. *Journal of Elder Abuse & Neglect, 5*(4), 35–57.

Taxel, P. (1998). Osteoporosis: Detection, prevention, and treatment in primary care.

Geriatrics, 53(8), 22–29.

Taylor, J. (1992). Medicaid fraud control. *FBI Law Enforcement Bulletin, 61*:17–20.

Teaster, P.B., & Anetzberger, G.J. (1992). Preface. *Journal of Elder Abuse & Neglect, 14*(2/3), xv–xviii.

Teitelman, J.L. (1999). Consensual versus abusive sexual behavior in adults with disabilities. Presented at the annual meeting of the Virginia Coalition for the Prevention of Elder Abuse, June 10.

The Economist. (1992). At the races: Death in life. 323(7753), A29.

The Virginian-Pilot. (1999, February 11). Americans face cross-border scams. p. A7.

Thomas, R. (2002). Law enforcement and the Elder Justice Act. *Journal of Elder Abuse & Neglect, 14*(2/3), 208–208.

Thomas, V. (2003). New program will seek to deter abuse of elderly. *Buffalo News.* October 22, B1.

Thompson, M. (1998). Shining a light on abuse. *Time, 152*(5), 42–43.

Tighe, T. (1994, January 30). Swindlers zero in on elderly. *St. Louis Post-Dispatch*, 1D+.

Tilden, V.P., Schmidt, T.A., Limandri, B.J., Chiodo, G.T., Garland, M.J., & Loveless, P.A. (1994). Factors that influence clinicians' assessment and management of family violence. *American Journal of Public Health, 84*(4), 628–633.

Tillman, R., & Pontell, H. (1992). Is justice 'collar blind'?: Punishing Medicaid provider fraud. *Criminology, 30*(4), 547–574.

Times Picaynne. (2003). Disrespecting elders. October 27.

Tisch, C. (2003). 82 year old beaten up, son help. *New York Times.* August 7, p. 1.

Tokarek, J. (1996). Keeping frail seniors independent through money management. *Aging, 367,* 84–86.

Tomita, S.K. (1990). The denial of elder mistreatment by victims and abusers. *Violence and Victims, 5*(3), 171–184.

Tomita, S.K. (1998). The consequences of belonging: Conflict management techniques among Japanese Americans. *Journal of Elder Abuse & Neglect, 9*(3), 41–68.

Tomita, S.K. (2000). Elder mistreatment: Practice modifications to accommodate cultural differences. *Journal of Elder Abuse & Neglect, 10*(3/4): 305–326.

Toseland, R.W. (1995). *Group work with the elderly and family violence.* New York: Springer.

Townsend, C. (1971). *Old age: The last segregation.* New York: Grossman.

Treas, J. (1995). Older Americans in the 1990s and beyond. *Population Bulletin, 56*(2), 2–46.

Tyasta, P., Robato, K., Duke, J., & Kim, K. (2000). Sexual abuse of older adults. *Journal of Elder Abuse & Neglect, 12*(3/4), 1–16.

Tyiska, C.G. (1999). *Working with victims of crime disabilities.* Office of Victims of Crime Report. Washington, DC: U.S. Department of Justice.

U.S. House of Representatives. (1992). Deceptive mailings and solicitations to senior citizens and other customers. Hearing before the Subcommittee on Social Security and the Subcommittee on Oversight of the Committee on Ways and Means. Washington, DC: U.S. Government Printing Office.

U.S. Senate. (1983). Consumer frauds and the elderly: A Growing Problem. Hearing before the Special Committee on Aging. Ninety First Congress. Washington, DC:

U.S. Government Printing Office.

U.S. Senate. (1991). Crimes against the elderly: Let's fight back. Hearing before the Special Committee on Aging. One Hundred First Congress. Washington, DC: U.S. Government Printing Office.

U.S. Senate. (1993). Consumer fraud and the elderly: Easy Prey? Hearing before the Special Committee on Aging. One Hundred Second Congress. Washington, DC: U.S. Government Printing Office.

Utech, M.R., & Garrett, R.R. (1992). Elder and child abuse: Conceptual and perceptual parallels. *Journal of Interpersonal Violence, 7*(3), 418–429.

Valentine, D., & Cash, T. (1986). A definitional discussion of elder maltreatment. *Journal Gerontological Social Work, 9*(3), 17–28.

Van Gigch, J. (1978). *Applied general systems theory* (2nd Ed.). New York: Addison Wesley.

Van Wyk, J., Benson, M., & Harris, D.K. (1998). Occupational crime by nursing home employees: Theft from patients. A paper presented at the annual meeting of the American Society of Criminology, Washington, DC.

Vaughn, D. (1983). *Controlling unlawful corporate behavior.* University of Chicago: University of Chicago Press.

Vezina, M., & Ducharme, G. (1992). The sad abuse of seniors. *Canadian Banker, 99,* 58–62.

Virginia Coalition for the Prevention of Elder Abuse. (1998). *Abuse hurts at any age: An information sheet.* VCPEA: Richmond, VA.

Viriginia Coalition for the Prevention of Elder Abuse. (1999). Annual conference handouts for annual meeting of VCPEA, Virginia Beach, VA, June 10–11.

Viano, E. (1983). Victimology: The development of a new perspective. *Victimology, 8,* 17–30.

Viano, E. (1996). Stereotyping and prejudice: Crime victims and the criminal justice system. *Studies on Crime and Crime Prevention, 5*(2), 182–202.

Vida, S. (1994). An update on elder abuse and neglect. *Canadian Journal of Psychiatry, 39,* S34–39.

Vinton, L. (1991). Abused older women: Battered women or abused elders? *Journal of Women and Aging, 3*(3), 5–20.

Voelker, R. (2002). Elder Abuse and neglect: A new research topic. *Journal of American Medical Association, 288*(18), 2254–2256.

Waldron, R.J., Uppal, J.C., Quarles, C.L., McCauley, P.R., Harper, H., Frazier, R.L., Benson, J.C., & Altemose, J.R. (1989). *The criminal justice system: An introduction.* New York: Addison-Wesley.

Waller, M., & Griffin, M. (1984). Group therapy for depressed elders. *Geriatric Nursing, 1984,* 309–311.

Walling, A.D. (1999). Abuse in elderly patients. *American Family Physician,* September 1, NP.

Wangrin, M. (1994, June 19). Addressing the elderly: Senior citizens a popular target for mail marketers. *Austin American-Statesman,* A1+.

Warren, K., & Bennett, G. (1997). Elder abuse: An emerging role for the general practitioner. *Geriatric Medicine, 1997*(3), 11–12.

Watson, W.H. (1991). Ethnicity, crime, and aging: Risk factors and adaptation. *Diversity, 15*(4), 53–57.

Webb, E.J., Campbell, D.T., Schwartz, R., & Sechrest, L. (1966). *Unobtrusive measures: Nonreactive research in the social sciences.* Chicago: Rand McNally.

Weber, M. (1976). *The agrarian sociology of ancient civilizations.* London: NLB.

Weber, M. (1975). *Roscher and Knies: The logical problems of historical economics.* New York: Free Press.

Wedge, D. (2003). Nephew held in widow's slaying. *Boston Herald.* November 28, p. 2.

Weiner, A. (1991). A community-based education model for identification and prevention of elder abuse. *Journal of Gerontological Social Work, 16,* 107–119.

Weishiet, R.A., Wells, L.E., & Falcone, D. (1995). *Crime and policing in rural and small-town America: An overview of the issues.* Washington, DC: National Institute of Justice.

Welch, C. (1998, April 7). Boarding home abuses spark change but critics say DSHS won't be enough. *The Spokane Review,* Newsbank Newsfile, n.p.

White, R.D. (2003). Former patients sue hospital. *Los Angeles Times.* August 16, p. 1.

Whittaker, T. (1995). Violence, gender and elder abuse: Towards a feminist analysis and practice. *Journal of Gender Studies, 4*(1), 35–45.

Wiehe, V. (1998). *Understanding family violence.* Newbury Park, CA: Sage.

Wierucka, D., & Goodridge, D. (1996). Vulnerable in a safe place: Institutional elder abuse. *Canadian Journal of Nursing Leadership, 9*(3), 82–91.

Wilber, K.H. (1990). Material abuse of the elderly: When is guardianship a solution? *Journal of Elder Abuse & Neglect, 2*(3–4), 89–104.

Wilber, K.H., & Reynolds, S.L. (1996). Introducing a framework for defining financial abuse of the elderly. *Journal of Elder Abuse & Neglect, 8*(2), 61–80.

Williams, F.P., & McShane, M.D. (1994). *Criminological theory* (2nd Ed.). Englewood Cliffs, NJ: Prentice-Hall.

Williams, G. (1998). How you could get nailed for patient dumping. *Medical Economics, 75*(7), 189–199.

Williamson, J.L. (1999). The siren song of the elderly. *American Journal of Law and Medicine, Summer-Fall,* 423–454.

Wilson, J.Q. (1968). *Police patrol work: A comparative perspective.* New York: Oxford University Press.

Wilson, J.Q. (1983). *Thinking about crime* (rev. Ed.). New York: Vintage Books.

Wilson, P., Geis, G., Pontell, H., Jesilow, P., & Chappell, D. (1985). Medical fraud and Abuse: Australia, Canada, and the United States. *International Journal of Comparative and Applied Criminal Justice, 9,* 25–33.

Winter, A. (1986). The shame of elder abuse. *Modern Maturity, 29*(5), 50–57.

Wivell, M.K., & Wilson, G.L. (1994). Prescription for harm: Pharmacist liability. *Trial, 30*(5), 36–39.

Wolf, R.S., Strugnell, C., & Godkin, M. (1982). *Preliminary findings from Three Model Projects on Elderly Abuse.* Worcester, MA: University Center on Aging. University of Massachusetts Medical Center.

Wolf, R.S., Godkin, M.A., & Pillemer, K.A. (1984). *Elder abuse and neglect: Final report from Three Model Projects.* Worcester, MA: University Center on Aging. University of Massachusetts Medical Center.

Wolf, R.S. (1988). Elder abuse: Ten years later. *Journal of the American Geriatrics Society, 36,* 758–762.

Wolf, R., & Pillemer, K. (1989). *Helping elderly victims.* New York: Columbia University Press.

Wolf, R.S. (1992). Victimization of the elderly: Elder abuse and neglect. *Reviews in Clinical Gerontology, 2,* 269–276.

Wolf, R.S., & Pillemer, K.A. (1994). What's new in elder abuse programming? Four bright ideas. *The Gerontologist, 34*(1), 126–129.

Wolf, R.S. (1996a). Elder abuse and family violence: Testimony presented before the U.S. Senate Special Committee on Aging. *Journal of Elder Abuse & Neglect, 8*(1), 81–96.

Wolf, R.S. (1996b). Understanding elder abuse and neglect. *Aging, 367,* 4–9.

Wolf, R.S. (2001). Support groups for older victims of domestic violence. *Journal of Women and Aging, 13*(4), 71–82.

Woodhead, G.A., & Moss, M.M. (1998). Osteoporosis: Diagnosis and prevention. *Nurse Practitioner, 23*(11), 18.

Yin, P. (1980). Fear of crime among the elderly. *Social Problems, 27*(4), 492–504.

Yin, P. (1982). Fear of crime as a problem for the elderly. *Social Problems, 30*(2), 240–245.

Yin, P. (1985). *Victimization and the aged.* Springfield, IL: Charles C Thomas.

Young, M.G. (2000). Recognizing the signs of elder abuse. *Patient Care,* October 20, n.p.

Zamana, K. (2003). Mountain view–3 arrested in death of elderly woman. *San Francisco Chronicle.* December 9, A 20.

Zborowsky, E. (1985). Developments in protective services: A challenge for social workers. *Journal of Gerontological Social Work, 8*(3–4), 71–83.

Zuzga, C. (1996). Challenges in prosecuting elder abuse. *Aging Magazine, 367,* 76–79.

INDEX

Wolf, Rosalie S., 33, 44, 137, 141 box, 147,
    180, 262, 263
Wood, L.A., 98

Y

Yin, P., 110, 112, 113, 129, 130
Young, M.G., 236

Z

Zborowsky, E., 14
Zevitz, R.G., 130, 170
Zingraff, M.T., 129
Zoabi, S., 265
Zuzga, C., 172

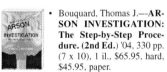
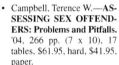
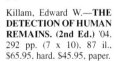
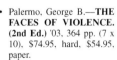

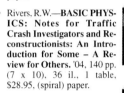
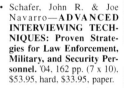
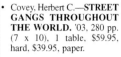
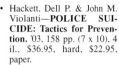
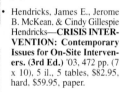
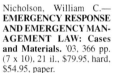
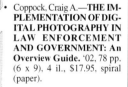
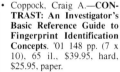